BY KEVIN BAKER

AMERICA
The Story of Us

AN ILLUSTRATED HISTORY

WITH SPECIAL INTRODUCTION BY PRESIDENT BARACK OBAMA

MELCHER MEDIA

ART AND PHOTOGRAPHY EDITED BY PROFESSOR GAIL BUCKLAND

The author and the publisher have made extensive efforts to ensure the accuracy of the information contained in this book. Any errors brought to the attention of the author or the publisher will be corrected in future editions.

Published in the United States by
A&E Television Networks, LLC.
235 East 45th Street
12th Floor
New York, NY 10017

Produced by Melcher Media
124 West 13th Street
New York, NY 10011
www.melcher.com

Publisher: Charles Melcher
Associate Publisher: Bonnie Eldon
Editor in Chief: Duncan Bock
Executive Editor and Project Manager: Lia Ronnen
Project Editor: Lindsey Stanberry
Map and Illustration Editor: David E. Brown
Line Editor: Bob Roe
Production Director: Kurt Andrews
Production Assistant: Daniel del Valle

Book design by Naomi Mizusaki, Supermarket
Maps by Nicholas Blechman
Illustrations by Don Foley

First edition, 2010

Library of Congress Control Number: 2010906734

Softcover ISBN 978-1-4229-8343-0

10 9 8 7 6 5 4 3

Printed and bound in the United States of America

CONTENTS

“OUR AMERICAN STORY HAS NEVER BEEN INEVITABLE.”

Over two hundred years ago, the world waited and watched to see if an unlikely experiment called America would succeed. It has—not because success was certain or because it was easy, but because generations of Americans dedicated their lives and their sacred honor to a cause greater than themselves.

This has been especially true in moments of great trial, like when a ragtag group of patriots overthrew an empire to secure the right to life, liberty, and the pursuit of happiness; when an Illinois rail splitter proved for all time that a government of, by, and for the people would endure; and when marchers braved beatings on an Alabama bridge in the name of equality, freedom, and justice for all.

Moments like these remind us that our American story has never been inevitable. It was made possible by ordinary people who kept their moral compass pointed straight and true when the way seemed treacherous, the climb seemed steep, and the future seemed uncertain. People who recognized a fundamental part of our American character: that we can remake ourselves—and our nation—to fit our larger dreams.

I hope you'll be inspired by these extraordinary men and women, and think about how this generation will write the next chapter in our great American story.

—President Barack Obama, 2010

CHAPTER ONE

REBELS

1497 TO 1733

A STAGGERING ABUNDANCE

THE WORLD COMES TO AMERICA

They came for freedom, and they came to get rich. The two desires were not necessarily distinct, nor was one or the other an unalloyed good. Or evil. They sought freedom of thought, of worship and speech and assembly, but also freedom from the feudal grip of Europe, freedom to rise as high as their talents and tenacity might lift them.

They made America the first wholly modern nation. As such, it was—and still is—all about change. Throughout history, Americans have transformed themselves, often with stunning rapidity, from peasants into city dwellers, from subjects into citizens, from illiterates into some of the most educated people the world has seen. In order to facilitate such transformations, each succeeding generation of Americans relied upon their immense ingenuity to make all things new—to invent incredible machines, raise fantastic buildings, even collapse time and space. Their inventiveness would also be applied to developing a level of civic equality and tolerance once considered impossible. This is the story of how they did all these things. This is the story of us.

They came from everywhere, the first immigrants, settling all about the perimeter of the continent: English in New England and the Carolinas; Dutch and Huguenots in what is now New York; Germans in Pennsylvania; Swedes in New Jersey; Scotch-Irish in western Virginia; Spanish in Florida and in California, Texas, and the Southwest; French voyageurs in the Northeast; Africans everywhere, almost always against their will. They also came from all social classes, and often from despised religious groups: Quakers, Mennonites, and Anabaptists in Pennsylvania; Puritans in Massachusetts; Catholics in Maryland; Baptists and Methodists in the South. Sephardic Jews, fleeing the Inquisition in Portuguese South America, were granted refuge in New Amsterdam by the Dutch West India Company over the violent protests of the city's volcanic, one-legged governor, Petrus Stuyvesant. There was a colony in Georgia intended for the "worthy poor," drawn from English debtor prisons by the general and philanthropist James Oglethorpe.

What they founded together was what F. Scott Fitzgerald would call "the last and greatest of all human dreams," bringing them "face to face for the last time in history with something commensurate to [man's] capacity for wonder."

Colonists approaching the New World could *smell* it miles out to sea, long before they could see it. The smell was sweet, the aroma of the vast primeval forests that covered almost half of North America. The continent they were approaching was twice the size of Europe and contained one-third of the world's freshwater. As many as 60 million buffalo thundered over its vast Western plains or wandered through its woodlands. East of the Mississippi, the woods were thick with deer and bears, squirrels and opossums, wolves and cougars; with fruit and nuts, and vines heavy with grapes.

The shores of Manhattan Island were ringed with tottering piles of oyster shells where the local Indian tribes feasted on them each summer, and John

Colonist and artist John White's depiction of the Algonquin people's three means of fishing, by spear, weir, and net. The fire in the canoe was used to lure the fish at night. The men shown hunted everything from crabs to catfish.

The manner of their fishing.
Cannow

HOOPOE

Some of the astonishing array of wildlife that Europeans encountered in North America: hoopoe, brown pelican, iguana, puffer fish, and box turtle. "For fish and fowle, we have great abundance, fresh Codd in the Summer is but course meat with us, our Bay is full of lobsters all the Summer and affordeth varietie of other Fish," reported Edward Winslow from Plymouth Bay. "...in September we can take a Hogshead of Eeles in a night, with small labour, and can dig them out of their beds, all the Winter we have Mussells and Othus at our doors..."

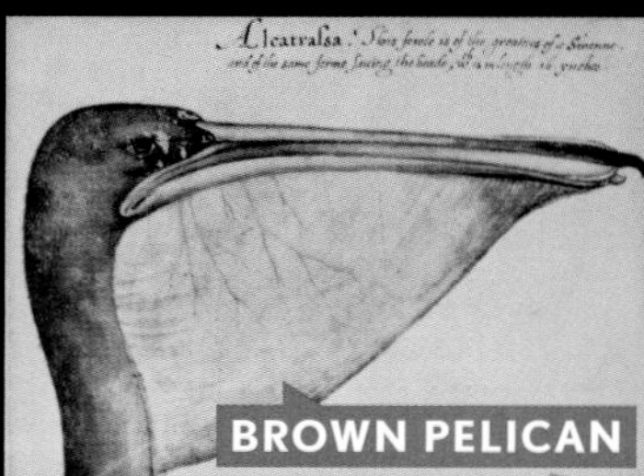

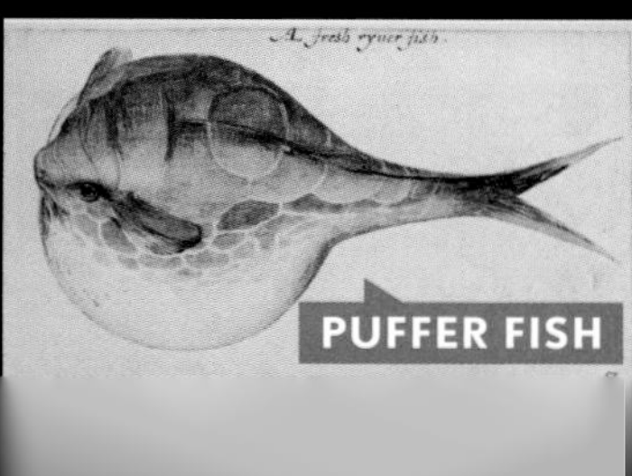

Cabot—originally Giovanni Caboto, the Venetian explorer charting the East Coast of America for England—found seas "swarming with fish, which can be taken not only with the net, but in baskets let down with a stone."

The commercial possibilities of such a cornucopia were not lost on Europeans. The Spanish grabbed up vast deposits of gold and silver in Central and South America. The French and Dutch were entrenched in the North American fur trade. But the English, who had truly developed their navies only in the latter part of the 1500s, were late to the game. This would have a fateful influence on how they operated in the New World. Every other European nation saw its American holdings chiefly as trading posts, designed to ship riches back to the mother country as cheaply and as quickly as possible. England would come to see America as a place to establish true colonies with large, self-sustaining populations.

Such numbers would be necessary to exploit what resources England could claim. For a small island nation, permanent colonies were also invaluable as a safety valve, drawing away tens of thousands of the poor, the ambitious, the religious dissidents, the radicals. Within half a century of the establishment of their first lasting outpost in America, the English had 90,000 colonists in the New World—enough to overwhelm every other nation with a claim to the continent. But they could not do that alone. For all of their numbers and their determination, for all of their greed and their faith, they needed help to tap the staggering abundance of the land around them.

The New World they discovered was not deserted. There may have been a hundred million people living in the Western Hemisphere before the sixteenth century. The majority were in Central and South America. But even in North America, there were cities like Cahokia, just across the Mississippi from St. Louis, which had 10,000 to 20,000 inhabitants. East of the Appalachians, there were some 400,000 Indians by 1600. They lived mostly in small tribes and were superb hunters, but they also built sturdy wooden wigwams and longhouses, cultivated and harvested grains, and set controlled forest fires to clear and replenish the soil.

They already knew about white men. By the seventeenth century, explorers such as Cabot, Giovanni da Verrazano, and Samuel de Champlain had been flitting up and down the East Coast of North America for more than a hundred years, and English and French fishing vessels had been plying the Grand Banks off eastern Canada as early as the 1480s. The Indians had met these men—and they were not impressed. As the historian Charles C. Mann writes: "Evidence suggests that they tended to view Europeans with disdain as soon as they got to know them," finding them "physically weak, sexually untrustworthy, atrociously ugly, and just plain smelly. (The British and French, many of whom had not taken a bath in their entire lives, were amazed by the Indian interest in personal cleanliness.)"

Watching these weak people flounder about in the "New" World, Native Americans decided that they posed little threat. They valued many of the tools and adornments the newcomers brought, and reasoned that they might be helpful in their own, internecine wars. It would prove a fatal miscalculation.

1585
TO
1609

PARADISE AND A FRIGID HELL

THE FIRST ENGLISH SETTLERS

Early English settlers were often woefully ignorant of the conditions in which they would have to live, and they had a disturbing tendency to brutalize the Native Americans they encountered. (An early Roanoke colony destroyed a village and burned its chief alive on the suspicion that Indians had stolen a silver cup.) For the colonists, just getting to the New World was an ordeal; it often meant living with a hundred or more people on a dark, airless deck, no more than 75 feet long and just five feet high. The voyage from England to Chesapeake Bay was 3,000 miles, and ships made as little as five miles a day—when they weren't being swept backward by the Gulf Stream. Food and water were limited, hygiene was abominable, and colonists usually arrived depleted and exhausted by disease.

The expense and risk of such expeditions was such that the English crown usually left them to chartered private companies of investors. One of these, the Virginia Company of London, managed to send three ships of new colonists out to the Chesapeake in 1607. This was the beginning of the Jamestown Settlement, the first enduring English colony in what would become the United States of America.

"What so truly suits with honour and honesty as the discovering things unknown, erecting towns, peopling Countries, informing the ignorant, reforming things unjust, teaching virtue and gain to our native mother country?"
—John Smith

JOHN SMITH'S VIRGINIA

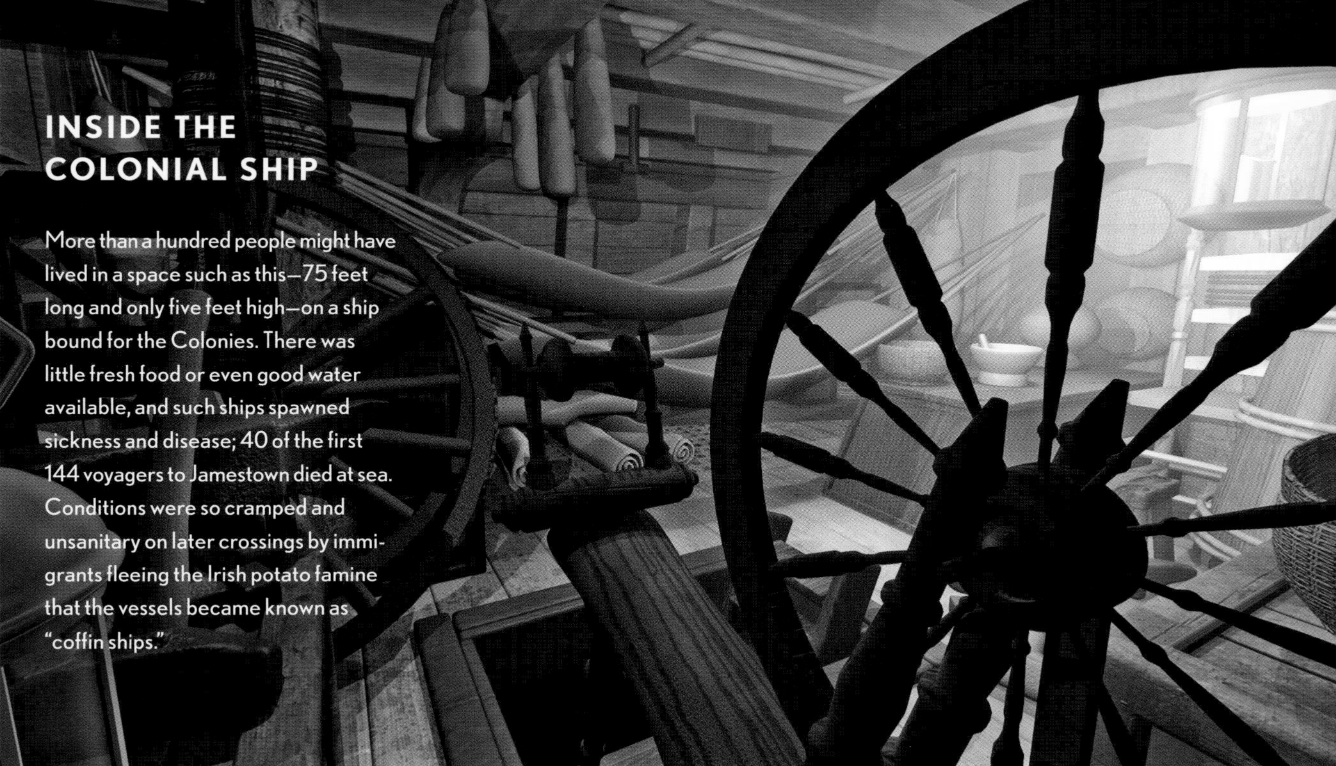

INSIDE THE COLONIAL SHIP

More than a hundred people might have lived in a space such as this—75 feet long and only five feet high—on a ship bound for the Colonies. There was little fresh food or even good water available, and such ships spawned sickness and disease; 40 of the first 144 voyagers to Jamestown died at sea. Conditions were so cramped and unsanitary on later crossings by immigrants fleeing the Irish potato famine that the vessels became known as "coffin ships."

Even before these colonists arrived, their expedition was a debacle—40 of the 144 men and boys died on board. The men who survived the trip were mostly tradesmen and laborers, soldiers of fortune, or the restless second sons of titled lords. They had little skill at agriculture, and spent most of their time looking for gold and quarreling among themselves. The land they had come to was, in the description of George Percy, a future governor of the colony, a "veritable paradise on earth," but it had its hellish side. The region was afflicted by drought, and at the time the Northern Hemisphere was in the grip of the so-called Little Ice Age, which meant that temperatures were on average two degrees Fahrenheit colder than they are today. The growing season was limited to five months, and producing any food proved almost impossible for the English. Afraid to venture close to Indian villages, they settled along the estuaries of the Virginia tidewater, where water supplies were stagnant and often undrinkable, not to mention a breeding ground for mosquitoes that spread malaria, yellow fever, and other diseases.

By January of 1608, only 38 people remained alive. Desperate, the colonists turned to their most audacious leader, a mercenary and adventurer named John Smith, who had a propensity for telling unbelievable stories about himself, many of which were actually true.

Smith immediately moved the survivors away from the deadly estuaries and up to land watered by fresh springs. He forced the settlers to build houses and tend crops, famously decreeing, in language borrowed from the Bible, "He who does not work, will not eat."

Smith would also leave us one of the first enduring legends of America. Captured by the Powhatan, the leading tribe in the area, he was supposedly saved by a young girl who threw her body between Smith and the chief's war club. She was the chief's daughter, Matoaka, whom the English would come to call by her teasing nickname, Pocahontas—which means, roughly, "little hellion."

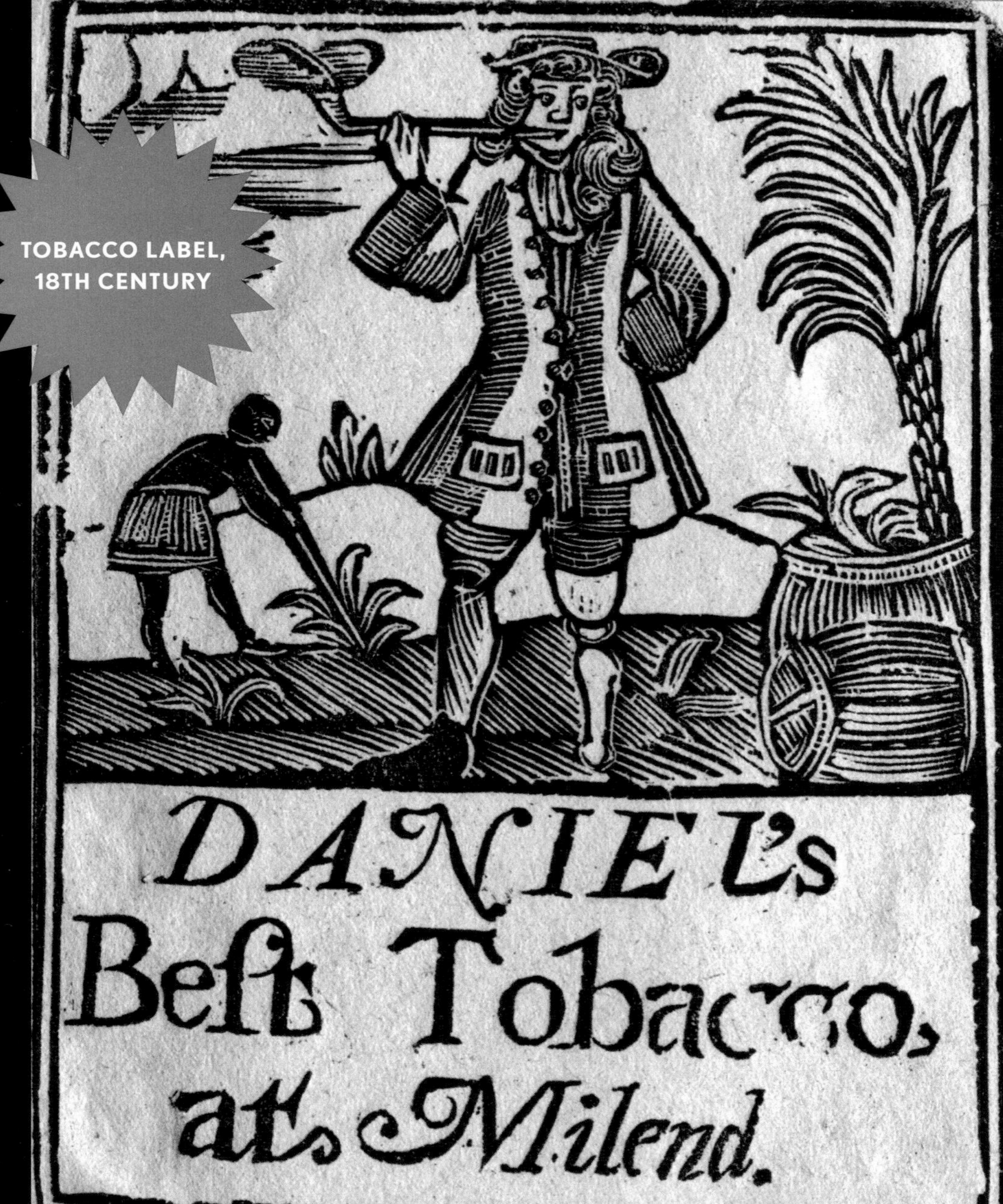

TOBACCO LABEL, 18TH CENTURY

1609
TO
1640

ROLL 'EM IF YOU'VE GOT 'EM

TOBACCO SAVES THE DAY AT JAMESTOWN

The English and the Powhatan eventually came to an understanding that would provide incalculable aid to the colonists. Chief Wahunsenacawh and his people dominated a loose confederacy of 14,000 Native Americans. They had been there for 16,000 years, and they had learned how to live off the land—knowledge they now shared with the English.

The Jamestown Settlement stabilized and grew, for a while, bolstered by the arrival of another 600 men, women, and children. The Powhatan soon became alarmed by the colony's rapid expansion, and relations took an abrupt turn for the worse, degenerating into open warfare. John Smith was badly burned in a gunpowder accident, and forced to return to England.

Jamestown now became an armed camp. Settlers were sentenced to death for any number of crimes, ranging from sodomy, rape, and adultery, to theft, to attempting to leave the colony. This last had become a pressing problem. Dozens of English settlers went to live with the Indians or took off for parts unknown. The colony continued to deteriorate, and by 1609 what would become known as the Starving Time had set in. The English went through their livestock, then resorted to eating vermin, fungi, shoe leather, excrement, and human corpses. Ships that reached Jamestown in 1610 found what seemed to be an abandoned fort, its gates swinging open. Only when they rang the chapel bell did the colonists slowly emerge from their crumbling houses, some of them naked and crawling, crying out: "We are starved! We are starved!" Only 60 remained.

The survivors dragged themselves onto the ships, determined to return to England. Then came deliverance—Lord De La Warr's supply ship *Deliverance* came sailing up the James River, along with its equally well-christened sister ship, *Patience*. De La Warr brought food, provisions, and new settlers, and persuaded the colonists to return to the settlement where they had suffered so mightily.

Among their number now was a man who held the key to Virginia's survival, a young English merchant named John Rolfe. Throughout their first years in America, the Jamestown colonists had chased mainly after the old myths of Oriental splendor, looking for gold, hoping to find the long-desired ocean passage to the East Indies. What Rolfe brought was a very different commodity: seeds of a particular strain of sweet tobacco, previously grown only by the Spanish on Trinidad. Largely due to the efforts of Sir Walter Raleigh, tobacco was already popular in Europe, where its nicotine served as a natural insecticide, and its smoke was thought to alleviate asthma and other afflictions.

Rolfe had been given his seeds by an English tobacconist. (Just how the tobacconist came to possess them is unknown; the Spanish guarded their supply jealously.) They were magic seeds indeed, and the plants grew like weeds in the rich soil of Virginia, springing up in the gardens and the marketplace of Jamestown. Rolfe called the brand Orinoco and cultivated it on his plantation 30 miles upstream from Jamestown. By 1617, he had packed the first shipment off to London. It was an immediate hit. By 1620, Virginia was shipping 50,000 pounds of Orinoco to England every year; by 1630, that figure had risen to 300,000 pounds; and by 1640 it was three million pounds, making the colony the leading tobacco supplier to all of Europe.

1620 TO 1621

SAINTS WITH GUNS

THE PILGRIMS AND THE PEOPLE OF THE DAWNLAND

Hundreds of miles to the north, in the area recently rechristened New England, a different sort of colony was taking shape. Its inhabitants had intended to land closer to present-day New York, but they didn't much mind the isolation. They settled at the foot of what is now Cape Cod, in Massachusetts, a place that John Smith had already dubbed Plymouth. They had come not to seek gold, but to found the New Jerusalem, the city of God on earth. Many of them were separatists and dissidents from the established Church of England, but the name they preferred was Saints, in keeping with their view of themselves as the elect of God. Their descendants would come to know them as Pilgrims.

The Saints were no better equipped to deal with this new country than their more worldly contemporaries in Jamestown. They expected to live off the land, but brought no livestock and few farming implements. They planned to support the colony by harvesting cod to be shipped back to England, but had brought the wrong kind of gear for fishing. They had set sail in September, and had arrived at the start of winter racked by illness. The land they had chosen was sandy and infertile, and the wilderness that surrounded their beachhead frightened them. They considered nature the Devil's realm and shivered at the sight of smoke from Indian campfires in the distance. "It was winter…sharp and violent, and subject to cruel and fierce storms," wrote William Bradford, the colony's second governor. "They died sometimes two and three a day." Before the winter was over, "[o]f 100 and odd persons, scarce 50 remained."

They seemed to have landed in a cursed place, the land around them covered with exposed human remains. The once-plentiful New England Indians had just been devastated by a plague, most likely what we now know as hepatitis A, probably caught from European fishermen. For 200 miles, from Maine to Rhode Island, the villages of the Native Americans lay silent and deserted. Up to 90 percent of the Dawnland, as the Indians called the New England coast, had perished, one of the great disasters in human history.

Their deaths, however, were the Saints' salvation. Desperately scavenging the deserted Indian villages, they turned up ten bushels of dried maize—American corn—that kept them going for weeks.

Then, in March of 1621, a demon emerged from the howling wilderness. He came in the form of a tall, sturdy man carrying a bow and arrows, his hair shaved in the front and long in the back, and naked save for a narrow belt. As he strode toward the gaping Pilgrim women and children, the men scrambled to intercept him, putting themselves between this apparition and the rest of the colony. The demon stopped—and said, "Welcome, Englishmen."

The mysterious visitor was Samoset, a brave of the Wampanoag nation, who had picked up a little English from fishermen in Maine. He eventually left the Pilgrims, but soon he was back, along with his chief, Massasoit, and a host of armed braves. He also brought a man who, like Pocahontas, would go down in American history as a friend of the white man… but under the wrong name.

This was Squanto. What he actually called himself was Tisquantum, meaning something akin to "the Wrath of God." Squanto had been a member of the Patuxet people, who lived near the very site the

Pilgrims had chosen. He had spent years among the Europeans, traveling for a while with the ubiquitous John Smith before being kidnapped by one of Smith's underlings, who tried to sell him into slavery in Spain. He had been rescued from that fate by Spanish friars, then worked for years as a guide, interpreter, and professional oddity in English manor houses.

The year before the Pilgrims' arrival, Squanto made it back home—only to discover that his tribe had been wiped out by the plague. He lived uneasily among the Wampanoag. Massasoit had brought him along to meet the Pilgrims because he needed a good interpreter, one who could help secure an important alliance.

Massasoit's show of force was a ruse, an attempt to disguise the weakened condition of his people. The Wampanoag had been hit hard by the plague, while their longtime enemies, the Narragansett, had not. What Massasoit offered the Saints was survival, in exchange for a military compact against the Narragansett. His offer was accepted, and Squanto went to live among the Pilgrims for long stretches of time, showing them how to raise maize by using fish for fertilizer—a technique, ironically, that he may have learned from European farmers. In return, the Saints gave Massasoit a surprisingly effective strike force, led by a mercenary named Captain Myles Standish.

Before long, Standish helped drive off the Narragansett, and Massasoit was pleased. He signed a treaty with the Saints, and a celebration was deemed in order. After a good harvest that year, in the fall of 1621, the Wampanoag and the Pilgrims celebrated what would come to be called Thanksgiving, eating venison the Indians had killed or dipping into pottage kettles stuffed with the migratory birds the Pilgrims had shot (yes, there were a few turkeys). It was a genuine celebration by allies who remained deeply suspicious of one another. Massasoit brought 90 Wampanoag, most of them young, armed braves. Standish and his Pilgrim militia marched about and made a great display of firing their guns. But whatever their reservations, each group had helped the other, and survived.

1630 TO 1750

MASS. REPRODUCTION

KING PHILIP'S WAR AND THE MAKING OF MASSACHUSETTS

The pact between the Wampanoag and the Saints lasted 50 years, but in Massachusetts, as elsewhere, there would come to be too many Englishmen for anyone else to coexist. In 1630, 11 ships brought 700 more colonists to the great natural harbor north of Plymouth, where they would erect Boston, the Puritans' shining city on a hill. Another 20,000 arrived by 1642, and they multiplied at a stunning pace, averaging six to eight children per family. The population of English America grew to more than 1.5 million by 1750.

Once they landed in the New World, the colonists made room for themselves. The typical settler cleared 15 acres a year. In Massachusetts, the Puritans turned 12,000 acres of woods into farmland in ten years, and established 230 villages and towns. Tribal continuity began to disintegrate, with some Native Americans converting to the Saints' religion and living in separate villages as "Praying Indians." The Wampanoag were pushed west, and more epidemics of European diseases continued to ravage them.

In 1675, Metacom, Massasoit's younger son, led a revolt that would later be known as King Philip's War (King Philip being the nickname bestowed on Metacom by the English). No one was spared; before it was over, 800 of the 52,000 English in the region and 3,000 of the 20,000 Indians were dead, making it the bloodiest conflict in the history of North America in proportion to the populations involved. The Puritan colonies suffered economic devastation, but the Wampanoag and their old rivals, the Narragansett, were all but annihilated. Metacom was shot dead in the war's climactic battle by a Praying Indian allied with the English. The chief's body was dismembered, his head set on a pike over Fort Plymouth, and his wife and son sold into slavery in Bermuda.

As costly as it was, the Puritans' victory was total, and it was achieved without any aid from across the Atlantic. As such, it may well have marked the start of a true American identity. More and more, the colonists began to think of themselves as *Americans*, with customs, laws, traditions, and priorities more closely shared with one another than with the country they had left.

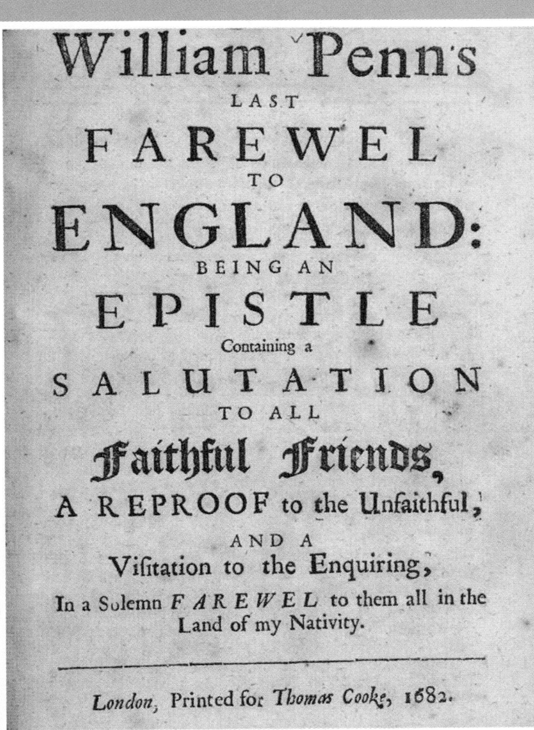
William Penn's

LAST

FAREWEL

TO

ENGLAND:

BEING AN

EPISTLE

Containing a

SALUTATION

TO ALL

Faithful Friends,

A REPROOF to the Unfaithful,

AND A

Visitation to the Enquiring,

In a Solemn *FAREWEL* to them all in the Land of my Nativity.

London, Printed for *Thomas Cooke*, 1682.

PENN WAS MIGHTIER THAN THE SWORD: THE VISION OF WILLIAM PENN

The Puritans weren't the only religious dissidents shooed out of England in the seventeenth century. In the 1650s, members of the Religious Society of Friends—better known as the Quakers—began filtering across the Atlantic, eager to escape Anglican oppression.

These were freethinking, forward-looking people, men and women whose notions of Christianity did not include clergy or rituals. They sought personal relationships with God, and they celebrated the "inner light," or divine spirit present in all people.

Advocates of pacifism, gender equality, and religious tolerance, the Quakers were natural enemies of the Church of England. They were subject to harassment and imprisonment. They didn't fare much better in Massachusetts, where their permissiveness irked the stodgy Puritans. In the early 1660s, after four of their members had been hanged, the Quakers left New England in search of friendlier neighbors. They found them in New Jersey.

Two decades later, they pushed farther west, moving into territory that William Penn, a rabble-rousing Quaker and son of a famed British admiral, had recently wangled from King Charles II. Charles had owed Penn's family 16,000 pounds, and by giving Penn the land that would become Pennsylvania—an enormous swath stretching between the Delaware and Ohio rivers—the cash-strapped monarch both settled his debt and rid England of a prominent troublemaker.

Penn envisioned a colony based on Quaker ideals, and before setting sail, he signed the First Frame of Government, a document that guaranteed Pennsylvanians a series of basic rights. He was especially committed to preserving religious freedom, and he named his capital Philadelphia, Greek for "the city of brotherly love." Penn welcomed immigrants from across Europe and extended his goodwill to Indians, brokering lasting peace with the Susquehannock, Shawnee, and Lenni-Lenape tribes.

Philadelphia would emerge as one of the New World's most diverse and important cities. In the 1770s, it became a gathering place for the architects of the American Revolution—men who, in drafting the Declaration of Independence and later the Constitution, borrowed heavily from Penn's concepts of government.

Although Penn would spend 11 of his final years in debtor's prison, poor business decisions did little to tarnish his name, at least among students of the Enlightenment. Writing in 1778, the French philosopher Voltaire credited Penn with "having brought down upon earth the Golden Age, which in all probability, never had any real existence but in his dominions."

The Quakers wielded political power until the 1770s, when their unwillingness to support the Revolution cost them their clout. They later recast themselves as social crusaders, championing women's suffrage and the abolition of slavery, and were renowned for their business acumen.

1619 TO 1800

TRIANGULATING EVIL

THE COLONIAL SLAVE TRADE

There was one social and economic institution that increasingly tied the colonies of the Atlantic coast together—an enterprise that would be the country's enduring curse. This, of course, was slavery.

The first Americans of African descent were brought to Jamestown in 1619, Angolans who had been seized from a ship transporting them from their native land to Veracruz. They were not slaves; such a designation did not yet exist under English law. Instead, they were considered indentured servants, in service to the master of the ship. This status provided the chance to work one's way to freedom, and to full citizenship. At least some of Jamestown's Angolans eventually became freemen, and as late as 1650, the colonists seemed to have little interest in slaves; there were only 1,400 in all the English colonies. African-Americans were often free, and some owned slaves themselves.

What spurred the growth of slavery was the notorious Triangular Trade, which ensnared all of the colonies in iniquity. Here is how it worked: By 1774, Massachusetts was manufacturing 2.7 million gallons of rum every year, most of it exported to the Slave Coast of Africa, where it was traded for human beings. This terrible cargo was conveyed in turn to the sugar plantations of the British West Indies, where those who survived the journey were put to work turning out molasses—molasses that went to Boston, where it was made into rum.

While the majority of slaves were worked to death on the brutal island plantations, more and more were imported to North America. During the eighteenth century, over 250,000 Africans were brought to the English colonies on the North American continent, more than all other immigrants who arrived during that time combined. Most American slaves were settled in the South, but there were nearly 50,000 in the North, owned by middle-class as well as wealthy families. The demands of the slave trade rippled out through the workforce, constituting an integral part of the Colonial economy. They provided work for loggers in the New Hampshire forests; for coopers, tanners, and rope makers along waterfronts from Maine to Rhode Island; for insurers, lawyers, and scriveners in the great Boston countinghouses. Fishermen on the Grand Banks and farmers in Vermont produced the salt cod used to feed the slaves on the Caribbean sugar plantations. The fortunes of the finest families in Massachusetts all were made in the slave trade.

The riches to be pulled from the triangle were so great that England was seduced by them too. But its more immediate concern was how to yank the Americans—now fattening on their slave profits—back within the royal orbit. Parliament curtailed emigration, but that loss was more than made up for by the colonists' birthrate, and by the tens of thousands of French Huguenots, Scotch-Irish Jacobites, and German religious dissidents who sought asylum in the new land. English kings began revoking colonial charters, installing new bureaucrats and governors, and insisting that American merchants return to the imperial system, trading only within the empire. Such restrictions limited the price Americans could get for their tobacco and other goods in Europe, and they bitterly objected. Many turned to smuggling; the beaches and seawalls of New England towns were honeycombed with tunnels through which they moved their illicit goods.

The British slave ship *Brookes*, with 292 slaves on two decks, 1788.

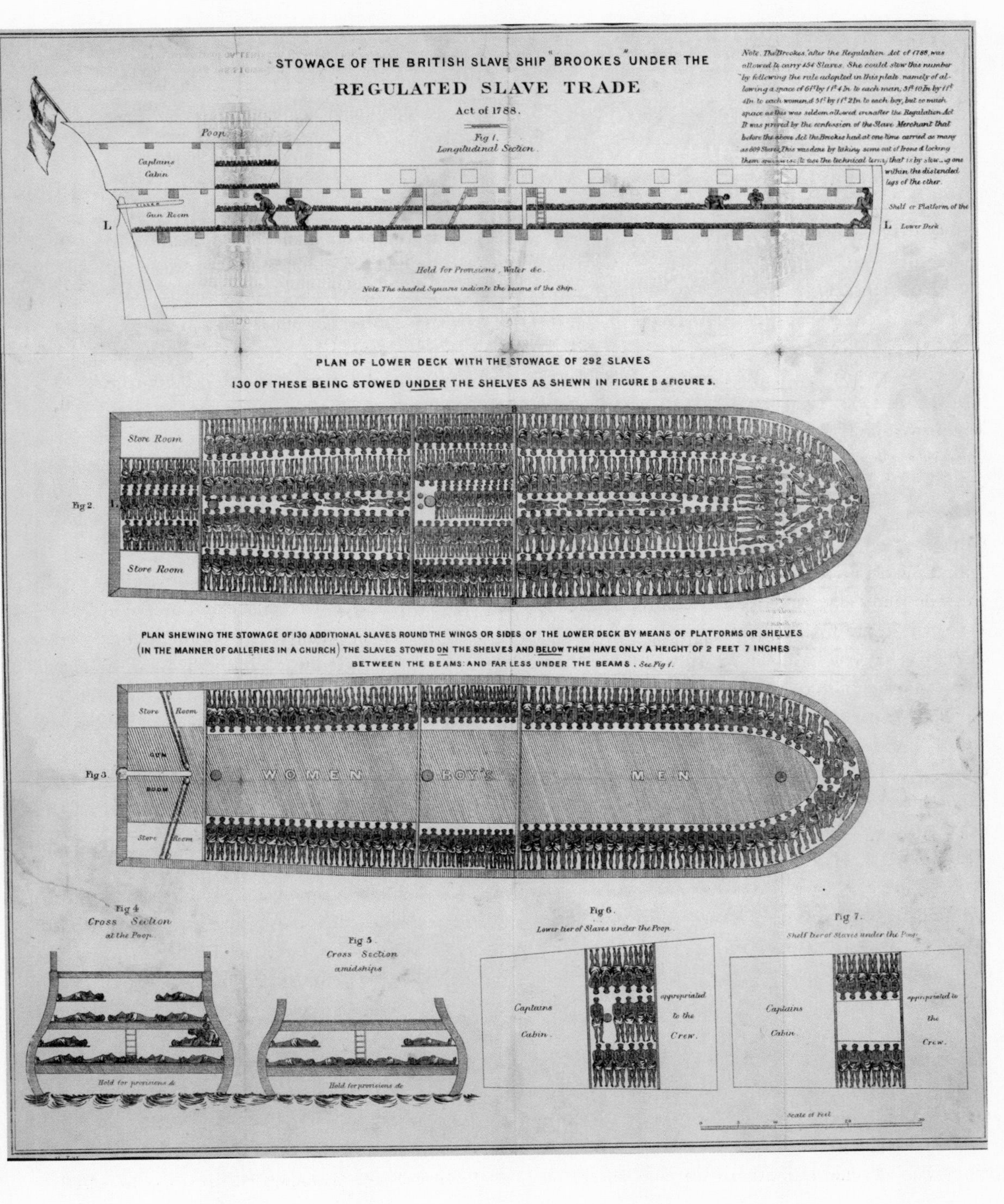

STOWAGE OF THE BRITISH SLAVE SHIP "BROOKES" UNDER THE
REGULATED SLAVE TRADE
Act of 1788.
Note. The Brookes, after the Regulation Act of 1788, was allowed to carry 454 Slaves. She could stow this number by following the rule adopted in this plate, namely of allowing a space of 6 ft by 1 ft 4 In. to each man; 5 ft 10 In by 1 ft 4 In. to each woman, & 5 ft by 1 ft 2 In to each boy, but so much space as this was seldom allowed even after the Regulation Act. It was proved by the confession of the Slave Merchant that before the above Act the Brookes had at one time carried as many as 609 Slaves. This was done by taking some out of Irons & locking
within the distended legs of the other.
Poop
Fig 1.
Longitudinal Section.
Captains Cabin
Gun Room
L
L
Shelf or Platform of the
Lower Deck
Hold for Provisions, Water &c.
Note. The shaded Squares indicate the beams of the Ship.
PLAN OF LOWER DECK WITH THE STOWAGE OF 292 SLAVES
130 OF THESE BEING STOWED UNDER THE SHELVES AS SHEWN IN FIGURE B & FIGURE 5.
Store Room
Fig 2.
Store Room
PLAN SHEWING THE STOWAGE OF 130 ADDITIONAL SLAVES ROUND THE WINGS OR SIDES OF THE LOWER DECK BY MEANS OF PLATFORMS OR SHELVES
(IN THE MANNER OF GALLERIES IN A CHURCH) THE SLAVES STOWED ON THE SHELVES AND BELOW THEM HAVE ONLY A HEIGHT OF 2 FEET 7 INCHES
BETWEEN THE BEAMS: AND FAR LESS UNDER THE BEAMS. See Fig 1.
Store Room
GUN ROOM
Fig 3.
Store Room
WOMEN
BOY'S
MEN
Fig 4
Cross Section
at the Poop.
Hold for provisions &c
Fig 5.
Cross Section
amidships
Hold for provisions &c
Fig 6.
Lower tier of Slaves under the Poop.
Captains Cabin.
appropriated to the Crew.
Fig 7.
Shelf tier of Slaves under the Poop.
Captains Cabin.
appropriated to the Crew.
Scale of Feet

1754 TO 1770

LIVE TAX-FREE OR DIE!

THE MOVE TO INDEPENDENCE

A new opportunity to remind the Colonials from whence they came seemed to arise with the outbreak in 1754, of the French and Indian War. In European eyes, this was largely a sideshow to the Seven Years' War raging on the Continent. But in North America, the conflict had been instigated at least in part by the colonists' desire to seize western lands claimed by the French, and to break the power of Louisbourg, Boston's trading rival to the north in French Canada. After a succession of frontier ambushes and attacks by the French and their Indian allies, Americans had to be rescued by English troops and ships. And by the time the war was brought to a conclusion, in 1763, the colonials identified themselves as British subjects more than they had for many years. Surely they would have to admit their dependency now—and accept new taxes to compensate England for the staggering expenditures incurred in winning the war, and for keeping an army and navy on hand.

Americans, though, were accustomed to being the least taxed people in the world. If they had benefited from the French and Indian War, well, so had England, by gaining huge new possessions in Canada. They saw no reason to keep troops and ships at the ready now that the war was over; all the redcoats seemed to do was evict Americans from the rich western lands they coveted, in order to uphold the crown's treaty obligations with the Indians. The colonists began to claim that they were, in the words of Rhode Island Governor Stephen Hopkins, "free-born subjects, justly and naturally entitled to all the rights and advantages of the British constitution." Some went even further, such as the Boston politician James Otis, devising what would become the rallying cry of the American Revolution: "Taxation without representation is tyranny!"

But representation would have done them little practical good. Even with their fast growth, the total population of the colonies was still only 2.5 million by 1775, many of them slaves, so their representatives would barely have registered in the English Parliament. Nor did England want them represented. To do so would have meant explaining to their own notoriously underrepresented boroughs why they could not have the say in Parliament they were due.

Instead, England began a long, largely fruitless effort to squeeze revenue out of the colonies through a series of taxes. The Sugar Act of 1764 laid down a tariff on molasses imported from outside the British West Indies—thereby alienating merchants in the Triangular Trade. The Stamp Act of 1765—the first tax directly applied to the colonists—placed a small toll on all legal documents and on each edition of Americans' beloved newspapers, thereby enraging the influential printing class; not a single printer in the colonies agreed to pay it. The Quartering Act of 1765 required Colonial governments to provide shelter and provisions for English troops stationed within their boundaries—thus annoying almost everyone. Meanwhile, the British troops who lingered in the New World were so badly paid that many were forced to take part-time jobs—thereby driving down the wages of working-class colonists.

In less than three years, Parliament had managed to unite nearly every class of America against the government. Parliament finally responded to the unrest by repealing the Stamp Act, but it placed new taxes on imports of glass, lead, paper, paint, and tea.

IN LESS THAN THREE YEARS, PARLIAMENT HAD MANAGED TO UNITE NEARLY EVERY CLASS OF AMERICA AGAINST THE GOVERNMENT.

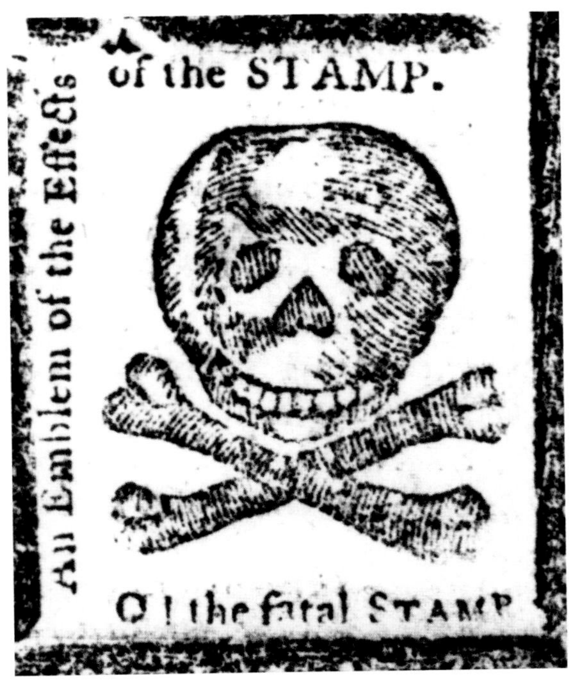

The last of those became especially contentious. Americans drank lakes of tea, importing 1.8 million pounds of it every year. Of that amount, however, only about 10 percent was actually declared and subjected to a tariff. Americans, and especially New Englanders, persisted in trading with other nations, smuggling in brands of tea (and almost everything else) produced outside the British Empire.

One of the leading practitioners of this illicit trade was John Hancock, a merchant whose family smuggling business had made him the richest man in Boston. When His Majesty's customs officials began trying to enforce the new tax on tea, Hancock swore they would not be allowed on his company's vessels. When an inspector did board his new ship, the *Liberty*, Hancock had his crew nail the man inside the ship's cabin until they could rush a hundred barrels of costly, contraband Madeira out of the hold.

The customs men were not amused. They had the *Liberty* impounded and towed out into the harbor by a British warship. But Hancock was a major sponsor of the city's patriotic societies, including the militant Sons of Liberty. When his ship was seized, some 500 of those men, who now called themselves Patriots, staged a riot on the dockside and attacked the homes of the customs men. Now it was the authorities' turn to overreact. Four full regiments of British regulars and part of a fifth—at least 1,200 soldiers—were ordered to Boston, where they began to arrive on October 1, 1768. Bostonians were outraged, considering themselves under military occupation.

"[They] formed and marched with insolent parade, drums beating, fifes playing, and colors flying," an engraver and silversmith named Paul Revere remarked, with obvious disgust.

The colonists decided to wage war—on England's pocketbook. They organized "non-importation" pacts—a boycott of English goods. They gave up fine clothes and finished goods in favor of homespun cloth and other products of American manufacture—inventing forms of nonviolent resistance to the British Empire that would later be used by such revolutionaries as Charles Parnell in Ireland and Mahatma Gandhi in India. English exports to America plunged, and angry merchants demanded that the government do something. Parliament capitulated. On March 5, 1770, it repealed most of the hated revenue acts—too late.

VIEW OF PART OF THE TOWN OF BOSTON IN NEW-E
TOWN OF BOSTON
TROOPS
2
3
4

ND AND BRITTISH SHIPS OF WAR LANDING THEIR TROOPS 1768

SMUGGLER

WHALE SHIP

MORE TROOPS

STILL MORE TROOPS

B

8

1

6

5

To the Earl of
Hillsborough, His
Majesty's Secry of State for
America. THIS VIEW
the only well Plan'd
EXPEDITION, formed fo
supporting ye dig
ity of BRITAIN
& chastising ye inso
of AMERICA, is humye
crib'd.

1770
TO
1774

THE STREET BRAWL HEARD 'ROUND THE WORLD

THE BOSTON MASSACRE AND A TEA PARTY

On the evening of that same March day, two armies ignorant of the repeal clashed in the frozen streets of Boston. Brawls between soldiers and workingmen had been flaring up for days. And now, on this cloudy, almost moonless evening, there was a confused, running series of altercations in the darkness. A mob of Patriot sailors, teenagers, laborers, and barflies broke into a church and rang the alarm bell, chanting: "Fire! Fire!" Hundreds of Bostonians came running out of their homes. Many joined the mob, surrounding a single British sentry at the Custom House who had just swatted a teenage Patriot in the head with his musket. The mob pelted the soldier with snowballs, and cursed him as a "Damned rascally scoundrel lobster son of a bitch!" among other things, until he feared for his life and yelled for help. Captain Thomas Preston rushed six more soldiers to the sentry's rescue but the mob kept growing and closing in, challenging the British soldiers with the usual, thoughtless courage of mobs: "Damn you, you sons of bitches, fire! You can't kill us all!" and, "Why do you not fire? Damn you, you dare not fire. Fire and be damned!"

When the crowd began to attack the redcoats with heavy sticks and clubs, one of them slipped or was knocked down. He came up firing, yelling for the other soldiers to do the same. After a confused pause, they did. Eleven men were left lying in the snow, five of them dead or dying.

Preston and eight of his men were charged with murder and manslaughter, but they were soon acquitted of the most serious charges. They were defended by a short, brilliant Patriot lawyer named John Adams, who had pointed out that the soldiers were attacked by a "motley rabble of saucy boys, negroes and mulattoes, Irish teagues and outlandish jack tarrs," thereby cleverly dissociating the mob from the respectable people of Boston.

In fact, the dead made up a telling cross section of the town. They included a 17-year-old boy, an Irish leather worker, a rope maker, and two sailors—one of them a hulking, six-foot-two black man named Crispus Attucks, who may have been an escaped slave, or part Indian, or both. They represented what was even then a diverse country like none other on earth, and their deaths shocked their fellow Americans. Paul Revere copied a popular sketch of the encounter, embellished it with a few details and captions to make it seem as if the British troops had fired deliberate, merciless volleys into the crowd, and called it "The Boston Massacre." Revere's incendiary print went out to the literate, news-hungry colonies by post rider. Other pamphlets ornamented by drawings of five black coffins soon followed, stirring fresh outrage.

The propaganda was effective, but only the most fanatical Patriots advocated breaking away from England. Both sides seemed to step back and take a breath. Then, a bit of political cronyism in London set events cascading downward again. The British East India Company, on the verge of bankruptcy, was desperate to dump 17 million pounds of tea onto the American market. Even with the revenue tax, it would be cheaper than smuggled tea. Parliament decided to allow it, thinking Americans could not possibly object to a cheaper version of their favorite beverage.

The colonists saw a trap. Accepting the tea, however cheap it was, would mean accepting the tax. Besides, it would wipe out many local merchants and enrich some of the leading, pro-English Tories in the colonies.

BRIAN WILLIAMS, *NBC Nightly News*: "These guys were revolutionaries, they were scallywags, they were rebels, some of them were gentlemen farmers, some of them were overeducated, some of them were undereducated. It really was the birth of a nation."

THEY CHOPPED OPEN ALL 342 CRATES OF TEA—90,000 POUNDS—AND DUMPED IT INTO BOSTON HARBOR.

When the East India Company shipped half a million pounds of their cheap tea to America, the Sons of Liberty were waiting. In New York, Philadelphia, and Charleston, South Carolina, they intimidated the company's retailers into refusing to accept the tea. But in Boston, these merchants fled to the protection of the British garrison, and refused to give up their consignment. The ships remained at the wharves.

On December 16, 1773, after nearly three weeks of stalemate and following a mass meeting of Patriots, a mysterious band descended upon the tea ships. These men had darkened their faces with burnt cork and clothed themselves in Indian blankets and a few feathers to disguise their identity. They chopped open all 342 crates of tea—90,000 pounds—and dumped it into Boston Harbor.

Parliament responded swiftly. By the spring of 1774, it put into place the Coercive Acts—known in America as the Intolerable Acts—designed to bring the wayward colony of Massachusetts into line, and to serve as a warning to everyone else. The colony's royal charter was annulled. The port of Boston was closed until the city compensated the East India Company and the customs office for their losses. The garrison in Boston was increased to over 3,000 troops. These were quartered throughout the town, and other colonies were told they could expect the same treatment, if warranted.

It was another misstep. The rest of America rallied behind Boston, sending the occupied city food and other necessities from as far away as the Carolinas. Representatives from every town in Massachusetts met outside Boston and resolved to neither pay the tea tax nor to compensate the East India Company. Instead, they would raise militia companies that would soon become known as Minutemen, supposedly able to respond within 60 seconds to any threat to their communities. Paul Revere took to his horse for the first time, spreading word of these Suffolk Resolves throughout the other colonies. Widespread literacy and printing presses enabled Americans to respond quickly to a challenge. Before the end of 1774, 56 delegates from 12 of the 13 colonies met in Philadelphia, in what would become the First Continental Congress—America's first national deliberative body.

Some of those gathered in Philadelphia were eager to take a bold step. A dazzling young Virginian named Thomas Jefferson argued that England's actions constituted "a deliberate and systematical plan of reducing us to slavery." But the congress did nothing more than petition King George III for relief, and hope for the best.

Meanwhile, events in the street were fast spinning out of control. Mobs throughout America were closing down royal courts and bullying English loyalists and officials, attacking their homes, and even tarring and feathering them—a sometimes fatal humiliation. The British House of Commons responded by ignoring the colonists' petition. Massachusetts was declared in rebellion, and the colony's fishermen were denied access to the Grand Banks. All the colonies were now forbidden to trade with anyone save for England and its Caribbean possessions.

The new military royal governor of Massachusetts watched all this with misgivings. General Thomas Gage had served in the Americas for the better part of 20 years, and he understood that the people he was dealing with were not a "Boston rabble," as the king's ministers believed, but "the freeholders and farmers

of the country." He had made a bold strike to confiscate Patriot munitions in nearby Somerville in September of 1774, and he knew the Sons of Liberty had, in response, built a formidable network of spies to keep track of British troop movements. Gage gave his king what would become the usual advice of a general facing an indigenous insurgency: Send more men. He figured he would need at least 20,000 troops to suppress the burgeoning rebellion: "If force is to be used at length, it must be a considerable one, and foreign troops must be hired, for to begin with small numbers will encourage resistance, and not terrify; and will in the end cost more blood and treasure."

THE DIFFERENCE BETWEEN THE COLONISTS AND BRITISH CITIZENS

By the eighteenth century, Americans were very different from Englishmen. They were taller; they ate better, breathed cleaner air, and drank purer water; they earned higher incomes and were ten times more likely to own land. Their children were more than twice as likely to see their 21st birthday. And they were also more literate, thanks to the Protestant insistence on reading the word of God for themselves.

	Colonist	British Citizen
Height (male*)	5' 8"	5' 5"
Literacy rate (male)	75%	60%
Life expectancy (male)	53.5 years	36 years
Death rate	25 per 1,000**	40–50 per 1,000
Fertility rate	7.2	5.1
Household size	6 people	4.5 people

* for a 21-year-old man, ** New England

MINUTEMAN!
MUSEUM EXTENSION PROJECT
WPA
DISTRICT 5
VINCE
AUT
MORIRE
LIBERTY
OR
DEATH
MINUTE MAN
1774
-75

1775

"YOU'LL HAVE NOISE ENOUGH BEFORE LONG!"

LEXINGTON GREEN AND CONCORD BRIDGE

King George's men decided Gage was too timid. He was ordered to arrest the rebellion's leaders and take the offensive. Gage received these orders on April 4, 1775. Patriot spies had already read them. On April 18, the Patriot leader Dr. Joseph Warren summoned Revere and William Dawes to his home, to tell them that the British would march on Lexington and Concord that night, to seize a suspected ammunition cache and arrest John Hancock and Samuel Adams.

The information triggered an elaborate early-warning system for the Patriots. Revere and Dawes were to leave Boston and make their way to Lexington and Concord by different routes, sounding the alarm in every town through which they passed. In case he was stopped before he could get out of the city, Revere arranged for the sexton of the Old North Church to hang two lanterns from the belfry when he saw the British begin to move. Dawes and Revere made it out of the city, mounted waiting horses, and sped off to warn their fellow Patriots. An ever-growing matrix of riders rode out from every village and town they stopped in, forwarding the message on through the rest of Middlesex County, and then to the rest of the colony. They did not shout "The British are coming!"—this would have seemed ridiculous to many colonists, who considered themselves British—but rather, "The Regulars are coming out!" When Revere pulled up before the house where Hancock and Adams were staying, a baffled sentry told him to stop making so much noise.

From "every Middlesex village and farm" came the Minutemen. Unlike other people who bravely stood up against the British Empire, most of them owned a gun, and they knew how to use it.

"Noise!" cried Revere. "You'll have noise enough before long. The Regulars are coming out!"

Dawes and Revere pushed on to Concord, but their work was done. Adams and Hancock had time to gather their papers and their wits and flee by coach, just as the Regulars came up the road to Lexington. It had been a hard night for the redcoats, who had suffered repeated delays and failed to get across the Charles River until 2:00 in the morning. It wasn't until 4:30, soon after first light, that an advance party under Major John Pitcairn of the Royal Marines arrived at Lexington Common. Pitcairn had 238 men, the first wedge of some 700 Marines and grenadiers that Gage had sent out. Facing him across the common were 60 of the Lexington Minutemen under their elected commander, Captain John Parker—a tall, weathered veteran of the French and Indian War, already racked by the tuberculosis that would kill him five months later. Pitcairn, a blunt, 53-year-old Scot, barked at them, "Lay down your arms, ye damned rebels!"

Parker ordered his men to stand aside, although they did not throw down their arms. Then someone fired. Who it was, on which side, was never determined, but it set off a sharp, deadly exchange. Most of the Americans turned and ran. The British kept firing, then charged forward, bayoneting some of the wounded where they lay. When the fighting on Lexington Green subsided, one Regular was mildly injured, while eight Minutemen were dead and nine were wounded.

The British searched for Hancock and Adams, then pushed on to Concord at 9:00 A.M. There they found no opposition; the outnumbered Concord militia was assembled across the North Bridge, over half

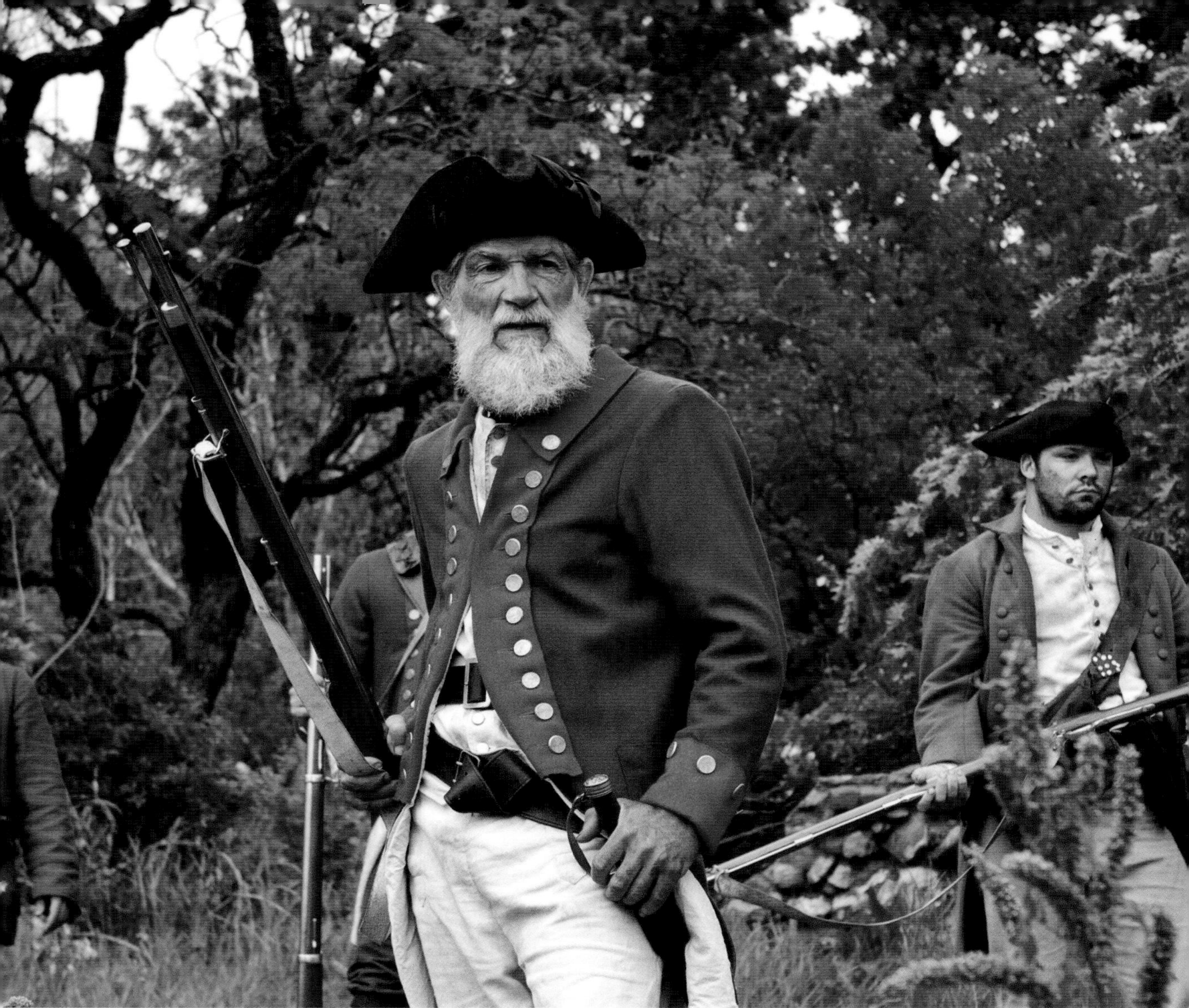

a mile from the center of the village. Pitcairn assigned a couple of companies to guard the bridge, then returned to seek out the rebel supply depot. The colonists had left little behind—some gunpowder and musket balls, a little food, and three artillery pieces that were too heavy to be easily carried away. The Regulars spiked the guns and tossed their wooden carriages into a pile in the village square, where they set them on fire.

Neither Pitcairn nor his commanders knew how well the Americans' early-warning system had worked. From all over Massachusetts, well-armed Minutemen were streaming into the woods and fields around Concord. Soon they were joined by Captain Parker and by 120 men from Lexington. Then someone noticed the smoke from the burning gun carriages. The Concord men, certain that the troops were burning their homes, surged toward the bridge, with hundreds of other Minutemen right behind them. Pitcairn's detachment, surprised, scrambled up to meet them and fired a ragged volley. The Minutemen suffered casualties but held their fire until they reached the bridge. Then they let loose, hitting 12 Regulars. Stunned and outnumbered by at least five to one, the British fell back, the Patriots sweeping across the North Bridge after them.

Suddenly, there was a war on, though neither side could quite believe it. Pitcairn's men continued to dally in Concord for another couple of hours before making their way back to Lexington, where they rejoined the rest of the Regulars. But now they were in real trouble. It was 17 miles from Boston, and thousands of local militiamen were still pouring into the hills and the woods around them. They constituted a force unlike any the British had faced. Throughout the eighteenth century, Regulars had crushed badly armed troops of rebels in the British Isles. The Americans they were facing now had their own firearms, and they knew how to use them. Many had fought in the brutal guerrilla campaigns of the French and Indian War, and they understood how to set an ambush and fire from cover.

Throughout that afternoon, they turned the retreating British column into a shooting gallery. The Regulars were saved only by a thousand reinforcements sent out from Boston equipped with cannons. One British commander reported that his men were under fire almost continually for 14 miles. Officers were a favorite target, most of them falling dead or wounded before the march was over. Enraged Regulars responded by looting and burning buildings along the way. By the time it was all over, the colonials counted 54 men dead or missing, with 39 wounded. The British had suffered 73 dead, another 53 missing, and 174 wounded; the remainder stumbled gratefully back behind their lines, exhausted.

The Battle of Lexington and Concord stunned everybody. The day after it ended, Bostonians awakened to find 15,000 rebels lining the hills and the rivers around them. They weren't going away; a revolution had begun. In Philadelphia, before the Continental Congress, a passionate Patriot from Virginia named Patrick Henry proclaimed: "The distinctions between Virginians, Pennsylvanians, New Yorkers, and New Englanders are no more. I am not a Virginian, but an American!"

Just what this meant would now be resolved in the terrible cauldron of war.

Above: A cartoon by Benjamin Franklin representing most of the colonies as a snake that might fight as one. "A military action...would make a wound which would never be healed," realized John Adams. "...It would render all hopes of a reconciliation with Great Britain desperate; it would light up the flames of war..."

CHAPTER TWO

REVOLUTION

A Declaration by the Representatives of the UNITED STATES OF AMERICA, in General Congress assembled.

When in the course of human events it becomes necessary for one people to dissolve the political bands which have connected them with another, and to assume among the powers of the earth the separate and equal station to which the laws of nature & of nature's god entitle them, a decent respect to the opinions of mankind requires that they should declare the causes which impel them to the separation.

We hold these truths to be self-evident; that all men are created equal; that they are endowed by their creator with inherent & inalienable rights; that among these are life, liberty, & the pursuit of happiness; that to secure these rights, governments are instituted among men, deriving their just powers from the consent of the governed; that whenever any form of government becomes destructive of these ends, it is the right of the people to alter or to abolish it, & to institute new government, laying it's foundation on such principles & organising it's powers in such form, as to them shall

[illegible] prudence indeed

[illegible] be changed for

[illegible] hath shewn that mankind are more disposed to suffer while evils are sufferable, than to right themselves by abolishing the forms to which they are accustomed. but when a long train of abuses & usurpations [begun at a distinguished period, &] pursuing invariably the same object, evinces a design to reduce them under absolute Despotism, it is their right, it is their duty, to throw off such [illegible] & to provide new guards for their future security. such has

ANNETTE GORDON REED, historian, Rutgers University: "Every group—blacks, women, gays, everybody—looks to the Declaration as a way of saying we are Americans too. The Declaration is the American creed."

1775
TO
1776

"WE ARE IN THE VERY MIDST OF REVOLUTION..."

WAR AND INDEPENDENCE

They came in the night, slipping through the Verrazano Narrows and into the harbor. New Yorkers looking out on the water the next morning—June 29, 1776—were stunned by what they saw.

"I was upstairs, and spied...as I peeped out the Bay something resembling a wood of pine trees trimmed. I could not believe my eyes," recalled Daniel McCurtin, a private in the new Continental Army, stationed in Brooklyn. "I thought all London was afloat."

What McCurtin saw was an armada of over 100 British warships, including five—the *Centurion*, the *Chatham*, the *Greyhound*, the *Phoenix*, and the *Asia*—that among them carried more firepower than all of the American guns arrayed to protect the city. These ships were the most fearsome, most modern machines of war available, used to project the power of the British Empire around the globe. Altogether, they carried 9,000 British Regulars. When, a few weeks later, the ships floated up, one by one, and dropped anchor off Staten Island, with "colors flying, guns saluting and the soldiers...continually shouting," the local militia defected almost immediately.

All summer long, the ships kept coming. By mid-August, there were more than 500 in the harbor, and some 32,000 British and German troops had been landed on Staten Island. "I feel for you and my other New York friends," an English sympathizer wrote to an American acquaintance, "for I expect your city will be laid in ashes."

After many delays and equivocations on both sides, the war was about to resume in earnest. But serious questions remained about just whom it was between—two nations, or a band of rebels and their rightful sovereign? And what its purpose was—the redress of grievances by loyal British subjects, or the suppression of a revolution? As the warships gathered in New York Harbor, a group of 50 mostly wealthy, generally conservative, but badly divided men likewise gathered in Philadelphia, rushing to resolve such questions once and for all.

In the 14 months since the first shots on Lexington Green, the Americans had scored one stunning success after another. British troops trying to storm Bunker Hill outside of Boston had lost 40 percent of their number, dead or wounded, the Americans retreating only when they had run out of powder. (Among the dead were Major Pitcairn, the crusty commander of the Royal Marines at Lexington, shot in the head by a freed black man, Peter Salem.) The attempt by a small fleet of British ships to capture the port of Charleston, South Carolina, had been repulsed. And a boisterous band of Vermonters who called themselves the Green Mountain Boys, under the command of Ethan Allen and a bad-tempered but audacious general named Benedict Arnold, had taken the key frontier post of Fort Ticonderoga by surprise. An enormous 25-year-old Boston bookseller turned colonel, Henry Knox, had then miraculously transported much of the heavy artillery at Ticonderoga across the winter snows of New England to the troops in Boston, where the guns' very presence was enough to break the stalemate and force the British out of the city. Only an ill-starred effort to seize Canada, and thus deprive the British of a base there, had ended in a setback for the colonials.

The Empire had regrouped in Halifax, Nova Scotia, putting together an enormous flotilla under

THE EXPEDITION HAD COST 850,000 POUNDS, A PRODIGIOUS SUM AT THE TIME—AND, AS SUCH, ONE THAT ILLUMINATED THE PROBLEMS ENGLAND WOULD FACE IN PROSECUTING THE WAR.

the command of two brothers, General William Howe and Admiral Lord Richard "Black Dick" Howe. By the time their expeditionary force was finally reassembled in New York Harbor, it would be the largest of any kind, anywhere, in the eighteenth century, and the largest such British force until the assault on D-Day during World War II. Its naval component alone constituted 40 percent of all the men and ships then active in the Royal Navy. It was also something of a bluff, one put together in the hope of ending the war without having to fire a shot.

The expedition had cost 850,000 pounds, a prodigious sum at the time—and, as such, one that illuminated the problems England would face in prosecuting the war. Many English workingmen openly favored the American cause, making recruitment difficult and forcing the purchase of thousands of mercenaries from Germany, primarily from the state of Hesse-Cassel. Sending so many Hessians and Englishmen across the Atlantic—and keeping them there—would bankrupt the crown before long. Scaring the rebels was preferable. General Howe, who was mildly sympathetic to American grievances, and who had seen every one of his aides killed or wounded at Bunker Hill, agreed. He made his preparations deliberately, sending out peace feelers, including a generous offer to the newly minted commander of the Continental Army, George Washington. Washington sent the offer back, unopened, establishing the primacy of civilian authority in the American government by informing Howe that only the Continental Congress had the power to consider such agreements.

Since May, the delegates of that Congress had been cloistered in Philadelphia's modest Carpenters' Hall, increasingly tormented by the summer heat and a plague of flies. Several colonies forbade their delegates to vote for any declaration of independence, but the Congress had appointed a committee to draw one up just the same. Its members had turned that job over to a handsome young Virginian squire and genius, Thomas Jefferson, who toiled away at it as the rest of Congress talked and talked.

July 1 dawned hot and humid, the delegates were bathed in sweat as the windows were kept closed against the fearsome flies. There was an added tension in the room. Everyone understood that the debate was close to reaching its conclusion, as rumors of the British fleet's arrival swept the city. Leading the opposition to independence was John Dickinson, a tall, gaunt, and very wealthy Philadelphia lawyer whom John Adams described as "a shadow...pale as ashes" throughout the debate. Dickinson had been a chief critic of the crown, but he still hoped for reconciliation. Couching his argument in practical terms, he pointed to the colonies' disorganization and weakness: "We are about to brave the storm in a skiff of paper."

Rising to debate him was John Adams, the touchy, querulous attorney who had defended the British soldiers in the Boston Massacre six years earlier. He worked his way through all the familiar arguments for independence, belaboring England's tyranny, calling for a new nation that would fit the tenor of a new time. "We are in the very midst of revolution, the most complete, unexpected, and remarkable of any in the history of the world," Adams told his colleagues. "The object is great which we have in view, and we must expect a great expense of blood to obtain it."

A thunderstorm had blown up at last, shattering the infernal heat, and as Adams spoke rain spattered against the windows and lightning creased the sky. Before he had finished, crucial new delegates came in, having just arrived after a hard journey through the night. Adams went through his arguments again for them, protesting that he felt like an actor hauled out to give an encore.

It would prove a fortunate delay. Before the Congress could adjourn for the evening, a dispatch from General Washington was delivered, confirming the arrival of the British fleet. Now Adams's words—combined with the looming threat of the invasion—concentrated the delegates' minds. The following day, the previously recalcitrant South Carolina delegation changed its vote, and backed independence. Delaware delegate Caesar Rodney, racked with pain from the facial cancer that would kill him, rode 80 miles through the rain and entered the hall in his boots and spurs to break a tie in his delegation, and cast his state's vote for independence. In the end, the vote was unanimous save for New York's abstention; the colony's Provincial Assembly, distracted by its flight from Manhattan to White Plains in the wake of the British fleet's arrival, had left its delegation without instructions. Jefferson's Declaration of Independence was approved.

A MAJOR MISTAKE

A Scottish native and career Royal Marine, Major John Pitcairn was sent by British commanders to disarm the colonists assembling near Concord on that fateful day in 1775. En route to Old North Bridge, Pitcairn and his three companies of Marines crossed through Lexington and met a band of rebels.

Pitcairn commanded the insurgents to lay down their weapons and ordered his own men not to shoot. Accounts vary regarding what happened next, but a volley of shots was exchanged, and eight Minutemen became the first American soldiers to lose their lives in combat.

The rebels would regroup and fire on the redcoats as they marched from Concord back to Boston. Shot twice, Pitcairn's horse bucked its master and made a break for the American side, supposedly taking with him the major's prized scroll-butt pistols.

Pitcairn's chance for revenge would come two months later. The rebels had taken Breed's Hill—mistakenly called Bunker Hill—and this time, Pitcairn wasn't holding his fire. The Marines broke through lines of infantrymen, but before they could reach the top, the major was shot.

He didn't die in the arms of his son William, as John Trumbull's 1786 painting *The Death of General Warren at Bunker's Hill, 17 June, 1775* suggests. After being shot by a freed black man named Peter Salem, he was carried to safety by the younger Pitcairn. The major lived just long enough to make it back to Boston, and when news of his death reached the front, William is said to have exclaimed, "I have lost my father!"

GENERAL
WASHINGTON

1776

NEW YORK CITY HAS FALLEN

WASHINGTON IN RETREAT

There was no abstention back in New York. On July 9, 1776, a crowd gathered before New York's City Hall to hear read aloud for the first time in Manhattan Jefferson's thrilling words: "We hold these truths to be self-evident, that all men are created equal, that they are endowed by their Creator with certain unalienable Rights, that among these are Life, Liberty and the pursuit of Happiness. . . ." They then marched a few blocks to Bowling Green, where they pulled down a statue of King George III, to raucous cheers. The statue's head was ultimately stuck on a pole outside an uptown tavern; the rest of it was melted down and shaped into more than 42,000 badly needed musket balls.

For much of the preceding year, the city's working classes had held what historians Edwin G. Burrows and Mike Wallace would call "an exhilarating, free-wheeling debate over fundamental political principles." But now, with the foe all too visible, the town was given over to chaos and paranoia. Colonial soldiers poured into the city, recently deserted by most of its inhabitants, chopping down the splendid trees New York had been known for as they advanced, and occupying and pillaging abandoned homes and businesses.

Their commanding general, George Washington, could barely control them, preoccupied as he was with building or strengthening 13 forts and defenses around the area. Many of his leading officers wanted him to leave the city (some advocated burning it, so that it would offer no shelter for the British), but Washington agreed with John Adams that New York was "a kind of key to the whole continent." All he had to defend it with, though, was a poorly organized, ill-equipped gaggle of men drawn from all over America on short enlistments, and ill-disposed to take orders from anyone beyond their immediate commanders. Washington had never led a force of this size, and getting his men the most basic provisions—such as clean water, a problem in Manhattan even in peacetime—proved difficult. By the end of the summer, dysentery and other illnesses had laid out a reported 9,000 of the 28,000 men Washington had on hand. Among them was General Nathanael Greene, his most capable subordinate and the man who had organized the defense of Brooklyn, then just a village at the western tip of Long Island, across the East River. Washington was forced to replace Greene with John Sullivan, a lesser general with no knowledge of the terrain on which he would be fighting.

On August 22, the British began to move. The Howe brothers landed their men on Long Island unopposed, and approached the defenses of Brooklyn. Probing about with the help of spies, they found a hole on the American left flank that remained open owing to a miscommunication. They exploited it expertly. Outnumbered and surrounded, the Americans were butchered at close quarters. "The greater part of the riflemen were pierced with the bayonet to trees," reported a Hessian officer.

Washington's army, on the brink of annihilation, was saved by a valiant counterattack led by 400 Maryland riflemen. Before their assault was over, all but nine of the Maryland men had been killed or captured, but they gave the rest of the Continentals time to escape and regroup.

For the first time in a major battle, colonials from all over America fought side by side. Watching their sacrifice, Washington reportedly cried out, "Good God, what brave fellows I must this day lose!"

THE AMERICANS PAID A TERRIBLE PRICE FOR TRYING TO DEFEND NEW YORK. THEY HAD LOST MOST OF THEIR MUNITIONS AND SUPPLIES, ALONG WITH 3,600 DEAD OR WOUNDED. THOUSANDS MORE HAD DESERTED. AND SOME 4,000, INCLUDING 300 OFFICERS, HAD BEEN CAPTURED.

Washington had lost 1,200 men—with another 1,500 wounded, captured, or missing—in his first major engagement, compared with just 60 British dead and 300 wounded or missing. His army was still facing imminent destruction, hemmed in on Brooklyn Heights with its back to the East River. Then, as he would do again and again throughout the Revolution, Washington saved himself and his men with an inspired bit of thinking. While some of his troops made a great demonstration along the lines, the rest sneaked off to longboats under the cover of rain and fog. This time, it was men from Massachusetts who saved the day, fishermen from Salem and Marblehead who pulled the troops quickly across the river and back to the temporary safety of Manhattan.

Here, the war paused for a moment, as Admiral Lord Howe sought again to fulfill the original, more wishful goal of his mission: to subdue the Americans without an extended conflict. The admiral hosted a delegation from the Continental Congress on Staten Island on September 11, 1776, plying them with good meat and wine, and implying that all would be forgiven if the Congress simply revoked the Declaration of Independence and swore allegiance to the crown. The two sides bantered. Howe told the Americans he was meeting with them not as members of Congress but as gentlemen of ability and influence. John Adams informed Howe that he could consider him in any way he pleased, save as a British subject. Later, as Howe remarked on how much pain ravaging America would give him, Ben Franklin replied that the Americans would have to take care to spare his feelings.

The gathering broke up with nothing achieved, and fighting resumed in the early-morning hours of September 15. Remembering Bunker Hill, General Howe still hesitated to assault New York City directly. Instead, he ordered General Henry Clinton to land his troops at Kip's Bay, a few miles up the East River from the town. Inadvertently, Howe had sent his men into just the sort of suicidal assault he wanted to avoid. The Americans had been strengthening their defenses in the area for weeks, and thousands of men now manned the parapets. Watching his Hessian troops clamber into their open boats and start across the river, Clinton thought it was the most dangerous attack he had ever witnessed. The Hessians themselves sang hymns to keep up their courage as they were rowed to shore. Yet, unlike at Bunker Hill, Howe had his brother's warships nearby.

"It was quite a dark night, and at daybreak, the first thing that 'saluted our eyes' was all the four ships at anchor, with springs upon their cables, and within musket shot of us," remembered Joseph Plumb Martin, a 15-year-old Connecticut farm boy fighting with the Continental Army. "The *Phoenix* lying a little quartering, and her stern towards me, I could read her name as distinctly as though I had been directly under her stern...."

Then the guns of the *Phoenix* and her sister ships erupted, firing 2,500 cannonballs into the American fortifications in an hour. The Americans had never seen anything like it, the deafening guns shattering their works and threatening to bury them alive in their trenches. The Continental soldiers broke and ran, abandoning their fortifications before the invasion force landed.

Where a few days earlier Washington had marveled at his men's courage, now he lashed at their

backs with his cane and threatened to run them through with his sword, cursing the "dastardly sons of cowardice." They ignored him, running on while he threw his hat to the ground and cried out, "Good God, have I got such troops as those?" His aides had to haul him away before he was captured by the advancing British.

Back in the city, General Howe's men chased the Americans north to about present-day 125th Street, where their buglers taunted the Americans by sounding the call traditionally heard at the end of a successful fox hunt. "It seemed to crown our disgrace," remembered Washington's adjutant, Joseph Reed.

Enraged, Washington ordered a brief counterattack that drove the British pursuers back. This victorious skirmish in upper Manhattan seems to have influenced General Howe to move more carefully than ever in pursuit, and may well have saved the Continental Army once more. Nonetheless, over the next two months the British smashed Washington's troops again at White Plains and grabbed up the considerable garrisons he had left on both sides of the Hudson. The Americans paid a terrible price for trying to defend New York. They had lost most of their munitions and supplies, along with 3,600 dead or wounded. Thousands more had deserted. And some 4,000, including 300 officers, had been captured.

A French artist's depiction of Patriots pulling down the statue of King George III—in a city that looks more like Paris than New York.

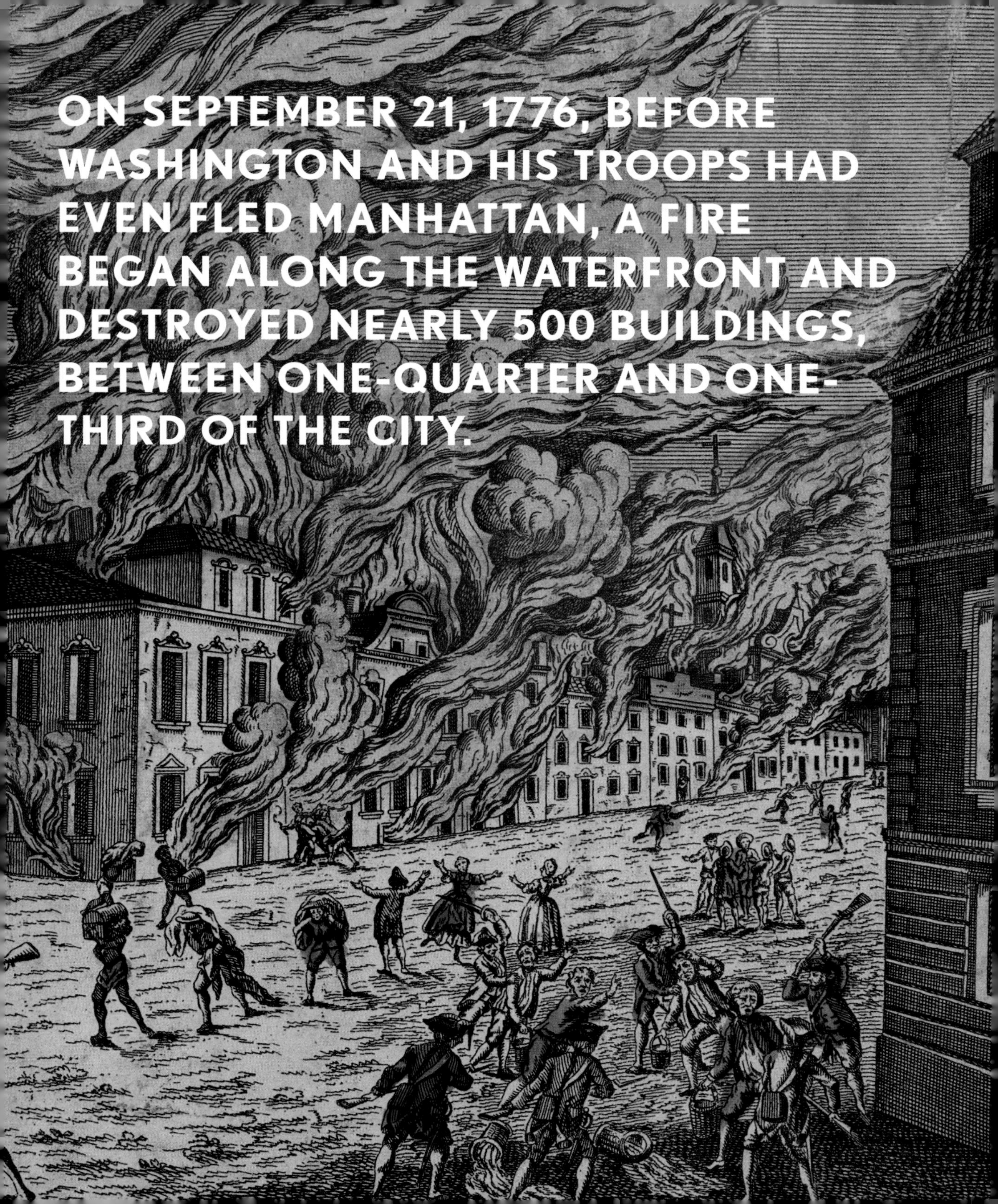
ON SEPTEMBER 21, 1776, BEFORE WASHINGTON AND HIS TROOPS HAD EVEN FLED MANHATTAN, A FIRE BEGAN ALONG THE WATERFRONT AND DESTROYED NEARLY 500 BUILDINGS, BETWEEN ONE-QUARTER AND ONE-THIRD OF THE CITY.

"What sobers the Brooklyn boy as he
looks down the shores
of the Wallabout and remembers the
prison ships,
What burnt the gums of the redcoat
at Saratoga when he
surrendered his brigades,
These become mine and me every
one, and they are but little,
I become as much more as I like."

—Walt Whitman, *Leaves of Grass*

1776 TO 1777

WASHINGTON DOUBLE-CROSSES THE DELAWARE

THE WAR TURNS SAVAGE

Most of the 4,000 men the British captured in the battles for control of Manhattan would die in incarceration, as part of the nightmarish experience that would now engulf New York. On September 21, 1776, before Washington and his troops had even fled Manhattan, a fire began along the waterfront and destroyed nearly 500 buildings, between one-quarter and one-third of the city. Another fire, two years later, destroyed a hundred buildings more, leaving much of the city a charred ruin. Arson by municipal patriots or Continental agents was widely suspected, but never proved. Among the suspects was Connecticut militia captain Nathan Hale, who was turned in to the British as a spy and conducted himself with notable dignity at his hanging, saying, "I only regret that I have but one life to lose for my country."

Before long, the city was overflowing with Tory refugees. Disease and privation were rampant. British troops and loyalist militias murdered and pillaged with impunity, while their officers held fancy-dress balls. Trade ceased, the wharves rotted, and the city and its suburbs were stripped of livestock and trees.

Out at Wallabout Bay, just off Brooklyn, thousands of American prisoners were kept on 20 rotting ships. They were held belowdecks, brutalized by guards, and deprived of adequate food and water. By the end of the war, 11,500 men had perished on the prison ships—more than the number of American troops killed in combat.

Washington could do nothing for them. His army retreated through New Jersey and into Pennsylvania during the fall of 1776, pursued by General Howe at his usual safe-neck pace. The Revolution seemed to be falling apart.

With just days left before many of his army's enlistment terms were to expire, Washington pulled off still another bold gambit. Calling on his Marblehead fishermen again, he crossed the Delaware—not once, but twice. The first crossing was on Christmas night, to attack the Hessian garrison at Trenton, New Jersey. Many of his men marched through a blizzard with only bloody rags wrapped around their feet, then charged through the streets of the town shouting one of Tom Paine's best lines: "These are the times that try men's souls." They took more than a thousand prisoners back to Pennsylvania, then recrossed the frozen river a week later, eluded a large force under Lord Charles Cornwallis, and overran the British at Princeton. As the British soldiers broke and ran, Washington stood up in his stirrups and remembered the buglers' slight from New York, shouting to his troops, "A fine fox chase, my boys!"

The British retreated almost the whole length of New Jersey. Yet the brief winter campaign of 1776–77 only underscored the unyielding obstacles facing both sides. Washington and his Continental Army had proved themselves to be resilient and determined, able to harass and even defeat limited British forces. But there were not enough soldiers, and they were not well-trained or well-equipped enough yet to win a decisive battle against the bulk of the king's army. The revolutionary government was all but dysfunctional. Politicking in Congress hindered the delivery of supplies, and Washington's rivals plotted constantly to replace him. American troops usually went home when their enlistment terms were up, to care for their families and farms.

1777

PLAYING SOME DEADLY LONG SHOTS

VICTORY AT SARATOGA ENTICES THE FRENCH

The British, meanwhile, faced the classic challenges of an occupying army far from home trying to suppress a guerrilla insurgency. Any territory they captured switched sides as soon as they were gone. Loyal Tories were outnumbered—and often put off by British arrogance. Efforts to recruit Indians and blacks (any slave was offered his freedom if he agreed to fight with the British) produced more troops, but further enraged the white colonists. The cost of the war kept rising, until it threatened to bankrupt the empire.

His Majesty's government resorted to the typical responses of the occupier: escalation and terror. Lord George Germain, secretary for America, accused General Howe of being soft on the colonists. What was required was more men, with fewer scruples.

The unlikely individual put in charge was John "Gentleman Johnny" Burgoyne, a flamboyant 55-year-old general who had ingratiated himself with King George III. Burgoyne was a flashy dresser and a ladies' man, "rumored to be illegitimate, rumored to be a little sharp at cards, known to be socially ambitious and badly in debt," according to historian A. J. Langguth. He was, as well, a veteran and innovative commander, one of the founders of the British light cavalry. Burgoyne witnessed the slaughter at Bunker Hill, and he had helped repel the rebel campaign against Canada, but he never seemed to have taken the fighting ability of the Americans seriously, betting an acquaintance 50 guineas that he would return from North America within the year, victorious.

Burgoyne's assignment was to lead an expedition south from Canada. Generals Howe and Clinton were to meet him at Albany, New York, and together establish a series of forts along the length of the state that would sever New England from the rest of the colonies. This was a dubious project to begin with, but at first, everything proceeded as planned. Burgoyne deftly recaptured Fort Ticonderoga before pushing on to Albany. There was little sign of the rebels, and the campaign seemed to be every bit the cakewalk he had anticipated. The officers' ladies accompanied the troops in carriages, singing and laughing. Burgoyne's army of some 7,700 men was towing an enormous baggage train, including 2,000 wives, mistresses, female servants, and other camp followers. Fifty teams of oxen were required to haul the artillery along, and there were 1,500 wagons packed with supplies—a full 30 of them devoted to the fine wines, delicacies, and other amenities to which Gentleman Johnny had become accustomed back in London.

Almost as soon as Burgoyne's sappers could cut a trail through the New York woodlands for this great caravan, Americans under General Philip Schuyler would close it again, felling trees across the road, destroying bridges, and removing or burning any produce and livestock in the path of the British. By August, the pace of the British advance had slowed to just a mile a day, and the column was beginning to run low on food and other supplies. When Burgoyne sent a force out to scour the countryside for provisions, the men were routed by a local militia at Bennington, Vermont. Gentleman Johnny lost over 900 men, killed or captured—nearly an eighth of his army.

Burgoyne's situation had suddenly become dire. Then, just above Albany, at a plateau known as Bemis Heights, the Americans manifested themselves again: A force larger than Burgoyne's, under General Horatio Gates, was dug in across the only possible

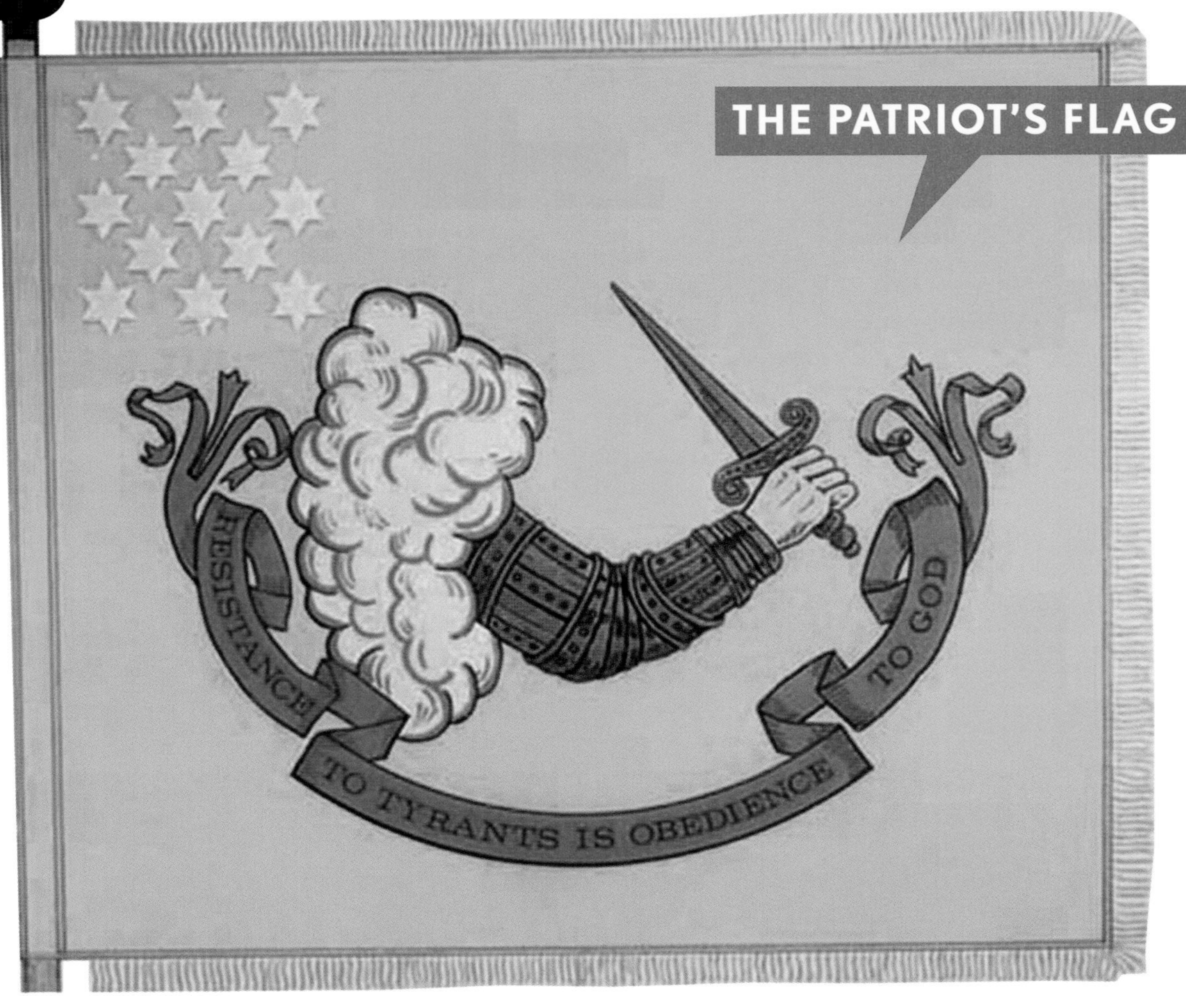
THE PATRIOT'S FLAG
RESISTANCE TO TYRANTS IS OBEDIENCE TO GOD

line of advance. What's more, they had an advantage Burgoyne had not counted on, one that was about to take a terrible toll on both his men and his ambitions.

Washington had created a special unit of some 500 of the Continental Army's best riflemen—the 11th Virginia Regiment—and placed it under the command of Colonel Daniel Morgan. There could have been no better choice. The son of Welsh farm laborers who had emigrated to New Jersey, Morgan had left home at 16 after a fight with his father and settled in the raw new town of Winchester, Virginia. He loved to drink, gamble, and fight, could barely read, and had never bothered to marry the woman with whom he lived. He insisted on cleanliness in camp, but refused to stand on military ceremony; like his riflemen, he usually dressed in buckskin shirts and leggings, coonskin caps, or even Indian gear. He was an easy disciplinarian, preferring to act as a father figure to his men, and was adored by them.

For all that, he cut a fearsome figure. Morgan's face had been badly scarred after he was shot through the cheek and neck during an ambush in the French and Indian War. On his back, he bore the marks of 499 lashes (Morgan liked to joke that "the king owes me a lash"), received for striking a British soldier during the same war. And despite his homespun ways, he was a military prodigy—according to one historian, "the only general in the American Revolution, on either side, to produce a significant original tactical thought."

Morgan had resolved upon a tactic that was considered virtually a war crime by many European armies. It would come to be known as sniping—deliberately taking out the most important targets in the enemy's ranks. During the last few days of the British march, his men had shot as many of Burgoyne's Native American guides as possible. The rest had abandoned him, leaving the British with no reconnaissance.

On September 19, 1777, as Burgoyne's men marched on Bemis Heights, the 11th Virginia confronted them across a 15-acre clearing known as Freeman's Field. When the British moved into the field, Morgan's riflemen, firing from the woods, killed or wounded every officer in the front line. Later, they took down the British general Simon Fraser, who was valiantly trying to organize a counterattack, and almost killed Burgoyne himself, shooting his horse out from under him. A wild charge led by Benedict Arnold left Burgoyne's men hemmed in against the Hudson,

THE PENNSYLVANIA LONG RIFLE

John Hancock called American riflemen "the finest marksmen in the world." Their weapons, a Colonial hybrid of Bavarian and English gunmaking, had rifled barrels up to four feet long that fired balls faster and more accurately than a musket. In the hands of skilled marksmen, these guns could bring down targets at 300 yards. That accuracy played a decisive role in several Revolutionary battles. Known as the Pennsylvania long rifle during the war, its popularity on the frontier in the nineteenth century gave it the name the Kentucky Rifle.

HOW A FLINTLOCK WORKS

When the trigger slams a small piece of flint against the steel frizzen, a spark ignites gunpowder in the flintlock pan—which then ignites gunpowder in the barrel.

where the British commander still refused to give up, hoping for relief from the armies with which he was supposed to join forces. Nearly three weeks dragged by, with Burgoyne's force steadily drained by casualties and desertions. Finally, exhausted and starving, the British surrendered in the nearby town of Saratoga, which would give the battle its name. Johnny Burgoyne had gone into the American wilderness and lost an army.

Saratoga was the pivotal battle in the American Revolution. The Congress's odd couple of diplomats—the worldly, sly Benjamin Franklin and blunt, fusty, provincial John Adams—had been in Europe for months, trying to recruit allies for their new nation. Now, with news of the victory, France agreed to send troops and ships in addition to the munitions and money it had already been secretly supplying. Spain also agreed to help, the Netherlands eventually provided money, and Russia gave its moral support—as well as refusing to sell Britain more mercenaries.

At last it appeared that the Americans might have the backing to win their revolution outright. But before any of these new allies could be brought into play, Washington's army would have to manage one more seemingly impossible feat: survive the winter.

BARREL RIFLING

The key to the long rifle was the spiraled grooves of its long barrel, which propelled balls at three times the velocity and five times the accuracy of smooth-bore muskets.

1777
TO
1781

THE LONG HAUL

BEYOND "THE SUMMER SOLDIER AND THE SUNSHINE PATRIOT"

All of the Continental Army's winter camps were brutal, but none was worse than that in Valley Forge during the winter of 1777–78.

The camp was just 18 miles outside Philadelphia, where General Howe's men were billeted in style for the season. Washington had chosen Valley Forge to make sure the British did not venture out and raid the rich farms of the Pennsylvania hinterlands. In preparation, his men had put up 900 cabins, each capable of housing 12 men, in just 40 days. But there was still so much they lacked: sufficient clothing, boots, food, even firewood. One man in five had no shoes. Just to feed the 11,000 soldiers every day required 35,000 pounds of meat and 168 barrels of flour; before long, they were out of meat and reduced to their last 25 barrels of flour, barely surviving on "fire cake"—a paste of bread and water.

"The Army which has been surprisingly healthy… now begins to grow sickly from the…fatigues they have suffered this Campaign," lamented surgeon Albigence Waldo, who was himself brought low with illness.

Unclean water spread typhus and dysentery, which killed hundreds of soldiers. Others were felled by hunger and exposure. Washington, horrified, moved constantly among his men, trying to rally them: "To see Men without Cloathes to cover their nakedness, without Blankets to lay on, without Shoes, by which their Marches might be traced by the Blood on their feet is a mark of Patience and obedience which in my opinion can scarce be parallel'd."

The camp faced another nemesis. A fresh smallpox epidemic was sweeping America; before it petered out, in 1782, it killed 100,000 people. In the eighteenth century, healthy Americans had a 15 percent chance of dying of the disease. Smallpox had already devastated the army that the Continental Congress sent to wrest Canada from the British, and thus changed history at least once. There was one thing that might stop the contagion: a primitive form of inoculation, in which pus from the pox of a victim who was no longer contagious was transferred to an open cut in an uninfected patient, thereby allowing him to build up an immunity to the disease.

It was one of the most daring experiments in American medical history, but necessary if Washington was to have an army left by the spring. His troops were inoculated, and once again his daring was rewarded. The Continental Army lost 2,500 men at Valley Forge, but only a few dozen died of smallpox after the inoculations.

Valley Forge, for all of its horrors, brought something positive to Washington's army as well. Ever since their arrival in Paris, Ben Franklin and the rest of his diplomatic mission had served as a sort of recruitment center for Europeans looking to fight in America. These individuals were idealists, knaves, adventurers, and soldiers of fortune. Most were aristocrats, usually true believers in the Enlightenment principles the Founding Fathers espoused. Some were looking to gain the military experience necessary to liberate their own nations; others just wanted a job. But whatever their motives, they brought much-needed enthusiasm and expertise to the American cause. Their ranks included a pair of young Polish officers, Tadeusz Kosciuszko and Kazimierz Pulaski, and a highly capable and enthusiastic young Frenchman, Gilbert du Motier, who would become beloved throughout America under his title, the Marquis de Lafayette.

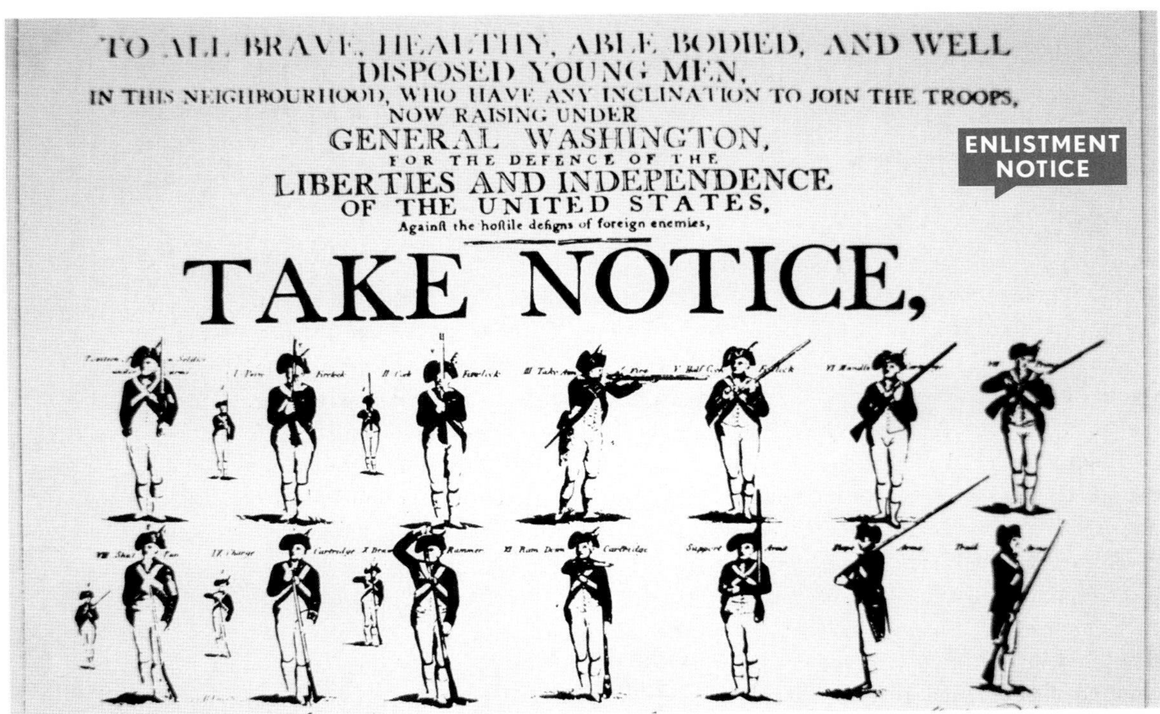

ENLISTMENT NOTICE

None of the contributions made by these men, however, approached those made by a comical, bulky Prussian fraud. When he appeared in America, in 1777, Friedrich Wilhelm Ludolf Gerhard Augustin von Steuben claimed to be a baron of the Holy Roman Empire, as well as former quartermaster general to Frederick the Great. He was neither of those things, but rather an eccentric captain who had been discharged for homosexual activity, and who went nowhere without his beloved Austrian greyhound and his entourage of younger officers—with two of whom he reportedly had an extended, "extraordinarily intense emotional relationship." What von Steuben had been, though, was a general staff officer in the best army in the world—something that made him an invaluable asset to the fledgling American military.

Von Steuben began by picking 120 of Washington's most capable officers and sergeants, and teaching them the basics of drill—not to mention how to care for their weapons and powder, how to kill with a bayonet, and, not least, how to lay out a sanitary and healthy camp. Von Steuben's apostles were then dispersed throughout the army, to spread the gospel through long winter hours at Valley Forge. They would emerge at the fore of a true modern army.

The war went on—and on. The action moved to the Southern states now, thanks again to the orders of Lord George Germain from London. He had been convinced by Southern exiles that most of the population there remained loyal to the king, and required only the presence of British troops to rise to the colors. Germain ordered Clinton—now in full command of the British forces in America—to mount an expedition. It was successful at first, with superior British naval and land power combining to take the ports of Charleston and Savannah, Georgia, and inflict the worst defeats the Americans would suffer throughout the war (some 5,000 Continentals surrendered at Charleston).

Then came the terror, as the British attempted to take the interior through a scorched-earth campaign. The contest soon devolved into a brutal guerrilla conflict. "We fight, get beat, rise, and fight again," the American general Nathanael Greene proclaimed. His relentless skirmishing through North and South Carolina—and a victory by old friend Daniel Morgan at the Battle of the Cowpens—cost Cornwallis some 2,000 casualties. Infuriated, Cornwallis dropped his baggage train, trying to catch up to Greene and deal his army one final, decisive blow.

"Then, he is ours!" exulted Greene when he heard the news of Cornwallis's actions, certain he could wear him down in the hostile country. The American commander maneuvered until he could fight Cornwallis on his terms, at Guilford Court House in North Carolina. The battle was another technical victory for the British, but Cornwallis lost 40 percent of his army, and his men were now badly in need of reinforcements and supplies. The British general resolved to push on into Virginia, and as he did so, nearly all of the commands he left behind him were defeated, with the British driven back to Charleston and Savannah.

Once in Virginia, Cornwallis linked up with troops under the command of Benedict Arnold, the most famous traitor in American history, who was now leading the depredations against his former country. But the British campaign had little remaining direction. Needing supplies, Cornwallis lurched toward the coast, where he could count on the protection of the navy.

Yet another British surge designed to suppress the rebellion had come to a very expensive and fruitless end. The empire's campaign in America hung by a thread. To cut it, Washington would need both luck and a little sleight of hand.

All through the Revolution, Washington and the rebels had shown themselves to be surprisingly adept at espionage. The man he placed in charge of intelligence was Major Benjamin Tallmadge, a close friend at Yale of Nathan Hale. Closemouthed, energetic, and clever, Tallmadge built a wide network of spies in and around occupied New York.

Yet the best intelligence coup that Washington pulled off was inadvertent. At the end of May 1781, he thoughtlessly wrote an uncoded letter to Lafayette in Virginia that was intercepted by a British patrol. It included the information that French and American troops intended to launch a major assault on the British army occupying New York. Thus alerted, Henry Clinton ordered Cornwallis to secure a base for the British navy near the Chesapeake, from which he could prepare to ship some 2,000 of his men back to Manhattan to help in its defense. Cornwallis balked and stalled, but then set about occupying and slowly fortifying Yorktown—not far from the site of the old Jamestown colony.

Unaware that Clinton was on to his plans and planning to bring up reinforcements from the South, Washington had his heart set on at last retaking New York before 1781 was out—in what almost certainly would have been a bloodbath. But his French allies had plans of their own. The commander of the French army in America, Jean-Baptiste-Donatien de Vimeur, the Comte de Rochambeau, had decided to march down to campaign instead in the South, and he had directed the commander of the French fleet in the West Indies, Admiral Comte François-Joseph-Paul de Grasse, to sail up and meet him in Chesapeake Bay. New York was off, at least for this campaign season.

Washington was furious, striding back and forth in his headquarters for half an hour, proclaiming before some astonished civilians that everything was lost. Then he collected himself, apologized...and began to plot the new strategy. He would move his army south and join with the French to trap Cornwallis where he sat encamped by the sea in Virginia. More disinformation—intentional, this time—soon followed. He marched men about as if they were preparing for an assault on New York. Known British agents were allowed to see documents indicating that Admiral de Grasse was sailing up to attack the British on Staten Island. Detailed plans for a camp that would hold a vast new army in New Jersey were drawn up, right down to the dimensions of ovens that could turn out thousands of loaves of bread. His soldiers were told nothing—even as he began to quickly, quietly march 3,000 of them south. "If we do not deceive our own men," Washington told his officers, "we will never deceive the enemy."

It was impossible to keep the movements of so many men—or of the 4,000 men under General Rochambeau who soon joined them—completely secret. Rumors of the allies' destination reached New York, where Benedict Arnold urged Clinton to attack the troops Washington had left around the city, in order to force him to stay in the North. Clinton responded by drawing up his own plans of attack, railing at his officers and the war ministry, and—on two different occasions—succumbing to temporary blindness. Within a few days, Washington was too far away to catch, and by August 29, Admiral de Grasse had arrived at Chesapeake Bay with over 30 ships of the line, and 3,200 additional French troops, bottling up Cornwallis in Yorktown.

THE REVOLUTION: BATTLE FOR A CONTINENT, 1775 TO 1783

The struggle for American independence was fought on every sort of terrain, from city streets to village squares to open fields, and deep in the frontier woods. On the high seas, Britain was rarely challenged by the fledgling American navy, but Captain John Paul Jones repeatedly defeated British ships of war around the Atlantic. On land, British regulars and German mercenaries routed American troops in most major engagements, but were unable to score a decisive victory or to hold territory without actively occupying it. Meanwhile Spanish forces aligned with the Americans routed British troops out of several Southern territories.

COLONIST VICTORY

BRITISH VICTORY

SPANISH VICTORY

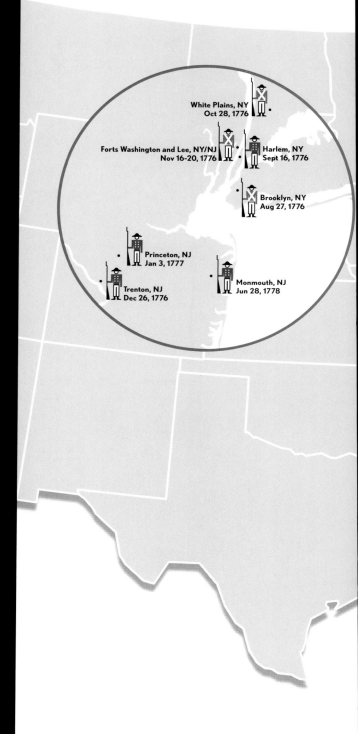

White Plains, NY
Oct 28, 1776

Forts Washington and Lee, NY/NJ
Nov 16-20, 1776

Harlem, NY
Sept 16, 1776

Brooklyn, NY
Aug 27, 1776

Princeton, NJ
Jan 3, 1777

Monmouth, NJ
Jun 28, 1778

Trenton, NJ
Dec 26, 1776

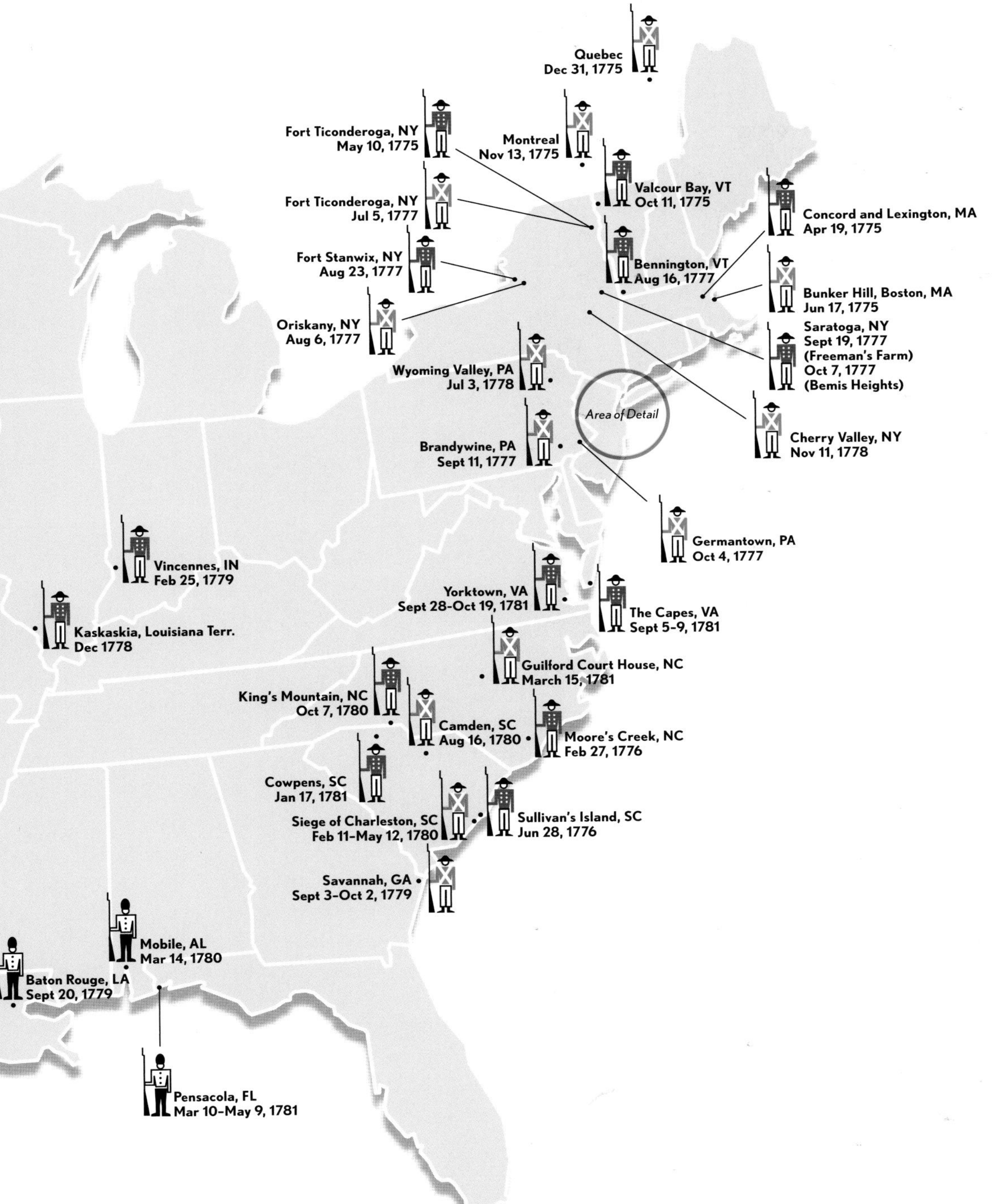
Quebec
Dec 31, 1775
Fort Ticonderoga, NY
May 10, 1775
Montreal
Nov 13, 1775
Valcour Bay, VT
Oct 11, 1775
Fort Ticonderoga, NY
Jul 5, 1777
Concord and Lexington, MA
Apr 19, 1775
Fort Stanwix, NY
Aug 23, 1777
Bennington, VT
Aug 16, 1777
Bunker Hill, Boston, MA
Jun 17, 1775
Oriskany, NY
Aug 6, 1777
Saratoga, NY
Sept 19, 1777
(Freeman's Farm)
Oct 7, 1777
(Bemis Heights)
Wyoming Valley, PA
Jul 3, 1778
Area of Detail
Cherry Valley, NY
Nov 11, 1778
Brandywine, PA
Sept 11, 1777
Germantown, PA
Oct 4, 1777
Vincennes, IN
Feb 25, 1779
Yorktown, VA
Sept 28-Oct 19, 1781
The Capes, VA
Sept 5-9, 1781
Kaskaskia, Louisiana Terr.
Dec 1778
Guilford Court House, NC
March 15, 1781
King's Mountain, NC
Oct 7, 1780
Camden, SC
Aug 16, 1780
Moore's Creek, NC
Feb 27, 1776
Cowpens, SC
Jan 17, 1781
Siege of Charleston, SC
Feb 11-May 12, 1780
Sullivan's Island, SC
Jun 28, 1776
Savannah, GA
Sept 3-Oct 2, 1779
Mobile, AL
Mar 14, 1780
Baton Rouge, LA
Sept 20, 1779
Pensacola, FL
Mar 10-May 9, 1781

1781

"MY DEAR LITTLE GENERAL!"

VICTORY AT YORKTOWN

Cornwallis still had one hope. Admiral Thomas Graves was on his way down from New York with the British fleet—but Graves had no idea of how dire the situation had become, unaware that de Grasse had arrived or that Washington was on the march. When he did make it to the Chesapeake, he let de Grasse slip out to the open sea, where his ships could maneuver. There, the two fleets engaged in 90 bloody minutes of combat, with the British taking somewhat the worst of it. The two fleets warily circled each other for a few days—then de Grasse slipped back into the Chesapeake, blocking the entrance to the bay. Still unaware of the urgency of Cornwallis's plight, Graves sailed back to New York to repair his damaged vessels and prepare to fight another day.

If a providential sign were required for the success of the American revolution, this was it. De Grasse's victory might not have been decisive, but it would serve—the one and only naval victory won by the French over the British since 1690. Meeting Washington a few days later, the tall French admiral embraced the American commander, kissed him on both cheeks, and cried, "My dear little general!" He could have kissed him a hundred times. Washington at last had a British army where he wanted it, pinned up against the water, with no navy to rescue it, and a force of veteran troops twice its size to contend with. It was almost the exact opposite of the battle that had started the war up on Long Island.

The British fortifications were extensive but spotty, and their forces were stretched thin. On September 30, Cornwallis abandoned three of their forward works—a move that allowed the French and Americans to move much closer. The British commander reassured his officers that Clinton had promised help would arrive soon. But in New York, a timber shortage was delaying Graves's ship repairs, and work had been suspended so that everyone could take part in two days of festivities honoring the visit of Prince William, King George's 16-year-old son. While the British officers gavotted in New York, the men in Yorktown, Virginia, munched the last of their bad meat and wormy bread.

Now, like a true professional army, the Continentals maneuvered closer still, digging a ditch for their siege guns and pounding the British defenses. Henry Knox, the old Boston bookseller, was on hand, an expert on artillery by now and soon to become the first American secretary of war. So was Plumb Martin, the Connecticut farm boy, who had become a sergeant in the Corps of Sappers and Miners. And so was Alexander Hamilton, a brilliant and dashing—if diminutive—24-year-old colonel. As a patriotic agitator at King's (later Columbia) College, he had attracted the notice of Washington and become a sort of surrogate son, serving for most of the war as his personal secretary. Fed up with desk work, Hamilton had demanded a field command, and the two men had quarreled.

Now he had his command: to lead the American troops in a night attack on one of two redoubts that were the keys to the British line. The French were to take the other, larger one. Before the assault began, Hamilton made sure that his men's muskets were unloaded; there was to be no chance of an accidental discharge that might alert the British. Their work was to be done entirely with bayonets, just as Baron von Steuben had taught them. "All the batteries in our line were silent, and we lay anxiously waiting for the signal," Martin wrote about the night of October 14, 1781. "The two brilliant planets, Jupiter and Venus, were in close contact in the western hemisphere.... I caught a glance of them, I was ready to spring on my feet, thinking they were the signal for starting."

Just after nightfall, 400 of Hamilton's men raced across a no-man's land strewn with enormous shell craters, drawing heavy British and Hessian fire. Martin and the other sappers and miners ran ahead with axes to batter down the enemy parapets, but when the troops began to pile up, they simply clambered over the wooden walls of the redoubt. Hamilton, too short to get over, ordered one of his men to kneel, climbed up on his back, and leaped over the wall. He and his men stood up under a final grenade assault by the British and captured or killed the entire garrison of the fort—all with bayonets. The attack led by the French was also successful.

Cornwallis, now as desperate as Washington had been in Brooklyn, tried the same tactic, attempting to slip his army across the James River under the inattentive noses of the French fleet. He got an entire division across before another providential stroke—a heavy thunderstorm, very much the opposite of the rain and fog that had helped Washington—intervened, making it impossible to complete the crossing. At two in the afternoon on October 19, 1781, with his supplies running out and facing annihilation, Lord Cornwallis surrendered his 8,400 remaining troops.

THE COST OF FINANCING THE REVOLUTION

With the powers established by the Articles of Confederation, Congress did not have the power to tax or regulate commerce, and states were required only to make voluntary payments to Congress for its war efforts. The bulk of the war's financing came from loans from France and the Netherlands, as well as from domestic loans, state requisitions, and the issuance of an increasing amount of paper money. As a last resort, Congress authorized the army to confiscate property. Money also came from public-spirited financiers like Haym Salomon, who found purchasers for government bills of exchange and lent his own money to the government. Britain financed their war efforts through an existing and effective tax system—but still suffered from a huge debt at war's end.

WHAT WAS SPENT

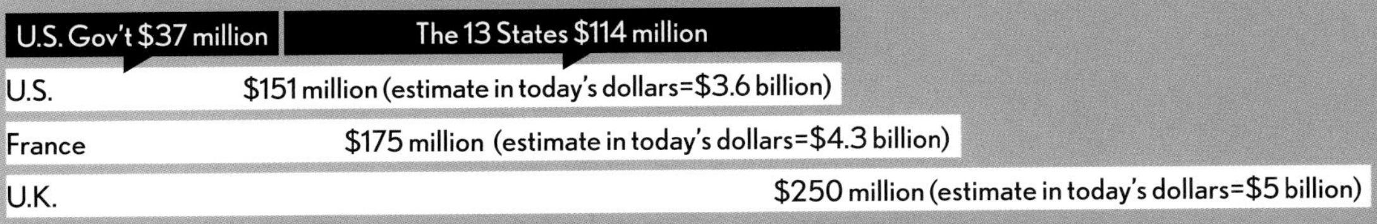

U.S. Gov't $37 million | The 13 States $114 million

U.S.	$151 million (estimate in today's dollars=$3.6 billion)
France	$175 million (estimate in today's dollars=$4.3 billion)
U.K.	$250 million (estimate in today's dollars=$5 billion)

1781
TO
1783

SORE LOSERS

THE END OF THE WAR

Even when it was over, there were insults and evasions. Cornwallis did not attend the surrender ceremony, pleading illness. He sent a subordinate, who tried to surrender to the French. Rochambeau insisted that Cornwallis's envoy surrender to Washington.

The war had been decided. George Germain resigned soon after the news from Yorktown reached London, and before much longer Parliament opened peace negotiations. King George III refused to accept this, egged on by a new acquaintance, Benedict Arnold, who assured him that America could still be regained. But under the terms of the Treaty of Paris, which formally ended the hostilities in 1783, all the king's ministers managed to hang on to was Canada.

Article 14th
No Article of the Capitulation to be infringed on pretext of Reprisal, & if there be any doubtfull Expressions in it, they are to be interpreted according to the common Meaning & Acceptation of the Words. —
Done at York in Virginia this 19th day of October 1781
Cornwallis
Tho: Symonds

CORNWALLIS SURRENDERS

The last plot of American soil to be occupied by the British was Manhattan Island. It was surrendered only after an estimated 35,000 loyalists were given free passage from the port by the British government. The city was in ruins, trenches dug across its main thoroughfares, its greatest church destroyed—and out on the prison ships of Wallabout Bay was an unspeakable horror.

The city's remaining residents still turned out to cheer Washington's Continental Army as it marched down Broadway.

"The [British] troops just leaving us were as if equipped for show," one witness wrote, "and with their scarlet uniforms and burnished arms, made a brilliant display. The troops that marched in, on the contrary, were ill-clad and weather-beaten, and made a forlorn appearance. But then, they were *our* troops, and as I looked at them, and thought upon all they had done for us, my heart and my eyes were full, and I admired and gloried in them the more because they were weather-beaten and forlorn."

The state of the nation was little better. Almost 30,000 soldiers, out of a population of 2.5 million, had died from wounds sustained in combat, from illness, or from the deprivations of captivity—the equivalent of close to four million deaths in today's population. Another 100,000 had died of the smallpox epidemic, while tens of thousands had fled the country. The new nation was held together by a barely workable framework known as the Articles of Confederation, its ruling legislature was barely functional and widely despised, and it was $150 million in debt. But like its leading city, it would overcome all obstacles, and rise again. America had begun.

DAVID BALDACCI, writer: “Washington was a genius in taking people in who didn’t seem like they could achieve great things, but under him they rose to the challenge, they rose to the occasion That’s what great leaders do.”

CHAPTER THREE

WESTWARD

HUNTERS IN THE CUMBERLAND GAP

1763 TO 1798

GO WEST, YOUNG BOONE

CROSSING THE CUMBERLAND GAP

Three hundred million years ago, a meteorite the size of a hundred football fields tumbled down toward what was then the treeless range of the Appalachian Mountains. It struck with incredible force, driving a deep wedge between the mountain peaks. For thousands of years, animals would use this opening to migrate west. Eventually men would follow, and they would give the crater a name: the Cumberland Gap. Through it would pour an empire.

Even before the Revolution, Americans had coveted these lands, chafing at the so-called Proclamation Line imposed by the British crown at the end of the French and Indian War, in 1763. The line reserved almost all territory from the Appalachians to the Mississippi for the Indian tribes that occupied it. But colonists had already founded small settlements in western Pennsylvania, Virginia, Ohio, and Kentucky. Neither king nor "savage" could deter them, and they were led by a man whose name would be legend.

On an early hunting trip over the Appalachians, Daniel Boone had run into a party of Shawnee who took his pelts and his horse, and warned him to stay away. He could not, drawn back again and again by what a companion, Felix Walker, described as "the pleasing and rapturous appearance of the plains of Kentucky."

It was also a hard land, and it would take much from Boone. He would lose his two eldest sons and a brother, killed by the Shawnee. Boone never held it against the Indians, later insisting that "they have always been kinder to me than the whites." Captured by the Shawnee at one point himself, he was adopted by the tribe and lived with them for five months.

Cumberland Mountain Hunters by Samuel M. Lee, 1830–1840 (detail).

Such episodes underscored the complex, interconnected nature of life on the frontier. Whites and Indians traded crops and livestock, intermarried, and often lived peacefully alongside one another. But they could be friends one day and mortal enemies the next. The Shawnee committed their periodic atrocities to send a message. They were enraged by the fact that various Iroquois and Cherokees had made treaties ceding to the British and the Americans land that was really theirs. They had been pushed west of the Appalachians only after a bloody battle with white settlers a hundred years before, and they were determined not to yield again. Boone knew they were doomed. The western lands were just too rich to resist.

Boone's original settlement, Boonesborough, established in Kentucky in 1775, held 200 souls. With the end of the Revolution, settlers flowed freely through the widened path that he and a team of axe-wielding men had cut along the Cumberland Gap, now known as the Wilderness Road. In 1795, 26,000 people went down that road in the space of two months. By 1800, there were 200,000 whites in Kentucky, and over 80,000 more in Tennessee.

It was the same old story—the Indians could not stand against such numbers, although they learned the lessons of their history and tried, by forming larger, more formidable coalitions. But Ohio fell in 1794, when Revolutionary War hero "Mad Anthony" Wayne and his Legion of the United States routed a strong confederacy of Shawnee, Delaware, Miami, and other tribes in the Battle of Fallen Timbers. In the South, beginning in 1798, white planters and their slaves began to swarm into western Georgia and into the territories of Alabama and Mississippi.

1810 TO 1813

ROCK STAR/ WARRIOR

TECUMSEH RALLIES HIS PEOPLE

At this point emerged perhaps the greatest leader Native Americans have ever produced to stand against the white man. Tecumseh was a Shawnee with Creek blood; some of his ancestors may have been white. Charismatic, slyly funny, tall, graceful, and relatively light-skinned, he would become every white man's favorite Indian, but his abilities and his accomplishments on behalf of his people were real enough. His father had been killed fighting the English, and his family was pushed from pillar to post during the vicious combat that took place on the frontier during the Revolution, his childhood homes repeatedly destroyed. Tecumseh seems to have held as little a grudge about all this as Daniel Boone did for his losses. Almost alone on both sides in the wars between Indians and whites, he would not tolerate the often barbaric abuse of the innocent and the helpless, repeatedly intervening to save the lives of hundreds of white prisoners.

What Tecumseh also would not tolerate was the theft of his people's lands. He pressed representatives of the American government to repeal the often dubious treaties they had made with Indians of one tribe or another.

When, in 1810, the government refused to reconsider the treaties, Tecumseh set about organizing the largest, most powerful Indian confederation ever seen in North America. He threw his influence behind the revelations of his brother Lalawethika, a one-eyed reformed drunk who claimed to have received apocalyptic visions from the Great Spirit. Calling himself "Tenskwatawa," meaning "the Open Door," Lalawethika demanded that Native Americans of every tribe give up anything related to the white man—clothing, customs, and especially whiskey. If they did, Tenskwatawa assured them, the whites' gunpowder would turn to sand, and their bullets would be useless against the Indians. They would be driven from the land, and the old ways would be restored.

It was a messianic appeal that bore a close resemblance to those expounded over 80 years later by the Boxers in China, the Zulu warriors in Africa, and the Ghost Dancers in the Dakota Territory.

Tecumseh seized on the message and ran with it, traveling relentlessly up and down the nations from the Great Lakes to the Gulf Coast, trying to bind them into one people—Shawnee and Creek, Cherokee and Mohegan, Miami and Delaware and Kickapoo, Choctaw and Chickasaw, Chippewa and Ottawa.

When a comet streaked across the heavens in 1811, the Indians murmured that it was Tecumseh's time (his name was generally interpreted to mean "Shooting Star" or "Panther Across the Sky"). But it was not to be. Tenskwatawa proved to be less of a tactician than a prophet, letting himself be drawn into a premature battle at Tippecanoe against William Henry Harrison, governor of the Indiana Territory, while Tecumseh was away trying to rally the tribes in the South. It was a disastrous defeat.

There was one last moment of hope, when Tecumseh made common cause with the British in the War of 1812. Congress had declared war ostensibly to stop the arbitrary impressment of American sailors into the Royal Navy, but its real purpose was to take care of some unfinished business from the Revolution: the seizure of Canada. From the start, the conflict was a fiasco for the Americans, with their slapdash armies disorganized, undersupplied, and erratically led. The invasion of Canada floundered, and in response British troops seized Washington, the country's new capital, and burned it to the ground. Save for a few notable events—the triumphs of a seemingly impenetrable warship, the *USS Constitution*, a.k.a. Old Ironsides; the defense of Baltimore (which gave us "The Star-Spangled Banner"); the noble death of Captain James Lawrence (which gave us the line "Don't give up the ship!"); and Andrew Jackson's mauling of a British army at New Orleans—U.S. triumphs of any sort were few and far between.

The war did, however, mark the effective end of armed Indian resistance in the Midwest. Fighting with the British, Tecumseh played a key role in forcing the surrender of a large American garrison at Detroit, and he would become a national hero in Canada for helping to preserve the identity of that nation. But as in the Revolution, Great Britain proved an unreliable ally to the Indian, and Tecumseh was killed in battle.

Afterward, Americans would speak of his bravery and his humanity, and would name their children and their schools and their towns after him. But they would not honor the ancient claims of his people.

1812 TO 1840

THE TRAIL OF TEARS

GENOCIDE AGAINST THE "CIVILIZED TRIBES"

Some Indians tried a different tack. Like all good Americans, they sued. Among those pursuing this approach were members of the so-called Five Civilized Tribes: the Cherokee, the Chickasaw, the Choctaw, the Muscogee (Creek), and the Seminoles.

By the 1830s, there were nearly 74,000 Indians at peace with the U.S., and still occupying large swaths of land from North Carolina down through Alabama and Mississippi, and in the newly acquired territory of Florida. The idea that red men should become white men would be a long-held dream of many well-meaning Americans, who hoped they would assimilate into the white population and disappear. And no people seemed more open to this idea than the Cherokee, who were then inhabiting much of the Appalachian foothills, from North Carolina into Georgia and Alabama.

The tribe had a long history of living at peace with whites, and they had already adopted many white ways. By the nineteenth century, Cherokees commonly dressed in modest, manufactured "white man's" clothing. Their women sewed and knitted, and their men raised crops of wheat and corn, and acquired pigs, cows, and other livestock. By the 1830s, an obsessed Cherokee silversmith named Sequoyah had worked out a written language for his people, complete with its own syllabary.

Almost overnight, the Cherokee went from an unlettered people to one that was more literate than the white Southerners around them, running their own printing press and publishing their own, bilingual newspaper, the *Cherokee Phoenix*. They also established a political capital, along with their own police, a National Council of Chiefs, and a National Committee. In July of 1827, they even held a constitutional convention, and ratified a document that defined their nation's permanent borders.

Far from disappearing, the Cherokee looked as if they were planning to stay forever—as Cherokee. But white farmers wanted their lands, and they got even hungrier for it once gold was found on Cherokee holdings in northern Georgia.

Fortunately for the Southern farmers, their greatest advocate was about to ascend to the presidency. Andrew Jackson was a man of the people—the white people. The popular movement he led had secured, for the first time, the right of all white men in the United States to vote, regardless of how little property they held. But Jackson was also a slaveholder and longtime Indian fighter. The Cherokee had fought alongside Jackson against the Creek in the War of 1812, but that made no difference now. In his inaugural address, Jackson called for the passage of an Indian Removal Act, which would force all Indians to move west of the Mississippi.

Jackson's bill was the subject of four months of bitter debate in Congress. It was opposed even by legendary frontiersman Davy Crockett, then a representative from Tennessee, and passed the House by just five votes. The Cherokee did not take this lying down. They submitted a petition with 16,000 names to Congress, asking to keep their ancestral lands. When that accomplished nothing, they went to the Supreme Court—and won. The great Chief Justice John Marshall ruled for the sovereignty of the Cherokee Nation. He was, however, ignored. President Jackson refused to enforce the court's rulings, and pressed ahead with the eviction of the Cherokee.

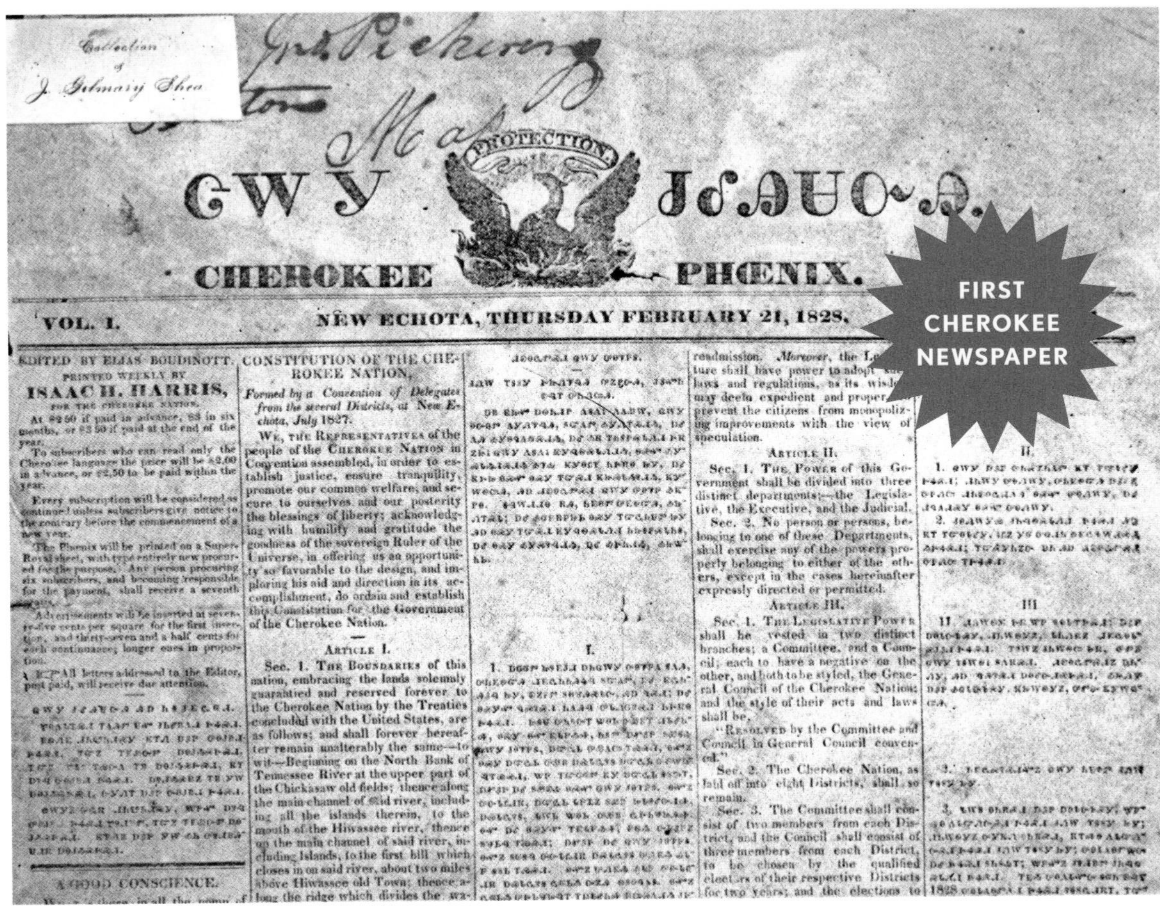

CHEROKEE PHŒNIX.

VOL. I. NEW ECHOTA, THURSDAY FEBRUARY 21, 1828.

EDITED BY ELIAS BOUDINOTT.
PRINTED WEEKLY BY
ISAAC H. HARRIS,
FOR THE CHEROKEE NATION.

At $2 50 if paid in advance, $3 in six months, or $3 50 if paid at the end of the year.

To subscribers who can read only the Cherokee language the price will be $2,00 in advance, or $2,50 to be paid within the year.

Every subscription will be considered as continued unless subscribers give notice to the contrary before the commencement of a new year.

The Phœnix will be printed on a Super-Royal sheet, with type entirely new procured for the purpose. Any person procuring six subscribers, and becoming responsible for the payment, shall receive a seventh gratis.

Advertisements will be inserted at seventy-five cents per square for the first insertion, and thirty-seven and a half cents for each continuance; longer ones in proportion.

☞ All letters addressed to the Editor, post paid, will receive due attention.

A GOOD CONSCIENCE.

CONSTITUTION OF THE CHEROKEE NATION,

Formed by a Convention of Delegates from the several Districts, at New Echota, July 1827.

We, the Representatives of the people of the Cherokee Nation in Convention assembled, in order to establish justice, ensure tranquility, promote our common welfare, and secure to ourselves and our posterity the blessings of liberty; acknowledging with humility and gratitude the goodness of the sovereign Ruler of the Universe, in offering us an opportunity so favorable to the design, and imploring his aid and direction in its accomplishment, do ordain and establish this Constitution for the Government of the Cherokee Nation.

Article I.

Sec. 1. The Boundaries of this nation, embracing the lands solemnly guarantied and reserved forever to the Cherokee Nation by the Treaties concluded with the United States, are as follows; and shall forever hereafter remain unalterably the same—to wit—Beginning on the North Bank of Tennessee River at the upper part of the Chickasaw old fields; thence along the main channel of said river, including all the islands therein, to the mouth of the Hiwassee river, thence up the main channel of said river, including Islands, to the first hill which closes in on said river, about two miles above Hiwassee old Town; thence along the ridge which divides the wa-

readmission. *Moreover*, the Le[...]ture shall have power to adopt [...] laws and regulations, as its wisd[...] may deem expedient and proper, [...] prevent the citizens from monopolizing improvements with the view of speculation.

Article II.

Sec. 1. The Power of this Government shall be divided into three distinct departments;—the Legislative, the Executive, and the Judicial.

Sec. 2. No person or persons, belonging to one of these Departments, shall exercise any of the powers properly belonging to either of the others, except in the cases hereinafter expressly directed or permitted.

Article III.

Sec. 1. The Legislative Power shall be vested in two distinct branches; a Committee, and a Council; each to have a negative on the other, and both to be styled, the General Council of the Cherokee Nation; and the style of their acts and laws shall be,

"Resolved by the Committee and Council in General Council convened."

Sec. 2. The Cherokee Nation, as laid off into eight Districts, shall so remain.

Sec. 3. The Committee shall consist of two members from each District, and the Council shall consist of three members from each District, to be chosen by the qualified electors of their respective Districts for two years; and the elections to

In 1838, under the administration of Jackson's handpicked successor, Martin Van Buren, 7,000 soldiers invaded the Enchanted Land, as the Cherokee called their nation, and forced its men, women, and children to march at gunpoint over a thousand miles, to the Oklahoma Territory. This trek became known as the Trail of Tears, and it may well have been the most shameful single episode in the history of the United States government. As always, it seemed, when a government action concerned the Indians, it was carried out with a maximum of disorganization, carelessness, and corruption. Dysentery broke out, killing thousands. More died from smallpox, contracted from blankets obtained from a white hospital in Tennessee—the infamous "plague blankets."

By the time the trek was over, more than one-quarter of the displaced Cherokees had died along the road. Similar fates awaited the other "civilized tribes." Only the Seminoles refused to surrender, waging a costly guerrilla war for years in the Florida swamps.

Of the nearly 74,000 Indians who still lived in the Southern states by 1830, over 14,000 had died and nearly all the rest had been transported to the Oklahoma Territory, their new home in perpetuity—until another land rush, in 1889, gave that, too, over to white settlement.

1797 TO 1806

NAPOLEON'S FOLLY

THE LOUISIANA PURCHASE

The instigators of the Louisiana Purchase were a nation of courageous ex-slaves, whose rebellion had sent a chill of fear throughout the American South. Toussaint Louverture, the leader of this revolution, wanted to secure freedom for his people but also maintain a good relationship with the old colonial masters in France, so that they might help develop the new, multiracial nation of Haiti. Instead, Napoleon Bonaparte had him seized at a parley under flag of truce, and Louverture was dispatched to live out his days in a chilly French prison. The emperor had decided to keep Haiti after all, as both a wealthy sugar colony and a base from which to harry the British in the West Indies. As Napoleon's own police chief would say in another context, this was worse than a crime—it was a mistake. After the loss of some 57,000 French soldiers to combat and yellow fever—and despite a campaign of atrocities by that former hero of the American Revolution, the Comte de Rochambeau—Napoleon decided to abandon his imperial ambitions in the New World.

MERIWETHER LEWIS

This meant surrendering France's vast holdings in the interior of North America. Rather than let this land fall into the hands of the British, Napoleon sold it to Thomas Jefferson and the fledgling American Republic in 1803: 828,800 square miles for $15 million dollars, or just three cents an acre. Predictably, the emperor chose to view it as a grand coup for himself: "This accession of territory strengthens forever the power of the United States, and I have just given to England a maritime rival that will sooner or later humble her pride."

RATHER THAN LET THIS LAND FALL INTO THE HANDS OF THE BRITISH, NAPOLEON SOLD IT TO THOMAS JEFFERSON AND THE FLEDGLING AMERICAN REPUBLIC IN 1803: 828,800 SQUARE MILES FOR $15 MILLION DOLLARS, OR JUST THREE CENTS AN ACRE.

The sheer size of the purchase was staggering, running from the port of New Orleans on the Gulf Coast up through Montana on the border of Canada. It would eventually come to make up all or part of 14 states, and constitute 23 percent of the landmass of the country. It was so vast, and so far from most of America's population, that the new nation had to send someone out to determine just what it had bought. President Thomas Jefferson selected a young Virginian friend and former army lieutenant, Meriwether Lewis, and Lewis in turn chose his former commanding officer, a veteran Indian fighter from Kentucky named William Clark. Together, they would head what they called a Corps of Discovery into the new lands.

It would take them two years, four months, and nine days to complete their mission. It was an incredible journey, over a daunting variety of landscapes—one that revealed the vast diversity of the continent the Americans had barely penetrated. In the end, the members of the Corps of Discovery ventured even beyond the vast territory that had been purchased from the French. They made their way down the Columbia River to the coast of Oregon, where Clark wrote in exultation: "Ocean in view! O! The Joy!" They spent another winter there, the first Americans to reach the West Coast by land. They gawked at the carcass of an immense beached whale and the huge buzzards that plucked at its flesh, and they found the Pacific (in Clark's words) "tempestuous and horrible," its breakers roaring in their ears for days. But they were there. America could now lay claim to the whole length of the continent.

INSIDE THE NOTEBOOKS OF LEWIS AND CLARK

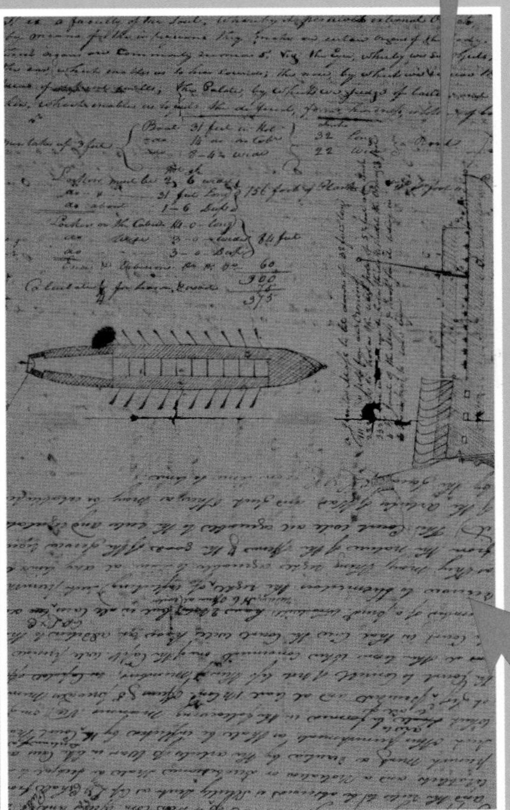

An excerpt from William Clark's journal, from January 17–20, 1804, detailing the construction of a large keelboat for his expedition with Meriwether Lewis and their Corps of Discovery into the new Louisiana Territory. It was built while the men wintered in the staging area at Camp Dubois in Illinois. Clark underestimated their journey to the Pacific by nearly a thousand miles, but they made it back to St. Louis by 1806 anyway, with the loss of only one man.

AMERICANS ON THE MOVE: THE WAY WEST, 1763 TO 1869

Through the Appalachians, 1763 to 1790
Even before independence, Americans began to move through the Cumberland Gap along the Wilderness Road to settle the territories of Kentucky, Tennessee, Ohio, and beyond.

To the Mississippi, 1790 to 1840
By the 1830s, over four million pioneers had moved west of the Appalachians into the rest of the Northwest Territory—Indiana, Michigan, Illinois—and beyond. In the South, they had settled throughout present-day Alabama, Mississippi, Arkansas, and Louisiana.

Lewis and Clark, 1804 to 1806
Meriwether Lewis, William Clark, and their Corps of Discovery made the first overland expedition to span the continental U.S.

Wagons Ho! 1841 to 1869
At least 400,000 people followed the Oregon Trail west from St. Louis, settling the Great Northwest, or turning off to head for California, Utah, and the Southwest.

Trail of Tears, 1831 to 1842
Over 75,000 peaceable Indians from the Choctaw, Cherokee, Chickasaw, Muscogee-Creek, Seminole, Fox, Sauk, Shawnee, Ojibwa, Potawatomi, and other peoples were forcibly removed from their lands.

The Mormon Exodus, 1847 to 1869
Seventy thousand members of the Church of Jesus Christ of Latter-day Saints trekked from Nauvoo, Illinois, and other points east to the Salt Lake Valley in Utah.

Gold Rush, 1848 to 1855
Some 300,000 Americans poured into California after the discovery of gold. Roughly half followed the Oregon Trail to Utah and then continued through the Sierra Nevada. The other half went by sea, through Panama or around Cape Horn.

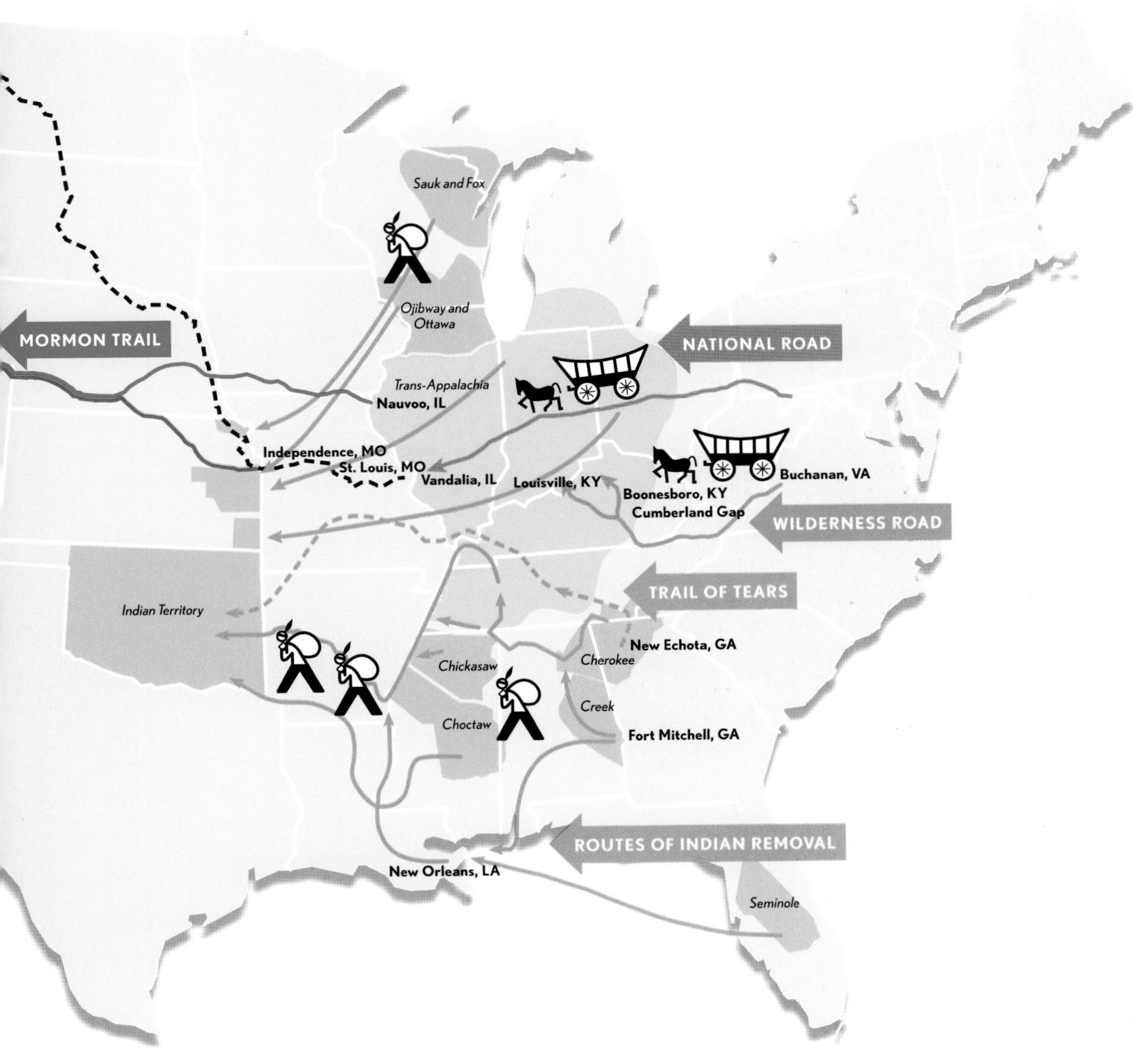

MORMON TRAIL
NATIONAL ROAD
WILDERNESS ROAD
TRAIL OF TEARS
ROUTES OF INDIAN REMOVAL
Sauk and Fox
Ojibway and Ottawa
Trans-Appalachia
Nauvoo, IL
Independence, MO
St. Louis, MO
Vandalia, IL
Louisville, KY
Boonesboro, KY
Cumberland Gap
Buchanan, VA
Indian Territory
New Echota, GA
Cherokee
Chickasaw
Creek
Choctaw
Fort Mitchell, GA
New Orleans, LA
Seminole

1807
TO
1840

THE STEAMBOAT SUPERHIGHWAY

THE TRANSPORTATION REVOLUTION

By 1820, one-quarter of the U.S. population was living west of the Appalachians. The phenomenal growth of these new states was not due solely to the richness of their soil, or to their inhabitants' penchant for hard work and procreation. With the Louisiana Purchase, Midwestern farmers had a ready distribution route for their goods, without the heavy duties charged by the foreign governments that once controlled it. This was the great highway of the Mississippi River, which led to the port of New Orleans.

The Mississippi creates the third-largest drainage basin in the world (exceeded only by those of the Amazon and the Congo), drawing over 40 percent of all the water in the contiguous United States. It is also a treacherous, changeable river, liable to sudden floods, constantly cutting itself new channels through the surrounding delta mud, and hiding any number of obstacles beneath its deceptive brown surface.

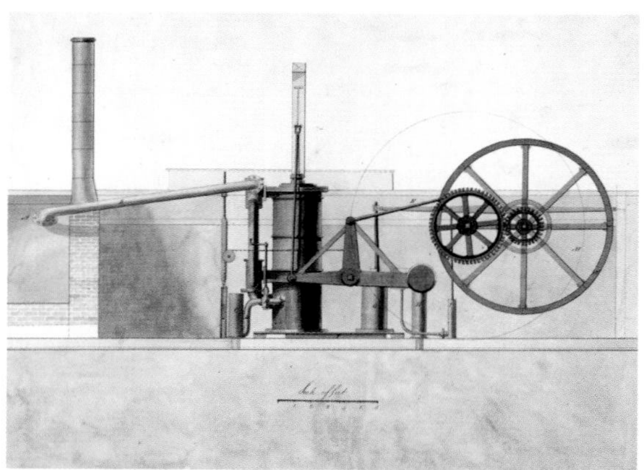

Robert Fulton's drawing of his steamboat engine, for his U.S. patent: It would be much disputed for the rest of his life by rival inventors. Earlier, he had tried to sell submarines, both to Napoleon and to the British.

For all its dangers, it was a godsend for the farmers of the Midwest, who found it easier to convey their goods all the way to New Orleans by flatboat than even 40 miles back through the mountains toward the big cities of the East. By the time he was 19, Abe Lincoln had been down the great river twice, helping local merchants pole their meat, corn, and flour to New Orleans. These were, for the most part, pleasurable trips, featuring stops to trade at the great sugar plantations along the river in Louisiana, though Lincoln was also brought face-to-face with a more disturbing side of the river's economy. On his first trip, his raft was attacked by seven black men, possibly escaped slaves; on his second, he was revolted by the sight of slaves at auction in New Orleans.

There was one enormous flaw in this transport system: For generations, Midwestern traders had been forced to sell their flatboats along with their goods after reaching New Orleans, and walk home. There was no other option—no wind- or oar-driven boat could beat its way back upriver against the Mighty Mississip'.

That changed soon after Robert Fulton put the first commercially viable steamboat in America, the *Clermont*, on the Hudson River in 1807. (Fulton had sailed a prototype down the Seine and invented a workable submarine when he was living in France, but the navally challenged Bonaparte had failed to grasp their usefulness.) Such boats transformed life along the Mississippi and every other navigable river in America. By 1836, there were 750 steamboats in the U.S., more than twice the number in Europe.

By the 1820s, the steamboat carried an average of 232 tons, and the new river port of St. Louis, Missouri, boomed, with an easy outlet now for its growing fur

and lead industries. Thousands of pioneers passed through the city every year, brought north by steam, on their way to points west in the Louisiana Territory. Wheat and timber poured down the river past them, making New Orleans the wealthiest and the third-most-populous city in the Union by 1840. The Mississippi had oriented the trade of much of the United States south, toward the Caribbean and the emerging republics of Latin America. The purchase of the Louisiana Territory pointed it west. In both directions, though, the U.S. was about to meet a new challenge.

U.S.M
QUEEN OF THE WEST

"The Mississippi River will always have its own way; no engineering skill can persuade it to do otherwise..." —Mark Twain
MORNING STAR

HOTEL.
Post Office.
NEWS!

1521
TO
1836

"SO FAR FROM GOD"

THE BATTLE FOR A CONTINENT

The Spanish had been the first Europeans to explore North America in any numbers, long before the tobacco growers of Jamestown or the Pilgrims of Plymouth Bay. In 1565, they established the oldest continuously inhabited European city on the continent, St. Augustine, on the east coast of Florida. Ponce de León first explored Florida even earlier, beginning in 1513, in search of gold and—perhaps—a fountain of youth, before dying from a poisoned Indian arrow. Hernando de Soto followed him in 1539, starting a four-year rampage from Florida to Texas, also in search of gold, that reduced the local Indian population from 200,000 to 8,500 through combat and disease. Around the same time, Francisco Vásquez de Coronado led an expedition up from Mexico—through Arizona and New Mexico and then on into Kansas—in search of El Dorado, a mythical city—or seven cities!—of gold. Still other priests and sailors would explore the West Coast all the way up to what is now Vancouver.

By 1821, though, Mexico was no longer just a launching pad for quixotic quests, but an independent nation, and there seemed to be no reason why it, rather than the United States, should not become the dominant power in North America. Its army, by 1845, was five times bigger, and its territory—which included some of the most fertile land and the richest mineral deposits on the continent—stretched from Panama to Oregon, including all of what is today California, Texas, New Mexico, Arizona, Nevada, and Utah, as well as parts of Colorado and Wyoming.

Mexico's war for independence, though, had been even more debilitating than America's—a desperate, 11-year struggle against Spain that left over one-tenth of its people and many of its most promising leaders dead. The country's population was reduced to just over six million (compared with almost ten million Americans), and the vast majority lived far from the territories north of the Rio Grande, separated by deserts, badlands, and hostile Indians, without the means or the inclination to overcome them.

Casting about for some way to hang on to this empire, Mexico looked to the success the U.S. had had in encouraging immigration. Anyone settling in the enormous Department of Tejas, for instance—home to only some 1,800 white Mexicans—was given 4,428 acres per family, and exempted from most taxes for years. The policy worked all too well. Some of the new settlers came from Europe, but 90 percent were from the American South, most of them adventurous young men seeking opportunity and/or fleeing debts or prosecution. They would tack up signs on their cabin doors with the scribbled abbreviation G.T.T. (Gone to Texas) and light out for the territories. By 1823, they had formed their own armed militia—the famed Texas Rangers—to combat Indians and outlaws. By 1835, there were 30,000 whites in the territory, nearly all of them transplanted Southerners.

They had also brought along 5,000 black slaves. Slavery had been banned throughout Mexico in 1829, but the new Tejanos ignored this law and agitated for its repeal. They were dissatisfied with the rule of the distant central government in Mexico City, and it seemed inevitable that Texas would break off and join the United States. But Northerners feared that admitting Texas to the Union would swing the balance of power to the slave states. Stephen F. Austin, the widely

War News from Mexico by Richard Caton Woodville, 1848.

TRAVIS SENT OUT A HEROIC APPEAL THAT ELECTRIFIED THE REST OF TEXAS, VOWING, "I SHALL NEVER SURRENDER OR RETREAT." HIS CLOSING WORDS WERE "VICTORY OR DEATH."

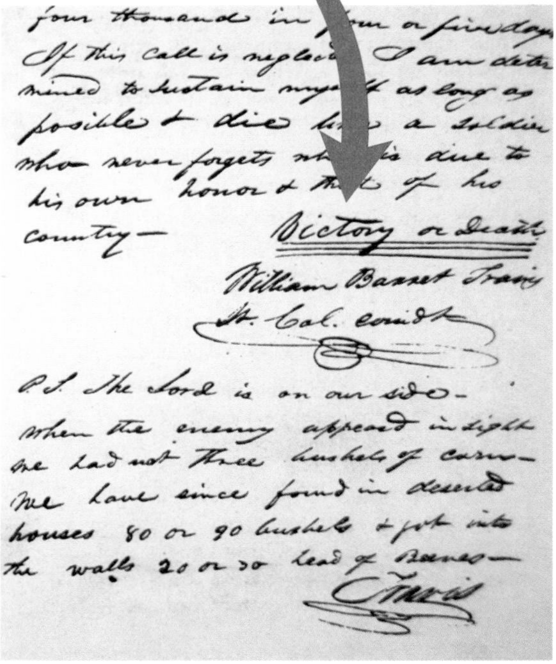

four thousand in four or five days.
If this call is neglected, I am determined to sustain myself as long as
possible & die like a soldier
who never forgets what is due to
his own honor & that of his
country — Victory or Death
William Barret Travis
Lt. Col. comdt.
P.S. The Lord is on our side —
When the enemy appeared in sight
we had not three bushels of corn —
We have since found in deserted
houses 80 or 90 bushels & got into
the walls 20 or 30 head of Beeves —
Travis

respected leader of the Texians (as they called themselves), urged conciliation and fealty to the Mexican government.

Enter Antonio de Padua María Severino López de Santa Anna y Pérez de Lebrón, the self-described Napoleon of the West. After seizing power, Santa Anna jailed Austin for over a year, centralized power in his own hands, and overturned the democratic Mexican constitution in favor of one that pandered to the richest families in the country.

Austin quickly dropped his opposition to independence. Rebellions by Mexicans enraged by Santa Anna's coup erupted throughout the nation, and the Texians were able to turn a slaveholders' protest into a battle for the rights of man. Even Hispanic settlers joined the insurrection. Oblivious, Santa Anna set out at the head of an army to subdue the rebellious province.

At San Antonio, just across the Rio Grande, he encountered a force of some 189 rebels under the command of a syphilitic 26-year-old lawyer named William Travis, whose company included the fabled frontiersmen Davy Crockett and Jim Bowie and at least eight Hispanic Tejanos. Travis, who had read too many romantic novels by Sir Walter Scott, persuaded the others to make a stand in a crumbling old mission known as the Alamo, reportedly drawing a line in the sand with his sword and inviting anyone who wanted to leave to cross it. Only one man did, and as Santa Anna's army of 2,400 closed in on his garrison, Travis sent out a heroic appeal that electrified the rest of Texas, vowing, "I shall never surrender or retreat." His closing words were "Victory or Death."

This was suicidal. The Alamo was indefensible, and the men inside were low on food and ammunition. The garrison might easily have been starved out, picked apart by the Mexican army's superior artillery, or removed with a negotiated surrender, but none of these options would have given the caudillo the dramatic victory he coveted. Waving a chicken leg at an aide who questioned his plans for a direct assault, Santa Anna berated him: "What are the lives of soldiers more than so many chickens. I tell you, the Alamo must fall, and my orders must be obeyed at all hazards."

Before dawn the following morning, March 6, 1836, Santa Anna's men swept forward in a direct assault. He had publicly sworn that no quarter would be given to any prisoners, thereby ensuring that most of the

Texians would fight to the death. His soldiers were badly led and badly equipped, with crudely improvised siege ladders that mostly fell apart. Roughly a quarter of his force was killed or wounded, many by friendly fire, but they managed to make it up the Alamo walls. A brief, bitter fight followed through the interior courtyard and the rooms of the old mission, with the few Texians who were taken alive promptly put to the sword, just as Santa Anna had promised.

A much worse slaughter followed later that same month at Goliad, where some 342 rebels were tricked into surrendering under the impression that they would be spared—only to be lined up along a dusty road, shot point blank, and then bayoneted. But far from terrorizing the Texians into submission, Santa Anna had only hardened their resolve. Less than two months after the Battle of the Alamo, his army was surprised and annihilated by a much smaller force at San Jacinto, and at the cost of only nine rebel fatalities. The Napoleon of the West had neglected to post sentries during the army's afternoon siesta, and a force under Sam Houston swept out of the trees upon them, shouting "Remember the Alamo!" and "Remember Goliad!" The great man was found hiding in a marsh in the uniform of a cavalry private and was hauled back before Houston—a political protégé of Andrew Jackson, and a general about as flamboyant as Santa Anna himself—where he promptly granted Texas its independence in exchange for his life.

Texas became an independent republic, with Sam Houston as its first president and Stephen Austin as secretary of state. Its population continued to increase exponentially, but it was beset by problems of administration and incursions by Mexican troops. Finally, in 1845, the U.S. Senate agreed to annex the enormous state, and soon thereafter President James Knox Polk—another Jackson protégé—baited Mexico into war over the question of its borders.

It was the first major conflict for the U.S. since the War of 1812, and many of the problems that bedeviled that effort had not been fixed. The army was still a hodgepodge of regulars, state militias, and volunteers, divided by religion and ethnicity. Opposition to the Mexican-American War was widespread in the North, where it was denounced by Abraham Lincoln, now a freshman congressman from Illinois, who said it had been thrust upon the country by "the sheerest deception"—even though he knew his words would cost him his House seat.

The Americans did possess at least one distinct advantage, which was a professional officer corps trained at West Point. Almost all of the leading commanders of the American Civil War—including Ulysses S. Grant, Robert E. Lee, and Thomas "Stonewall" Jackson, among many others—were first blooded in the Mexican War. The tactics they devised proved lethally effective, and their commanding officers, Zachary Taylor and Winfield Scott, pulled off some of the greatest feats of arms in American military history, driving deep into Mexican territory and taking Mexico City.

Santa Anna signed over a third of his country's territory, in another humiliating peace treaty. The United States used the war to seize California, too, and it would at last yield the prize that so many individuals—from Ponce de León and de Soto to the Jamestown colonists and the Georgians who had pushed the Cherokee out of the Enchanted Land—had sought for so long.

1848 TO 1860

HE WHO HAS THE GOLD

THE CALIFORNIA GOLD RUSH

In January of 1848, a transplanted New Jersey carpenter named James Marshall was supervising construction of a sawmill near present-day Coloma, California, for John Sutter, the local alcalde. Looking down at the channel being dug under his mill, Marshall saw something glimmer. When he told his boss, he tried to swear Marshall to secrecy. A runaway bankrupt from Switzerland, Sutter was a bluff, shifty, charming man, with ambitious but vague plans of starting an agricultural utopia on his huge homestead.

Sutter tried to buy as much land as possible before word got out, but it was too late. Marshall's construction crew had already quit to go searching for gold. Worse yet, his find had attracted the attention of Samuel Brannan, a wily apostate Mormon elder turned San Francisco entrepreneur and newspaper publisher. Brannan quickly claimed a mine in the area, built a store and a warehouse for prospecting equipment, and then went back to San Francisco, where he walked the streets, holding aloft a quinine bottle he had filled with gold flakes and calling out: "Gold! Gold! Gold from the American River!" Brannan next printed thousands of circulars, and had them spread around the country. The Great American Gold Rush was on, just 300 years too late for Coronado and Ponce de León.

The would-be prospectors were Missouri farmers, Yankee granite cutters, black slaves and freedmen, English shopkeepers, French peasants, Mexican miners, and Chinese laborers—the first considerable population of Asians to arrive in North America since the submersion of the land bridge over the Bering Strait. Two-thirds of the white male population of the Oregon Territory headed south. California's population grew to almost 243,000 by 1850, and to over 400,000 by 1860. For months after the first news broke, San Francisco virtually emptied out. In the countryside, crops rotted in the fields. Sailors desperate to get to the goldfields jumped ship, leaving some 500 vessels to molder in San Francisco Bay.

Nearly all of the new arrivals were young men, many of them armed and few of them with more than a notion of what they were doing. An estimated 20 percent of all prospectors perished within six months, most from the usual frontier culprits: dysentery, cholera, bad water, bad (or no) food, too much liquor, and frustration.

Marshall and Sutter both died in poverty, still trying to adjudicate their claims to the land the so-called forty-niners had shoved them off. A few did strike it rich. Some $500 million in gold had been extracted from the land by the start of the Civil War, in 1861. Some $220 million had made its way to the coffers of the federal government, repaying the financial cost of the Mexican War more than twice over.

The real money from the gold rush, though, was made by those who provided the prospectors with the goods and services they needed—often at extortionate prices. A loaf of bread that sold back East for five cents went for 75 cents. Apples went for as much as five dollars apiece; eggs, $50 a dozen. Blankets were $40; boots, $100 a pair. International businesses that thrive to this day had their origins in the California Gold Rush, including Wells Fargo Bank, Ghirardelli Chocolate Co., and Boudin Bakery, of San Francisco sourdough-bread fame.

An enterprising Connecticut peddler named Collis P. Huntington gave up on his prospecting

career after half a day, bought up every shovel in sight for $2.50 per dozen, and then resold them for $125 a dozen. Within ten years, he was one of "the Big Four"—tyrannical railway magnates who dominated California business and politics, and who would lay the first transcontinental railroad across the United States. Rascally Sam Brannan would clear $36,000 in his first nine weeks as a supplier to the miners. By the 1850s, he was a millionaire, controlling banks, a railroad, a telegraph company, huge swaths of land, and San Francisco's notorious Committee of Vigilance, which was designed to keep order in the boisterous new state, but which too often acted as a legalized mob. Brannan would, however, end up dying nearly as poor as Sutter and Marshall.

Many of San Francisco's merchants, saloon owners, and brothel-keepers regained their senses after the first news of the gold at Sutter's Mill hit, and drifted back to their once sleepy city, which they proceeded to convert into a riotous boomtown. In a year and a half, the town essentially burned down six times, but nobody much minded. Each time, it was built up plusher, louder, and grander.

Miners look for gold everywhere, even in the rocky streets of the mining town Grass Valley, California, 1873.

NEARLY ALL OF THE NEW ARRIVALS WERE YOUNG MEN, MANY OF THEM ARMED AND FEW OF THEM WITH MORE THAN A NOTION OF WHAT THEY WERE DOING.

It was a matter of covering two hundred and sixty miles...across an uninhabited and pathless land, of avoiding Indians, bears, panthers, wildcats, coyotes, and snakes of all kinds, including rattlesnakes," recalled Jean-Nicholas Perlot, a 28-year-old Belgian who arrived in Monterey in 1851 and headed immediately for the Mariposa gold mines.

The work was backbreaking at the best of times, bending over and sifting through pan after pan of "paydirt" in the freezing glacial runoffs or digging endlessly with pick and shovel. A few found their fortunes, such as a group of Mexicans who dug up $22,000 in gold out of a pit in Bear Valley. Most ended up with nothing.

1834 TO 1860

AMERICA'S LEFT COAST

THE PIONEERS

There were four basic land routes out West. A few pioneers, mostly traders, took the hazardous Santa Fe Trail down into the thinly inhabited Southwest. Another 50,000 turned north on the Oregon Trail from 1834 to 1860, to the rich timberlands and fisheries of the Northwest. By 1869, over 70,000 converts to a new, polygamous religious group calling itself the Church of Jesus Christ of Latter-day Saints—better known as the Mormons—had settled around the Great Salt Lake.

Some 200,000 people, though, followed the Overland Trail all the way to California before the Civil War, looking for gold but also soil, given that 60 percent of them were farmers. It was a journey of 2,000 miles, at the walking speed of an ox. Eight hundred miles across the treeless expanse of the Great Plains, against a pitiless sun, sudden storms and cyclones, and raging prairie fires. Through the towering Rockies, across scorching expanses of the Utah salt flats and the waterless desert of the Great Basin, then up again and over the snows of the Sierra Nevada, before winter blocked the way.

Usually the journey took five to six months—for those who made it. Contrary to the cinematic version, the main threats were not Indians but disease, illness, snakes, accidents, bad timing—and childbirth. These were tough, resourceful people, used to living off the land. Some had saved for as long as five years to make the journey, spending between $800 and $1,000 on their "prairie schooners." But, despite their preparations and their toughness, they were headed out into alien and hostile landscapes, regions much more arid and mountainous than anything they had ever experienced.

Yet for all of the terrible hardships they endured, for all of the human cost of winning the West, there were always more of them. The years from 1845 to 1855 witnessed the highest proportional rate of immigration in American history. Some 2.4 million immigrants—14.5 percent of the existing population—flocked to the young, muscular nation.

The physical size of the country, too, had doubled with the Louisiana Purchase, then doubled again after the Mexican War and with the acquisitions of the Oregon Territory and Florida. Between 1845 and 1849 alone, the nation had added 1.2 million square miles of territory. Just 75 years after Daniel Boone first blazed the Wilderness Road through the Appalachians, the United States was the size of the ancient Roman Empire at its zenith.

From 13 colonies hugging the East Coast along a strip of land barely 300 miles wide, the U.S. had become a continental nation, reaching from Boston to San Francisco; from the great forests of Oregon to the deserts of New Mexico; sweeping over the great mountain ranges of the Sierras, the Rockies, and the Appalachians, with the Mississippi—the Father of Waters—in between. America's expansion had exceeded the expectations of even its most visionary founders. And yet such rapid growth also stretched to the extreme the country's sense of itself as one nation. In the new state of Texas, for instance, there were already 58,000 slaves by the end of the 1850s—one more sign of a crisis deferred.

Ironically, Americans now faced much the same question that the vanquished Mexicans had confronted: How was this overnight empire to be held together?

INSIDE A COVERED WAGON

The typical "prairie schooner" was a masterpiece of utility. It was generally pulled by three to six mules or oxen. The wagon bed was nine-to-ten feet long and four feet wide, with a canvas cover waterproofed with paint or linseed oil. An adult could stand up inside—but mostly the wagon was for settlers' goods, not the settlers.

Pioneers might bring a few small pieces of furniture, bedding, clothes, and other finished goods that would be hard to obtain in the West, such as a Dutch oven, a skillet, a coffeepot, an oil lamp, a spinning wheel, a butter churn—and perhaps an early hot water bottle, made from India rubber. But mostly what they carried was food, to be augmented by whatever bison and deer they might shoot along the way.

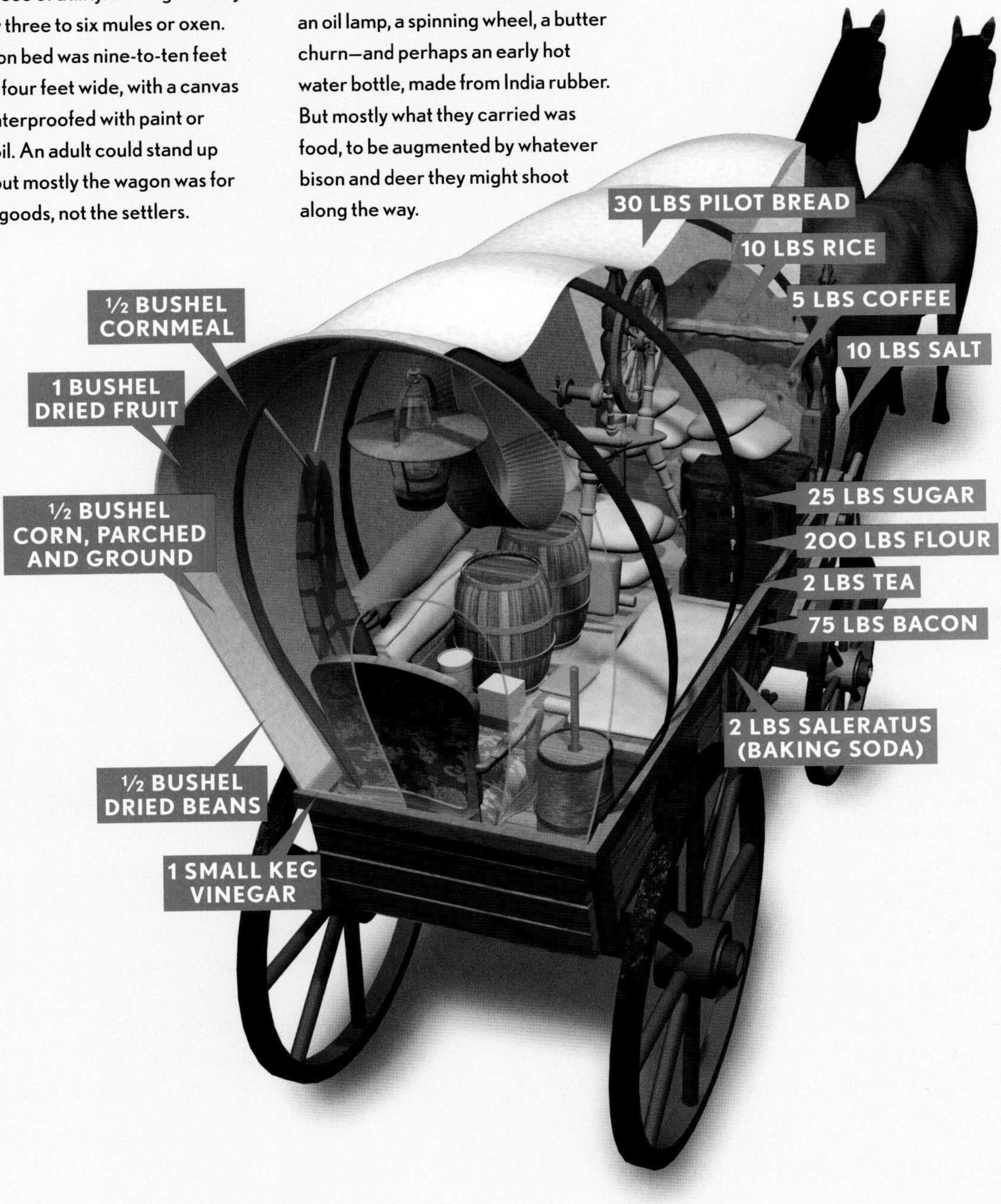

CHAPTER FOUR

DIVISION

1790
TO
1860

MAKING SLAVERY PAY

THE COTTON GIN REVIVES THE "PECULIAR INSTITUTION"

America had its continent. Now, what to do with it?

By 1849, just 60 years after the United States of America had formally constituted itself as one nation, its reach had exceeded the vision of even its most far-sighted statesmen, Thomas Jefferson and Alexander Hamilton. The destiny of the new nation has long been described—then and now—as a contest between their philosophies. Jefferson, the gentleman planter, believed that American democracy could be preserved only by a nation of yeoman farmers, each tending his own small holding; Hamilton, the lifelong city dweller, foresaw an industrial, urbanized America, forged by engineers and tinkerers.

In fact, the past would repeat itself. Colonial America had been built in part by the bartering of molasses, rum, and flesh—the notorious Triangular Trade; the independent United States would hoist itself to the top by means of a new triangle. This second triad was made up of cotton, manufactures, and slaves, and it would bestow upon the nation both untold wealth and its greatest tragedies.

The Founding Fathers had largely elided the issue of slavery because of its insolubility, but also out of the fervent hope that it might quietly go away. In the first decades after the Revolution, such a hope seemed justified. Slavery was slowly outlawed in the Northern states. It was forbidden in the new states carved out of the Northwest Territory. Both the United States and Great Britain outlawed the international slave trade in 1807.

By the time of the first U.S. census, in 1790, there were 700,000 slaves in the United States, the overwhelming majority of them in the South. They performed nearly every sort of task, from the most skilled crafts to the most tedious labor. But the economic viability of the South seemed to be limited. At the start of the nineteenth century, the South produced almost nothing that Europe—the biggest market in the world—could not find elsewhere at a lower price.

Hamilton saw a potential savior for his Southern brethren in a new crop that grew abundantly south of the Mason-Dixon Line, predicting, "[s]everal of these Southern colonies might some day clothe the whole continent." Cotton was already an important product in world trade, feeding the bustling cloth mills of England that were at the forefront of the Industrial Revolution. The only trouble was that most of the white stuff England was spinning into gold came from India.

From field to factory, cotton was a labor-intensive enterprise even in a slave economy. It took the most industrious person, working 14 hours a day, to pull all the seeds from the short, dense fibers of just a single pound of cotton. The South's cotton problem would be solved by a host of "Yankees," or "acute Yankees," the colloquial Southern term for inventive, shrewd-bargaining Northerners. One of these was a poor Yale grad from Connecticut, forced to travel to South Carolina in 1792 to take up a tutoring position. Finding that the job paid only half what he had been promised, Eli Whitney continued on to Georgia, to visit a plantation run by a remarkable woman he had fallen in love with on his boat trip south.

Catherine Littlefield Greene was herself a transplanted Yankee. The widow of Washington's favorite

Hauling the Whole Week's Picking by William Henry Brown, 1842 (detail).

general, Nathanael Greene, she was now managing her late husband's plantation. The question of how to make cotton pay bedeviled Greene and her neighbors. Soon after Whitney's arrival, she introduced him to local planters, telling them: "Gentlemen, apply to my young friend, Mr. Whitney. He can fix anything!"

What Whitney came up with was the cotton gin (*gin* being short for *engine*), a work of simple genius in which the picked cotton was fed through two counter-rotating drums edged with teeth. The invention soon spread throughout the South, and was improved upon by Whitney and others, especially with the substitution of a fine-toothed circular saw for the teeth. Using a hand crank, the amount of cotton that could be processed by an individual in a day rose from one pound to 50. Powered by horses, a water mill, or a newfangled steam engine, a bigger gin could clean up to 1,000 pounds of cotton a day.

Hand-colored daguerreotype of a nurse and child, circa 1850.

The cotton industry was transformed—as was the entire South. The share of all the world's cotton grown in the U.S. rose from 9 percent in 1801 to 68 percent by the start of the Civil War. In 1825, the U.S. shipped 171 million pounds of cotton to Great Britain, which was making more cotton fabric than the rest of the world combined. By 1860, the South was producing 2.275 billion pounds of raw cotton, which accounted for 60 percent of *all* exports from the United States. It was supplying over 80 percent of the cotton for clothing manufactured in Britain, and every bit of what was used in New England's fast-growing mills.

Hamilton's hopes for the new crop had been realized, but the triumph of mechanization had rendered slavery economically viable again. Freed from the time-consuming work of cleaning cotton, more slaves than ever could be put to work planting it, picking it, and clearing the land to grow still more of it. By 1800, there were fewer than 900,000 slaves in America; by 1860, there were nearly four million.

As remunerative as cotton was, slavery itself was the South's leading business by the Civil War, with total holdings in human beings estimated at $2 billion. Healthy adult male slaves usually sold at market for $1,000. With the African slave trade banned, the states of the upper South, less suited to the production of cotton, converted the supply of human beings into an industry.

ELI WHITNEY'S COTTON GIN

Eli Whitney's original, hand-cranked cotton gin could process 50 pounds of cotton a day. Plantations already used roller gins, designed to separate the hair from the cotton fiber, but these did not clean the South's short-staple, green seed cotton. Whitney's gin featured coarse wire teeth, which were later improved—by him, or by the South Carolina planter Hodgen Holmes—with the substitution of fine-toothed circular saws. Later generations of cotton gins were much larger and powered by steam—capable of processing huge amounts of cotton.

When the handle is turned, coarse wire teeth pull cotton bolls through a metal grate whose narrow slots separate out the green seeds. Cleaned cotton emerges from the other side of the gin.

The children of slaves—including those fathered by their white masters and overseers—were "sold down the river" to the great plantations of the South—a fate the most famous of escaped slaves, Frederick Douglass, would liken to "a living death." Slave coffles were a familiar sight along the primitive roads of the South—anywhere from a dozen to a hundred half-naked men and women, chained together in a line. They were marched up to 25 miles a day in this condition, and at the end of their trek lay the auction block.

The men at the top of the cotton world amassed enormous fortunes. By 1850, there were more millionaires per capita in the river town of Natchez, Mississippi—situated at a vital nexus of Delta cotton country—than anywhere else on earth.

Most of the great plantations had been carved out of the Mississippi Delta by shrewd, ruthless pioneers, including a few sons of Irish peasants and some transplanted Yankees. Yet the new planter class chose to identify itself solely with the romantic Cavaliers of the English Civil War. They fought duels, obsessed over honor, bred horses and dogs, and pumped millions into columned Greek Revival mansions.

Commerce was beneath these would-be Stuarts. Only about one in five of the great planters invested in anything other than land or people. There was no reason why the South should not have shipped all of its vaunted cotton directly to Europe from its ports of Charleston, Savannah, Mobile, and New Orleans. Instead, a planter class determined to keep its hands clean of commerce or toil cut deals with those acute Yankees.

1789
TO
1825

MAGNUS APOLLO MAKES A CITY

DEWITT CLINTON BUILDS THE ERIE CANAL

New York City had risen from the ashes of the Revolution thanks to another canny insight by the greatest advocate of urban America. In 1789, the city had been selected as the nation's first capital, but Alexander Hamilton soon horse-traded that honor with Thomas Jefferson, agreeing to move the government to a new, centrally located city in exchange for Jefferson's agreement to let the federal government consolidate the national debt.

Hamilton had traded the capital for capital—$80 million in government bonds that jump-started New York's financial exchanges. The bonds also set off an orgy of public speculation, by almost every class, which left the city nearly bankrupt. But it would quickly recuperate, thanks in no small part to the continual daring and innovation of its leading capitalists. In 1817, for instance, the New York–based Black Ball Line announced the first fixed shipping schedule for packet service between its home city and Liverpool, England. No more waiting for the hold to fill up with cargo; the boats would go on the date they said they would.

Reliable, regularly scheduled service secured New York's place as the leading port in the country, and lured Southern cotton ships into a 200-mile detour up the East Coast. Their white gold was transferred to Yankee ships, which sailed to Europe and returned with immigrants for the North and luxury goods for the planters of the Mississippi Delta. By 1822, cotton alone accounted for 40 percent of goods going out through the Port of New York. By the 1840s, it was estimated that cash-starved Southern planters were, on average, one year in debt—that is, they owed *one entire year's harvest* to New York financiers, who lent them money at 7 to 12 percent interest, with the loans secured by cotton crops.

New York's adventurous capitalists were soon casting about for new ways to multiply their cotton wealth. So was their mayor. DeWitt Clinton, or Magnus Apollo, was every bit the force of nature his nickname implied. Six feet three and powerfully built, he was not a man much crossed, even in the rough-and-tumble world of New York politics. Clinton had in mind a mad scheme to tie the city not only to the cotton fields of the South but also to the breadbasket of the nation, the prosperous new states clustered around the Great Lakes.

This was to be accomplished by means of a 363-mile, 83-lock canal, one that would cut straight across New York State from Lake Erie to the Hudson River, and along which goods could then easily be transported south to the city and its great natural harbor. Nothing like it had ever been built; its estimated cost was three-fourths of the total federal budget at the time. Opponents ridiculed it as "Clinton's Big Ditch." Even Thomas Jefferson protested: "It is little short of madness to think of it at this day."

Magnus Apollo was not to be deterred. He got himself elected governor of New York State in 1817, and within three months of his inauguration shovels were in the ground, the bonds for the canal guaranteed by the tolls it would charge. Eight years and four months later—two full years ahead of schedule—Governor Clinton poured two barrels of Lake Erie

It took more than 50,000 men to dig the Erie Canal. Many were Irish immigrants who lived in shanties "more like dog kennels than the habitations of men" and were kept going with 12 to 20 shots of whiskey a day.

MICHAEL DOUGLAS, actor: "The spirit of America is imagination combined with tenacity, a strong work ethic, a wonderful freedom of creation combined with the mental muscle."

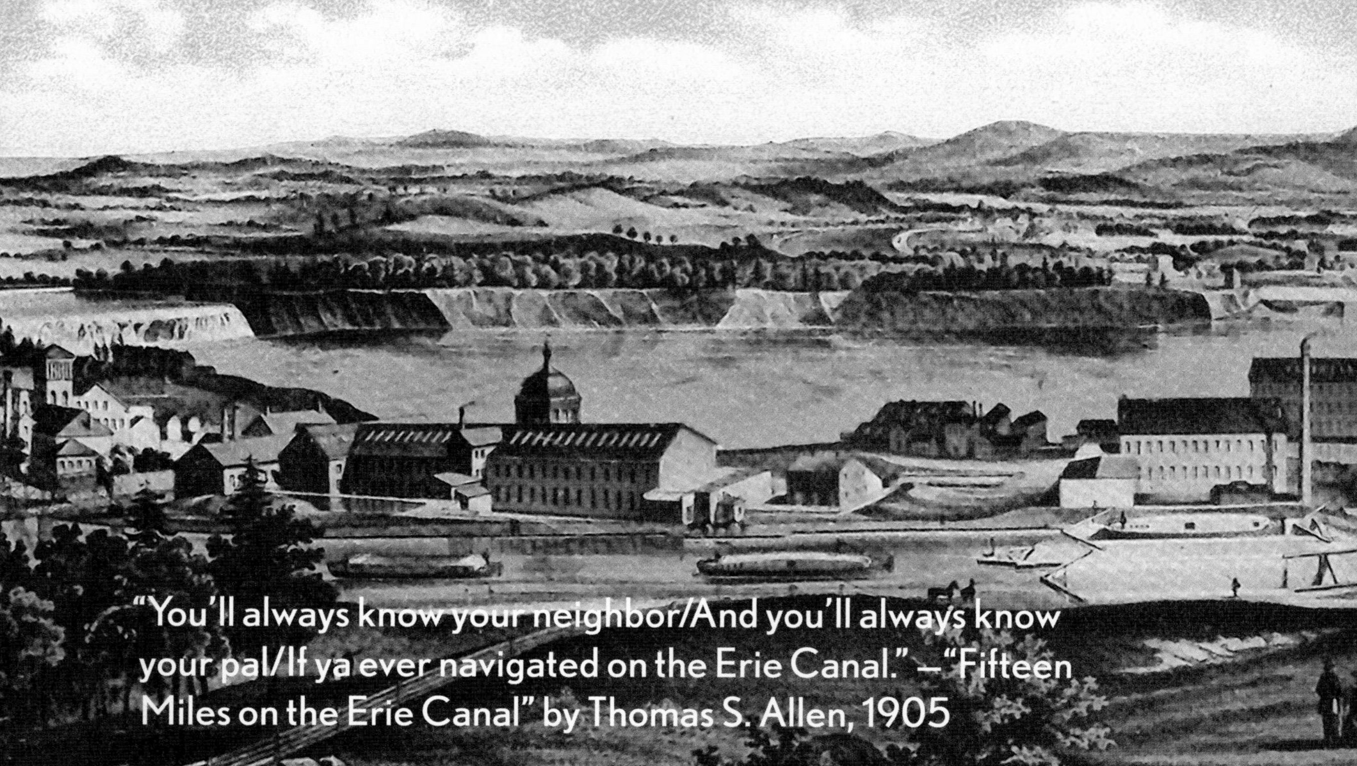

water into the Atlantic Ocean, thereby consummating "the wedding of the waters" and capping a triumphant, ten-day procession by canal boat from Buffalo to New York Harbor.

"You'll always know your neighbor/And you'll always know your pal/If ya ever navigated on the Erie Canal." —"Fifteen Miles on the Erie Canal" by Thomas S. Allen, 1905

Within a year of the canal's opening, 500 new mercantile houses had opened within the city, and 42 barges a day were being towed and poled along Clinton's Big Ditch. Shipping costs from Lake Erie to Manhattan dropped from $100 a ton to less than $9, and the time spent in transit dropped from weeks to a matter of days, enabling Midwestern farmers to get their crops to the coast before they could go bad.

In a stroke, New York City had, in the words of historian Mike Wallace, "adroitly positioned itself between three of the most dynamic regions of the early nineteenth-century global economy—England's manufacturing Midlands, the cotton-producing slave South, and the agricultural Midwest."

The entire flow of American commerce had been redirected. Within ten years after the wedding of the waters, one-third of all the goods America exported went out through New York Harbor, and two-thirds of its imports came in the same way. It would soon surpass London as the busiest harbor in the world, a title it would hold until 1960. The towering masts of the biggest and swiftest boats—the clipper ships built to sail all the way to China and back—would live on in the name given to the iconic buildings of the city they helped build. They were called skyscrapers.

The Erie Canal was the greatest engineering feat of its day—built by a country that, at the time, could barely boast a single trained engineer. It required the removal of 11.4 million cubic yards of earth and rock—and nearly all of it by hand. For this task, canal contractors turned to men who were eminently replaceable, and whose lives were considerably less valuable than that of a skilled slave: Irish immigrants.

Most of their work was done with what were fast becoming the traditional Irish tools of pick and shovel. But some of the hardest jobs required a

technology that was considerably more modern—and more dangerous. At the Deep Cut, near Lockport, New York, they had to go through three miles of hard blue limestone, then four more of rock and wet earth, to a depth of 26 feet. All in all, 450,000 cubic yards of rock had to be moved.

There was only one way to do this in the years before dynamite: black powder, a highly combustible mix of nitrate, charcoal, and sulfur, and all of it measured out crudely, packed into a drill hole, and set off by a twist of brown paper for a fuse. Often boys were used to light the fuse, on the theory that they could run away faster.

"On some days, the list of killed and wounded would be almost like that of a battlefield," recalled a Lockport woman named Edna Smith, adding: "[I]f the fuse went out or burned slowly, they would rush back recklessly to see what was the matter…often blowing on them to revive the dying fire. Many a poor fellow was blown into fragments this way."

Yet when they were done, the system of double locks at Lockport lifted canal boats a miraculous 60 feet up the Niagara Escarpment and then lowered them down again, enabling them to make their way to the Hudson and New York City. Many of the laborers followed, once their work was done, moving south to live in the slums around Manhattan's Five Points and Sixth Ward neighborhoods, or along the East River, with its permanent thicket of ships' masts. They spearheaded a Working Men's movement that made outrageous, radical demands for things like a ten-hour workday, abolition of prison sentences for debt, and public schools for all. The merchant class they had enriched denounced them as the "Dirty Shirt Party" and a "ring-streaked and speckled rabble." But slowly, surely, they pulled power to themselves, forming political clubs and trade unions, and volunteer fire companies. From the streets, they created a Democratic political machine that would dominate the city for a century.

A NATION OF COMMERCE: AMERICAN INDUSTRY IN THE 1850s

In the years leading up to the Civil War, the United States had already become a gigantic workshop, its manufacturing and agricultural production growing by leaps and bounds. In the South, farming predominated, particularly in cotton, the world's most important and lucrative crop. The West and Midwest yielded staggering harvests of wheat, corn, and timber. The Northeast was a hive of textile mills, factories, iron forges, shipyards, and a global center of industrial innovation.

Imports and Exports of Major American Ports, 1860 (in millions of dollars):

	Imports	Exports
New York, NY	233.6	120.6
Philadelphia, PA	14.6	5.5
Boston, MA	39.3	13.5
Baltimore, MD	9.7	8.8
Charleston, NC	1.5	21.1
New Orleans, LA	22.9	107.8
Mobile, AL	1.0	38.6
Savannah, GA	0.7	18.3

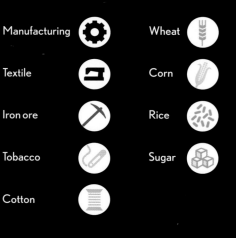

Manufacturing

Wheat

Textile

Corn

Iron ore

Rice

Tobacco

Sugar

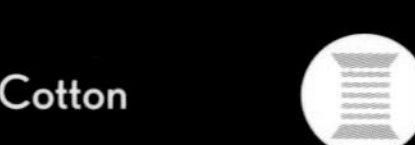

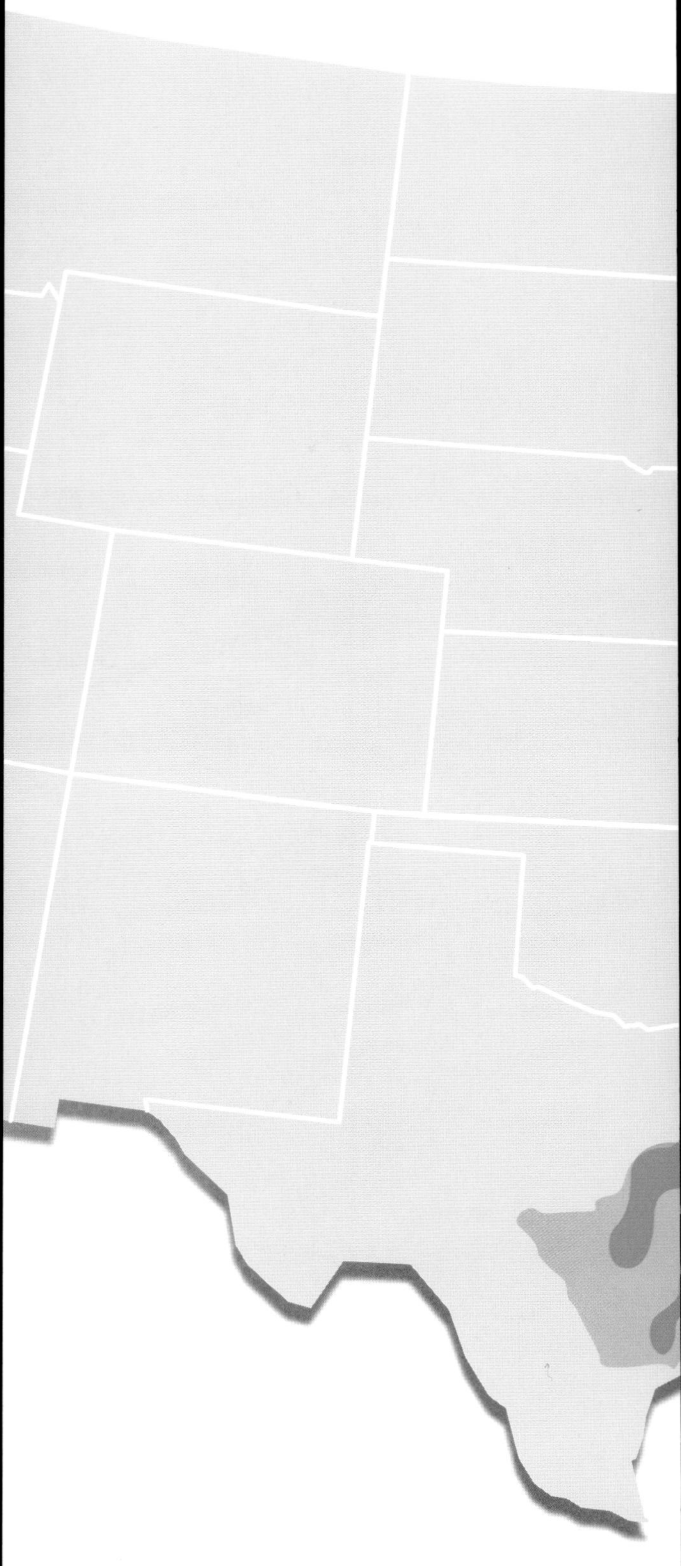

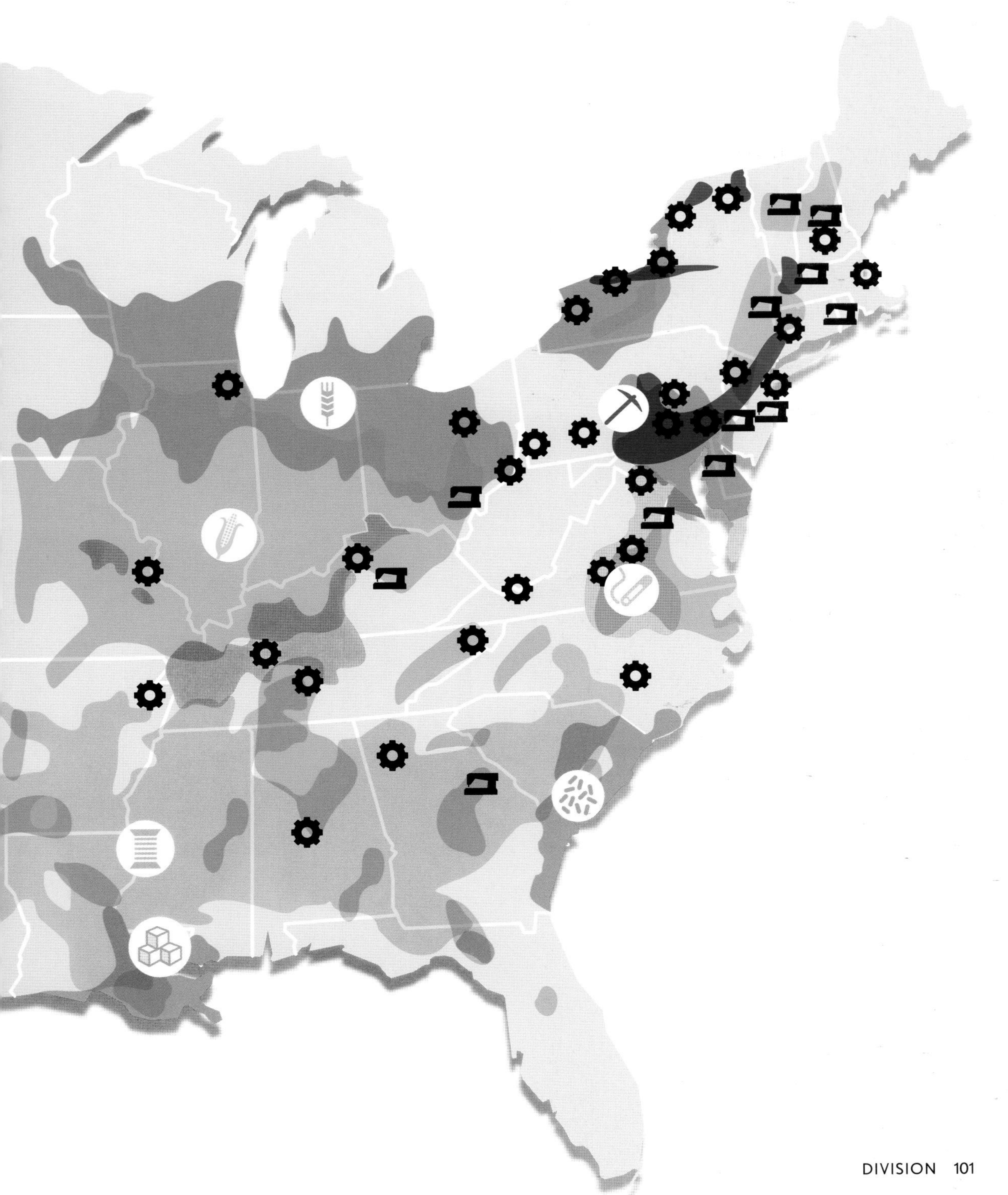

1789
TO
1860

WOMEN IN THE WORKPLACE

LOWELL AND THE MILL GIRLS

The Model City and the Kiss of Death Britain had clung jealously to its lead in the Industrial Revolution, particularly its monopoly control of the textile industry. Cotton cloth was the first great consumer product of the Industrial Age, and the technology that made it possible was a closely guarded secret. Textile workers were not allowed to emigrate, and suspicious travelers were searched at the docks in case they were smuggling out plans.

Samuel Slater, a 21-year-old apprentice engineer from Derbyshire, England, managed to slip out anyway in 1789, the first year of the United States, disguised as a farmer and carrying the plans for a cotton mill in his head. Slater formed a partnership with Moses Brown, one of four brothers from Providence, Rhode Island, who had made a fortune in the slave trade but who had become an abolitionist after converting to Quakerism. Soon Brown and Slater were building cotton-cloth factories throughout Rhode Island, Connecticut, and Massachusetts; at his death, in 1835, Slater—who became known as the Father of the American Industrial Revolution—had 13 mills and a fortune valued at $1 million, perhaps as much as $25 million in today's dollars.

Slater's industrial espionage was surpassed by that of Francis Cabot Lowell, scion of a prominent Boston family, who toured England for health reasons in 1810. Lowell and a family friend, Nathan Appleton, proceeded to Manchester—a strange place for the sickly to recuperate (during this period, it was described by Alexis de Tocqueville as a "foul drain" and by Friedrich Engels—not yet Karl Marx's collaborator but the son of a German cotton goods manufacturer who owned part of a Manchester factory—as a place in which it would be "impossible for a human being in any degree civilized to live"). Gaining access to the complex machinery of the new power looms there, Lowell committed to memory every inch, every moving part—and may also have made a sketch or two, later hidden away in the false bottoms of his steamer trunks.

By 1813, he was back in America, forming what would become the Boston Associates investor group with Appleton and a few other close friends and relations. After months of work with a brilliant mechanical engineer, Paul Moody, Lowell had a working model of a belt-driven power loom; a state-of-the-art factory soon followed in Waltham, Massachusetts. Meanwhile, Lowell used his political connections to erect a towering tariff wall against foreign cotton and British textiles. By 1815, 27 million pounds of raw cotton was being woven into cloth in New England. Lowell was dead by 42—he really *was* sickly—but the Boston Associates honored him by building a model factory town in a location even more ideal than Waltham, a spot 30 miles north of Boston where the onrushing Merrimack River dropped 32 feet before meeting the Concord. They named it Lowell.

The new town was designed to be a masterwork of American ingenuity. It was planned to accommodate 20,000 people, although its population would eventually exceed five times that number. Its four- and five-story brick factories were some of the largest buildings ever erected in the United States, outstretching the church steeples and rising for half a mile down the

Working conditions at mills continued to be dismal well into the twentieth century, as photographer Lewis Hine captured at Glenallen Mill in Winchendon, Massachusetts, 1911.

IN 1834 AND 1836 SOME 1,500 MILL GIRLS HAD GONE OUT ON STRIKE, PROTESTING WAGE CUTS, MACHINE SPEEDUPS, AND RENT HIKES.

Merrimack. Locks and dams stole the power of the river; a system of canals diverted it to waiting turbines and wheels. Above all, the Boston Manufacturing Company was determined to make Lowell a model city—nothing like Manchester.

This was out of necessity more than humanity. Sons could not be spared from farmwork, but some of the daughters could be. They proved eager for a measure of independence from families, and from the stifling monotony of rural life. Soon, over 70 percent of the mill hands in Lowell were single women, most of them teenage girls. Determined and industrious, they were used to hard work and long hours from their lives on the farm, but they had never experienced anything like life in the mills.

The day began before dawn with the ringing of the factory bells, giving them just enough time to scuttle from their boardinghouses to their looms by five o'clock. There was a half-hour breakfast break at seven, another break for lunch at noon—all but 80 minutes of a 14-hour day spent close at work, before the evening dinner bell rang at seven. There were bedtime curfews, mandatory church attendance, and very little contact with men. Dancing and other frivolous entertainments were frowned upon.

The company owned every inch of Lowell, and forced its employees to sign yearlong contracts. Working conditions were debilitating. Windows were nailed shut, even in summer—humidity kept the strands of cotton from breaking. There was the constant smell of burning machine oil, and fine cotton lint fell as thickly "as snow falls in winter." The lint filled up the girls' mouths, their nostrils, their lungs, to the point where they often vomited up small balls of cotton. Some used snuff to try to keep out the lint, but there was little recourse when it came to sucking threads through the narrow eyeholes of the machines' heddles, one of the girls' main tasks. They called it "the kiss of death," and it was not unknown for a woman to draw 43,000 pieces of thread through a heddle in the course of a week. Seventy percent of the workers would die from respiratory diseases.

Nonetheless, Lowell was a vast improvement over Manchester. The mill girls made two to five dollars a week, even after the $1.25 deducted for their room and board—less than a man made, but the highest wages known at the time for a woman on either side of the Atlantic. For many, this meant the chance to build up a good dowry with a year or two of work, before returning to farm, family, and new husband.

If they weren't too exhausted, the girls could go hear a visiting lecturer such as Ralph Waldo Emerson speak at Lowell Hall after dinner. They could also attend a meeting of the Improvement Circles to better their education and their social skills.

Reading was a passion among the young women of Lowell. Books were banned in the mills, but they would sneak them in amid the spindles and the cotton, then tear them up and pass them around page by page so they might read at any free moment. They did more than read, too—they wrote, starting their very own monthly literary magazine, *The Lowell Offering*, where their first-person accounts of life in the mills enthralled a visiting Charles Dickens.

These writers and readers soon shifted their attentions to a new, militant workers' publication, *Voice of Industry*. Already, in 1834 and 1836, some 1,500 mill girls had gone out on strike, protesting wage cuts, machine speedups, and rent hikes. They marched in the streets, made speeches around a water pump, and sang a satirical ditty, adopted from a popular Protestant song of the time called "I Won't Be a Nun":

> Oh! isn't a pity, such a pretty girl as I—
> Should be sent to the factory to pine away and die?

For many in the South, such actions justified their complaint that Northern abolitionists were hypocrites, condemning black slavery in the South while turning a blind eye to white "wage slavery" in the North. But what the South's apologists failed to understand was that the Northern wage slaves still considered themselves stakeholders in the republic. They had the right to improve their minds and express their thoughts, accumulate some capital, improve the lot of their children, and take off for the territories if all else failed.

Among other differences, the girls and women of the Lowell Mills—like Americans everywhere—continued to exercise their rights to read and write. The literacy rate in the country rose to almost 90 percent, a rate unheard-of anywhere else in the world. In cities and towns, working men and women of all descriptions started reading rooms and circulating libraries. Every town of any size had at least one newspaper. New York City had 17 dailies by 1860. Reading led to more thinking, and the consciousness forged in Lowell continued to express itself in bold new ways. The Lowell strikes were largely broken, but a few years later, in 1848, a convention of women drawn mostly from New England and upstate New York met in Seneca Falls, New York, to launch the first feminist movement in the United States.

NOT QUITE UTOPIA: INSIDE THE MILL TOWNS

From today's perspective, Francis Lowell's carefully planned mill town in Massachusetts was no worker's paradise. Textile weaving in Lowell was still intense physical work, with long hours and little hope of advancement. But compared with the mills of England, Lowell was indeed a huge improvement.

Lowell, Massachusetts	**Manchester, England**
10,000 workers	400,000 workers
70% women age 15–30	70% women age 15+ 15% children under 15
13–14 hours per day	14 hours per day
5 days per week plus ½ day Saturday	6–7 days per week
Wages: $2–$5 per week for women	Wages: About $2 per week for adults, about 50 cents per week for children
Living Conditions: Workers lived in boarding houses, four per room, with up to 40 in a house.	Living Conditions: Workers lived in slum houses, up to 12 to a room.

OVER 80 HOURS PER WEEK!

THE COST OF A PAIR OF SHOES WAS $1.50

1830 TO 1865

ADVENTURE CAPITALISTS

WHALING FUELS THE NATION

All this reading required fuel. An urban lifestyle was being forged in America, and candles would not suffice. The need for light, more light, sparked one of the most colorful and harrowing of all of America's emerging industries.

Whaling as a business was both a model of modern Yankee efficiency and a raw, atavistic throwback to prehistoric times. Harvesting the catch was a simple matter of sailing halfway around the world, flinging flimsy spears into the largest mammals that ever existed, then cutting them up and boiling them down to their every usable ingredient, on ships ingeniously fitted to serve as floating factories. Then doing so again and again, for three or four years, until the holds were full and the ships could head for home.

Each trip was a $50,000 investment, and a risky one: Forty percent of the ships did not return. But the profits were tremendous. By the 1830s, it was whale oil that kept the lights burning and the wheels turning in America. It shone brightly in the household lamps of the rich, in city streetlights, in the lighthouses that dotted the coasts and rivers, and in the headlights of the new locomotive engines chugging across the landscape. Whale oil was used to soften leather and thicken paint; it was congealed into soap, and used as a cleaning agent, a cosmetic, and a medicinal ingredient. Increasingly, it served as an industrial lubricant in the new factory towns of the North, greasing the spindles in the cotton mills and the gears of the trains and the steamboats.

By its peak, in the 1850s, whaling was the fifth-largest industry in the United States, employing over 70,000 people. It was also an industry dominated by America; of the 900 or so whaling ships in commission by 1846, 735 of them were American. Most of these were sponsored by early venture capitalists, local groups of Yankee businessmen plowing the fruits of previous shipping and manufacturing investments into new, high-risk, high-yield enterprises. They were owner-operated, as well—every hand on board got a share of the profits.

In such a world, there was room for a meritocracy that might overwhelm the worst prejudices of the time. Herman Melville made his fictional whaling ship, the *Pequod* (named after a vanquished Indian tribe), a metaphor for the republic; and it was true that, while the captains were nearly always old Yankee salts, the crews were a varied lot. There were Tahitians and other Polynesians, Portuguese and Azoreans and Cape Verdeans, New Zealanders and Maori, Peruvians and Colombians, West Indians and Western Europeans. "A coloured man is only known and looked upon as a man, and is promoted in rank according to his ability and skill to perform the same duties as a white man," one black whaler reported.

The hunt usually took place in the Pacific or the Indian oceans. When the famous cry "Thar she blows!" came from the lookout on a whaling ship, the crew launched its whaleboats, usually equipped with a small sail and six men at the oars. They rowed furiously, shouting, "A dead whale or a stove boat!" As soon as they were close enough, a man at the front leaped up, grabbed the harpoon—a rudimentary device, five or six feet of oak or hickory, with a single- or double-barbed piece of iron stuck into one end—and hurled it into the whale's back or flank with all his might.

Then the fun began. The whalers called it a

JAMES MEIGS, editor in chief, *Popular Mechanics*: "Whale oil opened up the night. And like so many really transformative technological innovations it expanded human freedom. It created a way for people to get more, do more, and achieve more."

"Nantucket sleigh ride," the desperate animal hurtling away, frantically trying to free itself. The whaleboat was tugged along at wild speeds, the sailors hurriedly dumping water on the harpoon line to keep it from bursting into flames as it unwound from the mast. Finally, many miles and hours later, the harpooned whale would start to slow. A ship's officer would then step forward with a lance, seeking to finish the whale off with a few expert thrusts under a fin and into its enormous heart. "The whale is a monster, terrible in his fury…able to shiver the boat in atoms by one stroke of his tail, and when in agony roaring like a lion in the forest," remembered John Thompson, an escaped slave turned whaler.

After finishing it off, the rest was easy—just a matter of six men grappling the leviathan to their small boat and returning to their ship over miles of open sea while beating back swarms of sharks or killer whales trying to devour their catch. Once back at the ship, all hands descended upon the carcass, hauling it up and hacking away at it with spades and knives and axes, rendering the oil from its blubber in the ship's special boilers.

Often these hunts didn't end well. In one particularly catastrophic encounter, a huge sperm whale, apparently incensed, turned around and swam straight for the mother ship, staving in its bow with its massive head. The ship, the *Essex*, sank within minutes, and its crew was barely able to scramble into the undersupplied whaleboats. Before they were picked up by another ship, many had died of starvation and exposure, the rest resorting to cannibalism.

Their story inspired Melville's epic novel, *Moby-Dick*, one of the first significant American novels. But with all it's dangers, whaling was still seen as a refuge by African-Americans escaping slavery.

Whalers whiled away the time making elaborate carvings on whale teeth—an art known as scrimshaw.

THE FLOATING FACTORY: INSIDE THE WHALING SHIP

Nineteenth-century whaling ships were floating flesh factories, in which almost every part of the whale was reduced to some useful commercial product. The whale was chained up along the starboard side of the ship, then cut into pieces by men wielding razor-sharp tools. A whaling voyage of three to four years might net 4,000 barrels of whale oil as well as whalebone, spermaceti, ambergris, and other raw materials.

The whale's carcass was literally unraveled as the crew cut and peeled four-to-six-foot-wide "blanket pieces" of blubber from it (1). These pieces were cut down to foot-square "horse pieces" (2), and then reduced to "bible leaves"—narrow strips of blubber with one end still attached to the skin, resembling the fanned pages of a Bible—on the mincing horse (3). Scraps were collected in a box (4) to be used as fuel for the "trying out," in which the oil was boiled from the blubber in immense, cast-iron cooking vats known as "trypots" (5). After cooling, the oil was stored in barrels to be lowered below deck (6). These barrels were often built with rings and staves (7).

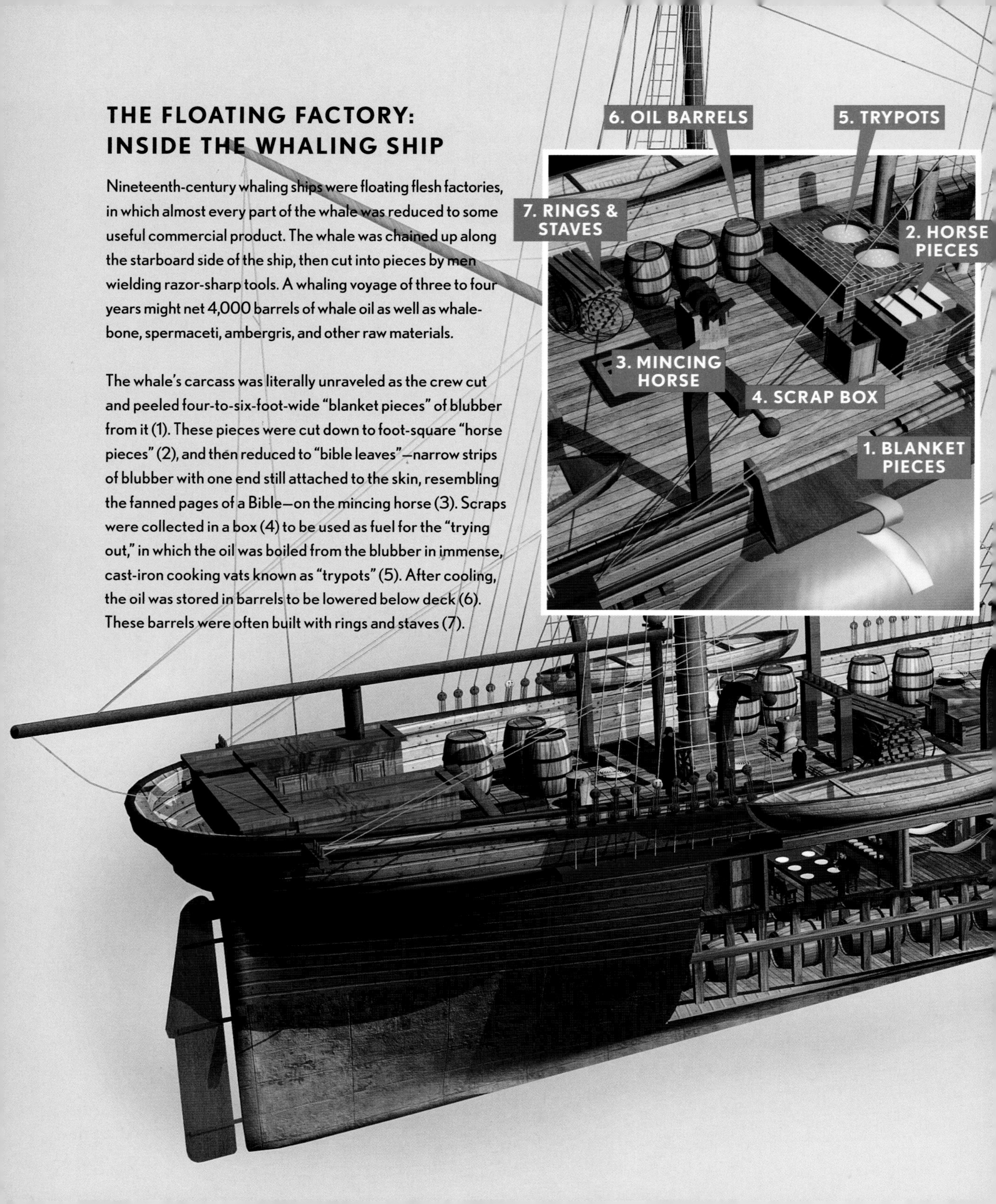

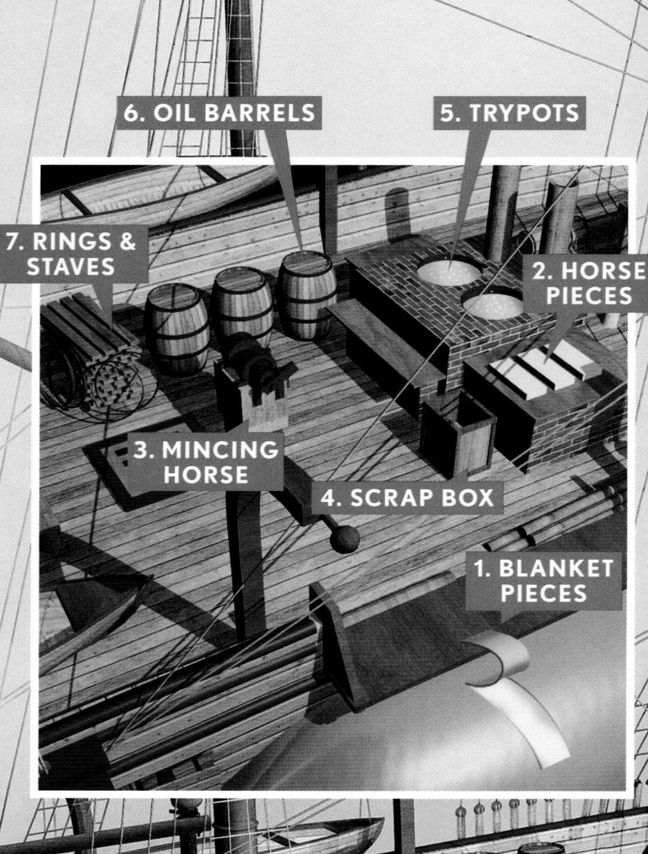

1822 TO 1860

"THESE HANDS DO NOT BELONG TO ME..."

FIGHTING THE SLAVE POWER

The South, by this time, had rationalized its "peculiar institution" into a religious and social imperative. Slavery did not simply enable the genteel, superior Southern way of life—it was good for all, saving the souls of millions of ignorant African heathens from hell, giving them a better life than the savage existence from whence they supposedly came.

Slave revolts, imagined or real—such as those of Nat Turner in Tidewater Virginia and Denmark Vesey in Charleston, or even the revolution in Haiti—sent shock waves rolling through the Southern states, leading to ever-harsher laws banning blacks from congregating or from learning to read and write. But how, then, were they to continue learning and practicing the Christianity that they had flocked to—and that whites liked to insist was the main purpose of slavery? How could they do the increasingly skilled tasks that many white masters hired them out to do?

"If there is no struggle, there is no progress." —Frederick Douglass

Daguerreotype of Frederick Douglass, circa 1847.

One skilled worker was Frederick Bailey, who by the age of 20 was a ship's caulker along the Baltimore docks. Like many slaves, young Bailey lived on his own, handing over nearly all of his wages to his master, who promised to free him by the time he was 25. Bailey did not trust him. He had been starved, whipped, and beaten, and deprived of so much as a blanket to sleep in or anything more than a long shirt to wear when he was young. He was fed cornmeal slush from a trough with other slaves, he wrote, "like so many pigs."

Having learned to read, he saved what pennies he could get to secretly buy newspapers, as well as a collection of speeches on liberty, democracy, and courage. Converted to Christianity at 16, he organized religious services for his fellow slaves, only to see them broken up by a white mob. Bailey was hired out to a poor farmer named Edward Covey, known as a slave breaker, who whipped and worked him nearly to exhaustion. From Covey, he learned something else: "Men are whipped oftenest who are whipped easiest." One day, when Covey began to tie him to a post for another lashing, Bailey turned on him.

"At this moment—from whence came the spirit I don't know—I resolved to fight," he later wrote. "I seized Covey hard by the throat, and as I did so, I rose."

Bailey fought Covey to a standstill for two hours, something that might easily have earned him the death penalty, save for the fact that Covey could not afford to endanger his livelihood by letting it be known he had failed to break a 16-year-old boy. Bailey resolved to escape to the North. Disguised as a sailor, and carrying the seaman's papers of a friend who was a freedman, he traveled by train to Philadelphia, a fast if harrowing 24 hours to freedom.

He later went to New York, and then to the home of another free black man, who found him work in the busy shipyards of New Bedford, Massachusetts, the great whaling port. To hide his identity from slave catchers, he changed his name to Frederick Douglass—inspired, ironically, by a character in *The Lady of the Lake,* by Sir Walter Scott, idol of the white South. But he would not stay in hiding. In 1844, Douglass wrote the story of his life. A friendly abolitionist advised him to burn it, lest he be captured and dragged back to bondage, but Douglass refused.

In 1845, 5,000 copies of *Narrative of the Life of Frederick Douglass, an American Slave* were printed. It was an overnight sensation, a bestseller on both sides of the Atlantic. It also attracted unwanted attention. Douglass was still a commodity, liable to capture and re-enslavement. His friends prevailed on him to travel to England and Ireland on a lecture tour, where he packed churches and lecture halls.

"I know there are some in this country who question my right...to myself," he pointed out, accusing himself of a crime: "I have run off with stolen property. These hands do not belong to me—they belong to Captain Hall [his former master]; well, I cannot believe it.... [I]t does not for a moment shake my opinion that I have the best right to myself."

British abolitionists bought his freedom, and Douglass returned to America officially a free man in 1847, where he continued to agitate for abolition, speaking wherever he would be heard, and publishing a newspaper, *The North Star,* with the masthead motto: "Right is of no Sex—Truth is of no Color—God is the Father of us all, and we are all brethren." For Douglass, freedom was indivisible. Speaking at the first American women's rights convention, in Seneca Falls, New York, in 1848, he told his audience, "In this denial of the right to participate in government, not merely the degradation of woman and the perpetuation of a great injustice happens, but the maiming and repudiation of one-half of the moral and intellectual power for the government of the world."

He was received rapturously. Northern women would provide a powerful impetus behind the abolitionist movement, and Douglass had started himself on a remarkable career, one that would see this former slave become an ambassador and an adviser to presidents. Narratives of escaped slaves became a popular staple in Northern bookstores. Douglass's memoir was followed by John Thompson's and Solomon Northup's, and by a melodramatic but well-researched novel by a white woman abolitionist, Harriet Beecher Stowe. *Uncle Tom's Cabin* sold over two million copies worldwide within two years, and was followed up by innumerable popular stage productions. Slowly, they were starting to move the stone. It would not budge easily, as Douglass often noted: "Power concedes nothing without a demand. It never did, and it never will."

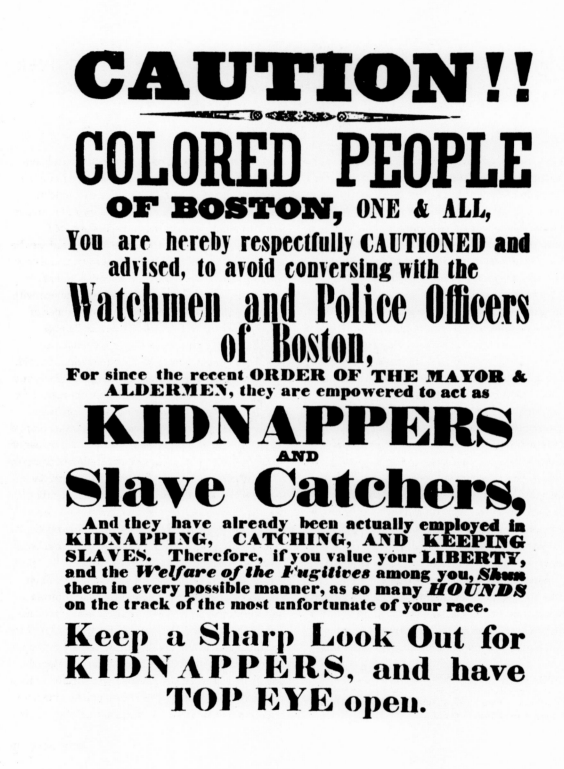

CAUTION!!

COLORED PEOPLE

OF BOSTON, ONE & ALL,

You are hereby respectfully **CAUTIONED** and advised, to avoid conversing with the

Watchmen and Police Officers of Boston,

For since the recent **ORDER OF THE MAYOR & ALDERMEN**, they are empowered to act as

KIDNAPPERS

AND

Slave Catchers,

And they have already been actually employed in **KIDNAPPING, CATCHING, AND KEEPING SLAVES.** Therefore, if you value your **LIBERTY**, and the *Welfare of the Fugitives* among you, *Shun* them in every possible manner, as so many ***HOUNDS*** on the track of the most unfortunate of your race.

Keep a Sharp Look Out for KIDNAPPERS, and have TOP EYE open.

Even in the North many still turned a deaf ear. Workingmen feared that freed slaves would compete for their jobs and drive down wages, and clung to their status as "white men." New York financiers feared that they might lose their investments if the South were driven to secede from the Union, while Yankee mill owners feared for their supply of cotton. The nation's two largest political parties, the Whigs and the Democrats, ducked the issue as much as possible. Mobs attacked black churches in New York, Philadelphia, and elsewhere. Abolitionists were still considered a small, fanatical faction in most places, their speakers shouted down and assaulted. The Reverend Elijah Lovejoy, an outspoken abolitionist, was shot by a lynch mob in Illinois in 1837.

The merchants of New England and the financiers of New York were reluctant to do anything that would interrupt the flow of cotton through the mills. They agreed with South Carolina's Senator John C. Calhoun, a fierce champion of Southern rights and customs, who was convinced that the South held in its hands the key to all world commerce—the one industry on the planet that was too big to fail. Seizing on a phrase first used by a Northern writer, James Henry Hammond expostulated: "No power on earth dares to make war upon [cotton]. Cotton is king."

Cotton is king. It became a rallying cry throughout the South. It was true that, by 1860, the export of raw cotton from the South would outstrip the value of all Northern exports by nearly four to one. Cotton made the Western world go 'round, but it created a boom mentality that had a lasting and deleterious effect on the South. It was a hungry crop, one that quickly leeched the richest soils of their waters and minerals. Eager to realize its value as quickly as possible, Southern planters rarely took the time to fertilize the land or bother with even the most fundamental crop rotation. There was always more land to be had, seized from the Indians or from others. The war with Mexico had opened up thousands of new miles of cotton-growing land in Texas alone. As Thomas Jefferson once noted, ruefully: "It is cheaper for Americans to buy new lands than to manure the old."

"This filthy enactment was made in the nineteenth century, by people who could read and write. I will not obey it, by God!" raged an incredulous Ralph Waldo Emerson, about the Fugitive Slave Act. "I think we must get rid of slavery, or we must get rid of freedom."

This mentality encouraged waste, transience, and exploitation. It also led to an ongoing argument over whether the new lands would be "slave" or "free." Always, the fear of the South was that its cotton empire would not have enough room to grow, and the fear of the North that its yeoman farmers could not compete with the great planters and their forced labor. Each side worried that a state or two more on the other side would tip the congressional balance for good.

For over a generation, a delicate series of political compromises had been orchestrated by the old lions of the Senate: Calhoun, Daniel Webster of Massachusetts, and Henry Clay of Kentucky. Their last deal was the Compromise of 1850: California would enter the Union as a free state, and slave auctions (though not slavery) would be outlawed within the District of Columbia. In return, slavery would not be restricted in the new territories of New Mexico and Utah. Northern states would be obligated to help return runaway slaves to their masters; anyone helping them to escape would face penalties of up to six months in jail and a $1,000 fine.

The compromise went down easily enough, but it did not sit well. To this day, apologists for secession contend that the American Civil War was fought over the issue of states' rights, not slavery. They are correct: The Civil War was fought over the right of the people of the North and the West *not* to have slavery in their states. The Fugitive Slave Act of 1850 was a visceral violation of traditional American notions of local autonomy. It meant that gangs of ruthless men from hundreds of miles away, carrying pistols, bullwhips, and manacles, could come into Northern towns and cart away their friends and neighbors if they happened to be black. Often it didn't matter whether the "fugitives" were runaway slaves or black men and women whose families had lived in freedom for generations; the sort of men who worked as slave catchers were rarely careful about such distinctions.

The law appalled Northerners, even those who cared little about the rights of black people. Attempts to send back escaped slaves set off mob action and near riots in Boston, where an Anti-Man-Hunting League effectively nullified the new statute. In Cincinnati, local blacks repeatedly battled lawmen to save fleeing slaves. Even federal marshals, confronted with their duty to help slave catchers find runaway slaves, sometimes tipped off the refugees in question.

Far from settling anything, the Compromise of 1850 only provoked an escalating series of crises that continued to fray the cotton thread and common civility. South Carolina Congressman Preston Brooks, incensed that an abolitionist senator from Massachusetts, Charles Sumner, had insulted Brooks's cousin, Senator Andrew Pickens Butler, sneaked up on Sumner while he sat at his Senate desk, and beat him severely with a heavy cane until he broke it over Sumner's head.

Brooks was exalted in the South as a hero, and was sent canes by hundreds of admirers. The South, though, had lost forever the support of New England mill owners. "We went to bed one night, old-fashioned, conservative, compromise Union Whigs, and we waked up stark mad Abolitionists," wrote Amos A. Lawrence, the son and namesake of one of Lowell's old partners at the Boston Associates. Such men had the greatest stake in slavery of anyone in the North. Now many of them began to break their old bonds in disgust.

More and more, Northerners resorted to civil disobedience. Abolitionists started the Underground Railroad, an ad hoc network of secret safe houses, to help slaves escape from the South and make their way to Canada. In hundreds of old New England homes, there can still be found false fireplaces, double closets, and attic and cellar hidey holes in which black and white "conductors" could shelter fugitive slaves before moving them along, usually at night, to the next "station."

As slaves continued to escape and new territories continued to line up to join the Union, the Compromise of 1850 continued to crumble. In 1854, the Democratic leader in the Senate, Stephen Douglas of Illinois, brokered a deal whereby the states of Kansas and Nebraska would determine if they would be slave or free when they entered the Union. This proved to be an even greater disaster. Free-soil Jayhawkers and pro-slavery Border Ruffians from Missouri competed to see who could rush the most men into the new territories. The Jayhawkers outnumbered the slavery

HEAVILY ARMED KANSAS SETTLERS, 1856

men, but the heavily armed Border Ruffians ran a fixed election set up a rump, pro-slave government and attacked, pillaged, and burned the Jayhawk capital of Lawrence, Kansas.

To the North, this was yet another violent, Southern outrage. One man decided to repay it in kind. John Brown was a hatchet-faced Connecticut Yankee and father of 20 children who, upon the death of Rev. Lovejoy at the hands of a pro-slavery mob, publicly vowed, "I consecrate my life to the destruction of slavery!"

That was almost 20 years earlier, and Brown had done little to destroy slavery. Now, at last, moving to Kansas with several of his sons and supporters, he determined to strike back. Late on the night of May 24, 1856, Brown and his men took five pro-slavery settlers from their cabins along Pottawatomie Creek and hacked them to death with broadswords. "We must fight fire with fire," Brown insisted, and "strike terror in the hearts of the pro-slavery people."

Brown led his men in several more engagements, as the conflict in Kansas broke into pitched battles, killing hundreds. He would lose a son in the fighting, but it would not deter him from leading a violent raid on Missouri, during which he freed 11 slaves. By this time, though, federal troops had managed to restore a shaky peace to Kansas, and the Jayhawkers won a fair election, allowing it to become a free territory. John Brown moved on to plot new ways of breaking the Slave Power; he would soon see an opportunity.

GOD'S CONDUCTOR: HARRIET TUBMAN

The most famous "conductor" of the Underground Railroad was a five-foot-tall disabled woman who came to be known as Moses. Harriet Tubman was born into slavery in Maryland, where as a child she was routinely beaten for such grave offenses as stealing a lump of sugar. A devout Christian, she began to see visions that she interpreted as messages from God. She also began to plot her liberation. "[T]here was one of two things I had a right to, liberty or death. If I could not have one, I would have the other." Hers was a 90-mile journey, moving by night on the edge of swamps and forests, following the North Star to the border of the free state of Pennsylvania. "When I crossed that line, I looked at my hands to see if I was the same person," she wrote. "There was such a glory over everything; the sun came like gold through the trees, and over the fields, and I felt like I was in Heaven."

She decided to take others there too. Back she went, 13 trips in all from 1851 to 1860, bringing 70 people out of bondage, including her parents, her four brothers, their spouses, and many of their children. She came in the winter, when the nights were long. She would lead people out on Saturday evenings, knowing that notices of their escape could not be printed in the newspaper until the following Monday. She employed disguises and prayed for guidance. "I never met with any person, of any color, who had more confidence in the voice of God, as spoken direct to her soul," wrote Thomas Garrett—but she carried a revolver, just in case.

Tubman was so good at what she did that no one ever figured out that it was she who was helping their slaves escape. "I was conductor of the Underground Railroad for eight years," she liked to boast, "and I can say what most conductors can't say—I never ran my train off the track and I never lost a passenger."

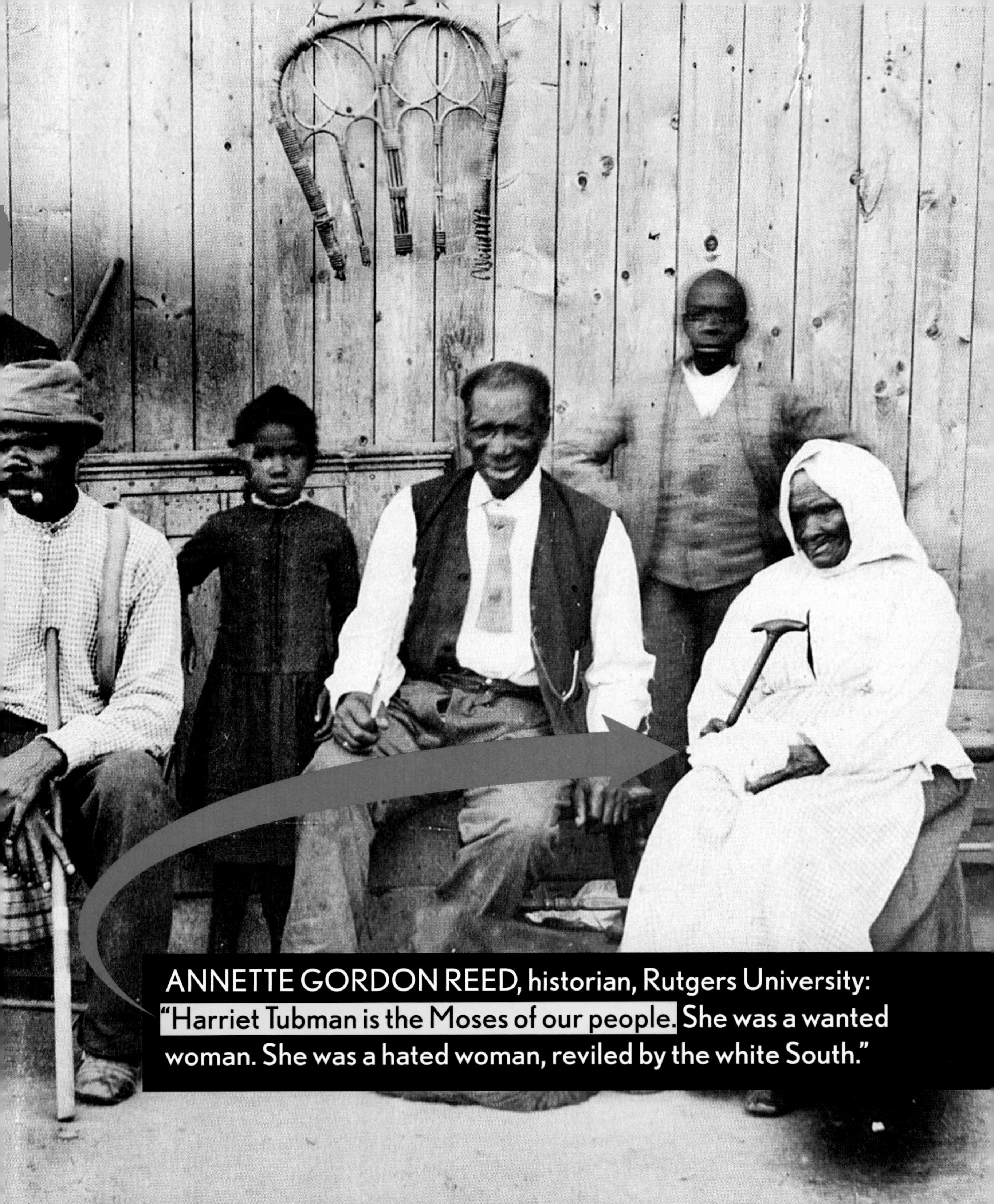

ANNETTE GORDON REED, historian, Rutgers University: "Harriet Tubman is the Moses of our people. She was a wanted woman. She was a hated woman, reviled by the white South."

1857
TO
1859

SUPREME COURT INJUSTICE

DRED SCOTT AND JOHN BROWN FRACTURE THE UNION

Dred Scott had been born on a Virginia plantation, but lived for years in the free states of Illinois and Minnesota with his army surgeon master. After the man's death, Scott sued for his freedom. Miraculously, the case made it all the way to the Supreme Court of the United States, where in 1857 Chief Justice Roger Brooke Taney wrote the majority opinion.

Taney was a brilliant legal mind and former Maryland slaveholder who had not only freed his slaves but also provided them with pensions, and who had written in a previous case that slavery was "a blot on our national character." But he had come to share the popular Southern sentiment that opposition to slavery constituted Northern aggression. Now he saw an opportunity to settle the whole question of slavery once and for all as fixed law.

The result would be the most disruptive decision in Supreme Court history. Going much further than the case required, Taney declared that for more than a century "every European nation" regarded blacks as "beings of an inferior order, and altogether unfit to associate with the white race, either in social or political relations, and so far unfit that they had no rights which the white man was bound to respect."

No rights which the white man was bound to respect. What's more, neither slaves "nor their descendants, were embraced in any of the other provisions of the Constitution"—not even those addressing noncitizens, such as Indians.

This was a willful misreading of history. Taney somehow missed the fact that when the Constitution was ratified, freed blacks had the right to vote in ten of the 13 states, owned property, spoke in public meetings, and sued in court.

Outrage rolled through the North. But once again, John Brown had a plan to do something about it. He declared war. Brown's plan was to seize the federal arsenal at Harpers Ferry, just over the Potomac River in Virginia. Slaves from miles around would flock to his banner. Brown would arm and then lead them into the hills and commence a guerrilla insurgency.

It was madness, and recognized as such both by the wealthy abolitionists whose backing he courted and by the slaves he hoped to rally. Brown gathered only 21 men—16 white and five black—for an operation he had originally planned for 4,500. Frederick Douglass, who always admired Brown's courage, warned him that he would be "going into a perfect steel-trap, and that once in will never get out alive...."

Moving on Harpers Ferry late on the night of October 16, 1859, Brown and his men quickly seized the arsenal, which was guarded by a single watchman. But the slaves didn't rise, and Brown was surrounded in the arsenal's engine house by a drunken mob of local militiamen, farmers, and townspeople. He and his men fought on for 17 hours, until the engine house was stormed by a contingent of U.S. Marines under the command of army colonel Robert E. Lee. Ten of Brown's men were killed in the fight, including two more of his sons, and another six would eventually be hanged for their insurrection. A wounded Brown was dragged out alive, deemed by Lee to be "a fanatic or madman."

If so, he was a canny one. Brown made his prosecution a show trial, and if it did not save him from the gallows, he did manage to put slavery on trial alongside him.

DRED SCOTT

For President

ABRAM LINCOLN.

For Vice President

HANNIBAL HAMLIN.

1860 TO 1861

IRREPRESSIBLE CONFLICT

SECESSION AND DEFIANCE

Southerners seized upon the raid at Harpers Ferry to prove what they had been saying all along, which was that Northerners did not care if they were all murdered in their beds by rebellious slaves. At the Democratic convention in 1860, the Southern delegates refused to agree on a candidate, fatally splitting the party. Meanwhile, that February Abraham Lincoln brought himself to the fore of the Republican party with his brilliantly reasoned address at the new Cooper Union, in which he decried the Dred Scott decision, pleaded for tolerance and restraint toward the South, but famously insisted, "Let us have faith that right makes might, but in that faith, let us, to the end, dare to do our duty as we understand it."

Lincoln won his party's nomination but drew less than 40 percent of the popular vote—and less than 2 percent in the South, where his name was generally not even allowed on the ballot. He still won handily against a badly divided opposition, continuing to plead for unity, and pledging not to interfere with slavery in the South.

Indeed, it would have been difficult for him to do so legally, considering the scope of Taney's ruling. By now, however, secessionists saw Southern independence as the only way to maintain their vaunted way of life, and they heard threats in Lincoln's words. South Carolina seceded from the Union before the year was out, and by the following spring it had been joined by ten more Southern states, constituting themselves as the independent Confederate States of America.

They expected little trouble. After all, cotton was still king on the world markets, and if Great Britain and France—the two leading world powers—did not act to keep the white gold flowing, their economies would be devastated. All the acute Yankees in their New England mill towns, holding Southern debt on Wall Street, would be ruined.

And if Lincoln resisted secession, as he claimed he would? Surely the superior civilization of the South would triumph over the money-grubbing Yankees and the immigrant wage slaves of the North—no matter that they held enormous advantages in everything necessary to fight a modern war. Secession propagandist Edmund Ruffin had predicted in his novel, *Anticipations of the Future*, that the Union would have to resort to a draft to get its urban immigrants to fight against the South, and this in turn would set off terrible riots, until "the great cities of Boston, New York and Philadelphia...[are] sacked and burnt, and their wealthiest inhabitants massacred, by their own destitute, vicious and desperate population."

At last, the bloody apocalypses of Ruffin and Brown were met. The world's first great democracy seemed to be dissolving into a welter of cultural hatreds. The reality would be so much worse than anything they had fantasized.

Abraham Lincoln had grown up in poverty on the frontier and had little formal schooling to speak of. By 1860, he was a wealthy railroad lawyer, and he had won the Republican nomination in the booming city of Chicago, which had not even existed before 1833.

CHAPTER FIVE

CIVIL WAR

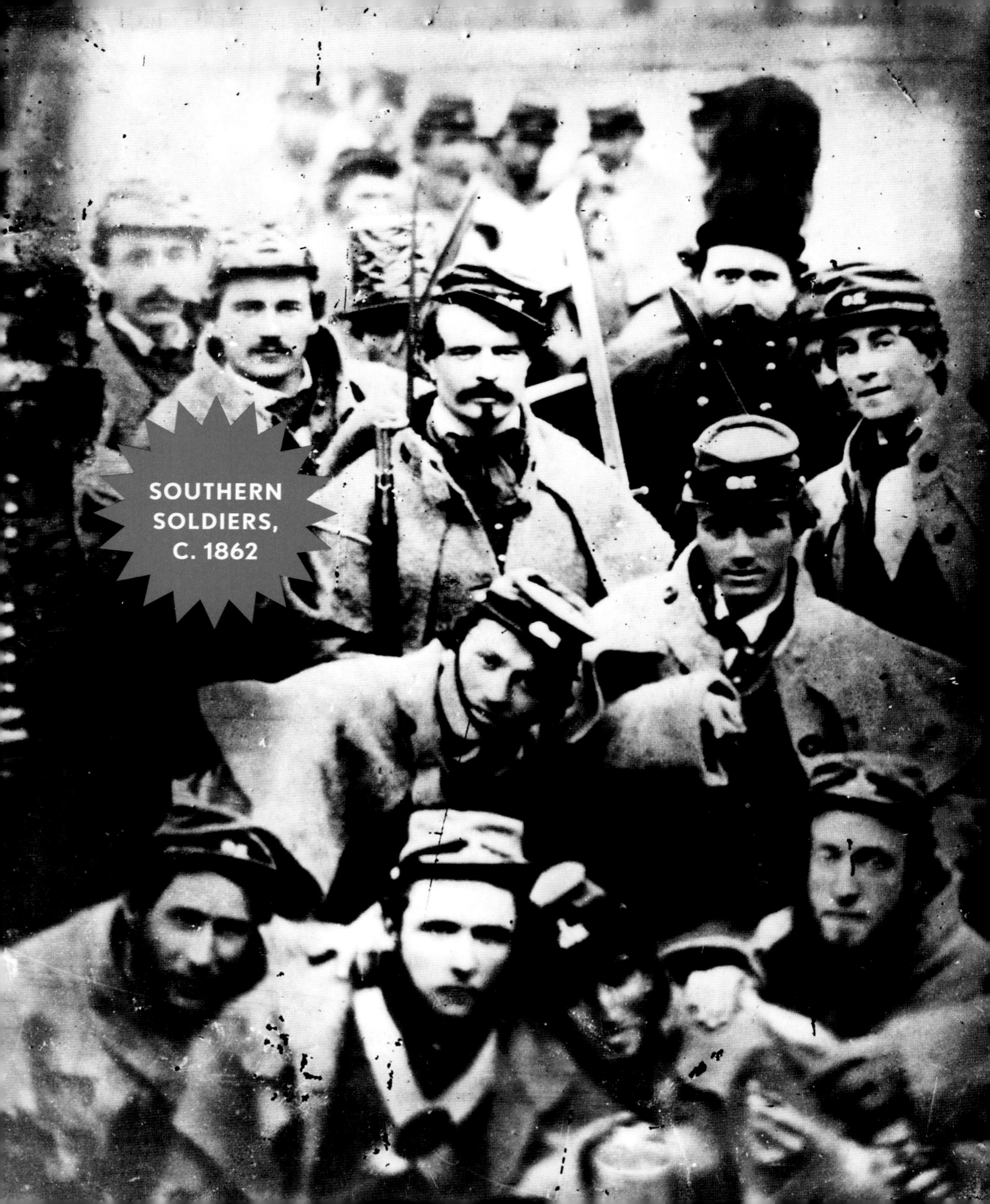

SOUTHERN SOLDIERS, C. 1862

1861

"THE THING IS AN IMPOSSIBILITY..."

THE WAR COMES

In his second inaugural address, delivered on March 4, 1865, just over a month before the effective end of the Civil War, Abraham Lincoln told a bone-weary nation: "[F]our years ago, all thoughts were anxiously directed to an impending civil-war. All dreaded it—all sought to avert it.... Both parties deprecated war; but one of them would *make* war rather than let the nation survive; and the other would *accept* war rather than let it perish. And the war came."

Once it did, both sides were woefully unprepared. They would compensate quickly. The Civil War would spur American ingenuity to some of its finest—and its most terrible—accomplishments. Over the course of four years, the United States would reinvent itself as one nation. From 1865 on, it would be referred to in the singular—"the United States *is*," as opposed to the old custom of saying "the United States *are*"—and the *is* for the first time included all black men as full citizens, at least in theory.

The Civil War would propel America into the modern Industrial Age, and it would provide a horrifying foretaste of twentieth-century combat, through the conflict's mechanized slaughter, its devastation, and its utter disrespect for prisoners and innocents alike. The war would bring about advances in medicine, health care, hygiene, manufacturing, agriculture, shipbuilding, communications, and finance. It would also give us the first carbine, revolver, and rifled musket; the precursors of the modern submarine, the machine gun, and the dumdum bullet.

Southern soldiers striking jaunty, confident poses before they knew what war was. Men departing for the front flocked by the thousands to the new photographic studios to have daguerreotypes or tin types taken for their loved ones.

On paper, at least, the American Civil War was one of the most uneven fights in history. The number of white males of fighting age in the Union outnumbered those in the Confederacy by more than three to one. The Northern states accounted for over 90 percent of the country's manufacturing capacity, and they produced 97 percent of its firearms, 93 percent of its pig iron, 94 percent of its cloth, and 90 percent of its boots and shoes. The North possessed two-thirds of the nation's railroad mileage, all built on the same gauge, unlike the tracks in the Confederate states, which had bought their rails from both England and the North before the war and had never bothered to coordinate them.

When it came to replacing all of the above, whether by buying it or making more, the North maintained stupendous advantages. There were more than 110,000 factories in the states remaining loyal to the Union, as opposed to fewer than 21,000 in the Confederacy; nearly 1.2 million industrial workers, compared with just 111,000. Union banks held over $207 million in deposits at the start of the war, versus $47 million in Confederate vaults. The Union had over twice as many horses, twice as many dairy cows, three times as many sheep. Every year, it harvested nearly twice as much corn, more than five times as much wheat, and seven times as many oats.

Yet bringing these advantages to bear was no easy task. At the beginning of the Civil War, the Union had little more than the munitions and uniforms necessary to arm and clothe its tiny, far-flung standing army of just 13,000. Northerners rallied immediately to President Lincoln's call for 75,000 volunteers, but most of these were on six-month enlistments; when

their time was up, entire regiments simply disbanded and went home. The textile factories of New England ground to a halt when the war started, much as the South had predicted they would when deprived of cotton. Wall Street financiers were left holding worthless pieces of paper signifying the massive debts they were still owed by Delta planters.

It might be tempting to conclude that all the South had going into the war were "cotton and slaves and arrogance," to quote Rhett Butler in *Gone with the Wind*, but the Confederacy was far from helpless. The advantages it held might be classified as solidarity, military leadership, daring, and size.

"They may overrun our frontier States and plunder our coast but, as for conquering us, the thing is an impossibility," the third Confederate secretary of war, George W. Randolph, wrote to his wife, Molly. "There is no instance in history of a people as numerous as we are inhabiting a country so extensive as ours being subjugated if true to themselves." Many historians and other observers agreed.

A week after Lincoln duped the South into starting the war by firing on Fort Sumter near Charleston, South Carolina, he adopted General Winfield Scott's Anaconda Plan, designed to slowly strangle the Confederacy by stopping traffic on its major rivers and

REBEL ARMIES REPEATEDLY LOOTED THE BALTIMORE AND OHIO RAILROAD; ON ONE RAID IN 1861, STONEWALL JACKSON MADE OFF WITH 14 LOCOMOTIVES AND 36 MILES OF RAIL, WHILE HIS MEN TORCHED ANOTHER 42 LOCOMOTIVES AND 386 RAIL CARS, BURNING 23 BRIDGES ALONG THE WAY.

blockading its ports. But in 1861, the North had only 42 ships to lock up 3,000 miles of coast and 189 ports, and for the first year of the war, nine out of every ten Confederate blockade runners escaped.

Some of the escapees would return with more than 600,000 small arms from Europe over the course of the war, along with untold amounts of ammunition, blankets, uniforms, and shoes. Who needed money or factories, when you had cotton to trade? Other Southern ships were commissioned to attack the Union's merchant marine; before the war was over, such ships would capture 247 vessels, including much of the North's vulnerable whaling fleet.

The North itself served as the South's commissary. Throughout the war, Confederate soldiers marched in Union shoes, wore Union uniforms, fired Union guns. Much of this bounty was reaped from Northern prisoners and Northern dead. Brilliant cavalry commanders, such as Nathan Bedford Forrest and James Ewell Brown "Jeb" Stuart, as well as the ruthless guerrilla leader William Clarke Quantrill, staged raids deep into Union territory and around Union armies, capturing supply trains and caches of supplies—and tying up tens of thousands of U.S. troops in the process. Rebel armies repeatedly looted the Baltimore and Ohio Railroad; on one raid in 1861, Stonewall Jackson made off with 14 locomotives and 36 miles of rail, while his men torched another 42 locomotives and 386 railcars, burning 23 bridges along the way. For every mile the Northern armies advanced into the South, their problems of supply and communication worsened. At the peak of the war, the Union was deploying 112,000 troops—one-third of all active soldiers at the time—to guard railroads and supply lines against an estimated 22,000 rebel raiders.

Jackson made his name in one of the war's earliest engagements, with his troops "standing like a stone wall" to win the First Battle of Bull Run. His battlefield aggression and his tactical brilliance were unsurpassed, and yet he was, along with James Longstreet and A. P. Hill, just one of three outstanding corps commanders under Robert E. Lee, who was in charge of the fabled Army of Northern Virginia. Lee was probably the greatest general America ever produced, and the South got the best part of the Union's West Point graduates and professional officers—the military being one of the few vocations considered fitting for the sons of plantation gentlemen.

The North was forced to rely much more upon "political generals," selected, at least at first, by a vote of their troops. Some of these men proved to be natural leaders; others were dismal. In the Eastern theater, especially, the Confederacy repeatedly out-generaled the Union for the first two years of the war—but the officers were only one part of the story. Undersupplied, underfed, and undershod, Confederate soldiers nevertheless fought with undaunted courage throughout the war, under good commanders and bad. Watching Lee's army on the move, one Northern civilian thought them "the dirtiest men I ever saw, a most ragged, lean and hungry set of wolves.... Yet there was a dash about them that the northern men lacked." They cared little for formal drill, and advanced in lines "crooked as a ram's horn." But they almost never broke or ran under even the heaviest fire, every man stepping up at his own pace, screaming the trademark, high-pitched rebel yell that sowed terror in their enemies.

THE DIFFERENCES BETWEEN UNION AND CONFEDERATE SOLDIERS

The Union had more than double the population of the Confederacy (including slaves), and almost four times the number of men of combat age. Even with only 50 percent of eligible men enlisted, relative to the Confederacy's 75 percent, the Union still had more than twice the number of soldiers. In total more than 600,000 Americans were killed in the war—at least 2 percent of the population.

	UNION	CONFEDERATE
Native-born Americans	45%	91%
Literacy rate	90%	80%
Profession	48% farmers	75% farmers
Death rate	23%	24%
Odds of dying from wounds	1 in 18	1 in 8
Odds of dying from disease	1 in 8	1 in 5

UNION
UNION
UNION

"Although a soldier by profession, I have never felt any sort of fondness for war, and I have never advocated it, except as a means of peace." —Ulysses S. Grant

TO BUILD A MORE PERFECT HELL

THE LOSSES MOUNT

To defeat such a people would take time, if it could be done at all. That was what the South was counting on. If it could simply keep the North from winning the war too quickly, the Confederate leadership felt, Britain and France would step in to guarantee their independence. Both European nations' economies relied heavily on cotton; in Britain alone, as much as 20 percent of the workforce depended on the textile mills.

The South also hoped to weary the North with the fighting, and with extraordinary death tolls. Early in 1862, Ulysses S. Grant, the Union's best general, was excoriated as a butcher by Northern newspapers and politicians, and temporarily relieved of his command after having *repelled* a savage surprise attack at Shiloh, in Tennessee. The reason for the reprimand was the bloodshed, of a magnitude unparalleled in American history at that time for a single battle; total casualties—killed, wounded, and missing—for both sides at Shiloh were 23,741.

Such casualty rates, though, would soon become the norm. In the fighting of the Seven Days' Battles, outside Richmond, Virginia (and just over two months after Shiloh), total casualties were over 36,000, with more than 5,200 dead. At the Second Battle of Bull Run, in August of that same year, there would be over 25,000 casualties, with more than 3,200 killed; at Chancellorsville, in 1863, there were over 30,000 casualties, and nearly 3,300 dead.

A new form of warfare was taking shape. The main cause was some of the terrible innovations in technology that Americans were both implementing and improving upon. Previous wars had been fought mostly with smooth-bore muskets, which had an effective range of only 100 yards. In the Civil War, both sides used new, rifled muskets with grooves inside their barrels, which had a range of 500 yards—greater, even, than the 400 yards of canister-firing artillery. They achieved this in part thanks to the ammunition they were firing: minié balls, pressed or molded lead bullets that had been invented in France and named for their cocreator.

A minié bullet changed shape when fired, the explosion of the gunpowder causing it to expand to fit the rifle grooves and sending it spiraling out of the gun at terrific velocity. Its lightness and its tendency to expand also meant that the minié ball often did not simply pass through the body, but flattened and burrowed into bone and tore through sinew, muscle, and organs. Over 90 percent of all wounds in the Civil War were caused by minié balls, and the new range that ammunition provided to infantrymen fundamentally changed the tactics of modern warfare. Ever since the Napoleonic Wars, generals had relied on offensive maneuvers, marching troops through artillery bombardments so they could get close enough to deliver withering, point-blank volleys, then charge with the bayonet.

Now the emphasis shifted back to defensive postures, with soldiers looking to take the high ground, and firing from behind fortifications and stone walls. Generals had to adjust to the fact that there were certain, well-defended positions that even the most determined troops could not take. It was not a lesson readily learned. At the Battle of Fredericksburg, in Virginia, Union commander Ambrose Burnside flung his Army of the Potomac again and again against Lee's well-defended position on Marye's Heights, leaving

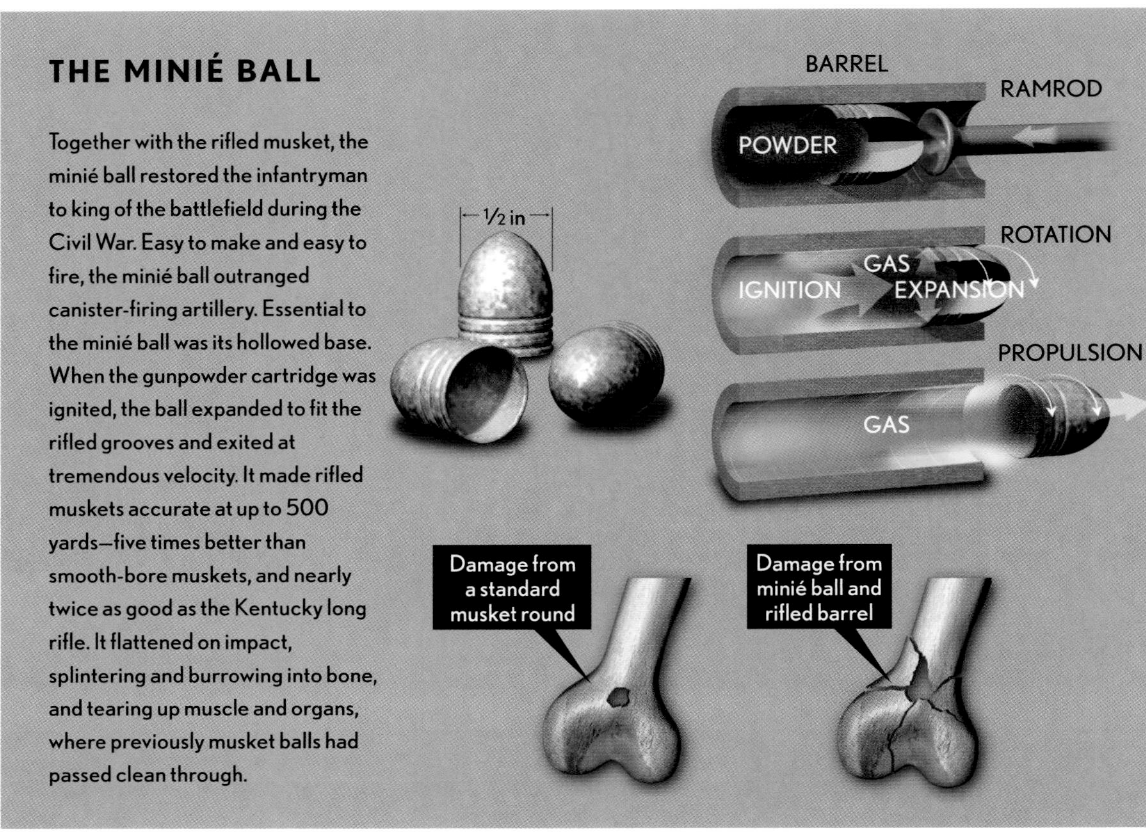

almost 1,300 of his men dead and 9,600 wounded, without reaching the Confederate line. Watching the dead pile up and the still-charging Union soldiers stumble about their bodies, Lee put down his field glasses and remarked: "It is well that war is so terrible. We should grow too fond of it."

THE MINIÉ BALL
Together with the rifled musket, the minié ball restored the infantryman to king of the battlefield during the Civil War. Easy to make and easy to fire, the minié ball outranged canister-firing artillery. Essential to the minié ball was its hollowed base. When the gunpowder cartridge was ignited, the ball expanded to fit the rifled grooves and exited at tremendous velocity. It made rifled muskets accurate at up to 500 yards—five times better than smooth-bore muskets, and nearly twice as good as the Kentucky long rifle. It flattened on impact, splintering and burrowing into bone, and tearing up muscle and organs, where previously musket balls had passed clean through.
½ in
BARREL
RAMROD
POWDER
ROTATION
GAS
IGNITION
EXPANSION
PROPULSION
GAS
Damage from a standard musket round
Damage from minié ball and rifled barrel

Robert E. Lee was offered command of all the Union armies by Lincoln at the beginning of the war, but he refused, claiming that he could not "raise my hand against my birthplace, my home, my children."

By *home*, he meant the Commonwealth of Virginia, where he had been brought up in the state's aristocracy. His wife, Mary Custis, was the great-granddaughter of Martha Washington, and his father was Henry "Light Horse Harry" Lee III, a dashing cavalry hero of the Revolution, whose penchant for games of chance and risky investments left the family almost destitute upon his death. Light Horse Harry's son, by contrast, maintained a rigid self-discipline, graduating second in his class at West Point without accumulating a single demerit, then serving with distinction in Mexico. He rarely drank, abstained from tobacco, and channeled his own love of gambling onto the battlefield, where he specialized in bold flanking and enveloping maneuvers that continually unnerved Union generals.

Within a single campaign season, Lee won worldwide renown, scoring victory after victory against larger, better-equipped Northern forces. White-haired, handsome, courteous, genteel, and deeply religious,

Lee was already the beau ideal of the Cavalier South. His first concern, though, was Virginia, and by the fall of 1862 his home state had been devastated by months of steady campaigning. Lee decided to take the fight to the enemy, moving his army across the Potomac into Maryland, a slaveholding border state that had been held in the Union mainly by force of arms. There, he hoped to raise thousands of rebel sympathizers to the cause, replenish his army's stocks, and maybe end the war with one decisive victory.

This was not beyond the realm of possibility. Disgust with the war's progress and anger over the mounting casualties were growing rapidly on all sides in the North. Lincoln's party was headed toward a smashing defeat at the polls that November. Meanwhile, Napoleon III, emperor of France, was eager to broker a peace in return for a Southern offer of 100,000 bales of cotton and recognition of his puppet regime in Mexico. In England, even with the 1.5 million bales that had made it past the Northern blockade, the textile industry was in turmoil. An estimated 500,000 men were out of work, and 35,000 former mill hands had been reduced to poverty.

Tracking Lee's march into Maryland, British Prime Minister Lord Palmerston wrote to his foreign minister, Earl Russell, that "even Washington or Baltimore may fall into the hands of the Confederates. If this should happen, would it not be time for us to consider whether in such a state of things England and France might not address the contending parties and recommend an arrangement on the basis of separation?" Russell agreed, adding that "in case of failure, we ought ourselves to recognize the Southern States as an independent State."

Abraham Lincoln was aware of such calculations. He thought that he had an answer. Soon after taking office, Lincoln had famously declared: "If I could save the Union without freeing any slave I would do it, and if I could save the Union by freeing all the slaves, I would do it. And if I could save it by freeing some and leaving others alone, I would also do that."

He had tried the first expedient already, doing nothing about slavery in order to keep the crucial border states of Missouri, Kentucky, Maryland, and Delaware in the Union. Abolitionists had been outraged, and as his armies advanced into the South, Lincoln's policy proved increasingly impractical. Slaves fled from their plantations to the soldiers they saw as their liberators—sometimes setting their masters' fields and their fine houses aflame before doing so. Union officers were under standing orders to return such "contraband" to their masters, but many officers were appalled by this idea.

By July of 1862, Lincoln had decided to try another of the alternatives he had laid out, this time freeing *some* of the slaves—specifically, all of the slaves in the rebel territories, the most he could legally do as president. The only question was timing. Union armies were stalled in the West and had been losing steadily in the East. As Lincoln's perspicacious secretary of state, William Henry Seward, pointed out, announcing the liberation of all Confederate slaves "would be considered our last *shriek*, on the retreat." He suggested that the president wait for a military victory. Lincoln agreed. But when would he have one?

1862 TO 1863

PLAYING THE EMANCIPATION CARD

ANTIETAM AND THE FREEING OF THE SLAVES

Everything seemed to revolve around a fidgety electrical device, one that had begun to forever alter American notions of time in the years before the Civil War, just as the steamboat and the locomotive had closed up the continent's enormous distances. Thanks to the telegraph, Lincoln was able to exert real-time control, in a way that no other commander-in-chief had ever done before. The contraption was the brainchild of yet another mechanical wizard from Massachusetts, Samuel Morse—ironically, an inveterate hater of Catholics and immigrants, and an advocate of the prevailing Southern belief that slavery had been brought about by divine wisdom. By 1860, there were over 50,000 miles of telegraph wire strung throughout the nation, most of it in the North, although Union armies added another 15,000 miles of it as they advanced, putting it up faster than even the most diligent Southern cavalry raiders could tear it down. Field telegraph tents in the Civil War, with soldiers bent over the small transmitters, tapping out Morse code, came to look surprisingly similar to modern field tents, with soldiers bent over their laptops.

The little telegraph office in the war office was the nerve center of the North's war effort. Lincoln used the instrument to question and goad his often recalcitrant generals into action—to meddle with them too much, some would maintain. He even monitored their telegraph communications with one another. But now he had to wait on the whims of his most maddeningly reluctant commander of all, George B. McClellan, as McClellan took on Lee near Antietam Creek in Maryland.

All through the day of September 17, 1862, Lincoln hovered about the telegraph room, waiting for the dots and dashes that could spell victory—or perhaps the end of the Union itself. By the evening, all he had to go on was a preliminary report from George Smalley—one of the hundreds of intrepid newspaper reporters embedded with the armies of both sides—that an army telegrapher diverted to the White House: "Fierce and desperate battle between 200,000 men has raged since daylight, yet night closes on an uncertain field. It is the greatest fight since Waterloo—all over the field contested with an obstinacy equal even to Waterloo."

Before the guns fell silent, over 3,600 men lay dead or dying, half again the number of Americans killed on the beaches of Normandy on D-Day. It was the worst single day of the war, the bloodiest day in the history of North America. But it was a victory—at least in the mind of George McClellan. The general's trademark timidity had squandered a rare opportunity to crush Lee's divided army before the two forces mauled each other to a stalemate. But Lee took his troops back to Virginia.

Lincoln had his triumph, or close enough, and on September 22, 1862, he issued what was, technically, a preliminary Emancipation Proclamation, announcing that on January 1, 1863, the actual proclamation would declare that all slaves in states "in rebellion against the United States, shall be then, thenceforward, and forever free."

"Whether we should survive or perish depended in large measure upon the coming of this proclamation," Frederick Douglass wrote, adding: "[T]here was room

Lincoln, with the general who drove him—but not the enemy—to distraction, General George B. McClellan, 1862.

PRESIDENT LINCOLN
GENERAL McCLELLAN

STEVEN JOHNSON, author: "[The telegraph] became the early version of email. Suddenly it was possible to get a message from someone in St. Louis to New York in a shockingly short amount of time."

to doubt and fear.... But would it come?" Douglass remembered waiting for the news to arrive over the wire on the first day of 1863. And then, when at last it did: "Joy and gladness exhausted all forms of expression, from shouts of praise to sobs and tears."

The final Emancipation Proclamation was a workmanlike, understated document, and it would have its critics: a few abolitionists who were angered that it did not free all slaves, Southerners who insisted that Lincoln was inciting murder, European newspapers who thought it was cynical. British Foreign Minister Russell pointed out that the proclamation contained "no declaration of a principle adverse to slavery," and a leading member of Parliament called it "the most unparalleled last card ever played by a reckless gambler."

Yet overnight, the whole nature of the war changed. After a heated cabinet debate, Lord Palmerston's government gave up any idea of recognizing the Confederacy or trying to mediate the war. The mill workers of England and France, in one of the great examples of human solidarity, closed ranks to express their approval of the proclamation. Even though the war had cost them their jobs and thrown many of them into abject poverty, they would not have their governments intervene on the side of slavery. In the Northern states, elated abolitionists pledged their devotion to the president, while in the South hundreds of thousands of slaves laid down their tools and fled the fields and the workshops of the Confederacy, grinding the Southern war effort under every footstep they took toward freedom.

The telegraph was used for more than just military purposes. Embedded correspondents used it to file over 100 million words of newspaper copy. The men are standing on tree trunks used a telegraph poles.

1861 TO 1866

PATENTS, PROFITS, AND PROFITEERS

THE INDUSTRIAL WAR

In other parts of the Union, though, there was a different feeling, sparked in part by another young technology and a brilliant artist. Mathew Brady was a leading society portrait photographer, a pioneer in the new art who had taken to it at the behest of Samuel Morse. He brought his camera to the battlefield, but his fading vision left him lost for days after the First Battle of Bull Run. Brady compensated by recruiting young photographers who would take his place in the field, and bring their images back to his National Portrait Gallery. All through the fall of 1862, New Yorkers visited the gallery to stare at the dead in the cornfields of Antietam. Photography was already popular when the Civil War began, and soldiers on both sides had rushed to the studios in their dashing new uniforms, striking heroic poses. Now they lay among the fallen corn, bodies distended by the sun, arms twisted over their heads, legs bent beneath them, bloated bellies pushing out past their shabby pants.

Beginning with the famous battle of the *Monitor* and the *Merrimack* (later named the *Virginia*) in 1862, the Civil War marked the dawn of ironclad ships. By 1865, the North had built 58 ironclads, including the USS *Carondelet* (above).

For working-class New Yorkers especially, the reminder was all too vivid. They were the ones who would have to go on fighting the war—and the war was far from over.

By the beginning of 1863, it was true, the North was beginning to make its vast industrial superiority felt. Yankee ingenuity was swiftly changing machine shops into gun shops, turning out over 1.4 million rifled muskets a year. Northern shipyards built ship after ship. By the end of the war, the U.S. Navy boasted 763 vessels of all kinds. By 1865, the number of ships reaching Southern ports had been reduced from 20,000 before the war to just 8,000, and many of these were smaller, swifter blockade runners, which could carry much less cargo and often ended up dumping it to escape capture.

The South was being slowly squeezed and starved to death, while in the North the war sparked an economic boom. Whole new industries emerged. Ready-made clothing, an enterprise founded to provide garments for slaves and pioneers, found a ready-made clientele during the war, becoming a $40 million business. Elias Howe's sewing machine reduced the time it took to make a man's shirt from 14 hours and 20 minutes to one hour and 16 minutes. One man operating a McKay sole-sewing machine could put together several hundred pairs of shoes a day—a production gain that meant the total number of shoes made in Northern factories would double to 1.5 million a year.

Over 5,000 U.S. patents were issued in 1864—a record—and not just for items directly related to the war. Americans were also hard at work inventing elevators, refrigerators, coal-oil lamps, clothes wringers and dryers, washing machines, fountain pens, flying

OVER 5,000 U.S. PATENTS WERE ISSUED IN 1864—A RECORD—AND NOT JUST FOR ITEMS DIRECTLY RELATED TO THE WAR.

machines, flypaper, ice and roller skates, stereoscopes, and steam-powered printing presses.

Some of the country's most famous business names got their start or their big break during the Civil War. Clement Studebaker made a fortune providing the military with wagons. J. P. Morgan helped secure British financing for the war effort as an agent for his family's banking business in Europe. Cornelius Vanderbilt, the great shipping and railroad tycoon, equipped the flagship of his private steamship fleet with a great ram, and put it at the disposal of the federal government for running down Confederate raiders. And Salmon P. Chase, as Lincoln's resourceful secretary of the treasury, rallied support on Wall Street, issuing war bonds and, for the first time in American history, large amounts of paper currency, also known as "greenbacks" or "shinplaster money."

Unscrupulous businessmen, known as "dead horse contractors," also abounded. J. P. Morgan was accused of selling faulty rifles. Others peddled sick livestock, bad meat, or defective gunpowder.

On Wall Street, stock traders made a carnival of their wealth, betting the Union up or down on the gold market. The traders made their fortunes at the same time that inflation was coursing through major Northern cities, leaving poor and immigrant families—many of them with their breadwinners away at war—all but destitute. Anger swelled, thanks to Brady's pictures, at the sight of maimed and crippled veterans flooding city streets, and at the soaring prices. Strikes, antiwar protests, and rising crime rates led to the arrest of one out of every ten adult New Yorkers at some point in 1862.

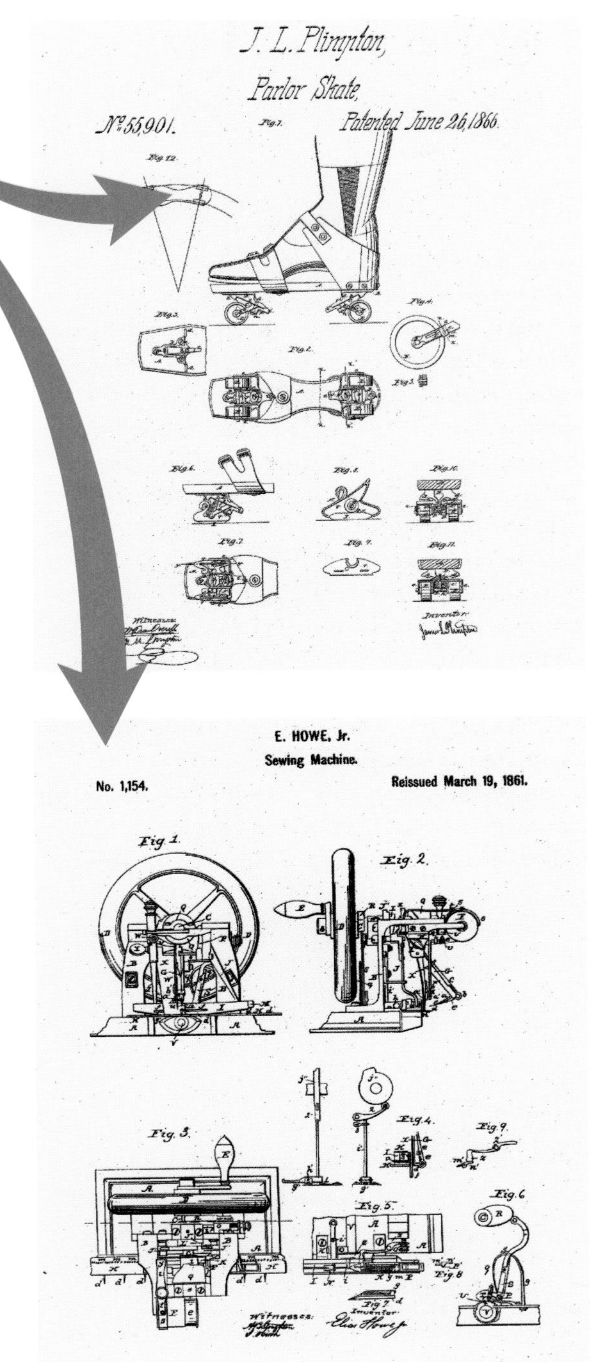

1862
TO
1863

LEE ROLLS THE DICE

THE TIDE TURNS AT GETTYSBURG

If the tide of the war was turning, it seemed to be doing so awfully slowly, particularly in the East. Lee resumed his string of victories, crushing two more federal commanders in the months after Antietam. In June of 1863, he turned north again, leading his army up into Pennsylvania this time, still seeking the one great battle that might decide the war. The rationale for this strategy was an imperative. In the Western theater, Vicksburg, Mississippi, the last major rebel redoubt on the river, was hanging by a thread, besieged by Grant's forces. Should it fall, the Confederacy would be cut in half. The aspiring nation was running out of matériel, men, everything.

Lee took the war back to the Union, replenishing his army by requisitioning food and livestock from Pennsylvania's citizens and seizing caches of uniforms and supplies. (As his troops marched, they also grabbed up any black person they came across, escaped slave or not, to be sold down South for whatever money they would bring.) Baiting the Army of the Potomac to stand and face him, Lee readied his men for one more throw of the dice.

In Pennsylvania, he finally got the federals to confront him outside the crossroads town of Gettsyburg. It was an accidental battle, started by a Confederate division seeking to plunder a shipment of shoes, and it left Lee on ground not of his choosing, facing a larger Union army in a well-defended position, anchored by hills and stone walls.

After two days of trying and failing to break the Northern lines, Lee might have taken the advice of General Jones Longstreet, his more defensive-minded adjutant, and at least sidled around the Union force, looking to resume the fight elsewhere. But by this time, Lee's deep religious convictions seem to have led him to believe that there was an almost mystical connection between himself and his cause, and with the founders of the country. The next day would be the Fourth of July, and as the historian Douglas Southall Freeman would write, Lee "had come to view duty as Washington did, to act as he thought Washington would." Now was the time to take a great, Washingtonian risk. His men had never failed him, accomplishing incredible feats against much larger forces, and surely Providence was on their side.

On the third and final day of the Battle of Gettysburg, Lee the gambler flung 11,000 men across three-quarters of a mile of open ground, against entrenched federal troops supported by artillery. Just over half of them returned. The failed assault, known as Pickett's Charge (named for one of the commanding Confederate generals), had come close to shattering the Army of Northern Virginia. It did not, and Lee limped back to Virginia. But never again would he go on the offensive. Never again would he fear coming to love war too much.

"As it is, the dead of the battle-field [sic] come up to us very rarely, even in dreams. We see the list at the morning paper at breakfast, but we dismiss its recollection with the coffee. There is a confused mass of names but they are all strangers; we forget the horrible significance that dwells amid the jumble of type," wrote *The New York Times*. "...Mr. Brady has done something to bring home to us the terrible reality and earnestness of war. If he has not brought bodies and laid them in our dooryards and along the streets, he has done something very like it." Photograph of the dead at Gettysburg by Timothy O'Sullivan

599

FORM 39.

Provost Marshal's Office,

10 District, State of New York

May 9, 1864

To Alex Joyce
Yonkers

SIR:

You are hereby notified that you were, on the 9 day of May, 1864 legally drafted in the service of the United States for the period of 3 yrs, in accordance with the provisions of the act of Congress, "for enrolling and calling out the national forces, and for other purposes," approved March 3, 1863. You will accordingly report, on ~~or before the~~ May 26, 1864, at the place of rendezvous, in Tarrytown, or be deemed a deserter, and be subject to the penalty prescribed therefor by the Rules and Articles of War.

W. W. Purson

Provost Marshal,

10 *Dist. of* N. Y.

1863

WAR IN THE STREETS OF NEW YORK CITY

THE DRAFT RIOTS

The next day, Vicksburg fell to Grant—the second, crushing loss for the Confederacy within 24 hours. The news was celebrated throughout the North by abolitionists. But in the poor immigrant wards of New York City, and in similar neighborhoods throughout the United States, no one was cheering. Instead, they read the long lists of casualties in the newspapers, and knew they could be next. The Union was running low on men. Already, delegations from distant Midwestern states were setting up tents next to Castle Garden, the immigrant-arrival station at the bottom of Manhattan, trying to persuade the greenest Americans to help them fill their enlistment quotas. It was not enough—and so President Lincoln had announced that there would be a draft, the first compulsory military service in U.S. history. Men could buy their way out for $300—a sum easily affordable for the rich, but as much as two years' wages for a workingman.

This was too much for working New Yorkers, and particularly for Irish Catholic immigrants. Despised for their religion and their poverty, discriminated against everywhere by many of the same people who seemed so concerned about the rights of black men, they had nonetheless enlisted in the army by the hundreds of thousands and fought bravely, often sustaining horrendous losses. They had thought they were fighting to preserve the Union, the country to which they owed so much. With Lincoln's Emancipation Proclamation, they were told the war was about freeing the slaves. Now, they would be *forced* to fight, while rich men could buy a way out for their sons.

When conscription began, New York exploded. For five days in July of 1863 draft riots rocked the city. It was the worst rioting in American history. The official death toll was 119, but it may have been closer to 500. Many of the victims were black; blamed for the war, they were horribly burned, mutilated, and hanged from lampposts. A mob even went to sack the Colored Orphan Asylum in Manhattan, chanting, "Burn the niggers' nest!" Federal troops had to be rushed to Manhattan to restore order, firing volley after volley into the frenzied crowds.

The army and the police stayed loyal to the government, suppressing the uprising. But that did nothing to solve Lincoln's manpower problem. Ever since hostilities had broken out, African-Americans in the North had been petitioning for the right to enlist and fight for freedom. Save for the famous Massachusetts 54th, an all-black regiment under white officers, they had been refused.

In the wake of the draft riots, New York and other states began to accept black recruits. Before the war was over, 180,000 had joined the Union armies, with another 19,000 going into the navy. Almost 40,000 of them died in service to their country. They were often paid less than whites, and treated savagely by white Confederates. Black prisoners were frequently slaughtered after they had surrendered, even burned alive. In battle after battle—at Milliken's Bend and Port Hudson in Louisiana, at Nashville in Tennessee, and at Cold Harbor and Petersburg in Virginia—they fought gallantly, despite taking heavy losses. The Massachusetts 54th lost half its men making one doomed assault after another on Fort Wagner in South Carolina.

By the end of the war, black soldiers had earned 16 Medals of Honor. They had also saved the country.

"Once let the black man get upon his person the brass letter, U.S., let him get an eagle on his button, and a musket on his shoulder and bullets in his pocket, there is no power on earth that can deny that he has earned the right to citizenship." —Frederick Douglass

"War is cruelty. There's no use trying to reform it.
The crueler it is, the sooner it will be over."
—William Tecumseh Sherman

1864

SHERMAN'S NECKTIES

TOTAL WAR

What were the rest of the American people fighting for? Lincoln tried to define it with his speech dedicating the military cemetery at Gettysburg, four months after the battle, which had left the field strewn with some six million pounds of rotting horse flesh and human remains. In one of the most famous speeches in American history, Lincoln now told his countrymen that they were fighting not just to preserve the Union, or even to free the slaves, but so that "government of the people, by the people, for the people, shall not perish from the earth."

Preserving that government would require the bloodiest, the most merciless combat this most deadly of wars had yet seen. Grant, now in charge of all Union armies, took the field in Virginia. After just over a month of fighting in the spring of 1864, he had nailed Lee into the Petersburg defenses around Richmond. The campaign cost the two armies 65,000 casualties. Two years earlier, such losses would have been unacceptable; now they were merely followed by ten months of brutal trench warfare. That September, Grant's ruthless cavalry commander, General Philip Henry "Little Phil" Sheridan, systematically destroyed the breadbasket of Virginia, seizing or burning crops and razing barns, mills, factories, and railroads along a 400-mile swath of the lovely Shenandoah Valley.

A few weeks later, Grant's hard-bitten right-hand man, General William Tecumseh Sherman, took off on his monthlong "scorched-earth" march from Atlanta to the port of Savannah, Georgia. His army lived off the land, taking livestock and crops from local farmers, burning, looting, and destroying anything they couldn't use. Upon reaching Savannah, they turned north and carved a path of destruction through South Carolina.

"We could do something in that line, we thought, but we were ashamed of ourselves when we saw how your men could do it," a Confederate captain told a Union officer just after the war. Instead of simply tearing up a rail bed, federal troops would use the wooden ties to start a bonfire, heat the iron rails in them until they were white hot, and then bend and tie them around nearby trees. These "Sherman's neckties" made sure the railroads stayed out of commission.

Sherman's troops also forced the dispersal of most of the remaining federal prisoners at Andersonville, Georgia. Prisoners on both sides were horribly neglected throughout the war, but conditions at Andersonville were the nadir, in a Confederacy increasingly unable to feed even its own troops and people. The camp was opened only in February of 1864, but before the war was over 45,000 Union troops had passed through it, with 13,000 of them dying of exposure, disease, and starvation.

Making "neckties": Sherman's men tearing up the heart of the South, 1864.

RAILROAD DESTRUCTION, ATLANTA, 1864

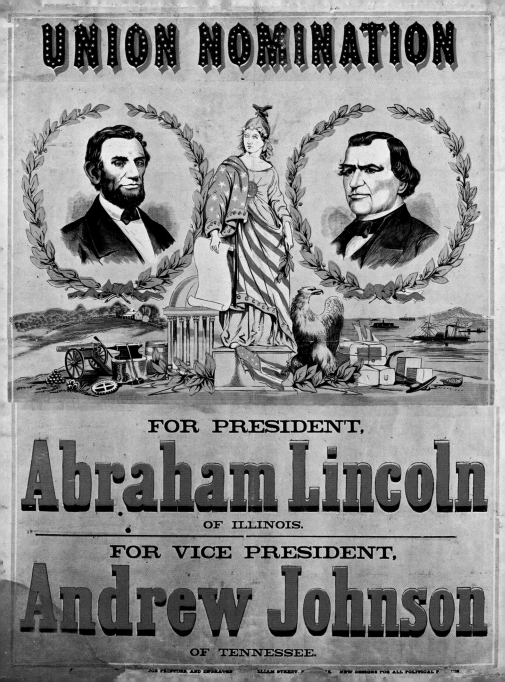

UNION NOMINATION

FOR PRESIDENT,

Abraham Lincoln

OF ILLINOIS.

FOR VICE PRESIDENT,

Andrew Johnson

OF TENNESSEE.

1864

FREE AT LAST... IN THEORY

LINCOLN'S VINDICATION

Lincoln, mindful of the toll the conflict had taken on his countrymen, feared that he would be turned out of office in November of 1864, and that a new Democratic administration might negotiate a peace that allowed the South to turn its imminent defeat into a victory. But Sherman's capture of Atlanta and Admiral David G. Farragut's victory at Mobile Bay in Alabama assured the president's re-election. He won a second term by over 400,000 votes, losing only three of the 25 states that remained in the Union. For the first time, soldiers were allowed to vote by absentee ballot, and Lincoln got 70 percent of their votes.

He had managed to bring the South to its knees, and he had done it by using every tool at his disposal as president of the United States. He had centralized power in the federal government as no American leader had ever done before, repeatedly citing the emergency of the rebellion as sufficient reason to suspend the right of habeas corpus for those suspected of plotting against the government—even expelling one seditious congressman, Clement Vallandigham, to the South. He had instituted the first military draft; started government-owned and -operated shipyards, gun factories, and meatpacking plants; imposed unprecedented taxes; and issued unimaginable amounts of debt. He had even overturned the basic social relationships of the country, freeing the vast majority of slaves, making many of them full citizens and putting rifles in their hands.

Before the war, Lincoln had believed blacks to be of a lower order than whites, and even during the fight he had suggested to a delegation of African-American leaders that they might be better off taking their people "back" to Africa. Over the years, through his friendship with Douglass and others, his views evolved, and he helped push through Congress the Thirteenth Amendment to the Constitution, banning slavery everywhere. In the next few years, the so-called Radical Republicans would pass the Fourteenth and Fifteenth Amendments as well, giving black men full voting rights and equality—again, at least in theory.

For the 1864 election, Lincoln replaced Hannibal Hamlin of Maine on the new Union ticket with Andrew Johnson, a rare Southern Democrat who had opposed secession. Petty, vengeful, insecure, and a white supremacist, he would prove a bad choice.

Lincoln understood how difficult it would be to reunite the country, given the bitterness that pervaded the South and the zeal for vengeance that motivated many Northerners. The South was ravaged—nearly one in five of its young men dead; its countryside, its fine mansions, and many of its cities laid to waste. Years after the war was over, an English traveler in Tennessee noted that "[t]he trail of war is visible throughout the valley in burnt up [cotton] gin-houses, ruined bridges, mills, and factories...and in large tracts of once cultivated land stripped of every vestige of fencing."

Everywhere, North and South, the streets were dotted with horribly wounded veterans begging for a handout. The orphanages were clogged, and there was so much to be done. Lincoln tried to make a start at his second inauguration, asking: "With malice toward none, with charity for all, with firmness in the right as God gives us to see the right, let us strive on to finish the work we are in, to bind up the nation's wounds, to care for him who shall have borne the battle and for his widow and his orphan, to do all which may achieve and cherish a just and lasting peace among ourselves and with all nations."

Lincoln lived long enough to see Lee's army broken at last in front of Richmond, to enter the enemy capital and sit, silent and contemplative, for a few minutes at the desk where his opposite number had sat before fleeing. Then he, too, was gone, shot—while watching a comedy at Ford's Theatre—by John Wilkes Booth, a histrionic actor who had been there for the horrible war's first act (he borrowed a militia coat to witness John Brown's hanging) and for its horrific epilogue (shooting the president of the United States in the back of the head at point-blank range) but had contrived to miss all the hard fighting and marching in between.

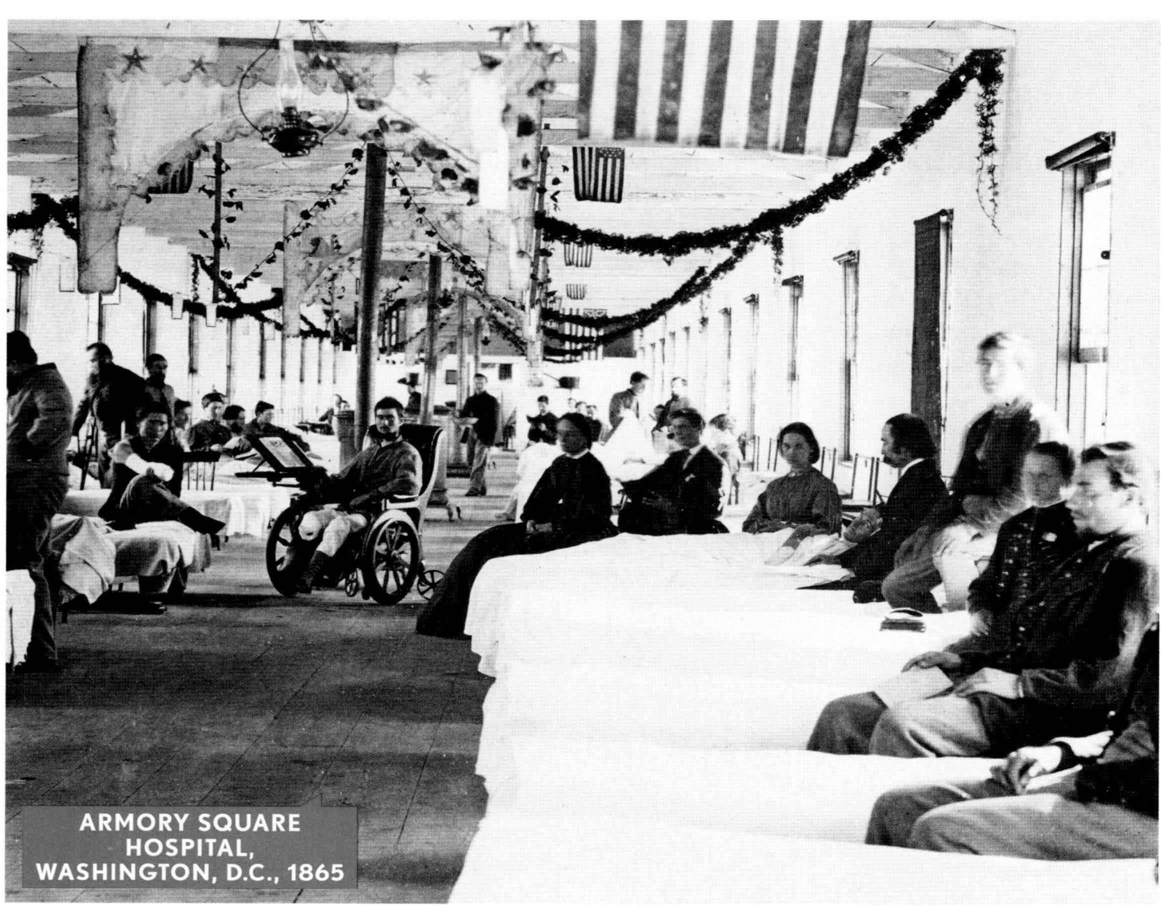

ARMORY SQUARE HOSPITAL, WASHINGTON, D.C., 1865

SURRAT.

BOOTH.

HAROLD.

War Department, Washington, April 20, 1865,

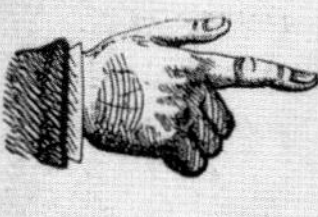

$100,000 REWARD!

THE MURDERER

Of our late beloved President, Abraham Lincoln,

IS STILL AT LARGE.

$50,000 REWARD

Will be paid by this Department for his apprehension, in addition to any reward offered by Municipal Authorities or State Executives.

$25,000 REWARD

Will be paid for the apprehension of JOHN H. SURRATT, one of Booth's Accomplices.

$25,000 REWARD

Will be paid for the apprehension of David C. Harold, another of Booth's accomplices.

LIBERAL REWARDS will be paid for any information that shall conduce to the arrest of either of the above-named criminals, or their accomplices.

All persons harboring or secreting the said persons, or either of them, or aiding or assisting their concealment or escape, will be treated as accomplices in the murder of the President and the attempted assassination of the Secretary of State, and shall be subject to trial before a Military Commission and the punishment of DEATH.

Let the stain of innocent blood be removed from the land by the arrest and punishment of the murderers.

All good citizens are exhorted to aid public justice on this occasion. Every man should consider his own conscience charged with this solemn duty, and rest neither night nor day until it be accomplished.

EDWIN M. STANTON, Secretary of War.

DESCRIPTIONS.—BOOTH is Five Feet 7 or 8 inches high, slender build, high forehead, black hair, black eyes, and wears a heavy black moustache.

JOHN H. SURRAT is about 5 feet, 9 inches. Hair rather thin and dark; eyes rather light; no beard. Would weigh 145 or 150 pounds. Complexion rather pale and clear, with color in his cheeks. Wore light clothes of fine quality. Shoulders square; cheek bones rather prominent; chin narrow; ears projecting at the top; forehead rather low and square, but broad. Parts his hair on the right side; neck rather long. His lips are firmly set. A slim man.

DAVID C. HAROLD is five feet six inches high, hair dark, eyes dark, eyebrows rather heavy, full face, nose short, hand short and fleshy, feet small, instep high, round bodied, naturally quick and active, slightly closes his eyes when looking at a person.

NOTICE.—In addition to the above, State and other authorities have offered rewards amounting to almost one hun-

1865

BLEACH'D BONES

TOTALING THE LOSSES

By the time the final Confederate armies were cornered and had surrendered in the spring of 1865, at least 620,000 men had died in the conflict—that is, 599 a day, nearly 2 percent of the total population, North and South. Taking into consideration the number of men who died later from wounds sustained in the war, and civilian deaths, the true death toll may have been as high as 750,000. Of the number killed in battle, Northern losses were almost twice as high as those sustained by the South.

Yet just as the leaders of the secession movement had miscalculated the power cotton gave them as the world's leading commodity, so did they also count too heavily on superior generalship. That two-to-one ratio was not nearly enough to overcome the Union's advantage in population. All told, 6 percent of Northern men ages 13 to 43 died in the war, compared to 18 percent of Southern men.

"...somewhere they crawl'd to die, alone, in bushes, low gullies, or on the sides of hills—(there, in secluded spots, their skeletons, bleach'd bones, tufts of hair, buttons, fragments of clothing, are occasionally found yet)," Walt Whitman would write years later. "Our young men once so handsome and so joyous, taken from us—the son from the mother, the husband from the wife, the dear friend from the dear friend...the single graves left in the woods or by the road-side...."

Most were buried where they were found, according to which side commanded the field. At Gettysburg, the Confederate dead were thrown into long trenches, while Union soldiers received individual graves. At Fort Wagner in South Carolina, Confederates tossed the stripped, looted body of Colonel Robert Gould Shaw, a 25-year-old white commander, in a common grave with his black soldiers of the Massachusetts 54th. Though the gesture was intended as an insult, Shaw's father wrote on hearing of it: "We would not have his body removed from where it lies surrounded by his brave and devoted soldiers.... We can imagine no holier place than that in which he lies, among his brave and devoted followers, nor wish for him better company—what a body-guard he has!"

For the many thousands of other dead men, the question remained: Who would go to gather them and account for them all? Clara Barton, who would later found the American Red Cross, organized the retrieval, identification, and reburial of many men. One hero of the dead was a remarkable 20-year-old named Dorence Atwater, who returned to his native Connecticut from Andersonville Prison and promptly collapsed from scurvy. Atwater brought something else with him: a list of the 13,000 Union dead at the prison camp and where they were buried, secretly copied by him while he was a prisoner there. He refused to give it up to War Department officers even after being court-martialed and sentenced to hard labor. Instead, he and Barton traveled together, back to the terrible camp, and there had individual headboards raised over each of the 13,000 who had perished, ensuring that their names did not vanish from history.

"Yet if God wills that...all the wealth piled by the bondman's two hundred and fifty years of unrequited toil shall be sunk...and until every drop of blood drawn with the lash shall be paid by another drawn with the sword, as was said three thousand years ago, so still it must be said: 'The judgments of the Lord are true and righteous altogether.'" —Abraham Lincoln

AT LEAST 620,000 MEN HAD DIED IN THE CONFLICT—THAT IS, 599 A DAY, NEARLY 2 PERCENT OF THE TOTAL POPULATION, NORTH AND SOUTH.

CHAPTER SIX

HEARTLAND

GRAND
CANYON,
1872

1853 TO 1863

THE GREAT ROAD WEST

PLANNING THE TRANSCONTINENTAL RAILROAD

The rare vision shared by both American presidents who waged the Civil War was of railroad tracks stretching across endless miles of prairie, from New York to New Mexico, from the Carolinas to California. Confederate President Jefferson Davis, in his earlier capacity as U.S. secretary of war, had lobbied successfully for the Gadsden Purchase of 1853–54, across southern New Mexico and Arizona, the very last slice of territorial acquisition for the contiguous U.S., so that tracks might be laid along the so-called Southern route, from California to Texas. Lincoln signed the plan for an alternative, central route—which would run through Nebraska and Wyoming—into law in 1862.

Both men knew that traversing the continent at the time was a terribly daunting enterprise. Getting from coast to coast meant a five-to-six-month trek by land across two mountain ranges; a four-to-six-month voyage through the turbulent waters around Cape Horn; or a weeks-long cruise down to Panama and back up the West Coast, interrupted by a 50-mile mule jaunt across the isthmus, during which travelers stood an excellent chance of contracting malaria or yellow fever. Even the fabled Pony Express, with its way stations of fresh horses, took 11 days to deliver a letter from St. Joseph, Missouri, to Sacramento, California.

The sheer ambitiousness of a transcontinental rail was stunning. Just a generation earlier, Americans had, with the Erie Canal, embarked on the greatest engineering project since Egypt's Great Pyramid; they now proposed to complete the most complicated one since the Great Wall of China. But *how*? How to build a railway through a mountain range?

A young Californian engineer, Theodore "Crazy" Judah, thought he had the solution. Originally from Connecticut, Judah had come west to build the Sacramento Valley Railroad, the first rail line west of the Mississippi, which was finished before he was 30 years old. But the project that possessed him was the transcontinental railroad. For weeks at a time, he would disappear into the Sierra Nevada with just his surveying equipment and a pack mule, taking measurements everywhere he went. The task seemed impossible. The Sierras were hardly railroad territory—coming out of Sacramento, they climbed a dizzying 7,000 feet in just 20 miles of impenetrable granite double ridges, sudden rock slides, and 30-foot snowfalls.

Then, in 1860, a storekeeper and miner from Dutch Flat, California, named Doc Strong took Judah up the Donner Pass (where, just 13 years before, the most infamous wagon train in history had resorted to murder and cannibalism). Judah realized that, approached from the west, the pass had a relatively gradual climb up a single ridge, then descended along the banks of the Truckee River and on into Utah. It still meant having to find a way through a thousand-foot rock wall past Donner Lake, but Crazy Judah had found his route.

Over the next two years, he was in constant motion, drawing up detailed maps and cost estimates for his proposed route and traveling repeatedly to Washington to lobby Congress and the president, all the while also rounding up California investors.

His chief moneyman was Collis P. Huntington, the shrewd hardware merchant who had made a fortune supplying the original forty-niners. After hearing Judah lecture on his favorite subject one night in

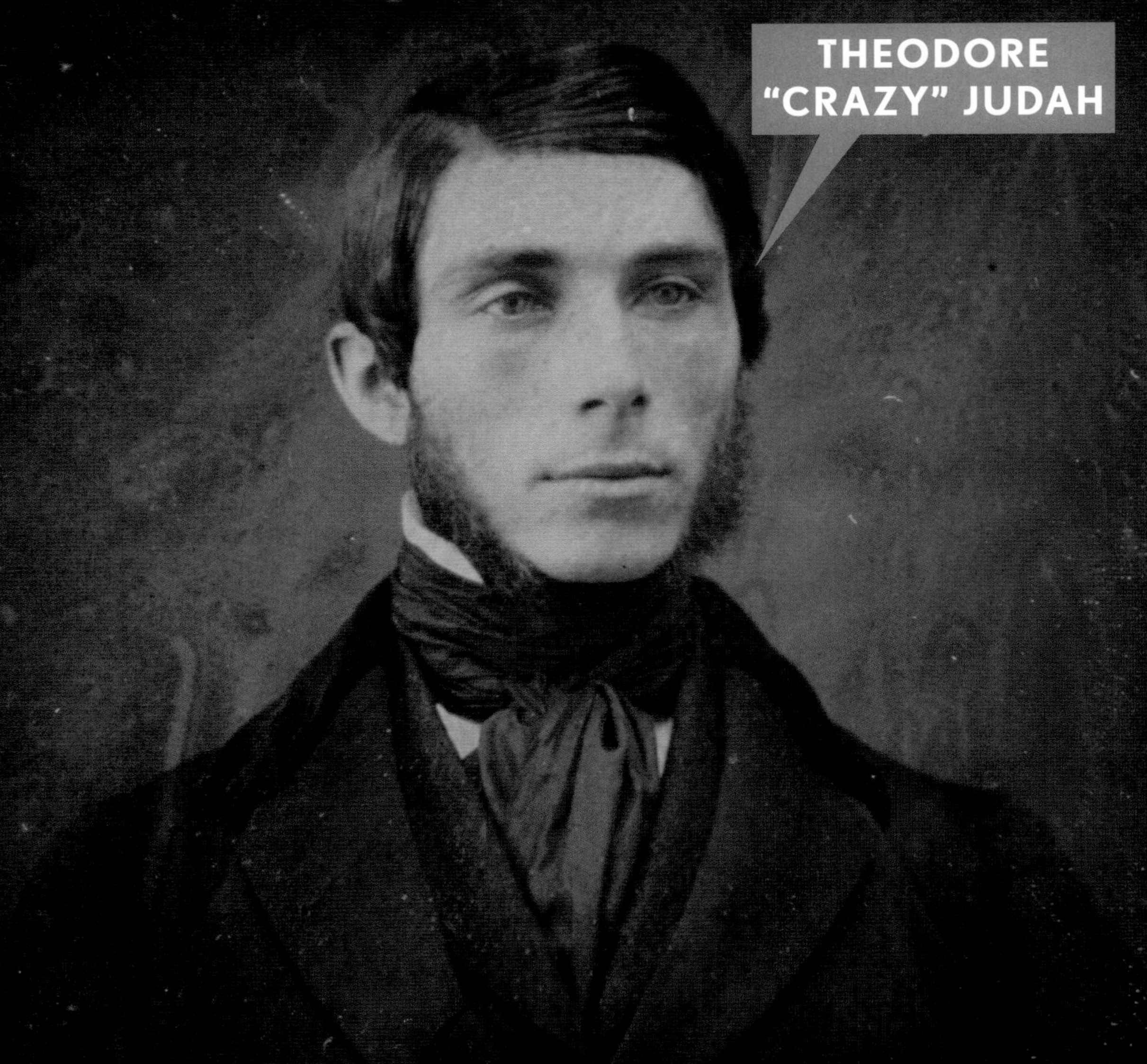

MICHAEL STRAHAN, former NFL Star: "You have to be brave in order to achieve in this country because nothing is set right there for you. You have to take chances and I think bravery and fear are the same things: It's just a matter of how you react to that same feeling."

THE BIG FOUR'S INITIAL INVESTMENT IN THE TRANSCONTINENTAL RAILROAD WAS ALL OF $1,500 APIECE.

San Francisco, Huntington brought aboard three other Sacramento storekeepers: Leland Stanford, a grocer turned politician who was about to be elected governor of California; Charles Crocker, a wealthy dry-goods merchant; and Mark Hopkins, Huntington's partner, a meticulous miser (it was said that he could "squeeze 106 cents out of every dollar"). They had the connections and the clout to make this happen; the men became known as the Big Four in the state they would transform.

Their initial investment in the transcontinental railroad was all of $1,500 apiece. Judah, after his years of tramping around the Sierras, did not have even that. But Huntington promised him an equal number of shares and a place on the railroad board. The bargain struck, Judah dashed back to Washington, where he dazzled Congress with a detailed presentation.

In 1862, Lincoln enthusiastically signed the Pacific Railroad Act into law. The U.S. government chartered the Union Pacific Railroad to build west from the Missouri River, and Judah's group, the Central Pacific Railroad, to build east from Sacramento. Both companies would be granted ten square miles of land for every mile of track laid—a potential bonanza in real estate. Government bonds would raise $16,000 a mile for construction over flatlands, $48,000 per mile for the passage through the Sierras. Crazy Judah cabled his partners from Washington: "We have drawn the elephant, now let us see if we can harness him up."

The Big Four might well have replied, "Whaddaya mean, 'we'?" They quickly pushed Judah to the margins of the Central Pacific; he responded by hopping on a steamer heading east, intending to raise enough money to buy out his erstwhile partners. In a brutal irony, he contracted yellow fever while crossing the Isthmus of Panama and lived just long enough to be carried ashore to New York's Metropolitan Hotel, where he died in his wife's arms, only 37 years old.

The directors of the Union Pacific Railroad confer in the comfort of their private train car, 1868. Construction on this section of the Transcontinental Railroad—which started in Omaha, Nebraska—was slow to begin, thanks in part to the Civil War and the corrupt finaglings of the railroad's main financier, Thomas C. Durant.

1862 TO 1869

THE ASIAN EXPLOSION... AND NITRO

THE CHINESE AND THE IRISH BUILD THE RAILROAD

Building the railroad from California would mean carving 15 tunnels just in the Sierra Nevadas, through some of the hardest rock imaginable. Cutting those required 13,500 men, all hacking away at a mountain with the most primitive tools: picks and shovels, wheelbarrows and one-horse dump carts. The longest tunnel, through the Number 6 Summit on the Donner Pass, had to be dug through 1,659 feet of solid rock. The dig advanced two to three inches a day, and the expenses made the Big Four frantic. Every length of track, every steel bolt, spike, and brace had to be shipped 18,000 miles, from Pittsburgh, around the Horn. As much as two years could pass between placing orders and receiving the material in question.

The answer, as it had been for the Erie Canal, was explosives. But the men building the Central Pacific had something 13 times more destructive than black powder. Nitroglycerin was a heavy, oily liquid that had been synthesized by an Italian chemist in 1847. Its explosive power was more predictable than that of powder, but it still had to be poured into holes 15 to 18 inches deep, capped, and set off with a slow match.

The other great energy source came from the Far East. The Central Pacific—like the Union Pacific and almost any other enterprise in America that had a hard, dirty, dangerous job to do—had started with Irish work crews. But after one fatal nitro accident too many in the Sierras, the Irish refused to work with the explosive. This motivated the Big Four to shift more of the workload to a new group of immigrants.

The Chinese had started arriving in California in large numbers during the Gold Rush. Whole villages of poor young men in Guangdong Province were drawn by tales of the *Gum Shan*, the Mountain of Gold, that awaited them across the Pacific. By 1864, there were almost 20,000 Chinese in the Golden State, nearly all of them single male laborers. Like nearly everyone else, they found little gold, and had to scratch out a living mostly by fishing or starting laundries, or by working as servants, cooks, gardeners, or day laborers.

Despised and mocked as "Celestials" and "coolies"—a racist epithet that may have come from the Hindi term *quli*, for "laborer," or from the Mandarin *ku li*, for "bitter toil"—they were willing to work for $30 a month plus room and board, as opposed to the $2 to $3 a day that Western laborers commanded. Chinese laborers had little choice: "Trading companies" from their homeland deducted all but $4 to $8 of their salary every month as repayment for their passage to the U.S. Like so many of the early settlers along the East Coast, they were essentially indentured servants.

The Chinese immigrants of the mid-nineteenth century tended to be small, nimble men—just four feet ten and 120 pounds, on average—but they possessed a wiry strength, and they worked carefully and well. They also took care of themselves, eating mostly rice and vegetables, occasionally augmented with the pigs and chickens they kept in camp. They washed their clothes and their bodies regularly; they preferred opium to whiskey, and boiled tea to water—thereby avoiding most of the dysentery that ravaged white work crews.

Railroad workers, c. 1875.

Before long, nearly 80 percent of the workers on the Central Pacific were Asian-Americans. Thanks to their efforts, and to the nitroglycerin, the daily pace of digging the tunnels improved from two to three inches to two feet. Working through the winter, the crews burst down out of the mountains and across the state line into Nevada in the spring of 1868.

Much farther east, the Union Pacific had got off to a laggardly start, thanks, in part, to the Civil War. But as the war ended, this road, too, suddenly sprang across the prairie. As the two railroad companies approached each other, they fell into a frenzied competition, vying to see which one could lay the most track in a single day. The Central Pacific men did six miles in a day, then the Union Pacific topped that with seven miles, until the Chinese-Americans on the Central put down a phenomenal ten miles. The two lines drew steadily closer and closer...

...and went right past each other, as both railroad companies tried to claim as much territory—and surrounding land—as they could. Finally, Congress had to step in, decreeing that the official meeting point of the lines would be Promontory Summit in Utah.

A grand ceremony was planned for the event, on May 10, 1869. Leland Stanford, president of the Central Pacific and now governor of California, raised a silver

The railroad was built along old wagon trails at times but also through fresh cuts into the rock and through thick brush and stands of trees. Wood and iron trestles as high as 70 feet and bridges over a mile in length spanned rivers and ravines.

It was usually simplest to cut tunnels straight through the granite rock. The longest, Tunnel No. 6, was 1,659 feet long, and had to be blasted out in part with nitroglycerin.

hammer to strike one final, celebratory gold spike…

…and missed. After a good deal of embarrassed laughter, Stanford drove the spike home. A one-word message flashed out over the telegraph from coast to coast: DONE. It set off fireworks and parades across the United States. In Philadelphia, the Liberty Bell was rung, and rightly so. The First Transcontinental Railroad was a seminal achievement. The Union Pacific had driven 1,087 miles from Omaha, Nebraska; the Central Pacific, 690 miles from Sacramento, but through the most formidable mountain ranges on the continent. The nation, so recently split apart, had been stitched back together by rail.

BUILDING THE MOUNTAIN RAILROAD

The Central Pacific Railroad's route over the Sierra Nevada was one of the wonders of the time. With 15 separate tunnels and scores of trestles, road cuts, and snowsheds, the mountain route required enormous engineering skill and the labor of thousands of men, many of them Chinese immigrants.

Most of these tunnels were built 6,000 to 7,000 feet above sea level, in the area of the mountains' greatest snowfall—not far from where the Donner Party had met its fate just 20 years before.

More than 50 snowsheds and galleries, running for a total of 37 miles, were erected through the mountain passes. They cost $2 million, but effectively prevented snow from clogging the tracks. "Chinese walls" (below the snowshed), named for the men who built them, were constructed in many places to prevent avalanches and erosion.

JOHN LASSETER, Chief Creative Officer, Pixar and Disney:
"It's interesting to think about what the railroads started to do to this country . . . and how similar it was to the Internet, how this technology connected people.... Never before in the history of mankind had there been that kind of connection."

THE LAST SPIKE:
MEETING OF THE RAILS
AT PROMONTORY
SUMMIT IN UTAH,
MAY 10, 1869

THE IRON HORSE: GROWTH OF THE RAILROAD, 1830 TO 1890

The U.S. railway system was a mind-boggling engineering project, built through mountains, over lakes and rivers, across canyons and deserts. By 1876, a trip from New York City to San Francisco on the Transcontinental Express would take just 83 hours and 39 minutes—only about 11.5 hours longer than on Amtrak today. Vital to stitching together this far-flung country, the railroad was subsidized with extensive government contracts and land grants, but it did not constitute a coordinated network. Controlled by scores of small companies, U.S. railways employed at least six different gauges (sizes), meaning that freight traveling from St. Louis to New York City might have to be unpacked and reloaded three or four times into different-sized trains. Railroads became notorious for stock swindles, underfinancing, and discriminatory rate scandals. Regulated by the federal government beginning in the Progressive era, and ruthlessly reorganized by magnates such as J. P. Morgan, the railroads were finally remade into a highly efficient national system until their decline (due to increased car and plane travel) in the postwar years.

Miles of Railroad in the United States

Year	Miles
1830	23
1850	9,000
1870	53,000
1890	164,000
1910	240,000
Today	140,490

ALL ALONG THE TRANSCONTINENTAL RAILROAD, LABORERS HAD STRUCK EACH RAIL SPIKE THREE TIMES; AT 400 RAILS TO THE MILE, THIS MEANT THAT THE HAMMERS HAD SWUNG 21 MILLION TIMES.

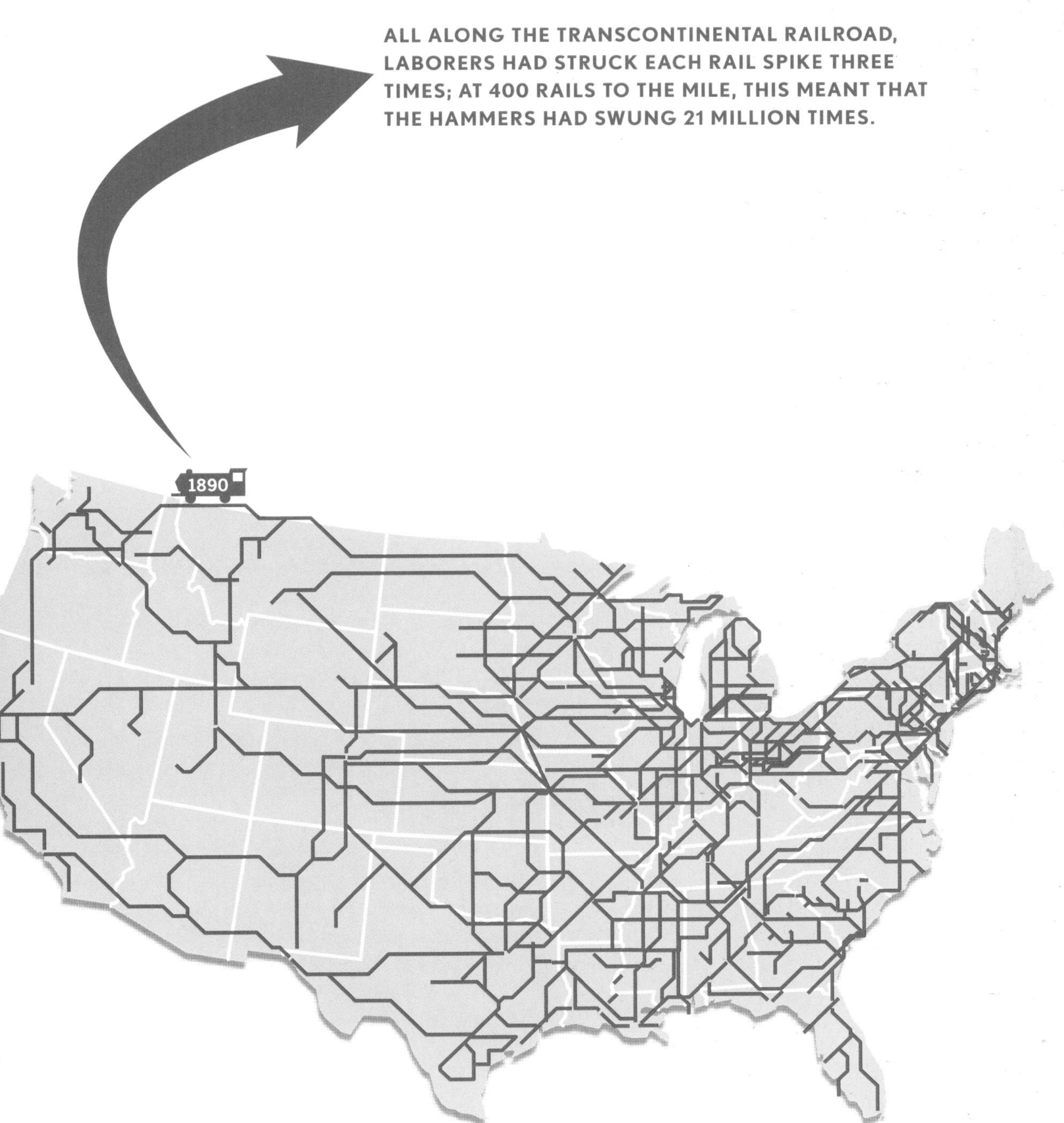

1820
TO
1892

A "PRAIRIE MADNESS"

SETTLING THE GREAT PLAINS

The primary reason to build a transcontinental railroad, at least for Lincoln, had been not simply to facilitate travel from one coast to the other but also to fill the vast lands in between. To this end, he passed two pieces of legislation in 1862 that would do much to shape the future of the country. One was the first Morrill Land-Grant Act, which made possible the founding or expansion of many of the great public universities in the United States. The other was the Homestead Act, which granted any citizen of the United States 160 acres of undeveloped land for just a $10 filing fee, provided the applicant agreed to occupy and farm it for at least five years.

It was the greatest land giveaway in the nation's history, and 1.6 million homesteaders took advantage of it, claiming 420,000 square miles, or one-tenth of the United States. In 1870, 40,000 settlers moved into Nebraska—many of them ex-slaves. This was the final shot of the Civil War: The offer was open to the freed slaves—but not to anyone who had taken up arms against the Union. The Northern ideal of the yeoman farmer had triumphed, and now it was going to be established for all time in the territories west of the Mississippi. But the land wouldn't yield to these pioneers without a ferocious fight.

As far back as 1820, an army topographic engineer probing the edges of the Mexican empire had labeled the High Plains region west of the Mississippi "the Great American Desert"—a seemingly endless grassland stretching from Iowa to Idaho and from Canada to northern New Mexico, covering more than a quarter of the North American continent. It was a delicate ecosystem inhabited mainly by those who lived lightly upon it—the fantastic herds of buffalo and the Indians who tracked them back and forth across the prairie.

Officially, the Great Plains could be classified only as semiarid, averaging less than the 20 inches of rain a year deemed necessary for farming, and with 20-year cycles of drought that could make even grazing cattle all but impossible at times. It was a daunting country, a place of almost constant winds and muddy, sluggish rivers, and some of the most violent weather on earth. Prairie fires lit by lightning swept hundreds of miles across the grass, moving faster than a galloping horse. Months of drought might be broken by hailstorms that devastated crops and killed livestock. Summer temperatures routinely reached 110 degrees; in winter, blizzards and bone-chilling "blue norther" storms swept down from Canada. When the cold and warm fronts collided, they created the phenomena that gave Tornado Alley its name. Over 1,000 twisters a year swirled across the Great Plains.

The solitude of the Plains stunned some pioneers into an enervating depression, a "Prairie madness." Others were overwhelmed by more material concerns. It quickly became apparent that it was not possible to make a living on just 160 acres. There was not enough moisture, nor was there enough topsoil—or enough trees and plants to hold the soil in place against the wind. Homesteaders, it was said, were "miles to water, miles to wood, and only six inches to hell."

The Homestead Act required settlers to erect a home on their claim, but with no trees in sight this usually meant digging up blocks of the prairie and forming them into sod houses. The blocks crawled with centipedes and other bugs, whose stinging and rustling drove the settlers to distraction. For fuel,

they relied mainly on dried "buffalo chips," picked up off the prairie and burned in stoves until the little houses were suffused with the scent of manure. And soon after they had moved onto the land, there came a biblical plague—the likes of which no white man in North America had seen before.

Locusts bred in the cool mountain streams of the Rockies. Then, thanks to a few years of particularly favorable weather, they hatched in record numbers, exhausted the local forage, grew wings, and hitched a ride east on the jet stream. One infestation in 1875 blackened the skies with an estimated 3.5 trillion locusts, forming a massive cloud half a mile high along a 110-mile front and trailing 1,800 miles back over the prairie. They even stopped the railroad, their crushed bodies greasing the tracks to the point where trains could not continue.

It was too much for some. During a single harsh summer in the 1870s, 30,000 sodbusters left the Plains. "In God we trusted, in Kansas we busted," read some of the banners on their wagons as they retreated back to Iowa. When more bad weather, more plagues of locusts, and a new phenomenon known as dust storms hit, half the population of western Nebraska surrendered and trudged back east. By 1892, one-third of the original homesteaders had abandoned their farms.

The four Chrisman sisters, daughters of a rancher, near Goheen settlement on Lieban Creek, Custer County, Nebraska, 1886. Each held claims under the Homestead Act.

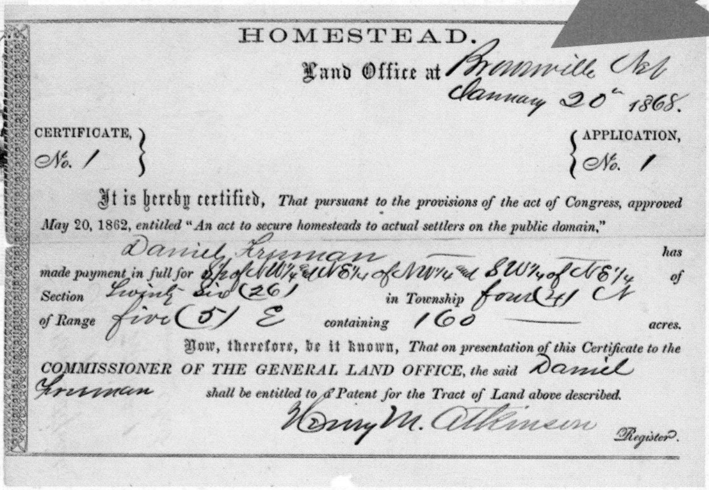

HOMESTEAD.

Land Office at Brownville Neb
January 20th 1868.

CERTIFICATE, No. 1

APPLICATION, No. 1

It is hereby certified, *That pursuant to the provisions of the act of Congress, approved May 20, 1862, entitled "An act to secure homesteads to actual settlers on the public domain,"* Daniel Freeman has *made payment in full for* S½ of NW¼ and NE¼ of NW¼ and SW¼ of NE¼ of *Section* Twenty six (26) *in Township* four (4) N *of Range* five (5) E *containing* 160 *acres.*

Now, therefore, be it known, *That on presentation of this Certificate to the* COMMISSIONER OF THE GENERAL LAND OFFICE, *the said* Daniel Freeman *shall be entitled to a Patent for the Tract of Land above described.*

Henry M. Atkinson *Register.*

IT WAS THE GREATEST LAND GIVEAWAY IN THE NATION'S HISTORY, AND 1.6 MILLION HOMESTEADERS TOOK ADVANTAGE OF IT.

J. F. GLIDDEN & P. W. VAUGHAN.

Machines for Making Wire-Fences.

No. 157,508. Patented Dec. 8, 1874.

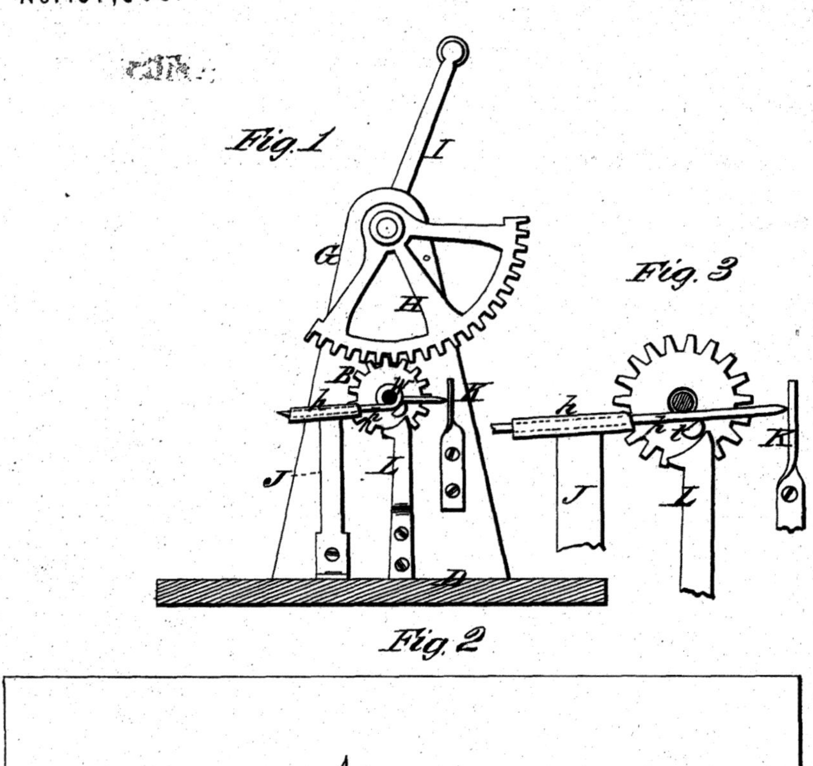

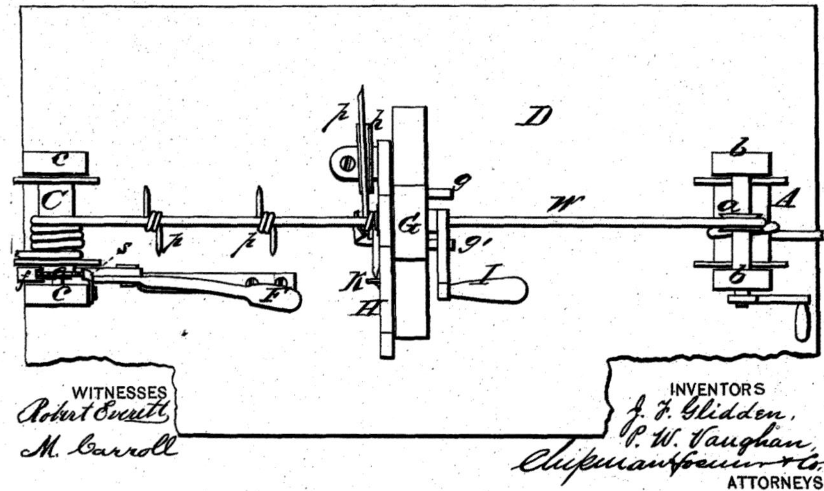

THE GRAPHIC CO. PHOTO-LITH. 39 & 41 PARK PLACE, N.Y.

1862
TO
1880

THE BARBED-WIRE FENCE MAKES GOOD NEIGHBORS

THE NEW HOMESTEADERS

And yet, the lure of owning land was too strong to stop new settlers from trying their luck. They were tenant farmers from the Midwest and the East who had never had their own places; immigrants from Scandinavia and Eastern Europe; or Germans moving en masse from the Russian steppes after the czar had revoked their rights. They reveled in the equality and opportunity of life on the frontier, whitewashing and plastering their sod houses to keep out the bugs. They burrowed dugouts down in the sod to survive the twisters and the prairie fires.

This wave of settlers brought the latest farm equipment ordered from factories in the East. If they had no water, they hired itinerant crews to drill down to the water table; these wells were then topped with little windmills that pumped the water out.

"In this country, we climb for water and dig for wood," farmers on the southern plains joked, referring to how they would dig down for mesquite roots and shimmy to the top of their windmills to get them moving during those rare moments when the wind stopped. They also plucked wood from the water—entire Northwestern forests were cut and floated downriver to Chicago by intrepid lumberjacks, then shipped out to the West. The lumber was used for barns and for the small, neat frame houses the settlers eventually built to replace their sod shelters.

Wood was still too expensive for all the fences necessary to enclose their rambling farms. But here, once again, technology had the answer. Born in New Hampshire, Joseph Glidden was a 60-year-old former schoolteacher turned politician and farmer living in DeKalb, Illinois, when he used his wife's coffee grinder to make pointed barbs of metal, which he placed at regular intervals along two intertwined wire cables. In 1874, Glidden persuaded a neighbor to chip in $265 to help start the Barb Fence Company. Soon they were employing steam-powered machinery to produce up to five tons of barbed wire a day, all of it snapped up immediately. Where it would cost a Nebraska settler as much as $1,000 to fence in his homestead with wood, he could do it with cheap, dependable, easy-to-erect barbed wire for only $300.

A firm from Worcester, Massachusetts, bought a half interest in Glidden's company for $60,000 plus 25 cents on every 100 pounds of wire produced. By 1880, the company was making 80.5 million pounds of it a year, Glidden was a very wealthy man, and barbed-wire fences stitched their way across the Plains, making it possible for farmers to keep cows and sheep out of their corn and wheat.

A homestead complete with windmill-operated well, circa 1886, which might be dug 30 to 300 feet to the water table. American farmers ordered listers, harrows, cord binders, threshers, silos, and plows from back East, making them the best-equipped farmers in the world.

1865
TO
1868

DRIVING A STEAK INTO AMERICA'S HEART

THE CATTLE BATTLES

Barbed wire also brought the plains "nesters" into contention with their main rivals. Ranchers had been on the prairies long before the farmers. As far back as the 1700s, Mexican vaqueros were raising a tough, scrawny breed of Moorish cattle in southeast Texas. Americans called these men cowboys (the English equivalent of *vaqueros*), and from them they would borrow much that would come to make up the familiar culture of the American West: roundups, rodeos, branding, lassos, chaps and other characteristic attire, and even "cowboy music," strummed on a guitar beside a campfire.

After the Mexican War, Texas cowboys crossed the Mexican cattle with more commercially popular Eastern cows to produce a remarkably strong, durable breed: the modern longhorn. Left largely to themselves, these animals began to cover the grasslands in western Texas and up the Panhandle; they were herded to markets when the price was right. Then came the Civil War. The Union stranglehold on the Mississippi cut off Texas from the rest of the starving Confederacy, and by the end of hostilities there was a glut of some five million head in the Lone Star State. Worth only $3 to $4 a head in Texas, they might fetch $35 up the Mississippi Valley, where the war had devastated local livestock.

The solution was the cattle drive. All through the winter of 1865–66, cowhands rounded up 260,000 of their longhorns from across the plains. When the prairie grass turned green, they headed the cattle north to the railhead at Sedalia, Missouri, over 500 miles away. It was exhausting, backbreaking—and neck-breaking—work; 11 cowboys were supposed to handle 2,000 cattle. The longhorns floundered in mud, and drowned in swollen spring streams; they were spooked into deadly stampedes by lightning and hailstorms, and bolted when confronted with the mysteries of crossing woodlands. The Cherokee demanded a toll of ten cents a head when the cattle were driven across a corner of Oklahoma's Indian Territory; angry Missouri and Kansas farmers, afraid that ticks from the longhorns would spread "Texas fever" to their livestock, shot animals and cowboys alike when they tried to cross their land.

Many thousands of longhorns were lost before they reached Sedalia, but the money was too good to resist. In 1867, Illinois meat dealer Joseph G. McCoy marked out a longer but friendlier route to the little Kansas railroad town of Abilene. It was in the middle of nowhere, but that was the whole point: "The country was entirely unsettled, well watered, excellent grass, and nearly the entire area of the country was adapted to holding cattle," wrote McCoy. The route would become known as the Chisholm Trail, after the legendary Texas rancher, and in 1868 some 75,000 cattle were driven up it with relatively little mishap.

For the next 20 years, the cattle kept coming. Abilene began to ship over 400,000 Texas beeves a year. Other Kansas towns soon followed as the herds grew and the farms multiplied, pushing the cattle drives ever farther west and south, to locations where no one's cornfield or wheat crop was yet in place to be trampled. In 1871, in a single, gigantic drive, 600,000 head were driven north from Texas.

Over ten million head would be herded through the chutes of Kansas rail yards. But like so much of

"Doggies" on the drive to market: "They feed in the coulees, they water in the draw/Their tails are all matted, their backs are all raw..."

JUDGE ROY BEAN'S COURTHOUSE AND SALOON, 1900

the legendary West—the Pony Express and the wagon trains, the Indian wars and the mountain men—the Long Drive was relatively short-lived; it lasted no longer than the golden age of the Hollywood Westerns that celebrated it, and was decidedly more prosaic than the movie version. At its peak, Abilene, Kansas, had all of three whorehouses and one dance hall.

Shootouts and showdowns were a myth. In all the cow towns, there were only 45 fatal shootings, 16 of them by lawmen. Only three men were executed, and only one man was lynched—none of them cowpunchers. After initial spates of violence, the cattle towns were invariably tamed by remarkably small but efficient police forces, thanks in large part to their strict gun control. Legendary gunslingers such as William Barclay "Bat" Masterson, Wyatt Earp, James Butler "Wild Bill" Hickok, and William Matthew "Bill" Tilghman disarmed violators by pistol-whipping them before hauling them off to jail. Neither Masterson nor Earp killed anyone while keeping the peace in Kansas.

Cowboys hitting town after months on the trail wanted whiskey and a woman, and to shout and raise hell, but they never matched the cinematic stereotypes of gunslingers and cardsharps. Wages were just $25 to $40 a month along the trail, plus meals from the company chuck wagon. In return, they would often spend 18 to 20 hours a day in the saddle—working so hard that "sometimes we would rub tobacco juice in our eyes just to keep awake," wrote E. C. "Teddy Blue" Abbott. "It was rubbing them with fire."

At work, they mostly wore overalls and old army coats, with a bowler hat that could be pulled down tight just above the eyes. This was understandable. According to Teddy Blue, the two "drag men" trailing the beeves would "come off the herd with the dust half an inch deep on their hats and thick as fur in their eyebrows and moustaches, and if they shook their head or you tapped their cheek, it would fall off them in showers." The trail boss would ride ahead, scouting for water; when he found it, the two point men up at the front of the herd, along with the four swingmen and flankers behind them, would then have the fearful task of turning the herd, pushing and bullying them to one side or another. Rounding up strays and stragglers was another arduous chore. Hernias, broken limbs, and worse were common. If the herd stampeded, a cowboy might be killed in an instant, going down under a sea of rampaging cattle.

The worst enemies of the cowboys were townsfolk and farmers. By 1884, nearly all of Kansas was fenced off, and the state was quarantined against Texas cattle, out of fear of the ticks. When Oklahoma was opened to the so-called Boomers, in 1889, cattle drives were banned from the territory.

The cattlemen took the hint, more and more of them starting ranches to raise their beeves closer to railheads in Kansas, Nebraska, Colorado, Wyoming, Nevada, New Mexico, and the Dakotas. Teddy Blue helped bring a herd through to the ample grasslands of Montana, where he got married and then settled in to ranching and politics. And the rails finally reached Texas, where vast new ranches were carved out of High Plains land. Profits for cattle ranchers reached 25 to 40 percent, with little risk. Wealthy Easterners, along with Scotsmen and Australians and the second sons of English lords, snapped up thousands of acres of ranch lands and poured in capital. Cowhands were reassigned to bailing hay and banging in fence posts.

The fencing of the prairie created years of new conflicts, as ranchers fought with farmers, sheepherders, and one another for land and water rights. Vigilantes and hired thugs would move stealthily across the plains—with handkerchiefs wrapped over their faces—cutting barbed wire, poisoning cattle, even murdering at times. Some of the most famous twice-told tales of the West would revolve around these "range wars." Henry McCarty, a slight orphan from the Irish wards of New York, would become forever famous as Billy the Kid, originally for his actions defending the rights of a transplanted English cattle rancher named John Tunstall during New Mexico's Lincoln County War, in 1878. The 1892 Johnson County War of Wyoming—in which big ranchers imported 50 Texas assassins to wipe out small ranchers, only to see their hit men trapped and shot up by their intended victims before being rescued by U.S. Cavalry—became a canvas on which authors and film directors would paint parables. It would spawn countless books, dime novels, and movies—including Owen Wister's *The Virginian*; the novel *Shane* and its movie adaptation; and the studio-killing flop *Heaven's Gate*.

These conflicts loomed larger in the retelling than on the plains. Before long, farmers and ranchers created a frontier example of commercial synergy. The ranchers' cattle fattened not just on prairie grass but also on the mountains of corn and other grains that the homesteaders and their successors produced, creating a permanent American yen for corn-fed beef. Countless boxcars of cattle and grain came pouring out of the Great Plains on the growing web of train tracks, along with the treasure gleaned from rich mineral deposits of gold, silver, iron ore, copper, and lead.

There were some sobering moments. Overstocking led cattle prices to crash. Then, in January of 1887, after a summer of intense drought, the worst blizzard on record ripped down the plains from the Dakotas to Texas, wiping out even some of the biggest ranchers. "Cowboys said they could walk the drift line, where snow piled up along fences north of the Canadian River, for four hundred miles, into New Mexico, and never step off a dead animal," wrote Plains historian Timothy Egan.

Then it was the farmers' turn. In the next decade came more drought, the last of the locust plagues, and more dust storms, driving thousands of people from the land.

Below: A posed photograph reenacting how homesteaders cut 15 miles of barbed wire around the large Brighton Ranch in Custer County, Nebraska.

KANSAS
COWBOY, 1880

1680 TO 1887

THE HORSE WHISPERERS

THE FIRST PEOPLES OF THE PLAINS

The first human inhabitants of the Plains might have told the settlers that this was a regular cycle. For millennia, the prairie Indians had lived as hunter-gatherers and occasional farmers on the margins of the Great Plains, constrained by the size of their environment. They hunted buffalo not much differently from how primitive man hunted woolly mammoths, driving them over the side of cliffs and down gulleys.

All that changed with a rider on horseback. In 1680, the peaceable Pueblo Indians of the Southwest finally rebelled after a century of oppressive Spanish rule, and drove the startled padres and conquistadors back into Mexico for a spell. The Spanish left behind many of their horses, which the Pueblo had little use for—but neighboring tribes could not get enough of them. By the time the Spanish returned, 12 years later, the Ute and Comanche were people of the horse, as sure on a mount as the Cossacks or the Mongols.

One by one, the ancient peoples came out across the Plains: the Kiowa and the Missouri, the Pawnee and the Plains Cree and the Arikara, the Crow and the Nez Percé, the Mandan and the Snake, Sarsi and Cheyenne, Sioux and Apache—31 tribes in all. The horse transformed them, enlarging the range of their wanderings—their trade, and their travels, and their wars—from 50 miles to 500. It was as if they were born to the saddle, or rather to the back of a horse, for often they required nothing more than the most rudimentary bridles and stirrups. The Comanche seemed so natural on horseback that whites often remarked that they looked awkward on foot. They were unmatched horse traders and horse thieves, expert riders who could dip down to fire arrows from beneath the neck of a galloping pony with deadly accuracy. They loved the lands they could now roam, and waged merciless war against the hunters, the stockmen, and the Texas Rangers who invaded this realm.

"They made sorrow come into our camps, and we went out like buffalo bulls when the cows are attacked," boasted Comanche leader Chief Ten Bears in 1867. "When we found them we killed them, and their scalps hang in our lodges. The white women cried, and our women laughed. The Comanches are not weak and blind like the pups of a dog when seven sleeps old."

Above: A family of the Gros Ventre, or A'ani ("white clay"), on the Fort Belknap reservation in Montana, 1904.

Opposite: A woman of the Nez Percé tribe, the people of Chief Joseph, who tried to escape to Canada in 1876 after being forced off their lands.

The wars between settlers and the Plains Indians were fierce. Like the Native American peoples east of the Mississippi, the Plains tribes were hopelessly outnumbered and outgunned, and unable to form lasting political coalitions. Yet thanks to their horses, their small numbers often worked to their advantage out on the prairies and along the mesas of the West. They were the best light cavalry in the world, able to strike suddenly and then fade away as quickly as they had come into a trackless land. They held Spanish, Mexicans, and Americans at bay for decades, against ridiculous odds. They seemed inured to fatigue and pain, able to ride or run incredible distances without food. Whites marveled at how the Native American children often did not cry out even when shot or operated on—though they might better have wondered on how so many of them came to have bullets in them in the first place.

A woman of the Lakota Sioux with a dog travois—the way in which the Indians moved most of their possessions across the prairie before horses. The photo was taken on the Rosebud Indian Reservation.

1872 TO 1889

THE KILLING OF YELLOW HAIR

LITTLE BIGHORN AND THE LAST STAND OF THE INDIANS

An estimated 1.5 million buffalo were shot in 1872, and more than that number the next year. Then, in 1874, the number of kills slumped to about 150,000. It wasn't from lack of trying. The buffalo were dying out. By 1889, approximately 1,000 buffalo remained in the United States. Starved out, nearly all of the remaining Plains Indians had been forced onto reservations. But even when they were restricted to the marginal lands the federal government allowed them to keep, the Indians were not let alone nor were their treaties honored. Crooked reservation agents stole constantly from their provisions, and whites intruded whenever there was something they really wanted. Just as they had pushed the Cherokee out of Georgia to get at their gold, white prospectors, backed by cavalry, invaded the Lakota reservation, on the tribe's sacred lands among the Black Hills of South Dakota.

COL. GEORGE ARMSTRONG CUSTER

Outraged, the Lakota left the reservation, led by medicine man Sitting Bull and their military leader, Crazy Horse. Moving into the Montana Territory, they joined large bands of Cheyenne and Arapaho. Reservation agents, trying to cover up their corruption and incompetence, told the U.S. Army that only about 800 Sioux were on the warpath. Instead, by the time Colonel George Armstrong Custer caught up to the warriors, they had become one of the largest aggregations of Indians in the history of North America—at least 7,000 and possibly as many as 10,000 to 15,000 people, including more than 1,800 warriors. Custer's Crow Indian scouts told him as much, but he decided to attack at Little Bighorn anyway. After less than an hour of fighting, the colonel and all 210 of the men under his immediate command were dead.

It would go down in history as Custer's Last Stand, but it was also the Indians' last stand. They had no strategy beyond this act of defiance—Sitting Bull's great confederation broke up soon after the battle, and before long most of the Lakota were brought back to the reservation. Within a few years, all the Indians of the Plains would be similarly confined. Well-meaning whites forced them to sell off their communal lands and gave each family individual plots, trying to make them into yeoman farmers—circling back to the dream that had inspired the Homestead Act. The Indian farmers had no more success than many of the white farmers, who by this time were in full-fledged, Populist revolt against the strictures on the slumping agrarian economy.

SITTING BULL'S FAMILY, 1891

THE BATTLE OF LITTLE BIGHORN

Perhaps the most intriguing fact about the Battle of Little Bighorn is that the Indians might have surrendered without a fight—if Custer had just asked them.

But George Armstrong Custer had made a career out of impetuosity. After a dismal record at West Point, where he finished last in his class, he redeemed himself by leading one headlong charge after another as a cavalry commander in the Civil War; at 23 he was made the youngest general of the war. After he was demoted to colonel in the postwar army, Custer's career stalled. He set off eagerly after Sitting Bull in the late spring of 1876, convinced that his Seventh Cavalry Regiment could handle any Indians.

He was wrong, obviously, but the many Sioux and Cheyenne who met him at Little Bighorn were not eager to fight. Feather Earring, a Miniconjou Sioux, told General H. L. Scott many years later, "If Custer had come up and talked with us, we had all agreed we would have surrendered and gone in with him." A number of other Indians at Little Bighorn confirmed that a diplomatic approach by Custer, especially under a white flag and accompanied by promises of more provisions and other reforms on the reservation, might well have brought the tribes in peacefully. They had no great plan, and no place to go. After slaughtering every man in Custer's detachment, these worried warriors soon drifted off in different directions.

After the battle, Custer's body, unlike those of many of his troops, was not scalped or badly mutilated—although some Cheyenne women did claim to have punctured his eardrums with a sewing awl. It was a symbolic gesture that recalled a peace meeting seven years before, in Oklahoma, when Custer was told that he would be killed if he ever made war on the Cheyenne again. The awl, they thought, might improve his hearing, because evidently he had not been able to hear what the Cheyenne had told him.

“They tell me I murdered Custer. It is a lie. He was a fool and rode to his death. . .” —Sitting Bull

1872 TO 1889

A GROCERY ON THE HOOF

INDUSTRIALIZING THE BUFFALO

The Plains Indians lived and died with the buffalo. Native Americans ate almost anything to be found on the prairie: wild grapes, plums, and currants; antelope; and, if they were forced to, even the local poultry—sage grouse, wild turkeys, and prairie chickens. But overwhelmingly, bison was the major food source on the plains—one that seemed as enduring as the sun and the grass and the endless Western sky.

The largest land mammal in North America after the Ice Age, the buffalo had come across the Bering Strait land bridge at roughly the same time as the first Indian peoples. They made their way as far south as Florida and Central America, and before the arrival of Europeans there may have been as many as 75 million of them on the continent. Standing over six feet high at the shoulder and weighing up to 2,000 pounds, they adapted readily to any number of ecosystems. But nowhere were they more at home than on the plains. By the end of the Civil War, 20 million buffalo still roamed there in massive herds, living off the tough, plentiful grasses. They were so numerous that for eons their main cause of death was drowning when they trampled one another while crossing a river.

A woman of the Gros Ventre drying meat on a reservation, 1906.

Even after the arrival of the Europeans, their comings and goings stopped boats in Western rivers, and halted or even derailed locomotives. Usually dormant animals, the buffalo started to run in spring, their hooves like rolling thunder across the plains, attaining speeds of 35 miles an hour, faster than any man.

With their horses, though, the Indians could keep up. Buffalo hunts evolved into fantastic athletic rituals. Tribes such as the Lakota Sioux would streak across the prairie, the painted warriors felling the great beasts with spears or arrows—of which they could fire off as many as 20 in the space of riding 300 yards. The bison served as a sort of mobile general store. Its nutritious, low-fat meat could be dried, smoked, stewed, or roasted. Its skin made a light, portable tepee, canoe casing, and even a coffin. Its stomach lining became food pouches and water canteens; its horns, spoons and cups; its sinews and tendons, fiber ropes, threads, and the strings of hunting bows.

Then came the white men. At first, they were mostly sportsmen, hunters from Europe and back east, who shot the buffalo from the moving carriages of the Kansas Pacific and left the carcasses to rot on the prairie. But contrary to popular wisdom, most whites put the buffalo to almost as many uses as the Indian did. They ate its tongue and its meat (one firm in Dodge City, Kansas, processed over 1.6 million pounds of buffalo meat during the winter of 1872 to 1873); pounded its bones into fertilizer or made them into buttons—or into calcium phosphate to make sugar white, or ash to make bone china. Hides were made into coats and robes and carriage blankets, or turned into the machinery belts that kept the mills of New England churning.

The problem lay not with what the white man did with the buffalo but in the efficiency with which he did it. Expert buffalo hunters, with their large-bore rifles and telescopic sights, shot the beasts through the lungs at 200 or even 300 yards. The bison bled a little through the nose and fell over dead; nearby buffalo—never the brightest of creatures—went on grazing, unperturbed. One expert hunter dropped 120 buffalo in 40 minutes.

"The whole Western country went buffalo-wild. It was like a gold rush.... Men left jobs, businesses, wives and children, and future prospects to get into buffalo running," remembered Frank Mayer, a 22-year-old New Orleans native. "They sold whatever they had and put the money into outfits, wagons, camp equipment, rifles and ammunition.... I did it myself. And why not? There were uncounted millions of the beasts—hundreds of millions, we forced ourselves to believe.... It was a harvest. We were the harvesters."

Mayer netted as much as $200 a day—over three times what the president of the United States made. Cartridges for his customized rifle cost 25 cents apiece. A pair of experienced skinners were another $60 to $100 a month. Working as a team, they could lift an 80- to 100-pound hide from a bull in five minutes. Pegged out on the ground for three to five days, it would lose half its weight, before being dosed with arsenic to kill the bugs, then sold for $2 to $3.

THE GREAT SLAUGHTER OF THE BUFFALO

IN 1800, THE BUFFALO POPULATION WAS 25 MILLION TO 30 MILLION
IN 1865 IT WAS 15 MILLION
IN 1880 IT WAS 400,000
IN 1890 IT WAS 1,000
IN 2010 IT WAS 430,000

The near extinction of the American buffalo—properly called bison—was the result of many powerful forces: A growing population needing meat and warm clothing, the needs of industries dependent on leather-belt-driven machinery, and cultural aggressiveness toward the lifestyle of the Plains Indians all contributed to massive over hunting. Drought, new cities blocking bison migration, and, after the Civil War, railroads sped up the pressure on the bison population. By the end of the century, only about 1,000 animals remained. Conservation during the twentieth century gradually increased the population, with 30,000 "wild" bison today, as well as about 400,000 raised as livestock.

1889 TO 1890

"A BEAUTIFUL DREAM..."

THE GHOST DANCE AND WOUNDED KNEE

In 1889, a Northern Paiute Indian by the name of Wovoka who was living among the Mormons recovered from a bad fever with the certainty that he was the Messiah. He'd had a dream: He had stood before God himself and was promised that if only the Indians would love one another, if only they would work hard and not cheat or steal or lie, and if only they would dance the Ghost Dance, the land would be theirs again, brimming with sweet grass and clear water, and the buffalo would come back. Wovoka walked his vision back across the prairie, and soon it ran ahead of him. The Ghost Dance spread everywhere, a shuffling, hypnotic dance much like other Indian circle dances that hundreds, even thousands of Native Americans would perform for hours until they had worked themselves into a state of religious ecstasy.

"...we took away their country and their means of support, broke up their mode of living, their habits of life, introduced disease and decay among them, and it was for this and against this that they made war. Could anyone expect less?" —General Phil Sheridan

It was the old dream, as well as a new one. The Ghost Dancers wore shirts dyed blue around the neck, with brightly colored suns, moons, and birds that they claimed made them invulnerable to the white man's bullets. This desperate mysticism panicked the reservation agent at Pine Ridge, South Dakota, a tenderfoot named Daniel F. Royer, whom the Indians called *Lakota Kokipa-Koshkala*—"Young-man-afraid-of-the-Indians." Royer called in federal troops, including Custer's old Seventh Cavalry. When a band of Sioux fled the reservation out of fear, the cavalry pursued and surrounded them near Wounded Knee Creek. A scuffle broke out as cavalrymen began to search the Indians' tents for weapons, and the edgy troopers opened fire with new, rapid-firing Hotchkiss rifles. Before the fighting was over, at least 200—and possibly as many as 300—of the 350 Indians there were dead, including women and children; 25 troops also died, many of them killed by their own crossfire.

"When I look back now from this high hill of my old age, I can still see the butchered women and children lying heaped and scattered all along the crooked gulch as plain as when I saw them with eyes still young," remembered Black Elk, a 27-year-old brave at the time of Wounded Knee, who had also taken part in the Battle of Little Bighorn as a boy. "And I see that something else died there in the bloody mud, and was buried in the blizzard. A people's dream died there. It was a beautiful dream."

The 1890 massacre spelled the end of any Indian resistance for nearly a century. The U.S. Census of that year found fewer than 250,000 Indians, down from the more than 400,000 just 40 years earlier.

BURY MY HEART AT FORT SILL: THE DEATHS OF CHIEFS

Many Indian leaders had a hard time living with the white man, mainly because the white man was so eager to kill them. Sitting Bull, after taking refuge for some years in Canada after the Battle of Little Bighorn, eventually surrendered on July 19, 1881, and moved onto the Standing Rock Indian Reservation, which straddles North and South Dakota. He was allowed to leave the reservation when he was signed up by Buffalo Bill Cody, to tour the East Coast and Europe with Cody's Wild West show. A source of constant fascination, Sitting Bull charged money for autographs.

After only four months on the road Sitting Bull returned to Standing Rock, where he was considered a troublemaker by the white reservation agent, James McLaughlin. On December 15, 1890, at the height of the Ghost Dance movement, McLaughlin sent 44 Indian police, including some of Sitting Bull's bitter enemies, to arrest him. They ended up shooting him dead, even though he was unarmed.

Many Indian chiefs died in custody, much as Osceola had in Florida, decades earlier, after going to negotiate under a flag of truce. Crazy Horse was bayoneted to death by his army guard; Gall, another leading chief at the Battle of Little Bighorn (or, as the Indians knew it, the Battle of Greasy Grass Creek), dodged a similar fate when the soldier who pinned him to the ground with his bayonet mistook him for dead. The great Apache leader Mangas Coloradas was shot to death while under guard, and the Kiowa chief Satanta went head-first out an army prison hospital window.

Geronimo, probably the most famous American Indian, managed to avoid assassination while a prisoner at Fort Sill, in Oklahoma. He was even trotted out to take part in Teddy Roosevelt's 1905 inaugural parade in Washington, D.C., then returned to his little house and his watermelon patch at Fort Sill—where he died, still officially a prisoner of war, in 1909.

Sitting Bull in a publicity photo with Buffalo Bill Cody, the one-time scout and buffalo hunter who turned impressario and toured for decades with his Wild West show. He took many of the West's most legendary figures on the road with him.

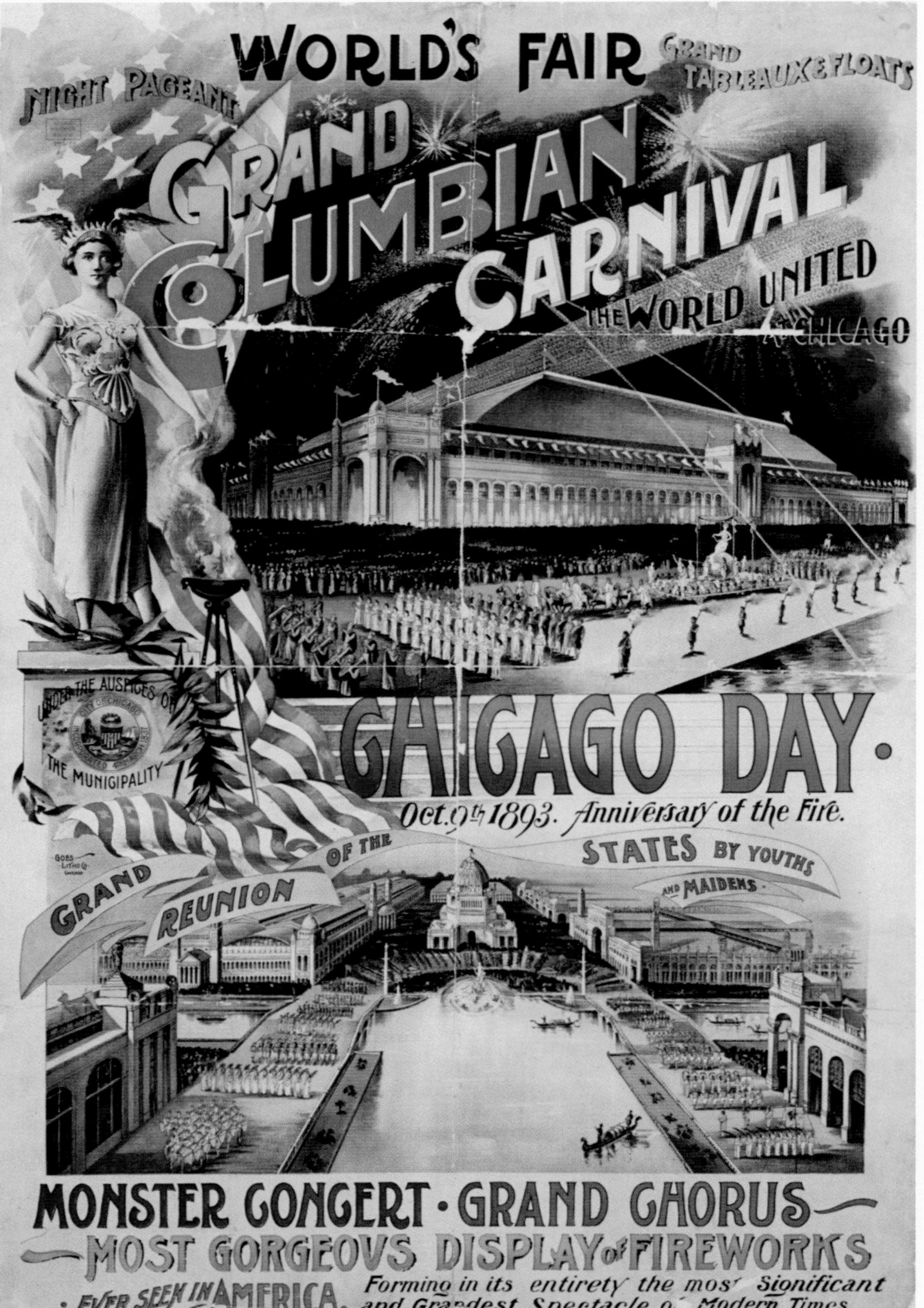
WORLD'S FAIR
NIGHT PAGEANT
GRAND TABLEAUX & FLOATS
GRAND COLUMBIAN CARNIVAL
THE WORLD UNITED AT CHICAGO
UNDER THE AUSPICES OF THE MUNICIPALITY
CHICAGO DAY.
Oct. 9th 1893. Anniversary of the Fire.
GRAND REUNION OF THE STATES BY YOUTHS AND MAIDENS.
GOES LITHO CO CHICAGO
MONSTER CONCERT · GRAND CHORUS
MOST GORGEOUS DISPLAY of FIREWORKS
· EVER SEEN IN AMERICA.
Forming in its entirety the most Significant and Grandest Spectacle of Modern Times.

1886 TO 1893

A CONTINENT TAMED

THE CLOSING OF THE AMERICAN FRONTIER

The 1890 census also declared the official end of the frontier. Within just four years, from 1886 to 1890, the buffalo had all but been finished off, the last Indian protest suppressed, the last cattle drive run, and the massive Dakota, Montana, Idaho, and Wyoming territories all granted statehood. No more could it be said that there was any unexplored wilderness in the contiguous United States. Every county in the nation now had at least six people per square mile. The great dream was indeed finished, just as Black Elk claimed. Or perhaps more accurately, many dreams—those of the Indians and the former slaves, of the buffalo hunters and the prospectors, of the cowboys and the ranchers, of the homesteaders and the loggers and the railway men—had been subsumed into one.

If a perfect democracy of independent farmers had not quite been forged on the plains, many had made a living, and a new life, there. The region had been converted into a vast, commercial enterprise, pouring its wealth into an American economy that had just surpassed Great Britain's to become the largest in the world (it would remain so for the next 125 years). By 1890, 160,000 miles of rail knitted the country together, with 12 lines crossing the Mississippi and five of them running from coast to coast. The railroads had become the Internet of their day, homogenizing national tastes, bringing new fashions and new ideas to many parts of the country—and even changing how Americans thought about time. Previously, the U.S. went by a patchwork array of 20 irregular time zones. Now, to facilitate railroad timetables, this was reduced to the current system of just four zones.

All of this came together in the booming, polyglot prairie metropolis that had been founded less than 60 years before, and that had just passed Philadelphia as the second-largest city in the country. More than 2,000 trains arrived and departed daily from Chicago. Its rail-yard silos processed 11.8 million bushels of grain a year. Its stockyards held 21,000 head of cattle, to be butchered on the spot, then shipped out in the new refrigerator cars—often as the popular patties of ground beef that became known as hamburgers.

At the World's Columbian Exposition, held in Chicago in 1893, a 32-year-old history professor named Frederick Jackson Turner delivered a paper titled "The Significance of the Frontier in American History." The frontier above all else, according to Turner, was what had shaped the distinctive American character—something he described as "that coarseness and strength, combined with acuteness and acquisitiveness; that practical, inventive turn of mind, quick to find expedients; that masterful grasp of material things...that restless, nervous energy; that dominant individualism."

The frontier, for Turner, meant the pioneering practice of "breaking the bond of custom, offering new experiences, [and] calling out new institutions and activities." It was the wellspring of American freedom and civilization. Without it, what would we be? And where would we turn for our next challenges?

Many of the answers were waiting in the very fairgrounds where Turner gave his speech, and where a model Beaux Arts city for America sat molded in plaster. Beyond it, though, rose buildings even more marvelous to behold, made of steel and brick, and rising higher than any structures ever had before. The only way to go, it seemed, was up.

CHAPTER SEVEN

CITIES

CHICAGO, POST-FIRE, 1871

1871
TO
1893

THE CITY BEAUTIFUL

REBUILDING CHICAGO

All autumn long, the winds had been blowing through the timberlands of the Great Northwest, and the rains had stopped falling. On that fateful Sunday, October 8, 1871, flames swept down both sides of Michigan's Thumb region, killing at least 200 people around Port Huron, Holland, and Manistee.

In Wisconsin, winds whipped the flames into a firestorm that William Lutz, a local historian, described as "a wall of flame, a mile high, five miles wide, traveling 90 to 100 miles an hour, hotter than a crematorium, turning sand into glass." People threw themselves into the water, but the flames grew more and more frenzied, tossing homes and even railcars into the air, jumping the waters of Green Bay to burn part of Wisconsin's Door Peninsula. The blaze, known as the Peshtigo Fire, burned up to 1.5 million acres—more than twice the size of the state of Rhode Island—and killed at least 1,200 (and perhaps as many as 2,500) people, making it the deadliest single fire in American history.

But the flames weren't finished. Down Lake Michigan lay the bustling new metropolis of Chicago. Forty years earlier, it had not existed; now it was the fifth-largest city in the country. For all that, it was still a rough, wooden city, like so many others in America. At about 9:00 p.m., *something*—a cow kicking over a lantern? a careless dice game?—happened in a shed owned by Catherine O'Leary at 137 DeKoven Street, and fire broke out.

Whatever the spark, the same devil winds that had set the north woods ablaze fanned the fire into a towering conflagration. It leaped the Chicago River and scorched a 34-block swath up to Fullerton Avenue. Before it burned itself out the following night, the Great Chicago Fire had incinerated an area four miles long and three-quarters of a mile wide, obliterating 17,500 buildings, including the city hall and most of the town's churches, theaters, and private libraries. The death toll was relatively light, "only" about 200 to 300. But 90,000 people, nearly a third of the city's population, were left homeless.

Chicagoans set about rebuilding at once, but the question remained: How could one of America's biggest and most important urban areas be so swiftly destroyed by an ordinary shed fire? The answers lay in the high winds and the drought but also in the workings of an indifferent urban government, one that—like nearly all city governments throughout the country—specialized in drawing power and money to itself while neglecting the most basic civic

Above: The White City, home to the 1893 World's Columbian Exposition, and a fantasy in white stucco and plasterboard. It, too, would burn and vanish, less than two years later.

Opposite: The *Chicago Tribune* building after the great fire. The total destruction was put at $222 million.

THE DEATH RATE IN NEW YORK IN THE 1850s OUTSTRIPPED THE BIRTHRATE; THE CITY KEPT GROWING ONLY BECAUSE OF THE ENORMOUS INFLUX OF IMMIGRANTS.

improvements. Chicago in 1871 was a city of wooden sidewalks, with hollow openings below them where all manner of trash could collect. Once the fire started, they served as enormous wicks. Nor was the city's amateurish, politicized fire department much help.

Most American cities at that time were slapdash affairs—little sanitation, less order, few green spaces (outside of their cemeteries), and some of the most corrupt governments in the Western world. The air of downtown Pittsburgh was dusky with coal dust by noon, and the city had the world's highest typhoid mortality rate. In New York, pigs ran loose in the streets until after the Civil War, and the city's sewers were so badly graded and so choked with butchers' offal that it was common to see little boys sailing paper boats in pools of blood. The death rate in New York in the 1850s outstripped the birthrate; the city kept growing only because of the enormous influx of immigrants.

The problem of what to do about the cities was the major conundrum facing reformers of all kinds. A pair of visionary landscape architects, Frederick Law Olmsted and Calvert Vaux, built a series of magnificent parks, parkways, and greenbelts throughout the country, including Boston's Emerald Necklace, San Francisco's Public Pleasure Grounds, and Manhattan's unparalleled Central Park. These green spaces were intended as social works as well as municipal ornaments, designed to provide cramped urban dwellers with recreation, fresh air, and access to neighboring museums and other cultural institutions.

Chicago's World's Columbian Exposition of 1893, celebrating the 400th anniversary of Columbus's discoveries a tad belatedly, featured 400 acres of gorgeous white-stucco buildings in a classical vein, interspersed with canals, lagoons, and public gardens, and brilliantly illuminated with electricity. Designed by Olmsted and the leading Chicago architect of the day, Daniel Burnham, the White City, as it came to be known, spurred a nationwide City Beautiful movement and became a model for world's fairs and amusement parks everywhere—as well as for L. Frank Baum's Emerald City and for Disneyland (Walt Disney's father supposedly helped to build the White City as a construction worker).

Chicago, meanwhile, had adopted a new building code and constructed wide boulevards and numerous parks. But its population had soared to over 1.1 million, making it the second-largest city in the country, behind only New York. How to keep it from strangling on its own growth? The answer would come from two basic elements: metal and light.

The masterpiece: Frederick Law Olmsted and Calvert Vaux's Central Park, 1863, intended as an exercise in social uplift as well as recreation. It even included a free dairy to serve New York's milk-starved children.

CENTRAL PARK.
Published by JOHN BACHMANN, 76 Nassau St New York.
PRINTED BY F. HEPPENHEIMER 22 & 24 N WILLIAM ST N.Y.

1835
TO
1875

THE ORIGINAL MAN OF STEEL

ANDREW CARNEGIE CONVERTS THE NATION TO STEEL

The harnessing of both elements was already well under way, thanks to two of the most extraordinary businessmen in American history. Both had worked their way up from next to nothing. Andrew Carnegie lived with his family in the single room of a Scottish weaver's cottage until he was 12 years old. Soon after the Carnegies emigrated to western Pennsylvania, he got his first job as a bobbin boy, changing spools of thread in a cotton mill. The teenage Andrew moved on to work as a telegraph messenger in Pittsburgh, where he memorized the faces of the city's most important men and the locations of their plants. Soon he was secretary to the head of the Pennsylvania Railroad, then supervisor of its Pittsburgh operations—at the astoundingly young age of 18.

A $500 loan from his mother, who had mortgaged the family home to get it, was turned into a stake in a small railroad company, which would eventually become a major holding in the Pullman Palace Car Company. Later, Carnegie made a killing in the new Pennsylvania oil fields, then developed steel mills and ironworks, a bridge-manufacturing company, and iron-ore fields around Lake Superior. "I determined that the proper policy was 'to put all good eggs in one basket and then watch that basket,' " he would famously remark, in a laughable misrepresentation of his own rise.

In fact, Carnegie had his eye on the connections between all eggs and all baskets. The nexus, for him, was steel. Supervising the Pittsburgh railroads, he had noticed that their iron rails needed to be replaced every six weeks to two months, especially around curves. After experimenting with steel-coated rails, Carnegie thought he had an answer. But where to get enough steel?

Carnegie traveled to England to see the latest technology, the Bessemer steel converter. Henry Bessemer and Robert Forester Mushet had come up with an ingeniously simple process in which molten pig iron was poured into a massive, egg-shaped converter and then blasted with air in order to remove the carbon impurities. When alloys were added to the molten metal, the iron was converted into steel. It could be done for as little as a sixth of the previous cost, and in enormous quantities.

Carnegie returned to the United States to recruit a small coterie of partners and build a $1.2 million steel mill just east of Pittsburgh along the banks of the

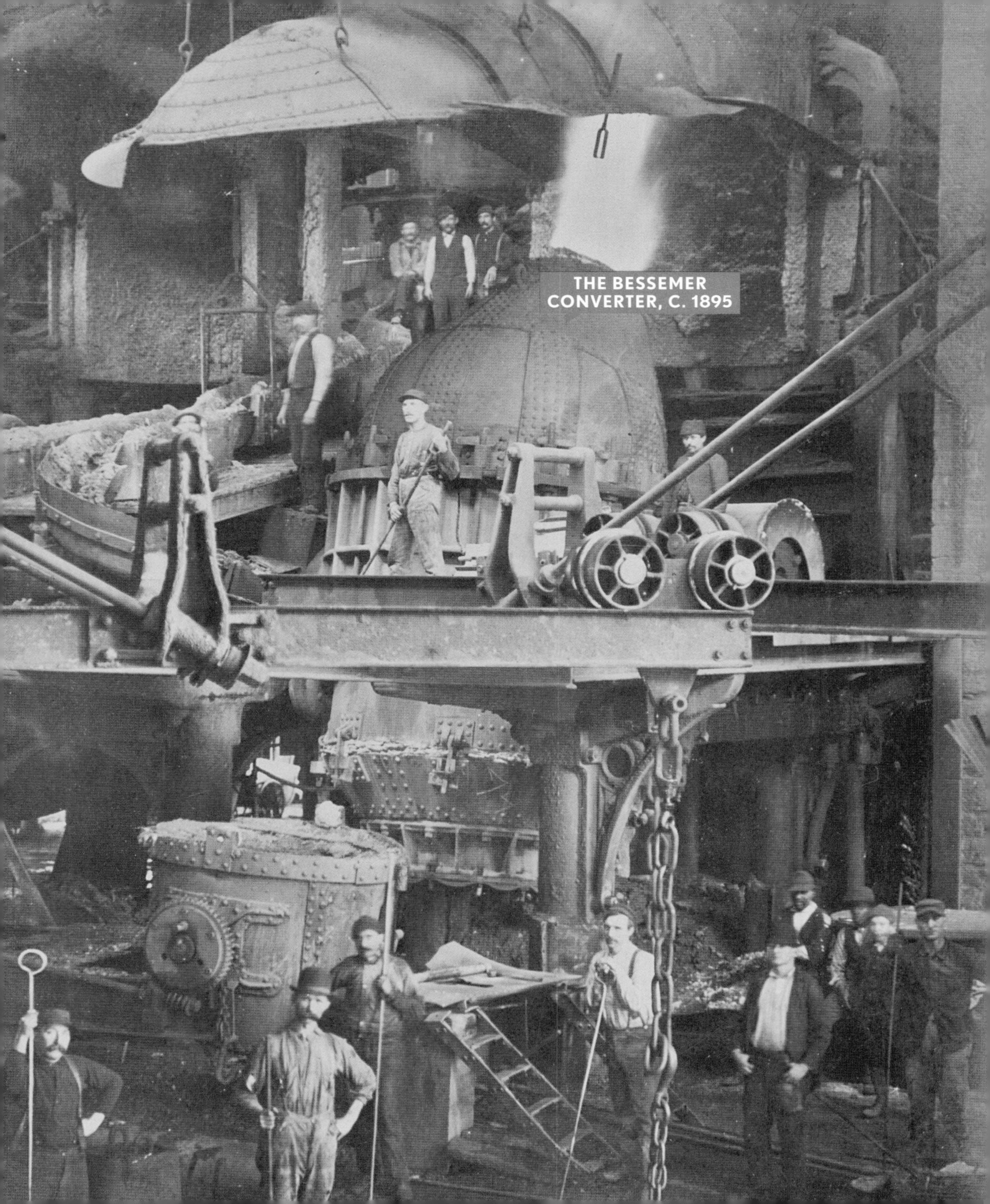

THE BESSEMER CONVERTER, C. 1895

Monongahela River. The workmen dug old bayonets and swords out of the earth. They were building on Braddock's Field, where the French and Indians had surprised General Braddock in 1755, and where George Washington had made his bones and won the moniker Hero of the Monongahela. Now it was the place from which Andrew Carnegie would lead the world into a new age.

Then, panic—literally. The colossal Wall Street Panic of 1873 sent American capitalism reeling. Carnegie embarked on a two-year battle to keep his steel mill on schedule and in his hands. Orders for rails and beams fizzled out as the economy melted down. Carnegie pursued debtors relentlessly, staved off creditors, and bailed two partners out of their obligations.

On August 22, 1875, he brought his great black egg hissing back to life, turning out the first steel for an order of 2,000 rails for the Pennsylvania Railroad. By the 1880s, Carnegie Steel Company was producing more steel rails, pig iron, and coke than any other firm in the world.

The United States—Pennsylvania in particular—would lead the world in steel production for most of the next century. Carnegie and his competitors were soon manufacturing countless miles of steel cable, which were used to build suspension bridges such as the wondrous new structure connecting Brooklyn and Manhattan. Steel rods and sheet steel went into making swift new ocean liners, powerful new boilers, engines, gears, and axles, as well as the turbines and generators used to convert the power of gigantic new dams. And steel beams made possible an entirely new sort of building, one that would usurp a term once associated with the tallest clipper ships: *skyscraper.*

THE BROOKLYN BRIDGE

A wonder of the modern world, the Brooklyn Bridge was the first major suspension bridge constructed, and the longest bridge in the world at the time, with a span of nearly 1,600 feet. Its woven steel cables could support nearly 19,000 tons, including wagons, pedestrians, trolley cars, and subway trains. The bridge took 14 years to build, and cost the lives of more than 35 men, including its designer, John Augustus Roebling. The main impediment was digging the foundations of its two towers underwater, especially on the deeper Manhattan side.

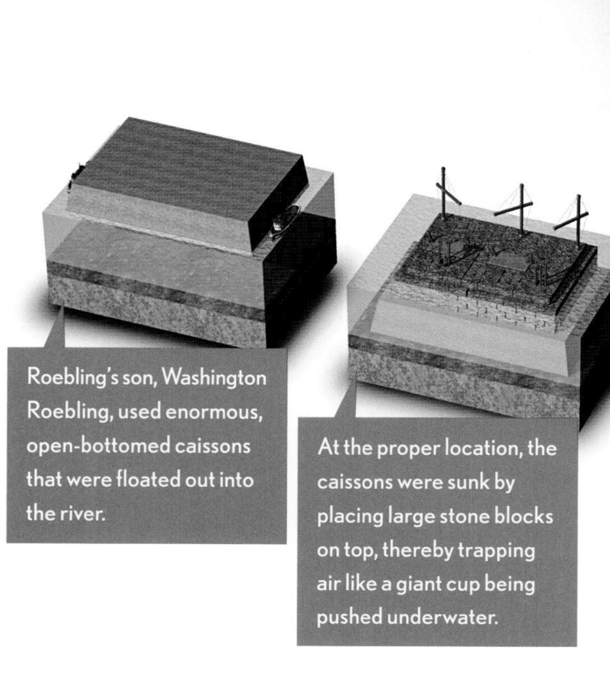

Roebling's son, Washington Roebling, used enormous, open-bottomed caissons that were floated out into the river.

At the proper location, the caissons were sunk by placing large stone blocks on top, thereby trapping air like a giant cup being pushed underwater.

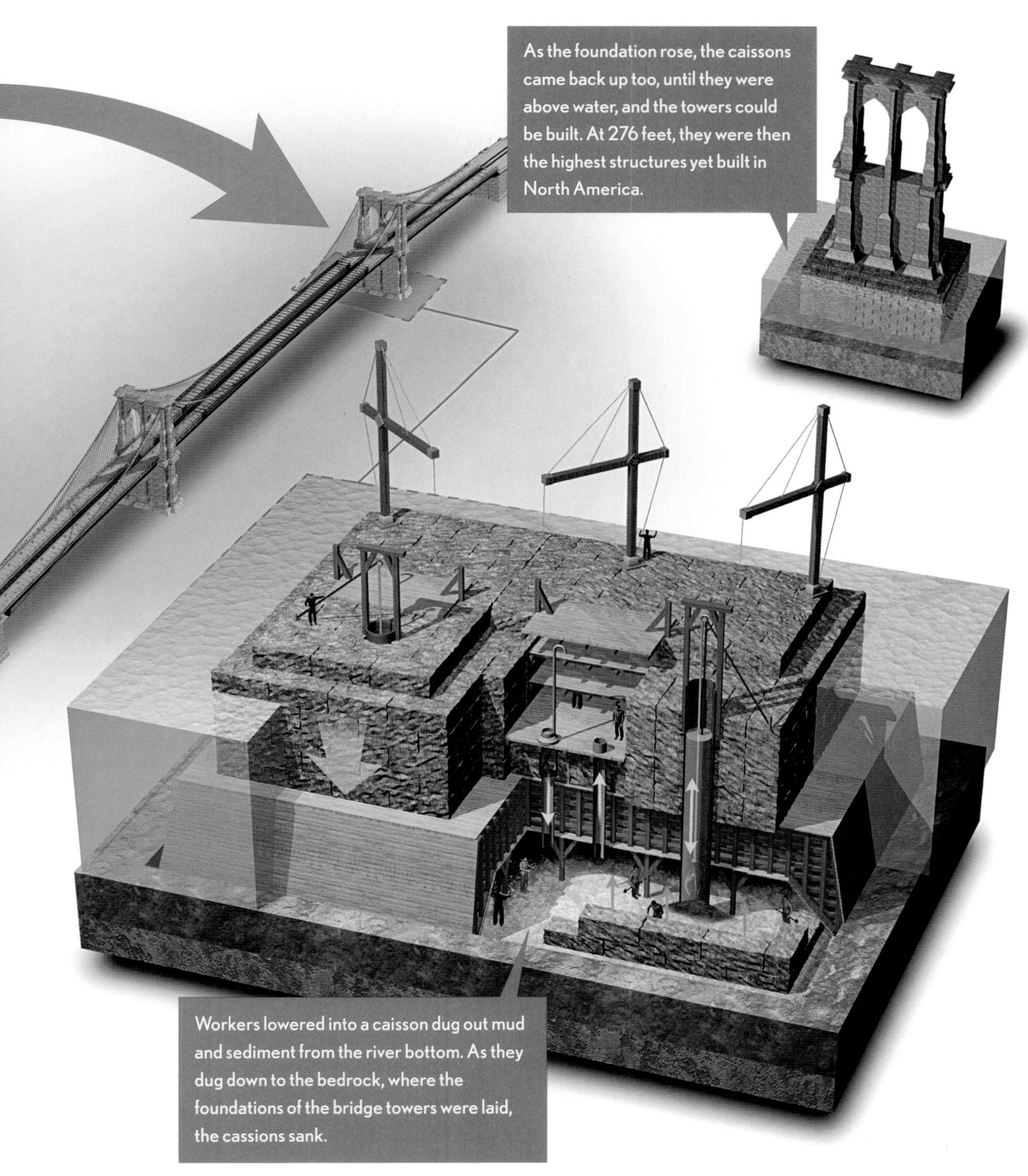
As the foundation rose, the caissons came back up too, until they were above water, and the towers could be built. At 276 feet, they were then the highest structures yet built in North America.
Workers lowered into a caisson dug out mud and sediment from the river bottom. As they dug down to the bedrock, where the foundations of the bridge towers were laid, the cassions sank.

1870 TO 1920

ABLE TO LEAP TALL BUILDINGS IN A SINGLE BOUND

THE BIRTH OF MODERN ARCHITECTURE

All over America, cast-iron buildings were slowly hauling themselves toward the tops of the church steeples that had, for more than a thousand years, defined the skyline in every Western city or town. These interlopers were office buildings, filled with workers in a host of emerging, white-collar businesses that would recast American working life in the century ahead. Publishers, insurers, financiers, retailers, and others—such as the incredible new Sears mail-order business, which combined all of these professions, along with shipping and manufacture—were grappling for more and more office space. Between 1870 and 1920, the percentage of white-collar workers—clerks, managers, assistant managers, salesmen, saleswomen, stenographers, and typists (or "typewriters," as they were then called)—grew to nearly 11 percent of the American workforce. Nowhere was the desire to go higher felt more keenly than in Chicago. "Chicago has thus far had but three directions, north, south, and west," noted the *Chicago Tribune*, "but there are indications now that a fourth is to be added...zenithward. Since water hems in the business centre on three sides and a nexus of railroads on the remaining, the south, Chicago must grow upward."

"Zenithward" it would go—and Chicago would become the birthplace of modern architecture along the way. At first this was achieved through existing technologies—office buildings taller than anyone had ever seen before could and would be built with iron and stone. But cast-iron construction had innate limits. Iron columns were less flexible than those made of steel, and harder to connect tightly; cheaply made iron turned brittle, and collapsed without warning.

In 1882, Daniel Burnham and his partner, John Wellborn Root Sr., erected something a little different: the ten-story Montauk Building, a structure so impossibly high that it would become the first to be referred to as a skyscraper. "What Chartres was to the Gothic cathedral, the Montauk Block was to the high commercial building," proclaimed one observer.

Yet the Montauk Building was still a building with load-bearing masonry walls—this was, essentially, how Chartres and every other building had been built since time immemorial. A greater innovation would be devised by one of the least spectacular of Chicago's many architectural lights. William Le Baron Jenney was an imperturbable Civil War veteran with funny pop eyes and a propensity for mangling the English language. While traveling in the Philippines with his father, a whaling captain, he had observed a native tribe that built its homes using tree trunks as supporting columns. Drawing another analogy from nature, the Major—as everyone called Jenney—proposed converting tall buildings from crustaceans (supported by their thick outer shells) to vertebrates (held upright by a hard, interior skeleton and covered with a much lighter skin).

In building his 12-story Home Insurance Building, Jenney let the interior beams—*not* the outer masonry wall—carry the weight of the building. Columns and floors connected to metal beams as if to make a gigantic birdcage. He made walls structurally insignificant, reduced to being merely a means of decorating and enclosing the building.

Still another step forward would come with Burnham and Root's Rand McNally Building, finished in 1890 as the first skyscraper with a frame made completely of steel. Others would soon follow. Tests

CHICAGO, C. 1880

showed that steel columns had 40 to 50 percent greater compressive strength per square inch than iron ones. What's more, steel, unlike iron, could be mass-produced so fast that Jenney's Fair Store was ready to open for business just three and a half months after the start of construction.

On and on, up into the sky the new buildings rose. The raw new town on the prairie had become the citadel of the world's most innovative architecture, with a pantheon of geniuses designing one masterwork after another. The man enabling them was Carnegie, his steel mills supplying the columns and beams used in 17 of the 29 classic Chicago School buildings erected between 1885 and 1895.

Yet as the skyscrapers rose ever higher, even Carnegie would have to scramble to keep up. Nervous municipal governments demanded greater load-bearing capacities, and his smaller, nimbler competitors turned from the Bessemer process to the open-hearth Siemens-Martin technique. The latter took longer to cook the metal, but it made steel that had even greater tensile strength. Carnegie struggled to convert his plants before finally selling out to J. P. Morgan in 1901 for $400 million, from which he personally netted a whopping $225 million, with this fortune he devoted the rest of his life to philanthropy.

THE FLATIRON, 1900

Chicago, too, would be surpassed. Civic leaders concerned about crowding out the sunlight would restrict the height of its downtown buildings to 20 to 24 stories until the 1920s. But the need to condense space would never be as compelling as it was back on the East Coast in Chicago's old rival—a city built almost completely on islands.

U.S. Steel, the industrial powerhouse that J. P. Morgan forged from the steel holdings of Carnegie and some of his rivals, was the world's first billion-dollar corporation. It was headquartered in Manhattan, of course—as were 69 of the 200 largest companies in America by 1901, including Standard Oil, General Electric, and American Tobacco. All this industrial muscle pushed real-estate prices upward. By 1910, frontage on Wall Street cost $25,000 a square foot. Within a few years after the turn of the century, there were already 66 skyscrapers in lower Manhattan, with more lumbering slowly up the island.

One after another, they emerged as the tallest structures not only in the city but also in the world, many of them holding the title for just a matter of months before they were replaced by something taller and grander. New York imported the Chicago School's skeleton-structure design and improved on it with "cage construction," in which Jenney's birdcage structure supported the interior but the steel exterior walls supported themselves, allowing ever-higher buildings. The city imported many of the Chicago School's architects as well. Indeed, the most extraordinary Manhattan skyscraper of all was Burnham's fabulous Flatiron Building, plowing into Madison Square (in the words of its greatest portraitist, the photographer Alfred Stieglitz) "like the bow of a monster ocean steamer."

Though at 285 feet and only 21 stories tall the Flatiron (officially the Fuller Building) was far from being the tallest structure in New York, no one had ever seen anything like it. Its shape both fascinated and appalled observers. It filled up a triangle of space where Fifth Avenue and Broadway intersect at 23rd Street, creating what one critic compared to "a stingy piece of pie." There, the Flatiron created its own *weather*—"scrap[ing] the wind off the sky and spill[ing] it in the street in long curly breezes," as the journalist Ellis Parker Butler wrote. Some New Yorkers of the time were terrified, afraid to walk too close to the thing. Other men loitered around its corners, hoping for a glimpse of stocking as the Flatiron's winds blew women's ankle-length skirts up a few inches. (The term *23 skiddoo*—long American slang for "Get outta here!"—was the cry of beat officers chasing away these voyeurs.)

The Flatiron was more than just a building—it was the shape of modernity coming into focus. Stieglitz captured it with the most modern of media, the camera. In his photographs, the Flatiron appears to float weightlessly above the snow-bowed trees of Madison Square and the passing, already anachronistic horse carriages. It was, he declared, "a picture of the new America still in the making.... The Flat Iron [sic] is to the United States what the Parthenon was to Greece."

THE GODS OF HIGH STEEL

By the turn of the twentieth century, the greatest theater in America could be seen hundreds of feet up in the air, over any city skyline. There worked the "roughnecks," grappling the great steel buildings of the Republic into place. Photographs would immortalize their risk taking and their insouciance: balancing calmly on a steel beam as it was hoisted high above the surrounding city; eating lunch out on the edge of a girder, feet dangling down into eternity. None wore the hard hats, the safety belts, or even the most rudimentary safety devices of modern construction workers.

They paid a price for this daring. By 1904, one in eight workers in high steel had been killed on the job, and the rule of thumb was that high-rises cost one life for each floor.

Veteran roughnecks were called "fixers"; novices, "snakes," because you wouldn't trust them with your life. None of their jobs required more exquisite skill and timing than those of the four-man rivet crews. High in the air, the "heater" would roast a rivet in a brazier until it was red hot. He would pull it out with a pair of tongs and flip it as much as 50 feet through the air to a "catcher," who would corral it in a metal bucket or megaphone-like device. Next the catcher would pull it out with his own pair of tongs, knock any cinders off against a beam, and place it in a beam hole. The "bucker-up" would hold the beams in place while the "gun man" drove it into permanent position with his hammer.

A veteran rivet gang could assemble steel with awe-inspiring speed—and with so little margin for error that many refused to work if one man called in sick. Most of them were of

THE SKYSCRAPER RACE

The new skyscrapers were elaborately clad and topped with marvelous frippery, serving as giant advertisements for the corporate giants they housed. Joseph Pulitzer's World Building was topped with a gold dome that could be seen 40 miles out to sea. The Metropolitan Life Building had clock faces bigger than Big Ben's, and a searchlight that signaled weather conditions to ships. Cass Gilbert's Woolworth Building, "the Cathedral of Commerce," was adorned with a white terra-cotta skin and gorgeous Beaux Arts interiors.

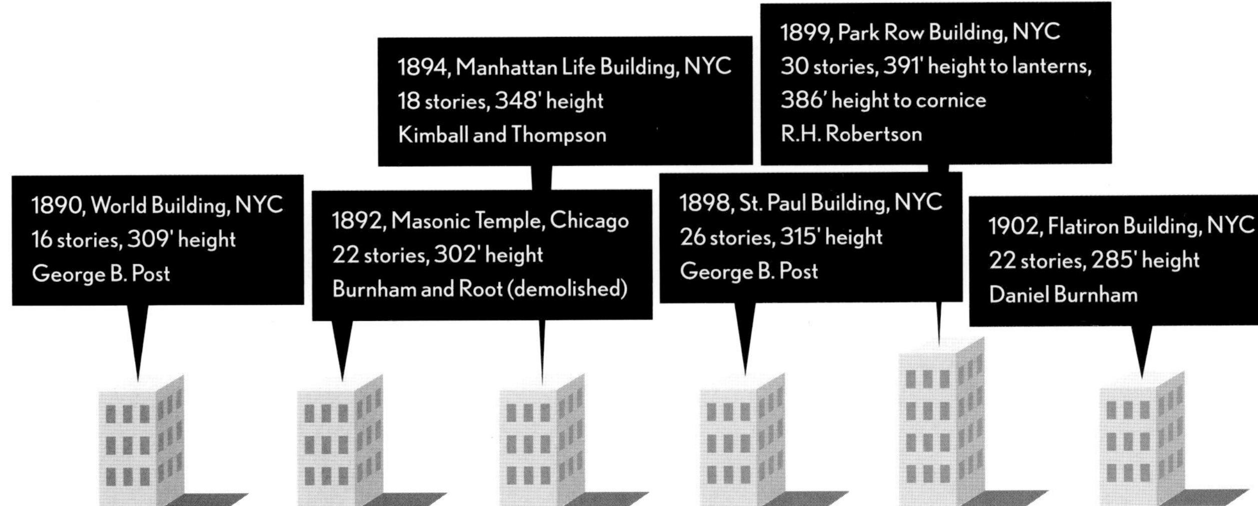

Irish ancestry, but of enduring fascination were the small minority of Mohawk Indians. They had come to this line of work in Canada, in 1886, working on the Dominion Bridge across the St. Lawrence River. The Mohawks would "boom out" across the U.S., working steel and iron construction from the Verrazano-Narrows Bridge in New York to the Golden Gate in San Francisco. By the 1930s, 700 Mohawks had settled in Brooklyn, where they were immortalized by Joseph Mitchell in his famous *New Yorker* essay "The Mohawks in High Steel," and by Gay Talese in his book on the building of the Verrazano, *The Bridge*. Rivet construction died out after the 1960s, but by the turn of the twenty-first century, 20 to 25 percent of Mohawk men were still working in steel construction. As Mitchell quoted an official from the Dominion Bridge, "Men who want to do it are rare and men who can do it are even rarer."

1908, Singer Building, NYC
41 stories, 612' height
Ernest Flag (demolished)

1909, Metropolitan Life Insurance Tower, NYC
50 stories, 700' height
Napoleon LeBrun and Sons

1913, Woolworth Building, NYC
60 stories, 792' height
Cass Gilbert

1930, 40 Wall Street, The Manhattan Company, NYC
71 stories, 927' height
H. Craig Severance and Yasuo Matsui

1930, Chrysler Building, NYC
77 stories, 1046' height
William van Alen

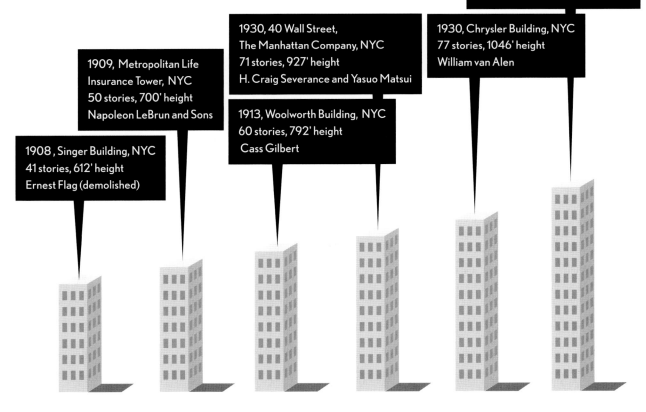

1931, Empire State Building, NYC
102 stories, 1250' height
Shreve, Lamb & Harmon

1847 TO 1912

BURNING THE CANDLE AT BOTH ENDS

THOMAS EDISON LIGHTS THE WORLD

All the last day and evening of 1879, special trains kept coming despite the growing snowstorm, bringing the curious to the little town of Menlo Park, New Jersey. By New Year's Eve, 3,000 of them had arrived, overwhelming the tiny depot and the rambling laboratory just up the hill, interrupting the ceaseless work of the engineers and mechanics there with questions. They had been coming for days, eager to see a miracle. Each night, after it got dark, they witnessed it, and their reaction had always been the same: delighted gasps of "Marvelous!" and "Wonderful, wonderful!"

The chief wizard of the Menlo Park laboratory flicked a switch, and on went 33 lamps inside the lab and its offices, as well as another 20 in adjoining houses and on the street leading back down to the depot. It was the miracle of light—of electricity—and afterward would come a full explanation and more demonstrations from the wizard, a courtly, nearly deaf young man who, at 32, was already the most famous inventor in America. Thomas Alva Edison informed them that what he called the "vile poison" of gaslight and all other means of illumination had had their day: "We will make electricity so cheap that only the rich will burn candles."

Much like Andrew Carnegie's, Edison's early life revolved around trains and the alluring magic of telegraph wires. In school in Michigan, he was so absentminded that his teacher called him "addled," and his formal education ended after three months. He went to work as a "butcher's boy" on the railroad, selling newspapers and candy to passengers, and caught a Horatio Alger–size break when he saved the three-year-old son of a stationmaster from a runaway train. The boy's grateful father taught him how to operate a telegraph, and Edison used this new skill to run an Associated Press bureau wire by the time he was 19—only to be fired when a sulfuric battery he was experimenting with dripped acid onto his boss's desk.

Penniless, Edison went to live in a friend's basement and kept up the experiments, most of them related to the telegraph. He made enough on an early stock ticker to move out of the basement and into his own laboratory, and by the time he was 30 he had invented a phonograph that recorded sound on tinfoil wrapped around a grooved cylinder. The first voice heard on it was his own, dolorously reciting "Mary Had a Little Lamb." It was a crude device, but it stunned the nation and earned him his nickname: the Wizard of Menlo Park.

The place itself was an invention, the world's first industrial research lab. There, teams of men toiled under Edison's supervision, branching out into many different fields. By 1877, most of their work was directed toward a goal that had eluded men of science for the whole of the century: the invention of a commercially viable source of incandescent light. The trick was finding the right filament, and Edison and his men tested any number of materials, going through everything from platinum to hairs from their own beards.

On October 22, 1879, they had it: A coiled carbon filament connected to platinum contact wires burned for 14.5 hours. A few months later, they switched to a

The new light, reported *The New York Times* in 1882, was "as bright as day, but without an unpleasant glare." It did not flicker, or give off extreme heat as gaslight did, but provided a glow that was "soft, mellow and grateful to the eye, and it seemed almost like writing by daylight..."

FIRST
MANUFACTURED
LIGHTBULBS

BALLOT
Millions of American women voted for President in 1920 and are finding time to take active interest in civic affairs
The suffrage and the switch
Woman suffrage made the American woman the political equal of her man. The little switch which commands the great servant Electricity is making her workshop the equal of her man's.
No woman should be required to perform by hand domestic tasks which can be done by small electric motors which operate household devices.
The General Electric Company is working side by side with your local electric light and power company to help lift drudgery from the shoulders of women as well as of men.
GENERAL ELECTRIC
One of a series of G-E Advertisements now appearing in General Magazines

By the 1920s, General Electric was advertising electricity as a feminist commodity, thanks to its labor-saving capacities. It had, in fact, transformed many households, although 50 million Americans still had no access to it.

carbonized bamboo filament, which lasted for 1,200 hours. Soon afterward, they were able to make their New Year's Eve demonstration, and then light up J. P. Morgan's mansion and the town of Menlo Park. (Morgan's house required 385 bulbs; all of Menlo Park, just 400.) But Edison and his team still had to come up with a distribution system. He had Morgan and the family of transportation and financial magnate Cornelius Vanderbilt behind him, so he shelled out $65,000 to buy two buildings on Pearl Street, in lower Manhattan, and got permission to light District No. 1 in the city. It was, as usual, a canny choice: That district included Wall Street and most of the city's many newspapers.

On September 4, 1882, the Edison Illuminating Company was ready, sending 110 volts of direct current to bulbs in 400 lamps belonging to 85 customers. The world had changed. Within a year, the Pearl Street station was lighting 10,000 lamps, although Edison's direct-current system could reach only customers within about a mile of a generating station. Like Carnegie, he, too, would be surpassed, as even geniuses regularly were in the cutthroat competition of New World technology. George Westinghouse would switch the world to a system of alternating current, patented by Philip Diehl and perfected by Nikola Tesla, that could be transmitted over much longer distances.

It was electricity that powered the skyscrapers' safety elevators, and all of the underground and underwater trains; it was electricity that ran the projectors that spewed forth the new century's boldest new art. "Incandescent lighting," cultural historian David Nasaw noted, "transformed the city from a

ON SEPTEMBER 4, 1882, THE EDISON ILLUMINATING COMPANY WAS READY, SENDING 110 VOLTS OF DIRECT CURRENT TO BULBS IN 400 LAMPS BELONGING TO 85 CUSTOMERS. THE WORLD HAD CHANGED.

dark and treacherous netherworld into a glittering multicolored wonderland."

It was the light that would usher in entire new entertainment districts, like nothing else ever quite seen before. The first electric sign appeared on Broadway in 1897, and by 1906 the Knickerbocker Theatre was advertising its production of *The Red Mill* with a windmill composed entirely of lightbulbs, the arms of which seemed to turn. By 1913, there were over a million lights along the Great White Way. They advertised the lure of a city that held more theaters than any other town on earth, a total capacity of nearly two million seats.

Who filled them? A whole new class of Americans: white-collar clerks and executives, secretaries and typewriters. Their hours were shorter than those of the vast majority of workers still toiling in factories or fields, and an unprecedented number of them were single men and women, living alone in the city. They needed something to do.

What they got was "the show business"—a professionalized, rationalized array of entertainments. Many of these were brand-new, including baseball parks (although the sport's troglodytic owners would not install lights for night games for another three decades), amusement parks, and vaudeville, as well as phonograph and kinetoscope parlors, where people could pay a nickel to stick an ear into a "listening tube" or peer through a peephole at a couple of minutes' worth of a flickering moving image. Edison soon turned Menlo Park's efforts toward making movie cameras and projectors.

All of these diversions were defined by their appeal to this new middle class. Most important, they were cheap. Vaudeville—from *voix de ville*, or "voice of the city"—cost between 25 cents and $1.50 for the top boxes. In return, it offered a vast array of constantly changing entertainments, including singers, dancers, comedians, jugglers, acrobats, minstrels, performing animals, freaks, and celebrities. "It may be a kind of lunch-counter art," the playwright Edwin Milton Royle wrote in *Scribner's* magazine in 1899, "but then art is so vague and lunch is so real."

The people who went to these entertainments had to be housed somewhere. All the new tunnels and bridges and train stations enabled hundreds of thousands, then millions of individuals to be whisked back and forth between work, pleasure, and their homes in the fast-growing suburbs. But who wanted to live in the suburbs? City residents would now get their own tall buildings: apartment buildings.

Four thousand of them went up from 1904 to 1912 along Manhattan's West Side alone, each with a hundred tenants or more. The new apartment houses offered something else of inestimable value against the loneliness of any great city: ready access to others. They were, as one commentator noted, home to "con men, clergymen; heiresses, actresses; fast people, slow people; good people, bad people; people you know, people you'd like to know, and people you don't want to know—but all of them interesting to look at, to think about."

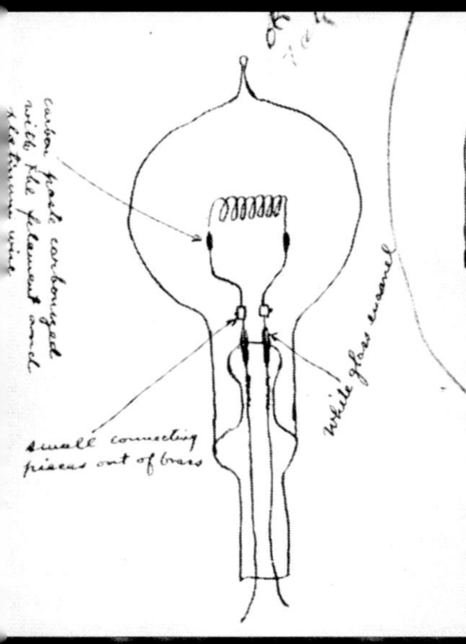

MENLO PARK: THE FIRST RESEARCH LAB

Thomas Edison's laboratory took up two city blocks, and he famously told reporters that he wanted it to have "a stock of almost every conceivable material," offering a reward to any visitor who could name something he did not have. An 1887 newspaper article claimed that Menlo Park already contained "eight thousand kinds of chemicals, every kind of screw made, every size of needle, every kind of cord or wire, hair of humans, horses, hogs, cows, rabbits, goats, minx, camels…silk in every texture, cocoons, various kinds of hoofs, shark's teeth, deer horns, tortoise shell…cork, resin, varnish and oil, ostrich feathers, a peacock's tail, jet, amber, rubber, all ores and minerals," and more. Edison registered an incredible 1,093 patents and started 14 companies over the course of his life. Above his desk, the Wizard of Menlo Park displayed a placard with a quote from Sir Joshua Reynolds: "There is no expedient to which a man will not resort to avoid the real labor of thinking."

THOMAS EDISON,
1880

1846
TO
1925

PITY THE POOR IMMIGRANT

NEW AMERICANS FILL THE TENEMENTS

Yet most urban Americans still lived under very different circumstances, jammed cheek by jowl into some of the worst slums in the history of the world. These were the tenements—minimal brick apartment buildings, four to six stories high, generally without elevators, hot running water, hall lights, or more than one cramped toilet per floor (if that). In New York City alone, 1.2 million individuals—about a third of the city's population—lived in 43,000 tenement buildings.

The vast majority of these people were new to the country, part of the greatest voluntary migration in human history. In the 1880s, over 5.5 million new immigrants arrived, or more than 10 percent of the U.S. population at that time. In the 1890s, almost 4.1 million more followed, even though the country was in a deep economic slump for much of the decade. All told, 30 to 32 million European immigrants arrived between 1846 and 1925, when the nation's first significant immigration restrictions became law.

The switch from sailing ships to steamships in the 1880s made this great influx considerably easier. It cut the length of a transatlantic voyage from three months (about what it had been for John Rolfe, en route to Jamestown) to just six days (what it is now) by 1900. Most of the immigrants arrived desperately poor, speaking little or no English. About half of the southern Italians, to cite one example, were illiterate even in their own language. They had few skills of use in an industrialized world, but they came anyway, fleeing the vendettas and the desolate soil of Sicily.

As late as the 1890s, it was common to see Italian immigrants working on street-construction projects under the supervision of padrones brandishing rifles and pistols. If they were lucky, the workers might get to sleep under a table or in the back room of one of their "patron's" enterprises. This was the nineteenth-century successor to indentured servitude—one more way in which the immigrants were preyed upon and exploited by their own.

Yet even under such conditions, Italian immigrants were able to send incredible sums of money back home—$85 million in 1907 alone. In this way, they paved the road for those who would follow. Indeed, much of this money was used to defray the cost of a steamship ticket in steerage for a relative or friend. By 1892, those hard journeys usually ended at Ellis Island. There, in a group of Victorian buildings in New York Harbor to which new Americans were taken by barge from their ocean liners, immigrants were made to wait in lines for hours; poked and prodded by doctors checking for mental illness, lice, and skin diseases; and had their eyelids pulled down with buttonhooks to check for trachoma. The backs of their coats and dresses were chalked with mysterious letters meaning acceptance, rejection, or a need for further examination.

Alone or with loved ones to help them make their transformation from "greenies" (short for *greenhorns*) into Americans, their journey was just beginning. Children lost parents who died prematurely from backbreaking labor, or who sometimes gave up and deserted their families. Parents lost children who Americanized before they did, or who died from the diseases that coursed through the slums.

Mulberry Street, on the Lower East Side of Manhattan, at the turn of the century. New York's slums at the time may well have been the most crowded in the history of the Western world.

IN 1900, THE AVERAGE RESIDENT OF MANHATTAN GENERATED 1,487 POUNDS OF WASTE A YEAR, SLIGHTLY MORE TRASH THAN THE NATIONAL AVERAGE TODAY.

MULBERRY STREET, NEW YORK, 1900

SCOTTISH

ALGERIAN

RUSSIAN

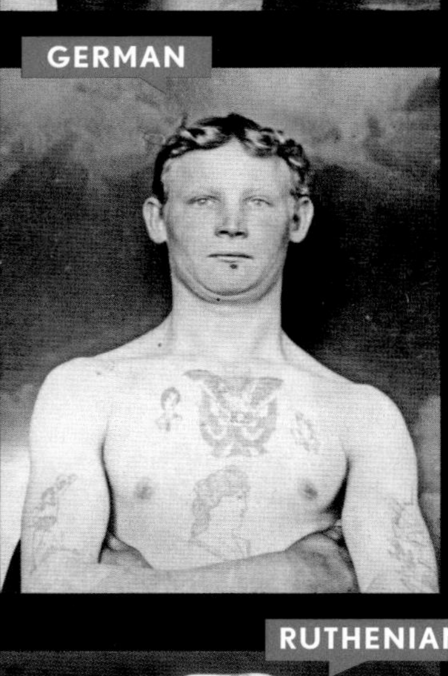
GERMAN

ITALIAN

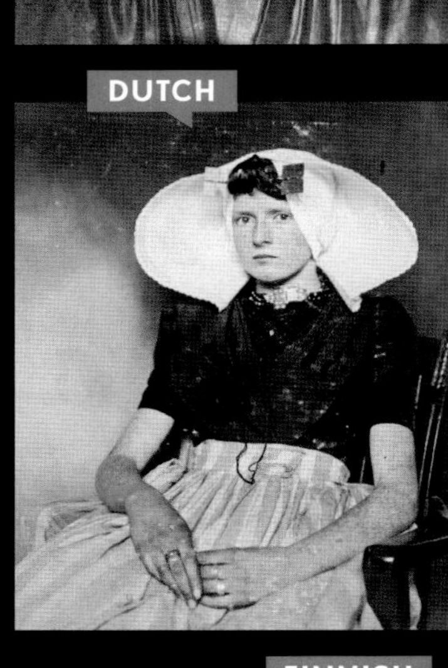
DUTCH

RUTHENIAN

FRENCH

FINNISH

DANIEL SILVA, author: "Imagine what it took for someone to leave Eastern Poland or Lithuania or some village in the mountains of northern Italy and come all the way to America with nothing—to come to this strange place. Imagine the drive, imagine the faith."

Leading statesmen disdained the immigrants. Henry Cabot Lodge, a powerful Republican senator, wanted to require a literacy test for immigrants, one that would weed out "the most dangerous elements… Italians, Russians, Poles, Hungarians, Greeks, and Slovaks who would wipe out the pure native breed." Less high-minded politicians—the sort of men who ran political machines, such as Charles "Silent Charlie" Murphy in New York and Michael "Hinky Dink" Kenna in Chicago—cast no judgments and provided considerable material relief, but always of the most transitory and dependence-inducing nature: bail money, a bucket of coal, a pair of shoes, the fabled turkey at Christmas. More substantial, transformative aid—a college education, a minimum-wage law—was out of the question. The city machines still ran on hierarchy and clan loyalty, like an Irish village, where anything might be granted as a privilege but nothing as a right.

Progressives, when they were able to gain power, built parks and playgrounds, took over private utilities and mass-transit systems, and regulated milk, food, and ice distribution to make it affordable for the poor. They attacked all problems with a logical eye, turning the latest scientific advancements to the aid of the people.

In New York, for instance, the city was more choked than ever by waste. By 1912, it would produce enough to fill the Great Pyramid of Giza three times over—every year. In wet weather, a greasy coating covered the streets and sidewalks. In dry weather, it became noxious dust. And in all seasons, it stank. Little was done. Garbage removal was performed by private companies owned by cronies of Tammany Hall, the city's notorious political machine, and by 2,700 street sweepers, who were political appointees and went about their work in a manner that could at best be called desultory.

In 1895, the reform administration of Mayor William L. Strong hired someone to do something about it: Colonel George Edward Waring Jr., a chemist and sanitary engineer who, in the Renaissance mode of the nineteenth century, had run a model farm, designed a flush toilet, built the drainage system for Central Park, and created its lovely lakes and ponds. Waring had also devised a sewage system for Memphis, Tennessee, that had rescued the city from its notorious cholera and yellow-fever outbreaks. He forced his sanitation workers into gleaming white uniforms, forbade them to drink or swear on the job or to beat their horses (he spied on them, disguised in a wide hat and a cloak), and called them his "soldiers of the public… defending the health of the whole people."

Before long, he had instilled his environmental awareness into the whole community, and New Yorkers were astonished at their newly cleaned streets. Waring even got them to separate their trash, in the ninteenth-century version of recycling.

Meanwhile, Dr. Hermann Biggs, head of New York's health department, hammered away at the city's most common diseases by quarantining cholera sufferers, scrubbing the tenements with disinfectant, supplying an antitoxin for diphtheria, and closely inspecting meat and milk for tuberculosis—all by way of trying to convince his fellow New Yorkers that "public health is purchasable." It was, at least in part, as the reforms of Biggs and Waring drove the death rate down in the 1890s.

BUILDING THE STATUE OF LIBERTY

The most famous statue in the history of the world was the brainchild of a French historian, Édouard René Lefèbvre de Laboulaye, who was moved by the sacrifice of the American Civil War and the death of Abraham Lincoln in 1865.

Laboulaye's dream was taken up by a young painter and sculptor, Frédéric-Auguste Bartholdi, who sailed to America to scout locations for the project. Bartholdi decided upon a speck of rock and landfill in New York's Upper Bay known as Bedloe's Island: "It is certainly here that my statue must rise; here where people get their first view of the New World, and where liberty casts her rays on both worlds."

"My statue" was to be a 151-foot-tall classical depiction of a woman representing *Liberty Enlightening the World,* taller than the Colossus of Rhodes. The statue's eyes are two and a half feet in diameter; the book she holds is taller than a two-story house. When Bartholdi displayed the finished head of his statue in Paris, his countrymen responded enthusiastically. Within two years, subscription drives across France had raised 600,000 francs from men and women eager to demonstrate their love for the United States.

Americans, by contrast, looked this gift horse in the mouth. One critic said the statue resembled "a bag of potatoes with a stick projecting from it." A penurious Congress voted to expend funds for an unveiling ceremony and maintenance, but nothing for the granite pedestal that architect Richard Morris Hunt had designed for it. New York's equally stingy governor, Grover Cleveland, vetoed the $50,000 the state legislature had voted to spend on it.

New Yorkers pumped for funds from around the country. Hunt donated his $1,000 fee back to the project, and agreed to make the pedestal out of concrete instead of granite. Still, by March of 1885, almost a year after the statue had been turned over to the U.S., the pedestal fund was $100,000 short of its $300,000 goal.

It was time for an immigrant to lend a hand. Joseph Pulitzer was a Hungarian Jew who had emigrated to the U.S. at the age of 17 and fought with General Philip Sheridan's cavalry. Arriving in New York in 1883, just 36 years old, he bought the *New York World* and quickly raised its circulation from 15,000 to 600,000 with a series of exposés, Sunday supplements, comic strips, and populist campaigns. Pulitzer decided that the Statue of Liberty would become another one of these: "The *World* is the people's paper, and it now appeals to the people to come forward and raise the money," he wrote in an editorial, adding: "It is not a gift from the millionaires of France to the millionaires of America but a gift of the whole people of France to the whole people of America. Take this appeal to yourself personally."

The people responded. Within five months, 121,000 of them—mostly working people and schoolchildren, from New York to as far away as Texas—had raised the $100,000.

On the afternoon of October 28, 1886, New Yorkers crowded the shorelines of Manhattan and Brooklyn to watch Bartholdi unveil his masterpiece. It stood 305 feet high on its pedestal, the highest structure in the nation at the time. Grover Cleveland, now president, gave the keynote speech honoring the instant icon he had declined to fund as governor.

BANDIT'S
ROOST,
NEW YORK,
1887

1849 TO 1914

THE SLUM OF ALL PARTS

JACOB RIIS AND THE FIGHT FOR REFORM

Others tried to bring the scientific method to the field of crime control, led by the New York Police Department's flamboyant chief inspector, Thomas Byrnes, who introduced to American policing mug shots, the third degree, telephone networks, and the whole idea of the modern investigative detective. Despite all of his contributions, Byrnes was forced to resign for rampant corruption by a new police commissioner, 37-year-old Theodore Roosevelt. Corruption was an endemic problem in urban American police forces, usually built into the system by the requirement that officers pay off their political sponsors—commonly referred to as "rabbis"—in return for their appointments and promotions.

Roosevelt tried the Waring method of spying on his cops in cloak and wide-brimmed hat. Venturing out at night, with a large revolver in his pocket, he sought the guidance of a crusading photojournalist whose church lectures and lantern slides had impressed him. This was Jacob Riis, already famous for his 1890 book on the slums, *How the Other Half Lives*. The two men became fast friends as they strolled the mean streets of lower Manhattan, discussing urban reform and checking for Teddy's missing policemen (nine out of ten, he was dismayed to find, were not walking their beats).

Riis made an excellent guide, having endured the worst of the immigrant experience himself. One of 14 children of a Danish schoolteacher and his wife, he had arrived in America with more advantages than many—namely, a skill (carpentry), the ability to speak and read English, and $40 in his pocket. Believing New York to be much like the dangerous and wild California he had read about in a prospector's memoir, he squandered half of his nest egg on a pistol.

"Bandit's Roost" was a largely Italian section of New York's notorious Mulberry Bend slum near Chinatown. Despite the nefarious appearance of its denizens, the city's murder rate was below even what it is today. The photo was taken under the direction of Jacob Riis.

Over the next few years, Riis worked as a carpenter, a traveling salesman of flatirons, a farmhand, and a journalist, and was repeatedly cheated, robbed, and bamboozled. He was reduced to sleeping on the street—and once on a tombstone—while living on windfall apples.

Through it all, Riis persevered, finally chancing upon a magic-lantern device that he and a friend used to put on shows for audiences out in the sticks on Long Island. He determined to use pictures to convey the sheer desperation of the slums. This would not be an easy task. One of the distinguishing characteristics of the slums was their lack of light (Riis later would often shock audiences by relating how, while trying to negotiate one tenement, he'd stepped on a baby lying on the stairs). Then, in 1887, he read about pistol-lamp photography—an early flash process that entailed firing cartridges from a pistol-like device into a mixture of potassium chlorate and antimony sulfide. Later, he tried lighting magnesium powder in a frying pan.

Both processes were highly volatile. On more than one occasion, Riis nearly burned down his subjects' firetrap buildings. But in the end, he gained access to a whole other world, one that most of his readers and audiences were only dimly aware existed, even though it was practically next door. In a single 12-by-12-foot room, Riis discovered five families—20 people in all—sharing two beds and the floor. The whole building was shot through with tuberculosis and malnutrition, and the result was a constant parade of hearses to the door.

Riis's accompanying text was simple, powerful, and sympathetic, but it was his pictures that told the story of the slums in a way that no words could. They brought home the claustrophobia of a world where families ate, slept, and toiled for endless hours within the same narrow, barren walls. He conveyed the full despair of men and women in dive bars and two-cent restaurants, opium dens and police lodging houses. But beyond these despondent scenes, he also humanized his subjects, showing them as proud, striving people. The most amazing aspect of the photos in *How the Other Half Lives* is how many people are smiling in them—the posed "street Arabs," as the newspapers liked to call homeless children, trying to keep from laughing as they demonstrate where they sleep on the street. The regal young Iroquois woman working around a table with her father and mother while her brother plays a fiddle. A teenage Jewish girl smiling between the scissors held up to her lips, paused for a moment while making knee pants at 45 cents a dozen in a Ludlow Street sweatshop.

Riis turned his subjects into people other people wanted to help, and so they did. His pictures and his words led to many of the reforms that he pressed for, letting light and air into the tenements, bringing in decent water and sanitation facilities, improving fire safety, limiting rent increases, and moving the awful work of the sweatshops out of people's living quarters.

Some of the 12 men and women Riis found in a Bayard Street room "not 13 feet either way." They paid five cents a night for the privilege.

"SAY WHAT YOU WILL, A
MAN CANNOT LIVE LIKE
A PIG AND VOTE LIKE A
MAN." —JACOB RIIS

1881
TO
1910

THE RICH WILL ALWAYS BE WITH US

CLASS WARFARE IN AMERICA

The tenements were only the tip of a deeper problem. The phenomenal industrial revolution that had made the U.S. economy the largest in the world had also created a gaping chasm in wealth, dividing the country as it had never been divided before—by economic class. Poverty was endemic in turn-of-the-century America. In 1890, *before* the devastating depression that racked the nation during the decade to come, the wealthiest 1 percent of American families owned 51 percent of all real and personal property. Another 12 percent, the "well-to-do" families, controlled 35 percent of the wealth, which translated to $16,000 per family. After that came the so-called middle classes, controlling just 12.8 percent of the wealth, or $1,500 per family. Last were the poor, nearly half the families in the country, who controlled just 1.2 percent of the wealth, at a mere $150 per household.

The mansion of William Kissam Vanderbilt, one of several his family owned along Fifth Avenue. Such homes lined the avenue for miles, but after the institution of a federal income tax in 1913, not a single new one was built.

A decade later, after the 1890s depression, more Americans lived below the poverty line than during the Great Depression of the 1930s, according to the calculations of the historian James Patterson. An ongoing brand of violent class warfare broke out. Between 1881 and 1905, there were over 37,000 strikes in the United States, many of them bloody struggles. Efforts to unionize were routinely met with clubbings, shootings, jailings, blacklistings, and executions, perpetrated not only by well-armed company goons but also by policemen, deputies, National Guardsmen, and even soldiers. Dozens of workers were killed in the Homestead and Pullman strikes and during strikes in Colorado at Telluride, Cripple Creek, Colorado Springs, and Ludlow.

Some unionists struck back with dynamite, now readily available at American construction sites. In 1905, a bomb ripped the legs off Idaho Governor Frank Steunenberg in his front yard, mortally wounding him, after he'd thrown a thousand miners from the Coeur d'Alene strike into makeshift jails for months without trial. Twenty-one men died when labor radicals blew up the headquarters of the rabidly anti-union *Los Angeles Times* in 1910. Relatively few workers were involved in such outrages, but millions did turn to the Socialist Party and to the militant International Workers of the World, organizations that promised to sweep away the capitalist system.

LOS ANGELES TIMES
BUILDING, 1905

1904 TO 1935

THE FIERY GIRLS' RIGHTEOUS FURY

THE TRIANGLE FACTORY DISASTER AND ITS LEGACY

Socialism was much on the mind of many immigrants in the big cities. On the Lower East Side of New York, Jewish immigrants had often been fighting for years for socialism back in the old country, where they saw it as salvation from the smothering persecution they faced within the Russian Empire. Giving in to what might seem a contradictory impulse, they were also unrivaled self-improvers, displaying a passion for education matched among the immigrant groups only by Germans. By 1904, though representing only 2 percent of New York's total population, they accounted for 8.5 percent of its college students.

Back in Eastern Europe, rigorous restrictions on what Jewish men could do to make a living had turned many of them into pure scholars, while the women in the family learned to be breadwinners. To the New World, these women often brought one skill of particular use: sewing. Their expertise in the needle trades reinforced their self-confidence and independence. Encountering the sweatshops they were expected to work in—apartments or cramped work spaces in which they were constantly "sweated," or pushed to work faster—many demanded a better life. They became known for their passionate speeches pressing for better wages and conditions, for a union. They would become known by the Yiddish term *fabrente maydlakh*—the "fiery girls."

During the bitter winter of 1909 to 1910, they tested their power, going out on strike in the "Uprising of the Twenty Thousand." The fearsome might of the sweatshop owners, the city government, the police, and the underworld were aligned against them. Cops allowed pimps to bring prostitutes to the picket lines, where they would attack the striking girls and women. Once an altercation had "broken out," the police waded in, clubs swinging, to beat and arrest the strikers. The fabrente maydlakh fought back by winning over hundreds of society women to their cause, including J. P. Morgan's daughter, the philanthropist Anne Morgan. Flummoxed, unable to attack wealthy society ladies, the police stopped making arrests. The strikers won concessions and recognition of their union at many of the small garment shops in the city.

One shop where they did not win was the Triangle Shirtwaist Factory. Like many sweatshops, it was run by former garment workers turned owners, Isaac Harris and Max Blanck. As many as 500 cutters, sewing-machine operators, and thread pullers worked at long rows of benches up on the eighth, ninth, and tenth floors of the building, where large windows brought in light and air. It was a vast improvement over a dark tenement sweat.

Yet little had really changed. The young women and girls who operated the machines still had to buy or rent their own equipment, were docked for any material they damaged, and were summarily dismissed if they could not keep up with the backbreaking grind of the busy season. When the orders piled up for shirtwaists—a type of woman's blouse popularized by the Gibson Girl drawings of Charles Dana Gibson—they routinely worked 16 hours a day, and were required to come in for a "half day" on Saturday that usually lasted until 4:45 P.M.

It was a few minutes before the end of work on one such Saturday, March 25, 1911, when the trouble began. Most of the Triangle workers were already starting to get up and put on their coats, when someone noticed a fire on the eighth floor—probably started by a cigarette

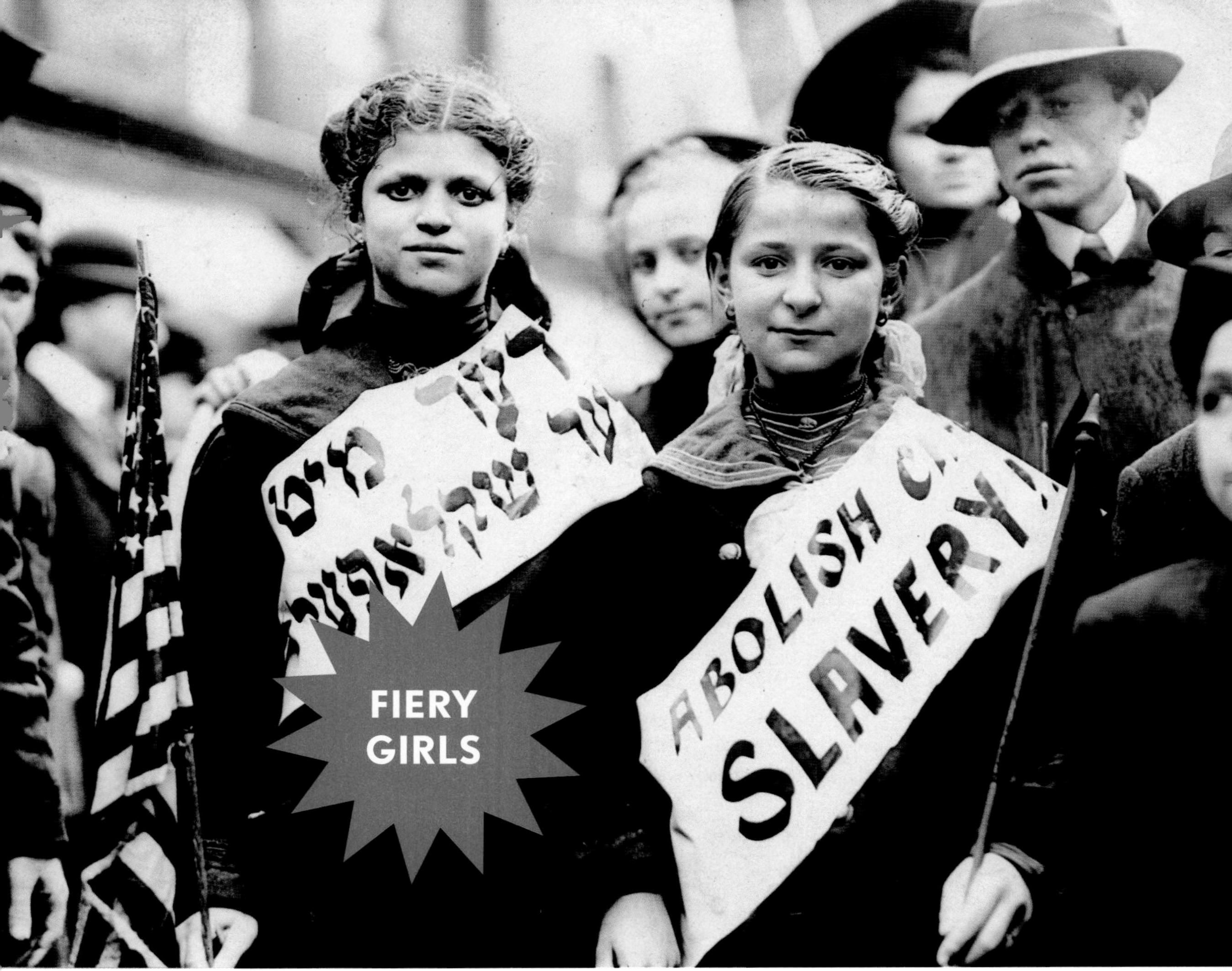

butt from one of the male pattern cutters. Men tried to throw water on the blaze, but there was over a ton of flammable cloth in the bins and machine oil everywhere, and the fire quickly spread.

It should still have been easy to put out the fire, or evacuate the factory, but the fire hoses didn't work, and there were no sprinklers. All the doors opened inward, and most were locked. There was a fire escape, but when two dozen women scrambled out onto its steps, it collapsed, pitching them down eight stories to be impaled on a spiked metal fence or to crash through the roof of a greenhouse.

At one point, the crowd that had gathered below saw what looked like a burning bundle come crashing through a window; many assumed it was the Triangle owners trying to save their stock. Only when it hit the paving stones did they realize that it was not a bundle at all, but a person.

Most of the workers on the eighth floor were able to make their way downstairs, and those on the tenth

The fabrente maydlakh, on strike for better wages and working conditions. Mostly teenagers, they would build the International Ladies' Garment Workers Unions (ILGWU).

BY THE TIME THE FIRE WAS OVER, 146 PEOPLE—NEARLY ALL OF THEM YOUNG WOMEN—HAD DIED IN THE SPACE OF 15 MINUTES. THE AVERAGE AGE OF THE VICTIMS WAS 19.

managed to get up to the roof and escape. But the ninth floor was a charnel house. The charred bodies of 25 young women were found huddled in the cloakroom. More were jammed up behind the doors that opened in the wrong direction—or did not open at all. Some got out in the elevators; as the last car descended, those packed inside could hear the bodies of their desperate friends and coworkers crashing onto the roof as they jumped down the shaft.

As the flames ripped across the factory floor, the trapped women turned to the windows. The people below shouted, "No, don't jump!" But they did, alone or with a friend, or sometimes with three or four young women together—holding hands, their long hair and voluminous Old World dresses streaming flames.

William Gunn Shepherd, a reporter who happened to be passing by, described the scene thus: "Thud—dead! Thud—dead! Thud—dead! Sixty-two thud—deads. I call them that, because the sound and the thought of death came to me each time, at the same instant." Shepherd called in the story as he watched it unfold, his voice breaking.

And then the window jambs broke. As Shepherd saw it: "Down came the bodies in a shower, burning, smoking—flaming bodies, with disheveled hair trailing upward." Shepherd counted 54 more going out the windows that way. By the time it was over, 146 people—nearly all of them young women—had died in the space of 15 minutes. The average age of the victims was 19.

Blanck and Harris were indicted for manslaughter, but they hired a shrewd lawyer, hid their assets, and beat the rap. The Asch Building, which housed the factory, was still standing—as it is to this day, its steel frame as fireproof as its architects had claimed. It was only everything inside that burned. In a city, where 300,000 workers already toiled in spaces seven stories or higher, the New York City Fire Department had no ladders that reached above the sixth floor.

From tragedy, though, would spring reform. The fabrente maydlakh turned the Triangle Shirtwaist Fire funeral processions into marches of protest and outrage. They were heard. Frances Perkins, a tireless social worker and community activist, happened to be in Greenwich Village when the fire broke out, and hurried over to witness it firsthand. She would serve on a committee investigating working conditions with the two leaders of the New York state legislature, Al Smith and Robert Wagner, and together they would secure the passage of 56 bills that limited working hours for women and children, provided workers' compensation, and set regulations for fire and workplace safety that are commonplace today.

Nor would they stop there. Smith, a scion of the old machine, would go on to become a reform governor of New York. Wagner would go to the U.S. Senate. And Perkins would become secretary of labor under President Franklin Roosevelt—the first woman to serve in the federal cabinet. Together, Perkins and Wagner would push through crucial legislation that guaranteed workers the right to organize and that initiated Social Security. American ingenuity would not stop at miraculous new buildings that seemed to hang in the sky, but would secure a social peace that protected the least of those working in them.

At the scene of a fire, hoses connected a hydrant or other water source to the pump (blue arrows). Steam from the boiler (red arrows) drove the pistons (black arrows), which kept the water pumping out.
Steam-pump fire wagons were pulled by horses, or propelled by the steam engine itself. At the firehouse, hot water was circulated continually through the pump, to make sure the engine was ready to go to work at a moment's notice. When a fire call came in, the pipes (to the right of the wagon) were disconnected, and the coal in the pump's boiler was lit.

THE INNER WORKINGS OF THE FIRE WAGON

John Ericsson, inventor of the ironclad *Monitor,* built a working steam fire wagon in 1841. But until the 1870s, most fire engines were pumped by hand and rushed through the streets by the colorful volunteer fire companies who worked them.

CHAPTER EIGHT

BOOM

SPINDLETOP

1859
TO
1975

OIL! OIL! OIL!

SPINDLETOP REFUELS THE NATION

The five men had been drilling into the earth for weeks, forcing pipe down through rock and sand, black dirt and shale. They had built their wooden derrick, piled slabs of pine into a boiler that fueled the steam engine powering their drill, and run lines down to a bayou for their water. At night, they slept in a moldy one-room shack that seemed to contain all the plagues of the Bible.

"We shared the shack with roaches and spiders... When we sat down to eat, frogs...the biggest we had ever seen...jumped down from the shack's rafters and landed on the table," remembered Curt Hamill about the little space that he shared with his wife and children, his brother Al, and Will "Peck" Byrd.

Such was the life of a wildcatter in 1900. For decades, men had swept across the Texas plains, searching to make a fortune in one commodity or another: cotton, cattle, slaves. Now they were looking for oil. Al Hamill had been hired by investors to dig into a salt dome at Spindletop Hill, just south of Beaumont. The Hamills were already known in Texas wildcatting circles for their use of a revolutionary rotary drill instead of the usual cable drill, but so far it had done them little good. Sand kept clogging their pipe and refilling their hole as fast as they could dig it. They were making headway at a rate of only two feet a day, and it seemed they might well make that most common of wildcatter discoveries: a dry hole.

On January 10, 1901, they attached one of their new bits and recommenced drilling. Suddenly, mud began to boil up out of the ground with such force that it pushed the pipe up through the derrick. As the Hamills watched, incredulous, the pipe knocked off the crown block of the derrick, then fell to the ground "like crumpled macaroni," taking out the boiler smokestack. Then came a deafening roar, and a geyser of mud that coated the three men. When it ceased, the wildcatters moved in to try to clean up what was left of their equipment, only to see more mud and blue gas flames shoot out of their six-inch drill hole with "an explosion like a cannon." Again, it was quiet, and again the team crept closer, peering down into the hole through the floor of the derrick.

First they could hear it, gurgling beneath the earth. Then they could see it—forced up with such pressure that the oil foamed as it came, blasting up into a 160-foot geyser.

Teddy Roosevelt, a New York aristocrat turned Progressive politician on the stump: "I have no idea what the American people think, I only know what they *ought* to think."

INSIDE AN OIL RIG

Wildcatters Al and Curt Hamill used a rotary oil rig like this to make the great Spindletop strike near Beaumont, Texas, in 1901, a find that transformed the American economy.

The drill was powered by a pine-fueled steam boiler. Rotating pipes were turned with the rotary table on the derrick floor, digging down into the earth with unequally spaced teeth that chipped away rock as it made a smooth, round hole.

The hollow stem of the drill enabled "drilling mud" to be pumped down into the hole, then back up through a slush pit , and down through the drill again. The circulating mud washed rock, sand, and other debris out of the hole, cleaned and cooled the drill bit, and helped prevent gushers as the drill descended.

It was a classic, cinematic strike. *Oil*. Only unlike in the movies, there was no way to contain it, the pipe and much of the derrick having been blown away. It rained down on Byrd and the Hamills, rained down on the crowds who flocked to see it. The Lucas Gusher, named for the head of the investor group, produced 900,000 to 1,000,000 barrels before it was finally capped—making it one of the most productive oil wells ever found. While it was flowing, it produced twice as much oil per day as all the wells in Pennsylvania, then the leading oil state. And save for 40 barrels (of 42 gallons each), it was all wasted. Soon after the Hamills got it under control the gusher shut down, and never produced any oil again.

But within the Spindletop field—just one mile in diameter, encompassing the crest of the dome and its flanks—lay the greatest oil strike anyone had ever made. After the Lucas Gusher, the next six wells drilled into the dome produced more oil per day than all the wells in the world put together, and helped triple total U.S. oil production by the end of the decade. The Spindletop field produced a record 21 million barrels in 1927, and would give up a total of 153 million barrels by 1985. Long before most of this was dredged out of the ground, though, what Spindletop indicated was the immense volume of oil to be found all over the world. And for the first time in human history, there was something to do with it.

The first oil strike in the United States had occurred in western Pennsylvania in 1859, producing all of 2,000 barrels. Oil's main value lay in the products that could be extracted from it for machine lubricant and for kerosene, a fuel for illumination that had effectively replaced whale oil but that

THE SPINDLETOP FIELD PRODUCED A RECORD 21 MILLION BARRELS OF OIL IN 1927.

produced a flickering, fuzzy light, and that was itself being replaced by Edison's wondrous electricity.

Most Americans associated oil with John D. Rockefeller, a spectral, pious, ulcer-ridden entrepreneur who had converted his stake in the early oil fields into the largest fortune in the world. Rockefeller had accomplished this through a series of business maneuvers that were canny, unethical, and sometimes illegal. The size of Rockefeller's enterprise had allowed him to pressure railroads into secretly charging his rivals more—and giving him the proceeds. Legislators had been widely bribed, and open combat had broken out between Rockefeller toughs trying to destroy competitors' pipelines and the men guarding them. In the mining fields of Ludlow, Colorado, Rockefeller's son, John D. Rockefeller Jr., presided over a 1914 strikebreaking operation that led to 25 deaths, including the massacre of 12 children, horrifying the nation.

By the beginning of the twentieth century, just two men—Rockefeller and J. P. Morgan, who had bought out Andrew Carnegie's interests and built U.S. Steel—either owned outright or exerted considerable influence over every part of the nation's economy. Such consolidated power gave Americans pause with regard to what they had long thought of as their laissez-faire system of business.

Populist and progressive reformers pushed through public ownership and regulation of utilities, the direct election of senators and the recall of governors, and a host of other reforms to combat the runaway power of big business. President Theodore Roosevelt and his handpicked successor, William Howard Taft, began to enforce long-dormant antimonopoly laws against the giant industrial trusts and corporations, forcing Rockefeller to split Standard Oil into several companies. When Roosevelt's attorney general, Philander C. Knox, set out to do the same with Northern Securities, a Morgan holding company that monopolized all transportation between the Great Lakes and the Pacific coast, Morgan hastened to assure the president, "If we have done anything wrong, send your man to my man and we can fix it up."

"We don't want to fix it up," Knox replied, "we want to stop it."

By 1912, Roosevelt was convinced that busting up the trusts and the cartels could never be more than a temporary measure against the enduring problem of bigness in American life. Running against both major parties on a "Bull Moose" Progressive Party ticket, he proposed a New Nationalism that would leave corporations to grow as big as they wanted to, but only in conjunction with an enhanced federal government large enough to regulate every part of the economy. He was defeated by Woodrow Wilson, who espoused instead Louis Brandeis's idea of a New Freedom, preferring to create what the economist John Kenneth Galbraith later called "countervailing power" through the likes of continued trust-busting, organized labor, the use of the individual states as "laboratories of democracy" (to use Brandeis's phrase), and a couple of new tools for the federal government—including a Federal Reserve Board and an income tax, recently made possible by constitutional amendment. But unions had to fight bitterly for recognition, the Federal Reserve had little real power, and the income tax did almost nothing to slow what the sociologist and economist Thorstein Veblen would call the "conspicuous consumption" of the upper classes.

1899
TO
1927

GO TO TOWN IN A BATHTUB?

THE ADVENT OF CAR CULTURE

Henry Ford, as usual, thought *he* had a better way. On January 5, 1914, he shocked his fellow industrialists and entranced the public by announcing that his Ford Motor Company would now pay workers the stunning wage of $5 for an eight-hour day. Ford had previously paid $2.38 for a nine-hour day, slightly below the industry standard. Now he proposed to more than double it. Ford announced grandly, "We believe in making 20,000 men prosperous and contented rather than follow the plan of making a few slave drivers in our establishment millionaires."

Adolph Ochs, publisher of *The New York Times*, asked, "He's crazy, isn't he?" *The Wall Street Journal* inveighed that "Fordism" was an application of "spiritual principles where they don't belong."

Ford may have been crazy, but his living wage was not an act of insanity, nor was it charity. What he was doing was cutting a grand bargain with his workforce, building a consumer base, and garnering a mountain of favorable publicity. The year that he announced his wage hike, every other car in the country was a Ford.

He rose on the shoulders of giants, working as a steam-engine machinist and demonstrator for the Westinghouse company in southern Michigan, then rising to become chief engineer at the Edison Company in Dearborn, Michigan. There, he met the wizard himself, who encouraged him to keep working on his "Ford Quadricycle."

By 1899, Ford had quit Edison and begun producing his own cars. Nobody worked harder, or thought further outside the proverbial box. Of all the great industrialists who transformed American life in the nineteenth and twentieth centuries, none was so involved in every aspect of creating, producing, marketing, and selling his product. Young Henry Ford not only designed his early cars but also worked side by side with his mechanics in assembling them. He thought up marketing strategies, wrote advertising copy, and even raced cars.

Yet at his first two companies, Ford grew dissatisfied, soon broke with his investors, and left. Most of the moneymen saw cars as playthings of the rich. Ford wanted to sell his cars to everyone—and control every aspect of the business. Everything would be made in-house, the better to integrate it into the assembly process. Always, he looked for ways to make his vehicles better and less expensive.

By 1908, his Model T was ready. It was the lightest, sturdiest, cheapest car anyone had ever seen, selling for $850 at a time when the average price of an automobile was $1,926. Even though a record number of Model Ts were sold in 1909 to 1910, sales nearly doubled the following season, and again the year after that. Now the Ford Motor Company was struggling to meet the demand. A new form of production would be needed. Ford already used an assembly line of sorts. Everybody did. A manufacturing process that featured interchangeable parts went all the way back at least to Eli Whitney's gun factory. In Detroit, Ransom Eli Olds had already introduced a production line to make his "Merry Oldsmobiles," and Henry Leland's Cadillacs were made with interchangeable parts.

Ford took things to another level. Back in 1908, he had produced a car on a *moving* line. In 1913, at the new plant in Highland Park, Michigan, Clarence Avery—a friend of Ford's son, Edsel—made the moving line into a way of life, timing every step with

DAVID KENNEDY, historian, Stanford University: "To be an assembly line worker you did not have to have a high degree of skill, you didn't have to be a card-carrying machinist or whatever, all you had to do was learn how to turn the same wrench on the same bolt, the same nut 5,000 times a day."

WHERE IT HAD ONCE TAKEN 12 HOURS AND 30 MINUTES TO BUILD A MODEL T, NOW IT TOOK JUST 90 MINUTES, AND THAT TIME WAS DROPPING STEADILY.

a stopwatch and regularizing the entire process. Everything would now be done on the same floor, with subassembly lines feeding into the main one.

The advance in production was stunning. Where it had once taken 12 hours and 30 minutes to build a Model T, now it took just 90 minutes, and that time was dropping steadily. Before long, Ford was producing half the cars in America with just 13,000 workers; the rest of the industry employed a total of 66,000 men. Ford sold just under 200,000 vehicles in 1913, and the base price per car dropped to $550, then to $440, then to $360 in 1915, and finally to $290 before the Model T was retired, in 1927.

Attracting—and retaining—the workers necessary to make this happen, however, was a problem. Turnover was high, with many employees leaving after just three months—all they could take on the monotonous assembly line. Ford's response was the $5 a day wage. Within three years, the $5 wage had become the industry standard. Ford even extended it to the few females in his company, an unrivaled salary for the many American working women.

The automaker was now one of the most revered men in America. This adulation confirmed Ford's always robust self-confidence—a trait that would eventually edge into egomania. Along with his new wage scale, Ford also endowed his employees with unheard-of benefits, including sick leave, health insurance, a company bank, free legal advice, and a lunch break. To reap such perquisites, however, Ford's employees had to submit to the intrusions of his new Sociological Department. Set up under the supervision of a well-intentioned minister, the department's investigators were soon visiting workers in their homes, quizzing them about their health, drinking habits, and marital status. Any sign of "unwholesome" behavior could mean probation. A failure to reform meant termination.

Yet to the public Henry Ford remained something akin to a god—and with good reason. Ford cars reinvented not only the American workplace but also American culture. Had the average person in any country, anywhere, ever been able to acquire something so personally empowering as *a car*? Long lines of Model Ts soon filled the Main Streets of American cities. When asked why she owned a car but not a bathtub, one woman supposedly replied, "You can't go to town in a bathtub!"

Ford altered the entire American economy. In 1900, of the 4,192 cars that had been made in the U.S., 78 percent were powered by either steam or electricity. But the advent of the Ford Motor Company came about at roughly the same time that the Spindletop strike drove the price of oil down from $2 a barrel to just *three cents* a barrel—cheaper than water in many places.

Ford cars would run on a synthesized oil product that would become known as gasoline. The overwhelming success of his third auto company ensured that all American cars, and virtually all cars in the world, would be powered by oil.

And just as Detroit and its surrounding cities and towns would be built by the auto industry, there was a new city on the West Coast that would come to run on oil. It was Los Angeles—no more than a sleepy village in Southern California a few years before the twentieth century began. But if it was to run on oil, it would also need water.

JUST TEN EASY PAYMENTS!

THE MAKING OF FORD DEALERSHIPS

In addition to all he did to design, test, and publicize his automobiles, Henry Ford also started a revolutionary franchise system, one that eventually put a Ford dealership in every city in North America and in major cities on six continents. The first franchise was started by William Hughson, the head of a machinery parts company, who opened a San Francisco lot in 1903 with 12 pre–Model T Fords. For three years, no one bought a car, and Hughson's business was then destroyed in the 1906 earthquake. But potential customers saw how well Fords operated in the rubble left behind by the quake, and the dealership was revived—and lasted into the 1970s.

In 1915, Roscoe Sheller began work at the Ford dealership in his little town of Sunnyside, Washington. His boss and friend, Bob Barnett, picked him up one morning, and on the way to the dealership Barnett taught Sheller to drive, although not before cracking his own head against the windshield and watching Sheller nearly veer off the road.

The two men failed to sell a single car during their first winter in business, and Barnett quit in frustration. Sheller found that teaching customers to drive was dangerous. "It seemed to me that I was spending about as much time in fields that bordered our rutted wagon roads as on them because of the unscheduled, cavorting expeditions through fences, over flumes and ditches, or wherever some iron-muscled, strong-willed driving student pointed the Model T," complained Sheller.

Nonetheless, on a single day in 1917, Sheller sold five Fords, and he knew the car was here to stay.

Model Ts became such a fixture of the American landscape that jokes about them proliferated. Comedians told of a Texan who had to abandon his Ford to escape Mexican bandits. They torched it, but when he came back for the car, it still started.

Henry Ford claimed to like the jokes as publicity, telling reporters: "The jokes about my car sure helped to popularize it. I hope they never end." But for many young Americans, such as the longtime *New Yorker* writer E. B. White, the car was not a joke at all, but a new kind of freedom: "Youth, I have no doubt, will always recognize its own frontier and push beyond it by whatever means are at hand. As for me, I've always been glad that mine was a two-track road running across the prairie into the sinking sun, and underneath me a slow-motion roadster of miraculous design—strong, tremulous, and tireless, from sea to shining sea."

CALIFORNIA
The Cornucopia of the World
ROOM
FOR
MILLIONS
OF
IMMIGRANTS
43.795.000.
ACRES
OF GOVERNMENT LANDS
UNTAKEN
Railroad & Private Land for a Million Farmers
A CLIMATE FOR HEALTH & WEALTH
WITHOUT CYCLONES
OR BLIZZARDS.
RAND MCNALLY & CO

1846
TO
1954

A POWERFUL THIRST

INVENTING LOS ANGELES

At the time of the Mexican-American War, in the late 1840s, Los Angeles was a mission town of about 1,600 whites and Indians, an oasis on the edge of a desert, made possible by the unassuming Los Angeles River. Unlike San Francisco, it had no harbor and was not close to any goldfields. Local rainfall averaged only 15 inches a year.

Then, beginning in 1882, the town was struck by a series of human tornadoes, itinerant adventurers who had wandered through much of America in search of a fortune and grabbed onto its very last opportunity. The first was Harrison Gray Otis, who bought a pair of tiny papers, the *Los Angeles Times* and the *Mirror*. Next was Harry Chandler, who had come west to heal his lungs after diving into a vat of starch as part of a college stunt. Working as a fruit picker, he saved up $3,000, which he used to buy the city's newspaper-circulation routes. Chandler married Otis's daughter, bought the *Times*'s printing plant, and helped put its main rival out of business. A newspaper dynasty was born.

Ambitious, authoritarian, and ruthless, Otis and Chandler were rabidly anti-union, organizing boycotts of all employers who dared to allow their workers to organize. They set Los Angeles on a path of continual conflict that culminated in the *Times* building's being dynamited by a pair of militant unionists in 1910, with a loss of 21 lives. But the two men were also relentless and savvy boosters of their adopted town. They pitched the city's near-perfect weather and coastal breezes to Midwesterners who had, for the first time, acquired enough wealth to be able to consider retiring to paradise.

By 1900, Los Angeles was "the best advertised city in the country," and its population was over 100,000. But not even Otis and Chandler could manufacture water to order. That would be up to another force of nature, the head of the city's new Department of Water and Power. William Mulholland was a blunt, pithy, hard-drinking Irishman, born in Belfast and raised in Dublin before coming to the United States as a young man. He had walked across the Isthmus of Panama, unable to afford the train fare. When he reached L.A. in 1877, it was still a little burg of just 9,000, and he decided to go back to the sea. On his way to take ship at the California port of San Pedro, though, he accepted a job digging a well.

Soon Mulholland was working at the privately owned Los Angeles Water Company, initially as a ditch cleaner. Within eight years, he had made himself an engineer and risen to the position of superintendent. When the city decided to take over its ramshackle water system, Mulholland was kept on as its chief. Honest and hardworking, he seemed to grasp the urgency of the situation. "The city is condemned to grow," he liked to say—but only if it got water: "If Los Angeles runs out of water for one week, the city within a year will not have a population of 100,000 people.... A city quickly finds its level and that level is its water supply."

But where to turn? All the land in sight looked to be even drier than the city itself. Mulholland's old boss at the water company, Frederick Eaton, thought he had a solution. Eaton's father had founded

To promote itself, Los Angeles hired a doctor to tell tuberculosis patients it was "the Italy of America." A special train toted about a "California on Wheels" exhibit distributing pamphlets with titles such as "Land of Heart's Desire" and "Land of Promise."

Pasadena, and at 14, Frederick had submitted the winning plans for L.A.'s city plaza. Turning politician, he got himself elected mayor of Los Angeles in 1898 and persuaded the local officials to buy up his old water company for $2 million. However, Eaton was much more interested in land over 225 miles out of town, in a high mountain vale known as Owens Valley, whose residents liked to call it "the Switzerland of California." Fed by mountain glaciers and the occasional storms that crept in through a pass in the mountains, the Owens River had been blocked from continuing down into the Southern California flatlands by a prehistoric lava flow.

Eaton and Mulholland began to make their way methodically through the valley, determining just what land they needed to acquire. Eaton purchased much of it with $30,000 of his own money, including the one good site for a dam. On July 27, 1905, Mulholland reported to the L.A. Board of Engineers, "The last spike is driven...the options are secure." Two days later, those irrepressible newspapermen Otis and Chandler let the cat out of the bag with the *Los Angeles Times* headline TITANIC PROJECT TO GIVE CITY A RIVER.

Mulholland then assembled a crew of 3,900 men—mostly Mexicans, Greeks, Bulgarians, Serbs, Montenegrins, and Swiss immigrants—to build a system across 230 miles of near-desert, bringing the water down at last from where it had been blocked by the ancient volcano. The aqueduct would follow a natural decline of 4,000 feet from the valley to the city, but getting it there was still an epic construction project. Mulholland's men laid 215 miles of road, planted 218 miles of power lines, and strung 377 miles of telegraph and telephone line. Ninety-eight miles of covered conduit were constructed, some of them wide enough to drive a car through. Most impressive of all were the 142 tunnels—43 miles in all—blasted out with six million pounds of powder and filled with the latest electrical equipment.

"This rude platform is an altar, and on it we are here consecrating this water supply and dedicating the Aqueduct to you and your children and your children's children—for all time," Mulholland told a crowd of 30,000 to 40,000 who showed up for the dedication ceremony on November 5, 1913. Mulholland, who had worked himself to exhaustion supervising every inch of the project's construction, then unfurled an American flag as the aqueduct's waters were unleashed into a canal, and told the mayor of Los Angeles, "There it is, Mr. Mayor. Take it."

The most telling aspect of that dedication ceremony was its location. The "altar" was at a reservoir in the San Fernando Valley, miles from downtown Los Angeles. Mulholland had predicted that by the day the aqueduct opened, L.A. would have a population of 260,000. In fact, it was 485,000, spurred by the development of a fledgling entertainment industry called "the movies," which had previously shot its films around the New York area but had discovered that California's long stretches of perfect weather could save it a fortune in production costs.

Yet somehow, despite this enormous, unanticipated growth, Los Angeles had yet to experience a water shortage. What was all the extra water for, then? Well, the future—the very near future. Chandler had begun to pump the mysterious "fertility" of the completely arid San Fernando Valley in the

Los Angeles Times, and it had already begun to leak out that much of the area had been bought up by a syndicate of the city's wealthiest and most powerful citizens. The aqueduct would not only allow L.A. to survive, it had also become the key to another land scheme—and one that set in stone the sprawling, car-dependent nature of the city, covering by far the largest physical area of any metropolis in the U.S.

By 1922, the population of Los Angeles was over one million, and the city was growing 11 times faster than New York was. Both L.A. and Owens Valley were now running seriously low on water, a problem exacerbated by the fact that the city's water system still lacked a dam and a storage reservoir to control the Owens River above the aqueduct intake. Eaton had made sure to buy up the one site suited for such utilities—but he wanted $1 million for it. Mulholland refused to give up the taxpayers' money to this extortion. Instead, the Department of Water and Power tried to maximize its Owens Valley holdings by purchasing still more land, pumping out groundwater, and buying options on the valley's main irrigation canal.

The valley's residents were desperate now. Farmers began illegally diverting water from the canal. Then, on the night of May 21, 1924, Tom Spratt and his nephew Lew, who worked as security guards at the Lone Pine aqueduct spillway, looked up from their nightly card game to find themselves facing a group of 40 armed men. The vigilantes cut the phone lines to the guard hut and politely led the Spratts away from their post at gunpoint, telling them: "We'll take you for a walk. There is going to be a dynamiting here." They then proceeded to expertly blow out 450 feet of iron pipe, before disappearing back into the night.

The dynamite attack caused $50,000 to $75,000 of damage and wasted almost 163 million gallons of water before the Spratts could drive the ten miles to

J. B. Lippincott, California manager of the new U.S. Reclamation Services, helped Eaton and Mulholland turn over Owens Valley's water in exchange for a well-paid consulting job.

BY 1922, THE POPULATION OF LOS ANGELES WAS OVER ONE MILLION, AND THE CITY WAS GROWING 11 TIMES FASTER THAN NEW YORK WAS.

get help. Its effects were not felt by Los Angeles homeowners, but it sent shock waves through the city's political establishment. Los Angeles decided to negotiate at first, offering to help promote the construction of a state highway to Owens Valley that would give the area a tourist industry. Valley residents refused. Led by a pair of local bankers, Mark and Wilfred Watterson, the residents demanded that the city purchase all the farmland it had made untenable and compensate everyone in the valley for their losses. To bring home their demands, Mark Watterson led 60 to 100 men to occupy the Alabama Gates, where they closed the aqueduct by opening an emergency spillway. A crowd of 700—including reporters from around the world—showed up to see "the Owens Valley War."

The trouble would continue for another three years. By 1927, there had been ten more dynamite attacks. Negotiations stalled; Mulholland received hundreds of threatening letters. In response, he sent deputies armed with machine guns and orders of "shoot to kill" to guard the aqueduct.

Then it was over. The Wattersons' banks collapsed, and they were indicted for embezzlement. Owens Valley was left completely destitute, the alkaline residue of its dry lake bed creating some of the worst air pollution in the country.

Mulholland, meanwhile, had decided to create his own storage reservoir, the St. Francis Dam, 40 miles north of L.A. It was built into the side of a canyon, and in March of 1928 it began to leak brown water—a clear indication that the canyon walls were on the verge of collapse. Mulholland went to inspect the dam, and found nothing wrong. Just hours later, on March 12, 1928, the dam gave way, killing 450 people and covering much of Ventura County in muck. It was one of the worst peacetime disasters in U.S. history, and a shaken Mulholland accepted full responsibility and resigned.

His old friend Eaton was finally able to sell his dam site to the Department of Water and Power. But he got only $650,000 for it—not enough, apparently, to recoup the losses he sustained—most of his assets—when the Wattersons' banks collapsed. He would live out his last years with his son, and died a bankrupt. But the city he and Mulholland had made would continue to be "condemned to grow," its political power and its water monopoly allowing it to absorb one suburb after another, expanding across mountains and valleys. It would become an unending cycle of acquisition and need, as "the water octopus of Los Angeles"—as the *Los Angeles Times* called it—extended its tentacles farther and farther in search of yet more water. It would reach 600 miles to the Feather River, then hundreds of miles more to a new dam the federal government was building on the Colorado River—a project that would give birth to still more sprawling desert cities in L.A.'s image, including Phoenix and Tucson in Arizona and Las Vegas in Nevada.

By 1954, the 2.3 million cars owned by Angelenos would form the greatest concentration of motor vehicles in the world. As *Time* magazine reported in 1970, "The Apollo 10 astronauts could see Los Angeles as a cancerous smudge from 25,000 miles in outer space."

Angelenos turn out to witness the dedication of their city's new aqueduct in 1913. Forty-three men died building it. But as William Mulholland said, "Whoever brings the water brings the people."

AL CAMARILLO, historian, Stanford University:
"One could argue that L.A. could not have developed the way it did without the aqueduct Mullholland built to bring water to the area."

USS QUISTCONCK

1914
TO
1919

WORLD WAR WON

THE U.S. EMERGES AS A WORLD POWER

Oil would rule, and its power would be demonstrated as never before during World War I, when the United States—by then the largest oil producer in the world—supplied a British Royal Navy that First Lord of the Admiralty Winston Churchill had converted from coal. The reasons for the switch were compelling: Ships accelerated faster and ran longer on oil, and they could be refueled at sea, eliminating their dependence upon networks of coaling stations around the world. Oil also helped draw the U.S. into the war, when its desire to keep dealing with Britain and France, its leading European trading partners, conflicted with Germany's attempts to cut off Allied shipping with a cordon of U-boats. It was the first U.S. involvement in a European conflict, one that led to more than 116,000 American deaths.

The war would also prove to be a windfall. At the outbreak of the fighting, the U.S. economy had been the largest in the world for nearly 40 years. It produced over one-third of all the world's goods and services—more than Great Britain, France, and Germany *combined*. Yet it was a predominance founded on foreign capital. Then, in the first three years of World War I, America went from being the world's leading debtor nation to being its largest—and *only*—creditor. Corporate profits tripled over the duration of the conflict, creating 42,000 new millionaires in the U.S.

For all its terrible deaths, the U.S. suffered nothing like the losses seen all over Europe, where a generation of young men was effectively destroyed. But faced with its first opportunity at global primacy, the United States...stepped back. The shortcomings of the Versailles Conference shattered Americans' illusions that they had been fighting a "war to end all wars." Their refusal to join the fledgling postwar effort at collective security, the League of Nations, likewise shattered their idealistic president, Woodrow Wilson, who sacrificed his health trying to sell the idea.

The great disillusionment stirred up a brace of fears and reactions that had been stewing for decades. Nearly all of this was directed against immigrants, people of color, union activists, and radicals—anyone and everyone who was perceived as less than truly "American."

Above: A doughboy of the New York 71st Regiment bids good-bye to his sweetheart before leaving for basic training.

Opposite: President and Mrs. Wilson christen the USS *Quistconck*.

1917 TO 1924

BRINGING THE WAR HOME

THE MODERNIZATION OF AMERICAN LIFE

World War I interrupted the almost constant, 70-year flow of large immigrant populations to the United States. The fight against Germany and then the rise of the Soviet Union had led to paroxysms of xenophobia unmatched in the U.S. since the anti-immigrant Know Nothing movement of the 1850s. Foreigners were suspected of being spies or radicals (or both), and a national vigilante group, the American Protective League, formed to root them out. Mobs attacked, beat, and even killed individuals for such offenses as refusing to kiss the flag, while leading leftists who had spoken out against the war—including the socialists Eugene V. Debs and Victor Berger—received prison sentences of 20 years or more. Publications deemed to be radical or seditious by the U.S. Post Office were confiscated, while teachers and other public employees were forced to swear loyalty oaths.

The nation's first Red Scare kicked off with a series of actions against suspected subversives and illegal immigrants—organized by a 24-year-old federal bureaucrat named J. Edgar Hoover, who had compiled the names of 150,000 targets. In December of 1919 and January of 1920, raids across the nation arrested 10,000 of the individuals on Hoover's list, including 4,000 of them in a single night. Some 556 people were deported, including the leading anarchists Emma Goldman and Alexander Berkman.

From the old textile mills of Lawrence, Massachusetts, to the steel mills of Pennsylvania, Ohio, and Indiana, to the shipyards of Seattle, Washington, unions in every industrial field were summarily smashed, usually with small armies of hired goons and Pinkerton detectives. Mine owners looking to finish a violent labor fight in the West Virginia coalfields even resorted to dropping primitive aerial bombs on their striking employees.

Independent labor organizations were replaced with farcical "company unions," under a system called, significantly, the American Plan. Congress finally obliged the long-standing nativist urge by passing draconian immigration laws in 1924 that drastically limited all immigration—but particularly restricted arrivals from non-"Nordic" nations.

Much to the dismay of the predominantly rural, reactionary elements that had spawned this legislation, the immigrant flow was replaced by the greatest internal migration in the nation's history. Whether or not they had seen *Paree*, it proved impossible to keep 'em down on the farm. Over 2,000 men and women *a week* moved to New York in the 1920s, swelling that city's population to over seven million by the end of the decade. More than ever before—fleeing the Ku Klux Klan and Prohibition, Babbittry and fundamentalism—the best and the brightest, the wittiest and the most alienated, the most talented and the most nakedly ambitious all came to the big city.

They created an intellectual ferment that made urban America the most creative and dynamic place on the planet in the 1920s. New industries and new ways of thinking seemed to be invented daily—in good part because there was a new mix of peoples in American cities that had never quite been seen before.

An early American Communist Party pamphlet. Official repression and sectarian fissures kept the Communists from ever approaching the following of other radical parties in the U.S. More-militant anarchist groups were probably behind the bombs that killed 38 people on Wall Street in 1920 and nearly assassinated the U.S. attorney general.

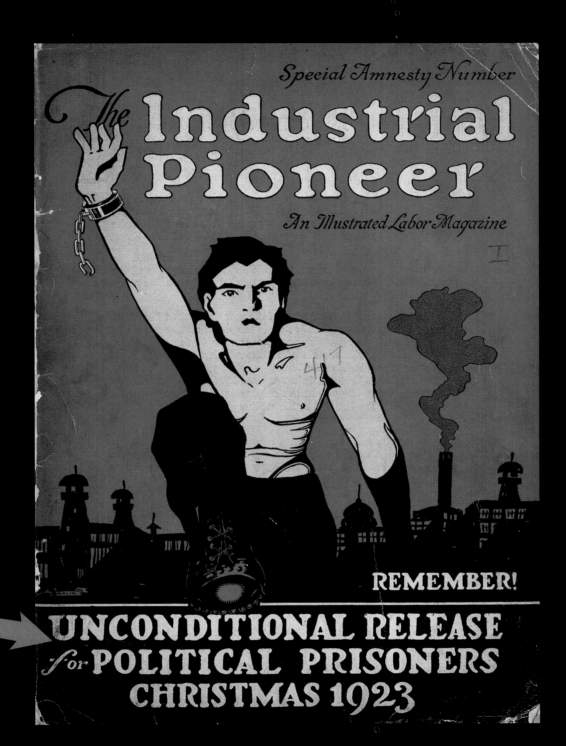

Special Amnesty Number

The Industrial Pioneer

An Illustrated Labor Magazine

REMEMBER!

UNCONDITIONAL RELEASE for POLITICAL PRISONERS CHRISTMAS 1923

1890
TO
1930

"I'D RATHER BE A LAMPPOST IN HARLEM..."

THE GREAT BLACK MIGRATIONS

From 1916 to 1930, over a million African-Americans fled from the South to Northern and Western cities. In 1890, only one in every 70 New Yorkers was a black person. By 1930, one in every nine was. The vast majority of them settled in Harlem, a community of vibrancy and accomplishment, where black people owned an unprecedented $60 million of property.

"I'd rather be a lamppost in Harlem than the governor of Georgia," the black migrants told one another.

Their neighborhood was soon called the Negro Capital of the World, but it was not without rivals. The black populations in other cities and districts, such as Cleveland, Chicago's South Side, and Detroit's Paradise Valley, saw even greater percentage increases. These people had come originally for new, war-related jobs; in 1910, annual wages still averaged only $376 in the South—less than one-third of the national average—and African-Americans were generally paid much less. Racial prejudice seemed to be increasing, not fading away. There were 40 major race riots—white-on-black riots—across the South from 1898 to 1908, as well as disturbances in Illinois, Ohio, Indiana, and New York. Lynchings—sadistic, orgiastic rituals often joined in by much of the white community—reached a high of 161 in 1892. A horrific outburst in East St. Louis, Illinois, in 1917, during which police joined rampaging white mobs, left 40 blacks and nine whites dead, and included terrible acts of mutilation and arson.

It was only a taste of things to come. During what the writer and activist James Weldon Johnson would label the Red Summer of 1919, returning African-American soldiers were greeted with a renewed campaign of lynchings and church burnings. Blacks raced for the North in segregated railcars that integrated as soon as they crossed the Mason-Dixon Line. At first the Northern cities seemed delightfully open, without the segregationist Jim Crow laws of the South. African-Americans reveled in the freedom to send their children to the same decent public schools that white children attended, and to sit where they wanted on streetcars and in restaurants. Above all, they exulted in the opportunity to better themselves, to get work that might provide more than a bare subsistence. For many, the immediate goal was the Ford plants in Michigan, which had become a paragon of workplace equality in America.

From the start of World War I to the end of the 1920s, over one-third of all black Americans migrating out of the South headed for Detroit, most of them settling in the city's Black Bottom and Paradise Valley districts, and often working at Ford. Originally, the company had lagged in hiring black workers; by 1916, it employed only 50 people of color, even though the automaker's total workforce had expanded to more than 32,000. This was to change rapidly. Influenced by a black cleric, Reverend Robert L. Bradby of Detroit's Second Baptist Church, Henry Ford was employing over 10,000 black workers a decade later—more than 10 percent of the Ford workforce and over one-half of all blacks employed in automaking.

The relative equality of blacks at Ford would carry over to the United Auto Workers and produce a black labor and political leadership unmatched anywhere else in the country. By 1967, a higher percentage of

A group of black migrant farm workers, on their way to Shawboro, North Carolina, to pick potatoes in Cranberry, New Jersey. Many more African-Americans left the South for good.

THE OFFICIAL DEATH TOLL FROM THE TULSA RIOT WAS 39. BUT SECRET MASS GRAVES MAY CONTAIN UP TO 3,000 MURDERED AFRICAN-AMERICANS.

S ON WAY TO
N HALL - DURING TULSA RACE RIOT
JUNE 1st 1921.

African-Americans owned their own homes in Detroit than in any other American city. The art and music communities of the city's Black Bottom district would come to rival Harlem's, their spirit of marvelous innovation reaching all the way through Motown and beyond.

At the same time, the rising number of black Detroit citizens stirred a vicious backlash. During the 1920s, there were over 40,000 Klansmen in Detroit, and a Klan candidate for mayor was nearly elected by way of a write-in campaign.

There were 25 major race riots in the country before the summer of 1919 was over. Nor would things stop there. Two years later, in Tulsa, Oklahoma, a black teenager found himself accused of molesting, in some never articulated way, a young white woman in the elevator of a downtown hotel. The accusation served as excuse enough for white citizens to launch a full-scale assault upon the town's prosperous black neighborhood of Greenwood, egged on by newspaper headlines such as TO LYNCH NEGRO TONIGHT. An armed mob of over 5,000 white men invaded Greenwood, in an attack that included six biplanes swooping in to fire on black citizens and drop crude firebombs on their homes and businesses. Before it was over, 35 blocks of Greenwood had been burned, leaving 10,000 people homeless.

The Red Summer coincided with a massive revival of the Ku Klux Klan, one sparked by the romanticization of the group's first incarnation in such works as D. W. Griffith's groundbreaking 1915 film, *Birth of a Nation*. The KKK was no longer just a Southern organization, it was a national movement. In the years just after World War I, the Klan "enrolled more members in Connecticut than in Mississippi, more in Oregon than in Louisiana, and more in New Jersey than in Alabama," according to the historian Stanley Coben. Klan political organizations virtually took over the state governments of Oklahoma, Oregon, and Indiana.

As the Klan spread out from the South, its grievances increased proportionately. The preoccupation with race was often supplanted by vehement campaigns against Jews, Catholics, "foreigners," and modernity in general. And as the fertile mind of Henry Ford slid into nostalgic paranoia, he funded the anti-Semitic weekly *The Dearborn Independent*.

To a modern observer, the most confusing of all the American political crosscurrents of the 1920s is surely the Klan's adamant support for suffrage. The Klan was as patriarchal as the next American institution, but giving women the right to vote meant a chance to institute the most radical social experiment in the nation's history: Prohibition. Like radicalism, unionism, Roman Catholicism, and subversion, alcohol had become inextricably linked in many American minds with shady foreigners. But as it turned out, getting women the vote wasn't even necessary. Enough Americans—enough of them, at least, in key positions of power—were already willing to believe that keeping people from their booze would transform the world.

Members of the Ku Klux Klan taking the oath at an initiation, 1923.

REVEREND AL SHARPTON: "The denial c white privilege clashing with the ambition of blacks looking for the promised land inevitab lead to an explosion."

A CONTENTIOUS DEMOCRACY: SOCIAL CONFLICT, 1900 TO 1930

n the first decades of the twentieth century, American ocial and political conflicts routinely turned violent. hese battles revolved around race, immigration, and abor. There were at least 1,886 recorded lynchings in his period, the vast majority of the victims black men ttacked by white mobs in the South. From 1898 to 908 alone, there were 40 major race riots—all white-on-black—in the South, and disturbances in Illinois, Ohio, Indiana, and New York.

Between 1881 and 1905 alone, there were over 37,000 abor strikes in the United States, many of them rou-inely suppressed with clubbings, shootings, jailings, lacklistings, and executions, perpetrated not only by vell-armed legions of company goons but also by police, leputies, National Guardsmen, and regular soldiers. Even without such conflicts, almost a hundred American vorkers a day died in industrial accidents.

Anarchists and radical unionists such as the Interna-ional Workers of the World (IWW, also known at the Nobblies) fought back, sometimes with dynamite, blow-ng up seven Chicago policemen, the *Los Angeles Times* building, and the governor of Idaho on various occasions between 1886 and 1910. A bomb left on Wall Street in 920 killed 38—the worst terror attack in the United States before the Oklahoma City bombing in 1995. The culprits were never found, but such incidents led to vaves of police and FBI raids, mass deportations of sus-bected radicals, and ultimately the first sweeping re-trictions on immigration in 1924.

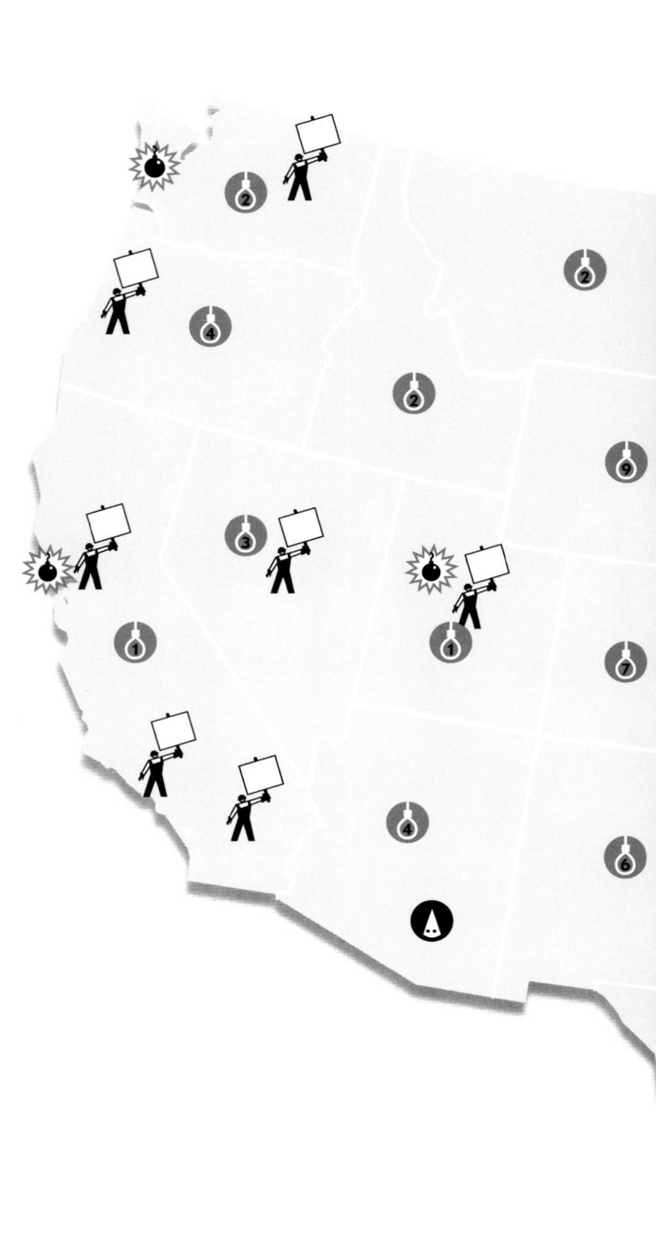

5
3
1
1
3
3
13
8
5
1
8
41
68
13
26
1
6
48
76
35
127
71
285
132
302
201
172
29
Strike
Bombing
Race Riot
Number of lynchings throughout state from 1900 to 1930

1840
TO
1920

THE REPOSITORY OF EVERY URBAN NIGHTMARE

THE TEMPERANCE CRUSADE

The roots of Prohibition, and of the Temperance Movement, went back at least 80 years, and were anchored in at least some genuine concerns about Americans' prodigious drinking. "We found intoxicating liquor used by everybody, repudiated by nobody," a young Abe Lincoln reported about Illinois. "It commonly entered into the first draught of an infant, and the last thought of the dying man."

Americans' level of imbibing inspired any number of personal and organizational campaigns against the demon rum, from Carrie Nation's hatchet attacks on bars to the decades-long battles of Frances Willard's National Woman's Christian Temperance Union. The latter, founded in 1874, had grown out of the Woman's Crusade, a movement in which women would drop to their knees and pray outside saloons and liquor stores.

FRANCES WILLARD

By the turn of the century, the consumption of hard liquor had dropped off to about what it is today. This was primarily because whiskey had been replaced by a substance that temperance crusaders considered to be still more pernicious. From 1850 to 1890, American consumption of beer rose from 36 million gallons a year to 855 million. This might have been considered an improvement, but beer's popularity reflected the steady rise in immigrants, many of whom were excellent brewers. And beer was served mainly in "the saloon," a murky, all-male preserve—"a black hole," as the historian Tyler Anbinder would write in another context, "into which every urban nightmare and unspeakable fear could be projected." It was a place where women were not permitted and foreign men might plot with ease.

The leading advocate for banning the sale of alcohol became the Anti-Saloon League (ASL), founded by a skillful attorney and strategist named Wayne Wheeler. Wheeler, much like Karl Rove decades later, was a saavy political operator able to mobilize the grassroots, while consulting closely with Washington politicians. Beginning in the ASL's Ohio office at the turn of the century, Wheeler gathered all the scattered strands of the Temperance Movement and wove them into an irresistible political force. He scared up enormous sums of money from the many wealthy men who felt that their own abstemious habits were the key to their success. Henry Ford and the steel magnate Henry Clay Frick—both of whom tried to stop their employees from drinking on *or* off the job—also chipped in.

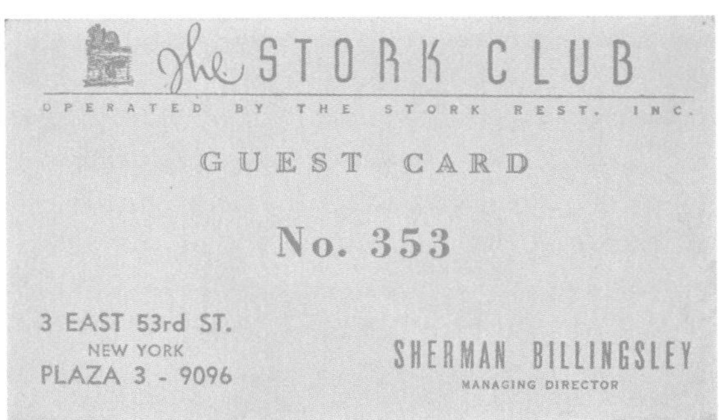

In the 1916 national election, the so-called drys won every statewide referendum, and candidates supported by the ASL swept the field. The Congress that Wheeler had got elected duly passed the Eighteenth Amendment—banning "the manufacture, sale, or transportation of intoxicating liquors"—by overwhelming margins. It was the first and only amendment to the Constitution to curtail personal freedom, and it would be treated accordingly. Many of its most fervent advocates did not believe it applied to them, most of its targets were bitterly resentful of the intrusion into their personal habits, and nobody wanted to pay to enforce it. "The drys have their law, and the wets have their liquor," went a popular saying, and so it was.

Americans smuggled liquor into the country by boat and by plane, by the carful and the trainful. They stomped and fermented their own wine in a million basements, mixed their own gin in a million bathtubs. They souped up their cars to outrun revenue agents, torqued up sharp little "cigarette boats" to outrun Coast Guard cutters.

Many state and local governments disdained enforcing the law at all. In New York City, there were at least 32,000 speakeasies, blind tigers, "drugstores," or other illegal drinking establishments; there may have been as many as half a million throughout the country. They were almost always let alone, as long as they made their payoffs to the local constabulary. This was the corrosive effect of Prohibition

The temperance crusaders had blasted open the dark, suspicious, all-male preserve of the saloon. Now young women in unprecedented numbers joined men in drinking at "speaks." Illegal and unregulated, bootleg booze might contain any number of nasty surprises. According to one statistic, alcohol poisonings increased from 1,064 in 1920 to 4,154 in 1925. Many thousands more were permanently crippled or blinded by wood alcohol and "jake," the slang name for a Jamaican ginger extract.

Worst of all, Prohibition would finance a generation of gangsters, and enable the rise of the Italian-American crime syndicates that came to be known as the Mafia.

Member cards for speakeasies. Some, such as New York's '21' or the Stork Club (above, left) became world famous.

1899 TO 1929

THE GANGSTER AS CAPITALIST

THE RISE OF AL CAPONE

By 1919, Alphonse Capone, barely 20, had already committed his first two murders, participated in innumerable thefts and shakedowns, and received, in an altercation over a woman, the long mark on his left cheek that would give him his famous nickname: Scarface. He had moved to Chicago from Brooklyn, and his mentor there, John "Papa Johnny" Torrio, took him in again—teaching him how to control his volcanic temper, listen to opera, dress well, and think like a businessman. It was Torrio, more than anyone, who put the organization into organized crime, both in Chicago and in New York. He saw the immense opportunity that Prohibition offered.

Torrio proposed his plan to the rainbow coalition of Chicago's criminal gangs: the Irish, the Poles, and his fellow Italians—they would all take a piece. Torrio and Capone's franchise on the South Side received the biggest cut, but that seemed only fair, since they had the biggest operation. Estimates about just how much money there was to be made in illicit liquor varied wildly, but a conservative estimate seems to have been $30 million a year. Torrio thought there was more than enough to go around, but he would have a hard time convincing his fellow gangsters, volatile men unaccustomed to accepting limits on anything.

Deany O'Banion, leader of a North Side gang, refused to play ball and instead had Torrio set up for a police raid and arrest, something he thought was a grand joke. Torrio showed his appreciation for it by having Deany whacked. O'Banion's esteemed colleagues retaliated by shooting Torrio in the street. Hit five times, Torrio miraculously survived, and returned to New York to spread the gangland gospel, counseling Charles "Lucky" Luciano and then the Genovese crime family in the ways of building criminal syndicates. He left Chicago to Capone, his protégé.

Capone inherited a wide-open town. Cops, judges, elected officials—it seemed that everyone in Chicago was on the take in the 1920s, their standard salute the extended hand, palm up. Of the more than 300 known gangland murders in the Windy City over the course of that decade, *none* were solved. Capone, meanwhile, made himself a veritable expert at public relations. He merely "supplied a legitimate demand," he insisted. "Some call it bootlegging. Some call it racketeering. I call it a business. They say I violate the prohibition law. Who doesn't?"

But the clamor for action against Capone finally grew too loud to ignore on February 14, 1929, when his gunsels, disguised in police uniforms, slaughtered five goons of the Bugs Moran gang and two relatively innocent bystanders. The St. Valentine's Day Massacre, as it would go down in gangland lore and gore, sent a delegation of Chicago's leading citizens to Washington, begging the feds to get involved. President Herbert Hoover, in his cabinet's morning exercise routine, pushed a medicine ball over to his attorney general every day and asked, "Have you got that fellow Capone yet?"

The most famous strategy was employed by a young Prohibition agent, Eliot Ness, who led his band of nine plucky Untouchables on flashy raids against liquor caches belonging to Capone and others. But the Untouchables never came all that close to touching Capone himself. The real spadework was done by the world's first forensic accountants. Capone was facing every American's worst nightmare: a relentless tax audit. It was news to most people—and to Al—that

THREE CENTS

THE CHICAGO DAILY NEWS

BLUE STREAK

YEAR—39. THURSDAY, FEBRUARY 14, 1929.—FORTY-EIGHT PAGES. FINAL EDITION

MASSACRE 7 OF MORAN GANG

HAFFA CHANGES HIS MIND; WILL FIGHT PRISON

Tells It to Friends. He Goes; Makes Bond, Prepares Appeal.

STAY IN COUNCIL

TWO OF VICTIMS AND SCENE OF LATEST GANGSTER OUTBREAK

KILLING SCENE TOO GRUESOME FOR ONLOOKERS

View of Carnage Proves a Strain on Their Nerves.

IS LIKE A SHAMBLES

It's too much to tell. You go into the door marked "S-M-C Cartage company." You see a bunch of big men talking with restrained excitement in the cigarette smoke. You go through another door back of the front office. You go between two close-parked trucks in the garage.

Then you almost stumble over the head of the first man, with a clean gray felt hat still placed at the ... angle of gangster toughness.

The dull yellow light of a ... daytime shows dark rivulets of blood heading down to the drain that ... meant for the water from ... cars. There are six of the red ... from six heads. The bodies—four of them well dressed in civilian cloth... —two of them with their legs ... as they wished to fall.

It's too much, so you crowd on past the roadster with bullet holes in it to the big truck behind.

Too Much for the Dog.

You look at the truck. It is something to look at because the men were fixing it. It's jacked up, with one wheel off. You look and the big man called "Commissioner" looks and a crowd gathers, and then it gets too much for the police dog you had failed to notice lying under the truck, tied to it by a cheap yellow rope.

It gets too much for the big brown and gray police dog and he goes crazy. He barks, he howls, he snarls, showing wicked white teeth in bright red gums.

The crowd backs away. The dog yowls once more and subsides.

Your thoughts snap with a crack back to the circle of yellow lamplight, where six things that were men are sprawled.

It's still too much. You push out into the fresh air.

Quiet in Mid-Morning.

You find that traffic was quiet in front of 2122 North Clark street at 10:30 o'clock this morning. A street-car rattled down the narrow way left by parked cars. Across from the high garage, two windows of one of those old-fashioned gray-stone apartment houses were open. Two women were exchanging go... despite the cold.

A blue and black sedan stopped in front of the garage. The women exchanged their curiosities about it and then went back to gossip.

They jumped as a muffled roar reached them. The blue and black car sped away and turned the corner.

VICTIMS ARE LINED AGAINST WALL; ONE VOLLEY KILLS ALL

Assassins Pose as Policemen; Flee in "Squad Car" After Fusillade; Capone Revenge for Murder of Lombardo, Officers Believe.

... were lined up against the ... at 2122 North Clark street ... them in police uniforms ... machine guns and sawed-... squad barked an ... the seventh three ...

... of a Mexican ... Capone-Lombardo ... was also the most ... land slaughters.

... were:

... gunman for the O'Banion ...

... of Peter. He died after ... talk, though conscious.

... side "alky" peddler.

MAY, JOHN, ... West Madison street, a $50-a-week mechanic, apparently killed to silence him.

CLARK, JOHN, brother-in-law of George ("Bugs") Moran, leader of the gang.

DAVIS, ARTHUR, west side racketeer.

FOSTER, FRANK, hoodlum.

War to Finish Russell's Plan

A hoodlum roundup unparalleled in Chicago's history—one that will far exceed the recent week-end wholesale arrests—was promised today by Police Commissioner William F. Russell the moment he looked upon the scene of the slaughter of six gangsters at 2122 North Clark street.

"It's war to the finish," the commissioner said. "I've never known of a challenge like this—the killers posing as policemen—but now that the challenge has been made it's accepted. We're going to make this the knell of gangdom in Chicago."

Immediately Commissioner Russell dispatched a runner to the city hall to send out a message on the police teletype to all ...

A second theory, advanced by federal prohibition agents, was that the massacre was perpetrated by a band of rum runners from Detroit and Ecorse to pay off the Moran gang for hi-jacking two truckloads of Chicago-bound Canadian whisky two weeks ago. This, the police agreed, would account for the boldness with which the killers operated.

Two other theories under consideration by the police are that the Moran gang and the Aiello clan, who have been working in harmony on the north side, may have fallen out with the Aiello gang, shooting first, and that today's slayings may have had some connection with the government conviction of Ald. Titus A. Haffa, in whose territory they operated. But little credence was given by the police to these theories.

The building at 2122 North Clark street, scene of the wholesale slaughter ...

STAYS GIVEN 2 OF 3 KILLERS DUE TO DIE TONIGHT

Shanks Faces the Electric Chair Alone; Seeks Sanity Test.

1929 FLAPPERS JUST EAT UP VALENTINES

Modern Greetings Take Line of Sandwich; Swains Spend $250,000 Here.

"I want a three-decker!" shouted a ...

DECIDE TO CUT COOK ADRIFT IN TAX TANGLE

Solons to Rush Laws to Avert Downstate Tieup; Aid County Later.

you could be nailed for tax evasion on income derived from doing illegal things.

Frank J. Wilson—a balding 42-year-old accountant with what one Capone biographer described as "cold eyes flinty behind wire-rim glasses"—found evidence of a sprawling criminal syndicate. By 1929, Capone's operation may have been taking in as much as $100 million a year. Much of this went right back out in protection money—an estimated $30 million in bribes and political cover.

Wilson was able to identify only a little over $1 million that Capone had made, meaning that he had cheated the government out of some $215,000 in back taxes—but it was enough for use in court. Capone was shipped off to serve a seven-year sentence in federal penitentiaries, his empire crumbling at his heels. Ravaged by syphilis, his mind also crumbled behind bars, and he emerged from prison in 1940 a feeble shell of his old self, dying of a stroke before he reached 50.

Al Capone had been tripped up by the income tax designed to keep Rockefeller, Morgan, and the other robber barons in line. America was, by the time he went to jail, a different place, well into the worst economic depression in the nation's history. The wide-open 1920s were over, and malefactors of great wealth, everywhere, would now be called to account.

Victims of the St. Valentine's Day Massacre, February 14, 1929, a scene so gruesome it led one investigating detective to proclaim, "I've got more brains on my shoes than I do in my head!" Not long before, Capone had pleaded, "We're making a shooting gallery of a great business," but some people just wouldn't listen.

JAMES CLARK
ADAM HEYER
JOHN MAY

CHAPTER NINE

BUST

THE EMPIRE STATE BUILDING, 1944

1929
TO
1931

EMPIRE FALLS

THE SKYSCRAPER REACHES ITS ZENITH

On August 29, 1929, a large truck rumbled up the marble steps of Manhattan's Waldorf-Astoria hotel and through its front door, drove across the front lobby, and turned down the world-famous passageway known as Peacock Alley—where, not long before, crowds had gathered to gawk at the cream of international society as they promenaded in all their finery. The truck halted in front of a bunch of reporters and a pair of leading Wall Street financiers, John Jakob Raskob and James Riordan, the hotel's only occupants at the time. Out hopped a crew of stonemasons, armed with special handsaws, who set about taking down the fabled veined-marble pillars of Peacock Alley. The pillars, Raskob proudly informed the reporters, would be preserved at his country home in Maryland, a permanent memento of the fabulous Victorian pile that stood around them.

The Waldorf-Astoria was coming down. On its site, at Fifth Avenue and 34th Street, would rise the tallest, most awesome skyscraper anyone had ever seen, designed to soar 85 stories and over 1,050 feet from the pavement to the tip of its crowning spire. It would accommodate over 60,000 workers in its offices—more people in one building than there were in more than half the counties in the nation.

The Empire State Building, Raskob had dubbed it.

Fabulous new skyscrapers were popping up in Manhattan like toadstools after a rain. Even as the Empire State Building was announced, a race was already on to erect the tallest structure in the world—a contest between those raising the Gothic Bank of Manhattan Building downtown and the sumptuous, 77-story Art Deco Chrysler Building in midtown, probably the most beautiful skyscraper ever built, with its crown of lights, its hubcap friezes, and such stainless-steel ornaments as gigantic radiator caps and gargoyles in the shape of eagles. At the last moment, its architect, William Van Alen, won the race to the sky by smuggling in a 185-foot-high steel spire that nipped its downtown rival with 117 feet to spare.

Not for long. Goaded by a long rivalry with Walter Chrysler, Raskob announced that *his* new building would be taller still, and that it would have its own steel spire—and this one would not be merely ornamental but would also serve as a mooring mast for the sleek silver airships that now regularly transported wealthy passengers across the Atlantic.

The Empire State Building would be built in a bad location, in an area that had never been a central business district, but its proprietor was certain that it would soon be bringing in $55 million a year. There was just one little surprise at the beginning: When Raskob's stonemasons bit into the marble columns of Peacock Alley with their special saws, they were covered in plaster dust. The pillars were fakes, a cunning bit of trompe l'oeil that had gone undetected for decades. Underneath a fabulous paint job, there was no marble at all.

Only five of the 3,400 men who built the Empire State Building died, a superb safety record at the time, and they built an edifice sound enough to withstand an airforce bomber crashing into it in 1945.

1927 TO 1929

A SPY IN EVERY POT

THE BOOM YEARS

John Raskob was not the sort of man to be deterred by such an omen. He was a determined, fearless, and furiously optimistic businessman. He never went to college, but he had worked his way up from serving as the personal secretary of the chemical magnate Pierre du Pont to becoming the chief financial officer of DuPont and of General Motors.

After quitting GM, Raskob had gone on to run the Democratic Party and speculate on Wall Street. While working there, he gave an interview to *Ladies' Home Journal* in which he claimed that every American could become wealthy by investing just $15 a week in common stocks. The article—titled "Everybody Ought to Be Rich"—was on the newsstands even as he stood in the echoing emptiness of the Waldorf-Astoria, watching the plaster chips fly. Raskob believed every word of it.

And why not? The great bull market of the twenties just kept going up and up and up. By the end of August 1929, the New York Stock Exchange had reached a record high, having added one-quarter of its total value just that summer alone. The new president, Herbert Hoover, had privately expressed concerns about runaway speculation, but during his campaign the year before, he claimed, "We in America today are nearer to the final triumph over poverty than ever before in the history of any land."

The most cautious of men might reasonably conclude that even the sky was no longer the limit for America's mighty industrial machine. "For urban workers, prosperity was wondrous and real," wrote historian David Kennedy in *Freedom From Fear*. "They had more money than ever before, and they enjoyed an amazing variety of new products on which to spend it." President Hoover's campaign might have promised a chicken in every pot and a car in every garage, but there was also, it seemed, a toaster in every kitchen, an electric iron in every cupboard, a vacuum cleaner in every hall closet.

There were also 26 million cars on U.S. roads, more than one for every five Americans. In Detroit, Raskob's GM and Chrysler's motor company were flourishing. In 1927, Henry Ford took the Model T off the line, and returned to the start of the alphabet, producing a brand-new Model A. With his new car came a spectacular new plant. Moving just across Detroit's city line to suburban Dearborn, River Rouge was the largest and most advanced industrial complex in the world.

The River Rouge facility employed over 100,000 workers at times of peak production, and it was an international phenomenon. Vacationing Americans came to tour it. Newspapers, magazines, and newsreel crews from around the world came to report on it.

Yet all was far from well inside the factory gates, thanks to the company's increasingly unstable boss. Ford hated accountants, crowding them into smaller and smaller spaces, hoping to get them to quit. He fired as many sales managers as possible; the man who had once done his own advertising and marketing was now convinced his cars would sell on their merits alone. His Sociological Department was converted into the 3,000-man Service Department, devoted solely to spying on Ford workers and uncovering the outside threats that Ford was sure lay all around.

The conveyor belts of Ford's new River Rouge plant, artfully photographed by Charles Sheeler in 1927. The complex contained 19 factories and 93 buildings, many designed by architect Alfred Kahn.

IN THE 1920s, ONE IN EVERY FIVE AMERICANS TILLED THE SOIL, AND 44 PERCENT OF THE POPULACE STILL COUNTED AS RURAL.

1918
TO
1929

RUNNING AGAINST THE GRAIN

FARMERS TEAR UP THE PRAIRIE

Out on the High Plains, another boom of sorts was going on. Ever since the end of World War I, the nation's farmers had been mired in a terrible depression, attributable to the basic conundrum of American agriculture. The harder the farmers worked, the more they produced; and the more abundance there was...the more food prices dropped. This was a serious problem for the entire nation: In the 1920s, one in every five Americans tilled the soil, and 44 percent of the populace still counted as rural.

Those rural people were in deep distress, with an average income only one-quarter that of industrial workers. Some 50 million Americans—almost all of them in the countryside—were still without electricity; 45 million lacked indoor plumbing. When World War I ended, in 1918, prices for many commodities dropped by one-half to two-thirds, and farmers were stuck with piles of debt for all their new tractors and toasters. Only one cash crop seemed to hold its value: The price of wheat had shot up from 80 cents a bushel in 1910 to over $2 by 1917, and wheat farmers were making eight times what Ford's $5-a-day men made on the assembly line. After the war, the price of wheat, too, began to come down, but not as rapidly as that of cotton or corn, and wheat remained relatively cheap and easy to grow.

By the mid-1920s, the breakfast tables of the nation were filled with cereal bowls, but grain prices continued to drop. Well, the answer to that seemed obvious: Just plant more wheat! And so, grassland that had stitched together the plains for 35,000 years was gone in an instant. The more experienced farmers knew that it was especially dangerous to plow up the earth in the late fall, when the winds of winter and spring—the "blowing season"—were right behind. But to save time, the more feckless wheat men burned their stubble to the ground after a harvest, or let their cattle nibble it all the way down, further loosening the topsoil.

The price of wheat kept plummeting—to $1.50 a bushel and then to 75 cents. The more it dropped, the more the farmers kept planting. Over the course of the 1920s, American farmers increased their output of wheat by 300 percent. It was a remarkable achievement, admired the world over. But wheat prices kept on dropping.

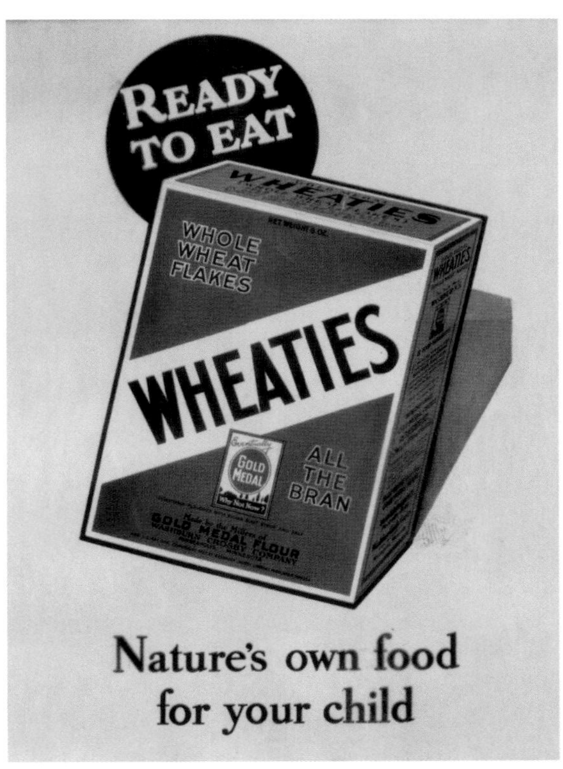

1919 TO 1930

HOLLYWOOD SWINGIN'

THE MOVIES ENTHRALL AMERICA

Few paid much notice to the price of wheat out in Los Angeles, where people's attention was more likely given to the constant clamor of construction all about them, or perhaps to the enormous, white-lettered sign that had appeared one day on nearby Mount Lee—another one of the increasingly flamboyant advertising stunts of the era.

It was, of course, all about real estate—and about Harry Chandler. The newspaper baron had erected the letters spelling out HOLLYWOODLAND on the site of his latest development venture. The sign itself was built with some of the jazziest materials available, because like everything else in L.A. it was supposed to be modern and stylish. The 13 letters were each 30 feet wide and 50 feet tall. At night, they were lit with 4,000 20-watt bulbs around their perimeters. The sign was supposed to stay up for only a year and a half, after which it would no doubt be pulled down by the members of the exclusive, affluent community it had attracted.

Of all the booms in all the towns throughout the United States in the 1920s, Hollywood's was unique, founded on entertainment alone. Before 1907, it had been a sleepy independent suburb of Los Angeles, composed mostly of orange orchards and grazing land. Then the Nestor Motion Picture Company (late of New Jersey) set up shop, producing a single-reel "Eastern," "Western," and comedy every week. By 1912, at least 15 studios had settled in, many of them turning old barns into sound—or, as it were, "silent"—stages. The film companies treasured the balmy weather and sunny skies. But they had also been driven out of New York and New Jersey by Thomas Edison, who was suing them for copyright violation. The Wizard of Menlo Park maintained that all filmmaking was derived from his Kinetoscope, and while the cases dragged on through the courts, moviemakers fled first to Cuba and then to Southern California.

By 1920, 40 million Americans—one-third of the population—were going to the movies every week. L.A. would grow throughout the following decade as no city ever had. Its population more than doubled, to over 1.2 million. But more remarkably, it added 80 square miles of area. Everyone wanted to live in Hollywood, drawn by the glamour of the movies. They flocked to the motion-picture companies that did, in fact, employ thousands of men and women in one capacity or another under the developing studio system—the artistic equivalent of River Rouge, producing over 800 movies a year, more than twice the number that Hollywood makes today.

For all the legendary restlessness of Americans, by 1930 two-thirds of people still resided in the state where they had been born. By contrast, only one in five Angelenos was from California. Many had come from Mexico, with half a million *Mexicanos* moving to the States in the 1920s.

Still "condemned to grow," still needing to hydrate, even after winning the Owens Valley water war, the octopus groped about for new sources. It seemed that the city had found a good one some 375 miles away, where surveyors were plotting a new dam meant to tame the Colorado River. It would be like nothing ever built before.

Those Hollywood hills. The sign would acquire its notoriety in 1932, when a 24-year-old veteran of the Broadway stage, Peg Entwistle, jumped to her death from the *H*, apparently depressed over her floundering movie career.

ORIGINAL
HOLLYWOODLAND

Average net paid circulation of THE NEWS, Sept., 1929:
Sunday, 1,535,775
Daily, - 1,311,806

DAILY NEWS

NEW YORK'S PICTURE NEWSPAPER

Copyright, 1929, by News Syndicate Co., Inc. Reg. U.S. Pat. Off.

Entered as 2nd class matter, Post Office, New York, N.Y.

PINK EDITION

Vol. 11. No. 107 48 Pages New York, Tuesday, October 29, 1929 2 Cents

LOSS IN STOCK COLLAPSE 10 BILLIO

Story on Page 2

(By Pacific & Atlantic)

PANTAGES SWINGS MOP.—Dejected at conviction on assault charge by Eunice Pringle, 17, Alexander Pantages (with cigar), theatrical magnate, is forced to mop up like other prisoners while awaiting sentence in Los Angeles jail. He is unable to eat prison fare. Here he is entering jail with deputy sheriffs. —*Story on page 37.*

(NEWS photo)

CLOUDS HAD GOLDEN LINING.—Mrs. Edith Murphy Belpusi Healy (above), came back from west yesterday with Reno divorce from Percy C. Healy, wealthy broker, and $500,000 alimony. Healy wooed her in plane. —*Story on page 16.*

1929
TO
1930

CRASHING THE PARTY

WALL STREET LAYS AN EGG

By the fall of 1929, America everywhere seemed poised to take the next step forward—and upward—to previously unimaginable heights of invention, accomplishment, and abundance. It had problems, even some big ones. But there was no reason not to believe, along with the country's earnest, optimistic president, that those difficulties could not be surmounted as they always had been, with an application of grit and ingenuity. Herbert Hoover had risen from being a penniless orphan to becoming an engineer drawing the largest salary in the world. His career had included surviving the siege of the Peking legations during the Boxer Rebellion; following the prints of a tiger's paws to discover an abandoned Burmese silver mine; and saving more people from starvation, during World War I and afterward, than any other man in human history. He seemed to be a combination of Horatio Alger and Indiana Jones. Wasn't he further proof that Americans were a good and great people, capable of anything? What new wonders would the future bring?

Then—crash. In the space of three weeks, the collapse of the great bull market in October of 1929 wiped out anywhere from $26 billion to $50 billion in market shares. Panicked crowds jammed Wall Street, and endless piles of ticker tape and sell orders piled up like snowbanks in lower Manhattan offices.

Then—nothing. Contrary to enduring rumor, bodies did not start cascading out of windows. The truth of the matter is that almost no Americans were in the market, and almost none had ever been. And the majority of those few, wealthy individuals who *were* in it owned mostly blue-chip stocks that may have lost tremendous value in the Great Crash, but that would (eventually) regain their value many times over—shares in such firms as General Electric, General Motors, Westinghouse, AT&T, and U.S. Steel.

The country was not without trepidation, but in October of 1929 the economy was thought to be healthy enough, with sufficient vigor to ensure against any real catastrophe. Unemployment did increase, but stocks also ticked steadily upward again, into the spring of 1930. "I am convinced we have now passed the worst and with continued unity of effort we shall rapidly recover," Hoover told the nation six months after the crash.

Then came another sickening slide. Or rather, the start of the longest, deepest slide America would ever experience. It was as if everything that the country had neglected during its headlong rush across the continent over the previous 130 years—everything it had botched, or ignored, or put off in its race to modernity—was coming back to haunt it. Over the next decade, Americans would have to wrestle with every contradiction of their democracy, and rework their every societal relationship. The worst of it would be the three years that followed, a time in which the nation's confidence in itself was tested as never before—save, perhaps, during the darkest moments of the Civil War.

A front page from October 29, 1929. In fact, much more had been lost, somewhere between nine to 17 times the federal budget at the time. But only one person went off a Wall Street building, and that may have been an accident.

1907
TO
1933

YOU CAN'T TAKE THAT TO THE BANK

THE CRISIS IN BANKING

America had endured depressions before. Just why this one was so long and so savage remains a matter of bitter contention.

One factor was surely the uneven distribution of income. Productivity rose by anywhere from 40 to 63 percent from 1920 to 1929, and corporate profits increased by 80 percent. But wages went up only 8 percent.

Then there was the nature of the country's financial system. This, despite the creation of the Federal Reserve Board before World War I, remained all but unregulated and unsupervised, even by its principals. Attempts by the House of Morgan to ape the actions of its founder back in 1907, and thus stop the crash by itself, failed utterly. The individual fronting this campaign, and much of Wall Street's subsequent PR efforts, was the vice president (and later president) of the New York Stock Exchange, Richard "Dickie" Whitney. Despite his insistence that the exchange was run by "gentlemen," Whitney himself ended up doing serious time in Sing Sing prison for embezzling money from just about every institution with which he was connected. Charles "Sunshine Charley" Mitchell, the influential head of what was then National City Bank—later Citibank, later Citigroup—was guilty of much more significant shenanigans in manipulating the market, and narrowly escaped jail time for tax evasion. He ended up settling with the government for $1.1 million in 1933.

Many of the shakier financial pyramids of the era went down under their own weight, once the market stopped soaring ever upward. Some were examples of the skulduggery still permitted on Wall Street in that era, such as "bucket shops," which essentially functioned as OTB parlors for stocks. Infinitely more damaging were the holding companies, the 1920s equivalent of securitized mortgage traders. Primitive by today's standards, they nonetheless served as well-disguised Ponzi schemes, opaque enough to wipe out major firms. Once the market went down, it was discovered that most of these holding companies had no real assets of their own, that they were just legal fictions created to enable speculation. Often, a holding company's "assets" consisted of stock in other holding companies, that were in turn composed solely of stocks in holding companies—shells upon shells upon shells, stacked up until the perfectly sound company at the bottom of it all would be crushed by how many times its stock had been sold over and over again.

Still, the collapse of the holding companies, in the wake of the crash, might have caused no more than acceptable losses, save for their relationships with the banks. Even in the best of times, U.S. banks failed in droves. The 1920s witnessed an average of over 500 bank suspensions a year; 345, with combined assets of $115 million, went down in the first six months of 1929 alone even *before* the Great Crash.

Most problematic of all was the plethora of rural banks, often with no more than $25,000 to $100,000 in assets. Senator Carter Glass of Virginia, father of the Federal Reserve, had long railed against them as no more than "pawnshops." A series of relatively small bank failures started in November 1930, in Tennessee. Then the National Bank of Kentucky, in Louisville, went down. This was an institution of some heft, and with it went affiliated banks in Indiana, Illinois, Missouri, Iowa, Arkansas, and North Carolina. Everywhere, it seemed, frantic men and women were mobbing teller cages demanding

BANK RUN IN THE BRONX, 1930

their money. The desperate banks, in turn, called in loans and peddled away assets in a weak market, depressing sound businesses in every field, creating a liquidity crisis to end all liquidity crises.

Rumors about the shakiness and overreaching of the Bank of United States had been circulating for months. Founded in 1913 by Joseph S. Marcus, it had been run prudently through its formative years. Despite its deliberately confusing name, Bank of United States was not a government institution of any sort but the private "Pantspressers' Bank," soliciting the business of garment workers. It was the Jewish equivalent of New York's Emigrant Savings Bank, which was run by and for Irish immigrants, or Amadeo Peter Giannini's Bank of America, which had started as a bank primarily for Italian immigrants in San Francisco, and would prove to be a pillar of integrity throughout the Depression. Like these other immigrants' banks, the Pantspressers' Bank expanded slowly and cautiously during its first years of existence,

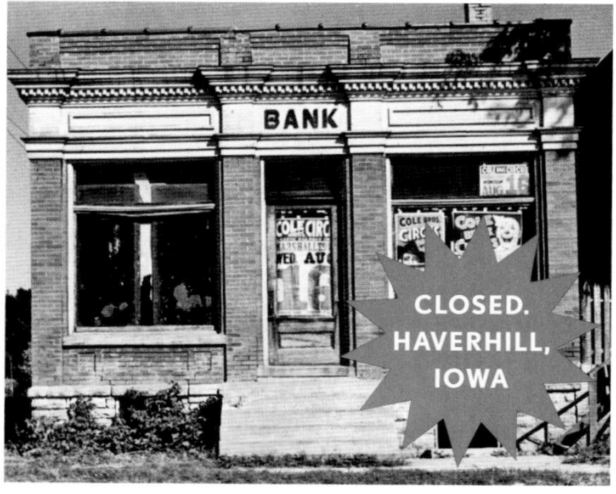

CLOSED. HAVERHILL, IOWA

making sure to safeguard its customers' money.

In 1925, though, Joseph Marcus died, and his son, Bernard Marcus, decided it was time to join everyone else in getting rich quick off the great boom. Moving swiftly, he acquired one smaller bank after another. By 1930, the Bank of United States was the twenty-eighth-largest bank in the country, with dozens of branches throughout the New York area. It was also heavily leveraged. In the summer of 1929, bank examiners were warning that its investment in real estate—45 percent of its assets, as opposed to an average of 12 percent at other New York banks—was too high.

The complaint seemed spurious, given that few long-term investments have ever bested Manhattan real estate. The bank's real-estate investments were not in marginal neighborhoods; they included spectacular new apartment buildings such as the Beresford, rising along Central Park West. But for whatever reason, Bank of United States stock dropped from $242 a share to $170 even *before* the Wall Street crash. Something wasn't right, and suspicions arose that the sell-off was the work of insiders, executives at the bank's newly acquired affiliates who had seen the figures and realized how precarious the conglomerate's finances really were.

Bank of United States officers responded by first using their depositors' money to buy the bank's stock and then setting up more holding companies in an effort to bolster the price per share. But after the crash in October of 1929, real estate also tanked—one bubble bursting alongside the other, much as they would 80 years later.

In September 1930, cash runs destabilized the Bank of United States, driving its stock price down to $20.

BY THE TIME THE EMPIRE STATE BUILDING OPENED, THERE WERE 82 BREADLINES IN NEW YORK, FEEDING 85,000 PEOPLE A DAY.

Then came what seemed to be a reprieve. On November 24, the bank announced an imminent merger with three other banks, a move that it was thought might provide it with enough hard assets to survive. But two weeks later, the deal fell through. The other banks argued that the Pantspressers' Bank's assets were too entangled in one holding company or another. It was impossible to determine just which holdings were good and which were worthless.

On December 10, over 20,000 depositors swarmed the bank's Southern Boulevard branch in the Bronx, frantically trying to retrieve their modest savings from a lifetime of backbreaking labor. They pulled $2 million out before mounted police charged into the crowd to drive them away. Word soon spread, leading to similar runs on other branches.

The Bank of United States announced the next day that it was closing its doors. They would never reopen. It was the worst bank failure in the history of the U.S., and it sucked what little available money there was left out of the sweatshops; some 10,000 of the 29,000 clothing factories in New York closed in 1930. Twenty years' worth of gains by the garment workers were wiped out.

Family finances began to collapse. By 1933, 17,000 New Yorkers *a month* were being evicted. They went to live wherever they could—hundreds of them squatting on the Great Lawn of Central Park, where they built two dozen brick-and-wood shanties directly under the gaze of the splendid, newly completed (and largely empty) Beresford apartment building.

Just as vacant was the new Empire State Building, opened officially on May 1, 1931. The skyscraper was a masterpiece of design and execution, built in just 410 days, topping out at 102 stories. But the structure would not turn a profit until 1950. The airship landings failed to materialize; instead, beginning on December 22, 1931, the building's upper floors were used to broadcast an experimental new medium, one that would also fail to turn a profit until after World War II. It was called television.

By the time the Empire State Building opened, there were 82 breadlines in New York, feeding 85,000 people a day. By April 1932, 1.25 million people—better than one-sixth of the city—were on public relief.

Bank runs continued throughout the country, with so many more going down in late 1932 and early 1933 that on February 14, 1933, the governor of Michigan declared an eight-day banking "holiday" to protect the solvency of the state's remaining institutions. State after state followed suit until, by the day of President Franklin D. Roosevelt's inauguration, on March 4, 1933, all the banks in 32 states and nearly all of them in six more had been shut down, and the New York Stock Exchange and the Chicago Board of Trade had suspended all trading. The following day, the new president invoked special wartime powers to temporarily shut every bank in the country. The American financial system had come to a full stop. The unemployment rate had almost tripled, to 8.7 percent, in 1930. In 1931, it nearly doubled again, to 15.9 percent; it reached 23.6 percent in 1932, and 24.9 percent in 1933. And most analysts felt that these figures were underestimates. Some guessed that as many as one in every three American workers was out of a job.

"I saw not a solitary thing but bare earth and a few lonely, empty farmhouses.... There was not a tree or a blade of grass, or a dog or a cow or a human being—nothing whatsoever, nothing at all but gray raw earth and a few farmhouses and barns, sticking up from the dark gray sea like white cattle skeletons on the desert." —Ernie Pyle, newspaper reporter

1930 TO 1938

THE DIRTY THIRTIES

THE DUST STORMS RAVAGE THE PLAINS

The agony was often worse in the countryside than in the cities. By 1933, one-quarter of all remaining American farmers had lost their land. They fought back as best they could, trying to save their neighbors from eviction. One judge in Iowa was dragged from his bench, had a rope placed around his neck, and was told he would be lynched if he did not stop foreclosing on farms. Other evictions were essentially thwarted through "penny auctions," in which a farmer would win a sheriff's auction with a rock-bottom bid. Thus, the $800 mortgage on Walter Crozier's farm outside Haskins, Iowa, was redeemed for $1.90, and the property was promptly handed back to Crozier. In case any outsiders didn't grasp how the system worked, a well-placed noose or two might appear dangling from a barn or a tree during the bidding.

Edward O'Neal, president of the American Farm Bureau Federation, warned Congress, "Unless something is done for the American farmer we'll have revolution in the countryside in less than 12 months." John A. Simpson, leader of the National Farmers Union, echoed the sentiment, proclaiming: "I feel the capitalistic system is doomed. It has as its foundation the principles of brutality, dishonesty, and avarice."

What the farmers were undergoing in Iowa, though, was nothing compared with the ecological catastrophe rapidly evolving on the Great Plains. By 1930, the rain had stopped falling—as it always had, every 20 years or so, going back to prehistoric times. Two years later, the parched soil began to fly.

A duster rolls over Naponee, Nebraska, 1935.

They were called dust storms, and they were the most terrifying things anyone had ever seen on the High Plains: billowing clouds of dirt up to 10,000 feet high. They sometimes came accompanied by lightning and thunder; more often, and more eerily, they came in silence—moving at speeds of more than 100 miles per hour, outracing cars and shorting their ignitions with static electricity. Awesome to witness, the dusters were hell to experience.

"This is the ultimate darkness," one Kansas woman wrote in her journal. "So must come the end of the world." People sat for days in the gritty, perpetual twilight, faces covered with wet cloths and towels. It did little good: "The door and windows were all tightly shut, yet those tiny particles seemed to seep through the very walls," recalled a woman quoted in the *Kansas City Times*. "It got into cupboards and clothes closets; our faces were as dirty as if we had rolled in the dirt; our hair was gray and stiff and we ground dirt between our teeth."

It got into lungs, too, killing hundreds, maybe even thousands, with the "dust pneumonia," and choking countless livestock. There seemed no end to it, and nothing to stop it. On the morning of May 9, 1934, the wind began to tease up the topsoil of Montana and Wyoming. Soon, 350 million tons of dirt were hurtling eastward on the jet stream. By late afternoon, the dirt reached Chicago, where 12 million tons were deposited on the Windy City. By noon the next day, it had darkened the streets of Buffalo, New York. And by May 11, it had descended on New York, Washington, Atlanta, and Savannah, Georgia, and then blew out over the sea for at least 300 miles, coating the ships of mystified sailors in dust.

THE WINDS STIRRED UP BY THIS EPIC COLLISION RAISED UP ENOUGH DUST TO BLACKEN THE SKIES ALL THE WAY DOWN OVER DENVER, AND THEN INTO NEW MEXICO, KNOCKING CARS OFF THE ROAD, AND EVEN DERAILING A LOCOMOTIVE.

One of the worst "black rollers" came on April 14, 1935, a day that would be known as Black Sunday. In two hours, the temperature plunged 30 degrees when a cold front moving down from the Yukon ran head-on into a high-pressure system crouched over the Dakotas. The winds stirred up by this epic collision raised up enough dust to blacken the skies all the way down over Denver, and then into New Mexico, knocking cars off the road, and even derailing a locomotive.

A huge oval out on the plains—roughly 100 million acres, 400 by 300 miles in size—now lay desolate. Associated Press reporter Robert Geiger dubbed it "the Dust Bowl," and so it was. The dust was everywhere, covering farm machinery and entire houses, piled up against barns like Saharan sand drifts. By the end of 1938, the top five inches or more of soil from ten million acres was gone.

Annual precipitation in some counties dropped to nine inches in 1934, while summer temperatures reached an unbearable 118 degrees in Nebraska and 115 degrees in Iowa—the heat broken only by occasional showers of softball-size hail.

The folks who worked this land knew it was a hard land, but they loved it nonetheless, doing everything they could to stay on it. Now, though, with no water, no animals, no seed crop, and nothing to grow it in, they were at last reaching their breaking points. Banks offering 160 acres for as little as $25 found no takers. "Unless something is done," the U.S. Forest Service warned, "the western plains will be as arid as the Arabian desert."

Fortunately for the region's inhabitants, the 1932 elections had brought to power a president who believed in doing something, and who had a special predilection for conservation. Franklin Roosevelt commissioned a wide-ranging interagency report that confirmed at last the basic nature of the High Plains. "The Federal homestead policy, which kept land allotments low and required that a portion of each should be plowed, is now seen to have caused immeasurable harm," read the Great Plains Drought Area Committee's memo, "The Future of the Great Plains." "The Homestead Act of 1862, limiting an individual holding to 160 acres, was on the western plains almost an obligatory act of poverty."

Hugh Hammond Bennett, a genial, dedicated apostle of soil conservation, taught farmers to plow and reap in ways that would preserve the land as much as possible. New strains of buffalo grass were planted to bind the prairies up again, and FDR indulged his personal obsession by having Civilian Conservation Corps workers plant a "shelter belt" of 220 million trees around the Dust Bowl.

Most of this worked—immediately in terms of saving the region's people, and eventually in the case of healing the land. Despite the return of the regular, 20-year drought cycles over the decades ahead, nothing like the dust storms of the "Dirty Thirties" recurred, as the winds could no longer find enough soil for the plucking.

STUCK WHERE THE SUN DON'T SHINE: LIFE IN THE DUST BOWL

Life in the Dust Bowl was Kafkaesque. The dusters left a greenish-purple haze in the sky, and the air was so heavy with static electricity that people regularly gave each other painful shocks when they shook hands. Insects proliferated as the dusters drove off birds and rattlesnakes; tarantulas and black widow spiders, perhaps blown in by the storms, suddenly appeared in places where they had never been seen before; and, much worse, the locusts returned from the Rockies—14 million to a square mile, devouring everything still above the dust. Local governments responded by spraying as much as 175 tons of insecticide on each square acre, effectively killing whatever the grasshoppers hadn't eaten. And there were jackrabbits everywhere, overrunning the land. Towns organized massive rabbit slaughters, advertised with newspaper headlines such as "Big Rabbit Drive Sunday—Bring Clubs." The locals would form a wide circle and slowly begin to tighten it, driving the long-eared rabbits before them, smashing their heads with clubs and baseball bats as the animals screamed and darted frantically about. Initially, the motivation for these drives was to have the hard, cathartic pleasure of doing something about the disaster that had engulfed them. Eventually, though, hungry people started coming for the food the slaughtered rabbits provided.

1930 TO 1941

BORDER WARS

HEADING FOR CALIFORNIA

America in the 1930s was a country in motion again, full of people looking for jobs, looking for better land, looking for a fresh start somewhere, somehow. White Southerners and African-Americans were heading north again, as the farm crisis led to the eviction of thousands of tenant cotton farmers from their land. Young men and boys, refusing to further burden their families, were riding the rails and filling the hobo jungles. And the Exodusters, the Arkies, and the Okies were piling up their pickup trucks and their old Model Ts: More than 440,000 people had left Oklahoma before the 1930s were out, and 227,000 had fled Kansas.

Where were they going? West, of course, where Americans usually went when things went bust. Nearly half a million went up to the Pacific Northwest, where they helped build the great Bonneville and Grand Coulee dams, or worked the timberlands, or picked beets and hops. Another 300,000 headed out on Highway 66 to California—86,000 of them in a single 15-month period at the height of the High Plains dusters—lured by countless flyers extolling the sunshine and bounty of the state, just as the Los Angeles Chamber of Commerce had been singing its virtues for decades...

...only to find that they were not welcome. Comfortable Midwesterners with plenty of disposable income were one thing. Penniless, dirt-covered Okies were another. The new flyers had been plastered across the Dust Bowl by California's unscrupulous factory farms, which violently suppressed every attempt by their migrant pickers to win decent wages and working conditions, and which now wanted excess labor to keep their costs down.

Angelenos were horrified. James E. Davis, one in a long line of essentially lawless L.A. police chiefs, sent 125 city cops out to patrol the borders of Arizona and even Oregon—800 miles away!—and keep all "transients" out. By order of the LAPD, Okies entering California were required to prove that they had sufficient cash, friends, relatives, or job offers so as to avoid becoming a burden on the city of Los Angeles. Meanwhile, city authorities rounded up entire trainloads of Mexican-American (later called *repatriados*) and shipped them back south of the border.

Many Okies got through anyway, and the city continued to grow. It would become more vital than ever to provide its residents with enough water. Fortunately, that was on tap. Faced with an economic crisis the likes of which had never been seen before, President Hoover had faltered at critical moments, but one thing he did do was facilitate the completion of federal public-works projects. The greatest of these was a dam on the Colorado River that would slake L.A.'s thirst and at the same time give birth to an even more unlikely city of its own.

A Mexican migrant farmworker holds his baby before a shack at the edge of a pea field in California's Imperial Valley. A pickers' strike for the most basic wages and working conditions was brutally crushed by the growers in 1934. This picture was taken by Dorothea Lange, who with her fellow Farm Security Administration photographers recorded the most indelible images of the Depression.

TRITON
MOTOR OIL
THIS SIDE UP
114
2M 93 97

JAMES MEIGS, editor in chief, *Popular Mechanics*: "The Hoover Dam was a statement of America's fortitude, of our integrity, of our talent for hard work, and our willingness to transform the environment around us."

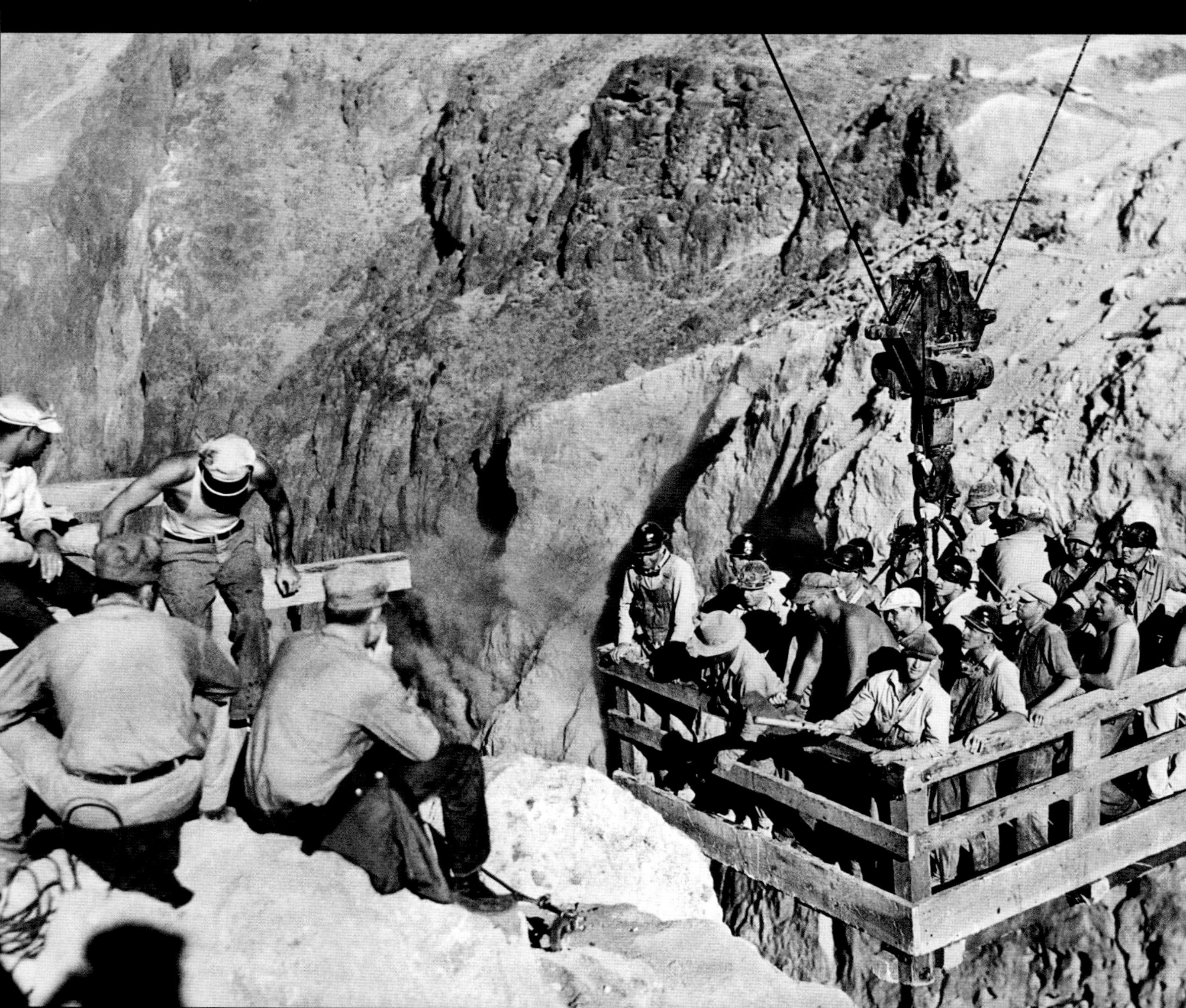

1931 TO 1942

A DAM-GOOD IDEA

THE NEW DEAL BUILDS MODERN AMERICA

It was called Boulder Dam, named for the canyon that was originally supposed to be its location, though when the surveyors were done they had moved the site eight miles downstream, where they thought the dam could better control the river. The very idea of anyone or anything controlling the Colorado River would have bemused Jedediah Smith, the mountain man who first saw it in 1826, or Major John Wesley Powell, the one-armed Civil War hero whose ten-man expedition became the first to extensively chart it in 1869 (losing two of their number along the way). One of the wildest rivers in the world, the Colorado's waters tore through the canyons at speeds of up to 175 feet per second. Each year, its rampant flooding killed hundreds and drowned thousands of acres of farmland. The river seemed to have a will of its own, and at the rate things were going it was feared that it would plow a canyon a mile deep and hundreds of miles long.

It would have to be dammed. And the government thought it had just the man for the job.

Frank "Hurry Up" Crowe was a tall, stately, 50-year-old Quebecois. He had moved to the West nearly 30 years before, all on fire to build dams. He had built the Jackson Lake Dam in Wyoming, the Tieton Dam in Washington, the Arrowrock Dam in Idaho—six dams in all, every one of them brought in on time and under budget. But just like Theodore Judah looking to build the Transcontinental Railroad, he had gone out West with one big job in mind. "I'm going to build Boulder Dam," he told people as early as 1921.

Crowe could be a hard, even brutal, man (his motto: "To hell with excuses—get results"). But he won the job as the consensus choice of a six-company consortium contracted to do the work. He and his family were housed in a custom-built mansion in a sleepy nearby road town known as Las Vegas. Most of the men he would be bossing were not so lucky, living in a wretched working camp known as Ragtown, where they had gone on strike in reaction to the bad food, worse drinking water, and multiple fatalities sustained from working in 130-degree summer desert weather. Crowe broke the strike by summarily firing everyone, then sending in company goons with guns and clubs to clear out Ragtown. He hired the men he wanted, putting them in a new town the Nevada authorities were hastily building that would become known as Boulder City.

Crowe quickly became a familiar figure, pacing around the work site in his trademark boots, spotless white shirt, and Stetson hat. Every detail required—and got—his close attention.

As 1931 gave way to 1932 and the unemployment rate rose above 20 percent, men from all walks of life headed for the dam site, just as they swarmed anyplace where there was the promise of a job. "They hired anyone who didn't have brains enough to be scared," claimed one workman. This held true even for those parts of the job that meant tunneling through solid rock, and might better have been reserved for the likes of professional miners. Erma Godbey, wife of one of the dam builders, remembered: "There were college professors. There were

Building the Hoover Dam, circa 1932: An intricate system of cables enabled 5,000 workmen to maneuver a 4,000-foot canyon floor at Hoover Dam. They dug out more dirt and rock than were excavated to build the Panama Canal. It was finished two years ahead of schedule.

lawyers and everybody and—and they didn't know a damned thing about mining."

Yet the dam kept growing. Crowe was indeed an engineering genius, as well as a wizard at logistics. The dam was to be 45 feet wide at its rim and 660 feet thick at its base. It would require 6.6 million tons of concrete, enough to lay a four-foot sidewalk around the earth at its equator. Simply pouring that amount of concrete—accurately—presented an immense logistical problem, but there was another factor to be considered. Hardening concrete not only contracts but also involves a chemical reaction that releases heat. Crowe's engineers calculated that the amount of concrete needed for the Boulder Dam would take 125 years to cool and harden—and that it would crack in the process, rendering it useless.

Crowe and his team had the solution: 230 wooden box molds, each equipped with one-inch pipes and thermometers—582 miles of pipe throughout the entire dam. The concrete was poured into sections five feet deep. Refrigerated water was then pumped through the pipes to cool it down. When the thermometers indicated that it was cool enough, grout was pumped into the pipe sections—thereby further strengthening the dam—and the next section was poured. Thanks to the grout, the dam's concrete continues to cure and strengthen with the passage of time.

Boulder Dam was finished in 1936, two years ahead of schedule, and upon its completion it was the largest concrete structure in the world, as well as the largest dam and the greatest single generator of power. Over half the power it generates now goes to Los Angeles and elsewhere in Southern California, although there has been plenty left over to light that sleepy little town Frank Crowe and his family stayed in, even as it has grown exponentially. Since the company town of Boulder City had banned gambling, prostitution, and the sale of alcohol, Las Vegas established itself as the local sin city—although its boom years had to wait for another world war, and for the Mob.

"This morning I came, I saw, and I was conquered, as everyone would be who sees for the first time this great feat of mankind," intoned President Roosevelt at the dedication ceremony for the dam. But the great dam was part of his predecessor's vision. And when political passions cooled, he would be honored for it, with the structure renamed Hoover Dam in 1947, a name it bears to this day.

Asked how he felt when his dam was done, Frank Crowe replied, "I feel like hell." But he added, "I'm looking for a job, and I want to go right on building dams as long as I live."

The building, of all kinds, would go on, in countless places and in countless ways. Dams, aqueducts, highways, roads, airports, bridges, tunnels, pipelines, sewer systems, schools, (local and national) parks, playgrounds, post offices, government buildings of all sorts, and even a few model towns—the New Deal would lay the foundations of a modern infrastructure in America. Its programs kept tens of millions of people in their jobs, kept millions more in their homes, made work for millions who had no jobs, and provided outright relief for those who had no recourse.

The construction projects would prove a huge boon to those who lived and worked in the industrial cities. New York, in particular, would become "the model New Deal city" under its feisty, frenetic mayor, a

CONSTRUCTING THE HOOVER DAM

A masterpiece of engineering, the Hoover Dam (originally called the Boulder Dam) was finished in 1936, two years ahead of schedule. It employed as many as 5,000 men at a time—96 of whom died building it.

Constructing the 726-foot-high dam meant first diverting the turbulent Colorado River. This was done by digging four immense tunnels (far left), two on each side of the river, with the use of dynamite and electric drills.

Once the water was diverted downstream (far right), workmen could dig down to bedrock, removing 1.5 million cubic yards of rock and soil, more material than was dug out of the Panama Canal.

Two of the 230 wooden box molds into which the original concrete for the dam was poured. Water circulating through the pipes in the boxes cooled the concrete, and then was replaced by grout, which continues to cure the concrete and harden the dam.

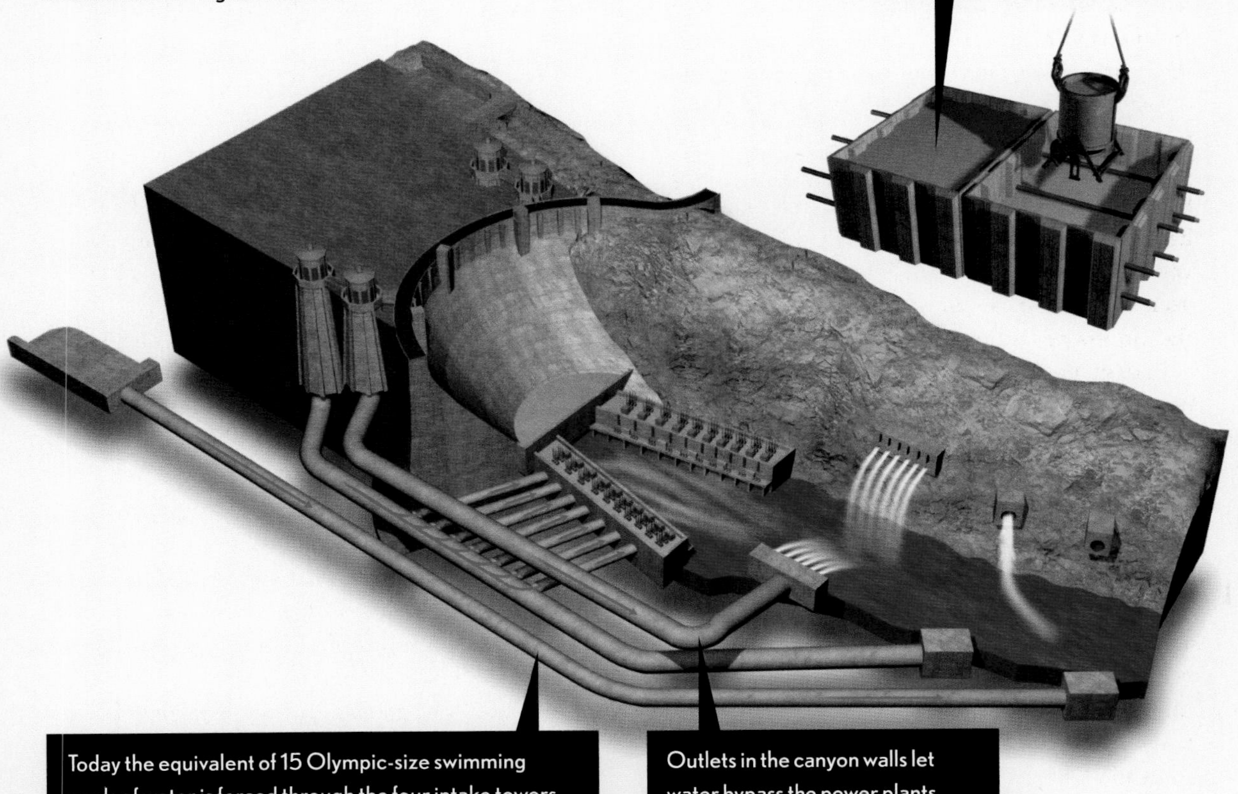

Today the equivalent of 15 Olympic-size swimming pools of water is forced through the four intake towers above the dam every minute and down through the 17 generators just below the dam (on both sides of the river) to produce 2,080 megawatts of power—the rough equivalent of that produced by two nuclear plants.

Outlets in the canyon walls let water bypass the power plants during floods or for maintenance.

onetime immigration inspector at Ellis Island named Fiorello La Guardia. Embodying almost the entire American experience in a single squat, pudgy body, La Guardia was of Jewish-Italian ancestry, a baptized Catholic and practicing Protestant, who spoke half a dozen languages—and always spoke up for social justice. With the help of the federal government, he would remake New York physically and morally, turning it into a great, middle-class city—and eventually into the de facto capital of the world.

Ben Shahn's poster for the Resettlement Administration. New Deal agrarian reforms did little to help many Dust Bowl victims stay on the land, but they did help resettle them in more-prosperous urban existences.

For the elderly and the disabled, there was a new federal pension system known as Social Security, designed in part by Secretary of Labor Frances Perkins, the first woman cabinet member and a witness to the 1911 fire at the Triangle Shirtwaist Factory; the bill that created the fund was pushed through Congress in good measure by Senator Robert Wagner, who had served on the Triangle Fire's investigating committee with her. For many of the migrant pickers, sweltering in California's San Joaquin Valley or ousted from their tenant farms in Southern cotton fields, there were the Resettlement Administration and the Farm Security Administration, which would help to rescue them from the road or from the squalid "ditch camps" where the growers had forced them to live to keep them away from union organizers. Now they would be provided with sustenance and the start of a new and better life.

Many of the former Okies and Exodusters would end up taking jobs in the defense plants that had sprung up in and around Los Angeles. Even Hollywoodland was eventually filled up. The development's sign had begun to crumble by 1939, and the last four letters were discarded after the war—but like so many Angelenos, it survived mudslides, fires, earthquakes, and neglect. What was intended as an 18-month publicity stunt ended up set in stone, as it were, rebuilt eventually in concrete to serve as an enduring symbol of a dream.

CHISELING MOUNT RUSHMORE

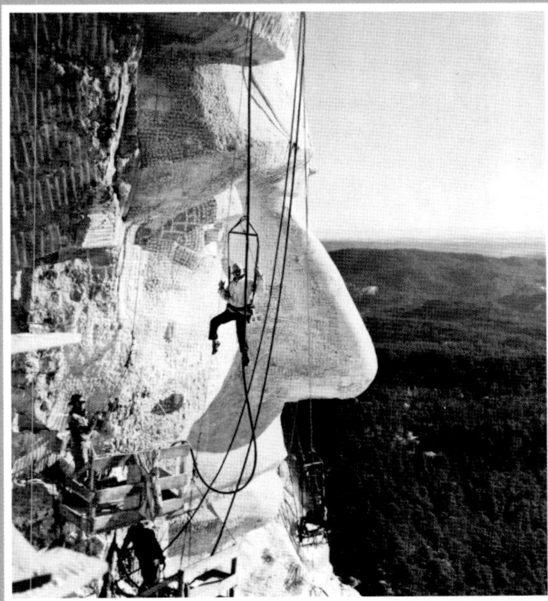

Mount Rushmore's progenitor was a mass of contradictions: a son of Danish immigrants who was also a leading Klansman; the designer of both a tribute to the Confederacy to be carved on Georgia's Stone Mountain and a memorial to the anarchists Sacco and Vanzetti. Gutzon de la Mothe Borglum had trained under Rodin, and he was determined to create art that was "American, drawn from American sources, memorializing American achievement."

Borglum enjoyed working on patriotic themes—as he defined them—and always on a colossal scale. He was just the man Jonah LeRoy "Doane" Robinson was looking for. The aged state historian of South Dakota, Robinson, envisioned giant sculptures of leading frontiersmen and Indian chiefs carved into a section of the Black Hills. Inspecting the site, Borglum decided that the granite was too flinty, and that, in any case, he had no intention of carving a bunch of regional heroes. Instead, he informed Robinson, he would carve the heads of the nation's greatest presidents along the face of Mount Rushmore, which had a southeastern exposure and picked up plenty of sun, making it visible for miles around. "America will march along that skyline," he told Robinson.

Beginning in 1927, workmen used dynamite to remove 90 percent of the 450,000 tons of rock that had to be cleared away. The first head, George Washington's, was dedicated on July 4, 1934. But after two years of work on Thomas Jefferson, the underlying granite unexpectedly cracked so badly that the head had to be destroyed and work begun again.

Objections came from the Lakota Sioux, who were outraged by the construction of a patriotic memorial on what they still considered to be stolen, and sacred, land. A congressional rider mandated that a head of Susan B. Anthony—the great feminist leader—be added, but this was voted down. Borglum was forced to embark repeatedly on extended fundraising trips, leaving his son, Lincoln, in charge.

Somehow, it all got done. Jefferson's head was finished in 1936; Abraham Lincoln's the following year; Teddy Roosevelt's in 1939. The lack of funds actually ended up putting a welcome cap on Borglum's ambitions. He had originally planned to sculpt the four presidents all the way down to their waists, and to add a gigantic plaque in the shape of the Louisiana Purchase, on which would be carved the words of the leading patriotic documents of American history, including the Declaration of Independence and the Constitution. Instead, the much more impressive heads were all that had been completed when Borglum died of an embolism in 1941. With the bulk of the work accomplished, his faithful son was left to finish up.

"I had seen the photographs, I had seen the drawings, and I had talked with those who are responsible for this great work, and yet I had no conception, until about ten minutes ago, not only of its magnitude but also its permanent beauty and importance," said FDR, moved to give an impromptu speech at the dedication of Jefferson's head in 1936. "...I think that we can perhaps meditate on those Americans of 10,000 years from now...meditate and wonder what our descendants—and I think they will still be here—will think about us. Let us hope...that they will believe we have honestly striven every day and generation to preserve a decent land to live in and a decent form of government to operate under."

BUILDING MODERN AMERICA: PUBLIC WORKS IN THE DEPRESSION, 1933 TO 1942

By the 1930s, the United States was still a nation where tens of millions of citizens lacked modern amenities such as decent roads, electricity, or even plumbing. The vast public works projects that came to characterize the New Deal would change all that in less than ten years, and build the framework for the dynamic American economy that was about to emerge. Huge new dams and rural electrification projects would transform the nation, modernizing and enriching the South and the West, in particular. In the cities, massive improvements in infrastructure and housing, and the building of countless areas for rest and recreation would pay dividends for decades to come.

The Public Works Administration alone would complete 11,428 road projects, 7,488 school buildings (70 percent of all such buildings constructed between 1933 and 1939); and one-third of all hospitals built during the same period. It also built the first federally financed public housing in American history, totaling 25,000 units, most of which are still in use today—and several warships that later saw service in World War II. The Works Progress Administration (WPA) tended to build or renovate smaller projects, such as the Dock Street Theater in Charleston, South Carolina, the Merritt Parkway in Connecticut, the Griffith Observatory in Los Angeles, and the Timberline Lodge in Fort Hood, Oregon. It was the largest single employer in the nation between 1935 and 1942, putting eight million people to work.

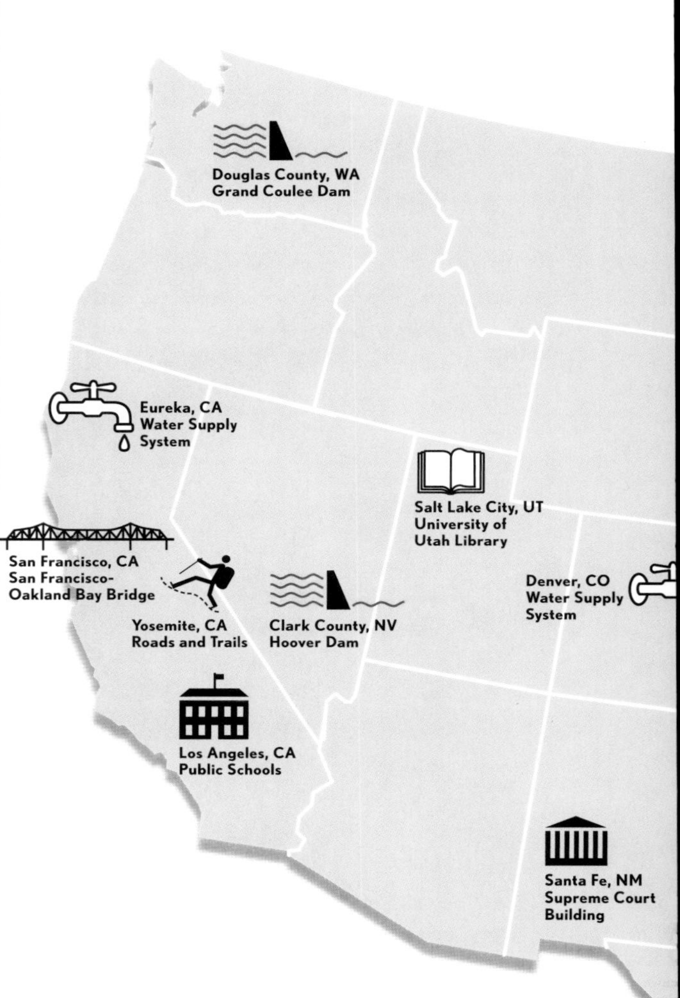

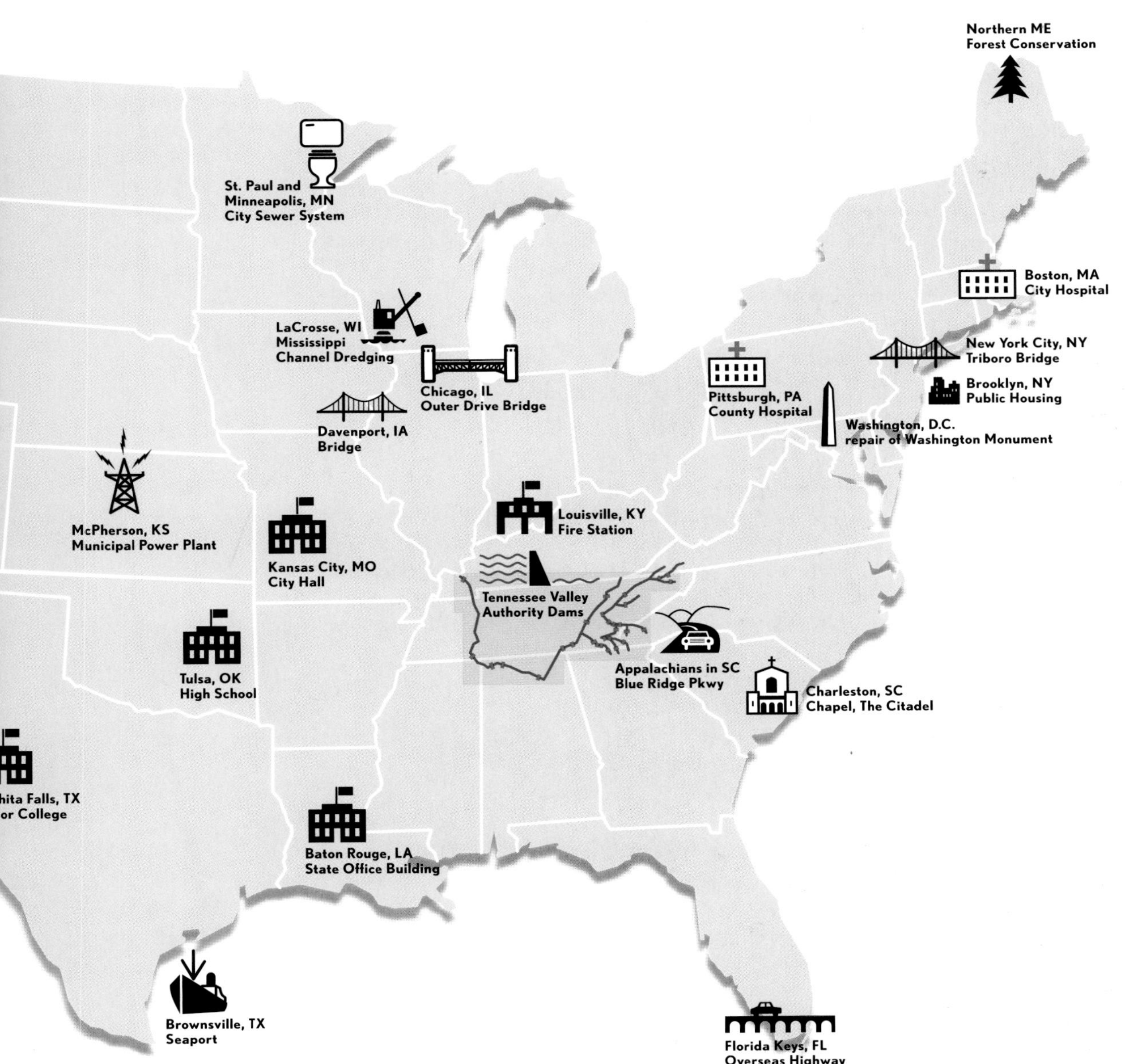
Northern ME
Forest Conservation
St. Paul and
Minneapolis, MN
City Sewer System
Boston, MA
City Hospital
LaCrosse, WI
Mississippi
Channel Dredging
New York City, NY
Triboro Bridge
Chicago, IL
Outer Drive Bridge
Pittsburgh, PA
County Hospital
Brooklyn, NY
Public Housing
Davenport, IA
Bridge
Washington, D.C.
repair of Washington Monument
McPherson, KS
Municipal Power Plant
Kansas City, MO
City Hall
Louisville, KY
Fire Station
Tennessee Valley
Authority Dams
Appalachians in SC
Blue Ridge Pkwy
Tulsa, OK
High School
Charleston, SC
Chapel, The Citadel
chita Falls, TX
ior College
Baton Rouge, LA
State Office Building
Brownsville, TX
Seaport
Florida Keys, FL
Overseas Highway

Work Pays America!

PROSPERITY

WORKS PROGRESS ADMINISTRATION

1930
TO
1955

PEOPLE HAVE THE POWER

THE TRIUMPH OF AMERICAN DEMOCRACY

As talented and visionary as many of America's leaders proved to be during the Great Depression, the real change was brought about by the people. It was they who pushed presidents and governors and congressmen as much as they were led. The New Deal was ultimately less about providing for material needs as it was about the great opening up of American democracy. This was a process that had been going on in fits and starts for decades, but thanks to the Depression there would now be monumental advances in securing the rights of millions of Americans to have a say in their lives, and a real opportunity to succeed.

Out on the plains and down in the cotton fields, the Agricultural Adjustment Act of 1933 would give farmers the chance to work together, to decide collectively how much they would grow and harvest, instead of working the land in a mindless competition that, the more they grew, only impoverished them more quickly. In the cities, government jobs and welfare programs would break the hold of the political machines and leave American citizens free to vote for whom they liked. Federal crime-fighting efforts, along with the repeal of Prohibition (also ratified in 1933), would return a sense of order and respect for the law. Progressive tax codes, a Federal Reserve with real teeth, and a strict separation of savings and investment banks under the Glass-Steagall Act would all greatly level the economic playing field, return sanity to the nation's banking system, and prevent the recurrence of another financial meltdown for 75 years—until after Glass-Steagall was repealed.

Under the guidance of selfless, hardworking administrator Harry Hopkins, the WPA proved adept at putting people to work in a hurry.

In all of these reforms, it was the people who provided the thrust, and the people who would seize the chances offered. Courageous men and women in ten thousand workplaces made the union movement a reality. In Detroit, that meant a grueling, extended battle to organize the so-called Big Three automakers. At General Motors, it culminated in a six-week fight in which thousands of workers not only walked the picket lines but also occupied the plants where they worked, staging "sit-down strikes"—a tactic that soon spread around the country. Armed with fire hoses and car-door hinges, the strikers fought police, deputy sheriffs, and company goons firing tear gas and live ammunition at the company's Fisher Body plants in Flint, Michigan. When Frank Murphy, now the governor of Michigan refused to intercede on GM's behalf, the company gave up and recognized the union.

Henry Ford was the last of the Big Three automakers to surrender. His Service Department savagely beat and bloodied union organizers, resisting the United Auto Workers with a brutality that shocked the nation. Nonetheless, on May 21, 1941, Ford workers voted for the union. A stunned Ford at first offered his men the most generous contract in Detroit, then swore that he would close the company before he recognized the union. At this, his long-suffering wife, Clara, threatened to leave him if he did not keep his word. He folded and honored his contract offer.

Unions in every industrial field scored comparable successes. By 1955, 35 percent of the private-sector workers in America were unionized, wages had skyrocketed, and the U.S. was in what seemed like an economy of permanent prosperity.

It was just one success of many that would come

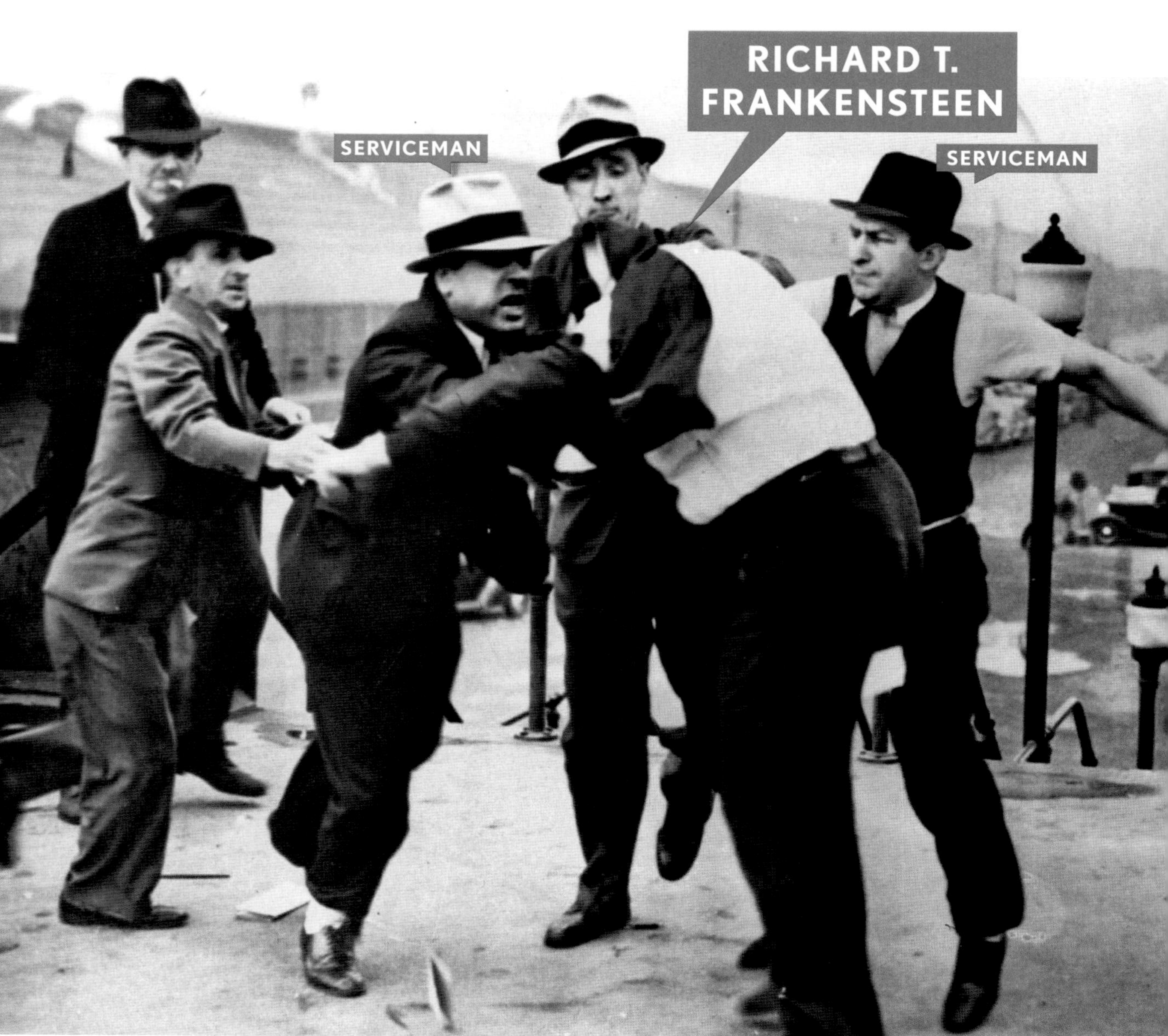
SERVICEMAN
RICHARD T. FRANKENSTEEN
SERVICEMAN

out of those darkest days. Americans had long shown that they were as good as—or better than—anyone at inventing things and at overcoming almost any natural obstacle in their way. But now they had displayed their ingenuity by reinventing the way they lived and how they ran their society.

America's greatest accomplishment was in fighting its way through the Great Depression without becoming fatally polarized (like, say, France, Spain, or Austria) or a totalitarian state, such as Germany, Italy, Japan, and the Soviet Union, all of which were held up at various times as the light guiding the world to its future. Every American organization or demagogue who suggested a less democratic path—Father Coughlin, Huey Long, the Liberty League, et al.—got nowhere.

At the same time, though, the American people pulled back deeper into isolationism. Americans in the 1930s were loath to accept the idea that the bank failures in their country, the only creditor nation left in the world, had helped push banks throughout Europe into failure too, and that in the modern scheme of things the destinies of the U.S. and the Continent were now inextricably linked. One spending program of FDR's that Congress had quickly nixed, after the building of a couple of aircraft carriers, involved significant American rearmament. It was an admirable gesture, but one that would leave the Great Republic less prepared than it should have been as it turned to face the war clouds that, as the 1930s slipped away, were bearing down on it as rapidly as any black roller.

Richard T. Frankensteen, organizational director of the U.A.W., is attacked by men from Ford's Service Department, at the gate of the Ford River Rouge plant in Dearborn, Michigan, May 27, 1937. Sixteen people were injured in this outbreak of violence.

WHAT ENDED THE DEPRESSION?

Almost as controversial as the theories about what started the Great Depression are the theories about what ended it. During Franklin Roosevelt's first term, his administration achieved annual growth rates of 9 percent—albeit from the rock-bottom low that economic activity had reached when he entered the White House. Unemployment dropped from between 25 and 33 percent to 14 percent—and even to 9 percent, if one counts those workers employed in government programs, as they would be in any calculation of unemployment from the end of World War II until the present day.

"We *planned* it that way!" crowed overconfident New Dealers—words that would come back to choke them. FDR, a fiscal conservative at heart, promptly cut the federal budget. Unemployment shot up again in the double-dip Roosevelt Depression of 1937 to 1938.

The truth was that neither Roosevelt nor his predecessor, Herbert Hoover (not to mention most of America), was ready for the sort of sustained, Keynesian deficit spending at a level that might have kicked the slump for good. Renewed public spending cut unemployment again and shot the rate of growth back up to 11 percent, but full employment would be realized only after 1941.

CHAPTER TEN

WWII

CHARLES LINDBERGH

1919
TO
1941

COMING ON THE RUN

THE LONG TRUDGE TO WAR

"In the final enumeration of Hitler's mistakes in waging the Second World War," wrote military historian John Keegan, "his decision to contest the issue with the power of the American economy may well come to stand first."

Yet for more than two years, it remained uncertain that Hitler would even get to make that contest. Most Americans had watched with growing revulsion as fascist regimes came to power in Germany, Italy, and Japan and then began their campaigns of aggression against China, Ethiopia, Libya, Spain, Czechoslovakia, and Albania. But even after German armies sliced across the Vistula River into Poland in the early morning hours of September 1, 1939, most Americans did not feel the war directly concerned them, and were determined to stay out.

Isolationism, after all, was in America's DNA. Most Americans had come to their land seeking to be rid of the Old World and its age-old national conflicts. America would do best to avoid "the toils of European ambition, rivalship, interest, humor, or caprice," George Washington had warned. Besides, what was the need for what Thomas Jefferson had disparaged as "entangling alliances"? A young Abraham Lincoln had declared, back in 1839: "All the armies of Europe, Asia and Africa combined, with all the treasure of the earth (our own excepted) in their military chest; with a Buonaparte [sic] for a commander, could not by force, take a drink from the Ohio, or make a track on the Blue Ridge, in a trial of a thousand years."

Contemporary isolationists ranged from former president Herbert Hoover to respected Socialist Party leader Norman Thomas. They were all sure that America would be kept safe by its oceans, or that a bayonet was a machine with a worker on either end, or that everything was an English plot.

The U.S. experience in World War I tended to underscore such convictions. That war came to seem like just one more tortured exercise in European

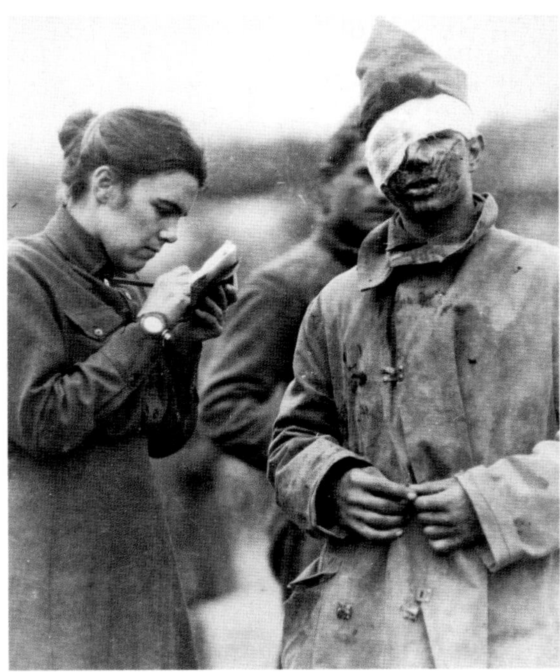

Above: War and rememberance: A Red Cross volunteer writes a letter for a blinded American doughboy in World War I. Although the U.S. was only in the war for 19 months, it suffered twice as many fatalities as it would suffer in the entire Vietnam War, and left many Americans weary of any conflict.

Opposite: Charles Lindbergh, the first man ever to fly across the Atlantic Ocean, speaks out at an America First rally. An admirer of the Nazi regime in Germany, Lindbergh vehemently opposed U.S. entry into World War II.

big-power rivalries, and a horrible waste. The overwhelming verdict of American arts and letters was that the First World War had been a fool's errand—"No European country is our friend nor has been since the last war and no country but one's own is worth fighting for," no less belligerent an individual than Ernest Hemingway asserted. "[I]n modern war there is nothing sweet nor fitting in your dying. You will die like a dog for no good reason."

The Senate passed a series of Neutrality Acts throughout the mid-to-late thirties that made it virtually impossible for America to aid any foreign country. President Roosevelt complained that the first such act was "more likely to drag us into war than keep us out," but signed it into law anyway. He loudly proclaimed, "I hate war!" in 1936, and told the mothers of America during his run for an unprecedented third term in 1940, "Your boys are not going to be sent into any foreign wars." Behind the scenes, he searched for some U.S. role in strengthening the West's security against the dictators but was hard-pressed to find one.

The start of open warfare in Europe, with Hitler's startling victories, helped sway American opinion—up to a point. By 1941, FDR was clearly hoping to instigate some provocation—most likely the same sort of German submarine attacks that had drawn the U.S. into World War I. In August, he traveled secretly to meet with British Prime Minister Winston Churchill off the coast of Newfoundland. There, the two leaders acted like de facto allies, singing "Onward Christian Soldiers" on deck during a religious service with sailors and staff, and signing the Atlantic Charter, a bold imagining of a democratic postwar world even as the fascists were advancing everywhere in the present one.

But for all of his seeming intention to stir up incidents in the Atlantic, Roosevelt regarded them charily when they happened. The reason for such reticence may have been the continuing strength of the isolationist movement. Even as U.S. sentiment moved closer and closer to all-out support for war in defense of Britain—which was still bravely holding out as the last Western defender against the Nazis—the Committee to Defend America First, now led by the flying hero Charles Lindbergh, continued to draw big crowds and big donations, and to make congressmen tremble. Lindbergh undermined his cause with a radio address in Des Moines, Iowa, in October 1941 that lurched into crude, anti-Semitic railings against supposed Jewish control of the U.S. media and government, but the so-called America Firsters still commanded a large audience.

Like its president, America seemed to consider war inevitable, but it could not quite bear to take the final step without some overwhelming reason. "I am waiting to be pushed into the situation," Roosevelt confided about the war to his friend and secretary of the treasury Henry Morgenthau Jr. But the push would come from an unexpected direction.

Roosevelt and Churchill confer aboard the HMS *Prince of Wales* in Placentia Bay, off Newfoundland, August 1941. Most of those present would die within a few months when the battleship was sunk by the Japanese.

ROOSEVELT
CHURCHILL

1919 TO 1941

CAUGHT NAPPING

THE ATTACK ON PEARL HARBOR

An ancient nation, the Japanese Empire had moved into the modern technological world with breathtaking speed, but the development of its government had lagged behind. Japan was controlled by a gaggle of military factions that revered but largely imprisoned the emperor, despised most civilians, and ruled more by coup and assassination than by law or parliamentary procedure. Fanatical cliques of younger officers urged both domestic reforms and incredible schemes of empire. Secret military societies pressed for the invasion of China, or Manchuria, or Siberia, or for a vast Pacific war with the U.S. and Great Britain.

A racist caricature of Isoroku Yamamoto, the great Japanese admiral, who did not want to fight the U.S.

The order to plan for a surprise attack against the United States was passed down to the extraordinary commander of Japan's Combined Fleet, Admiral Isoroku Yamamoto. A lover of baseball and bridge who had studied at Harvard and hitchhiked across the U.S., Yamamoto had objected so vociferously to the idea of war with America that he had to be ordered back to sea, lest army factions try to assassinate him. Undeterred, Yamamoto told his government that, unlike him, they had never seen firsthand "the automobile factories in Detroit and the oil fields in Texas." He warned, "If I am told to fight regardless of consequence, I shall run wild for the first six months or a year, but I have utterly no confidence for the second and third years."

His superiors noted his protests, and told him to get planning. What he came up with was typically audacious and brilliant, a first strike not at the obvious target—the 30,000 American troops stationed in the Philippines—but at Pearl Harbor in Hawaii, nearly 4,000 miles from the home islands of Japan.

Yet unbeknownst to Yamamoto, the U.S. Army had just installed a radar system in Hawaii, including three fixed sites and five mobile ones. The best situated was the Opana Mobile Radar Station on the northern tip of Oahu, on the other side of the island from Pearl Harbor. On December 7, 1941, the Opana station was manned by a pair of privates, Joseph L. Lockard and George E. Elliott Jr., who were about to shut it down at 7:00 A.M.—the hour when, inexplicably, the radar was always shut down for the day.

USS WEST VIRGINIA
USS TENNESSEE
USS ARIZONA

the United States of America was simultaneously and deliberately attacked by naval and air forces of the Empire of Japan.

The United States was at the moment at peace with that nation and was continuing the conversations with its Government and its Emperor looking toward the maintenance of peace in the Pacific. Indeed, one hour after Japanese air squadrons had commenced bombing in Hawaii and the Philippines, the Japanese Ambassador to the United States and his colleague delivered to the Secretary of State a formal reply to a former message from the Secretary. This reply contained a statement that diplomatic negotiations must be considered at an end, but contained no threat and no hint of an armed attack.

It will be recorded that the distance of Manila, and especially of Hawaii, from Japan make it obvious that the attacks were deliberately planned many days ago. During the intervening time the Japanese Government has deliberately sought to deceive the United States by false statements and expressions of hope for continued peace.

Just at that moment, Private Elliott spotted a blip on their oscilloscope, then another, and another; the planes were 132 miles away and coming in fast. Private Lockard, the more experienced of the two radar operators, took a look, but thought they should close down the device as scheduled. Elliott insisted that they report it to the Information Center at Fort Shafter, 30 miles from Opana and just a few miles from Pearl Harbor. The switchboard operator at Shafter, Private Joseph P. McDonald, took the call and quickly informed the only other man on duty at the Information Center, Lieutenant Kermit Tyler. Tyler was charged with helping the flight controller get planes up in the air to meet any incoming threat, but that morning there was no controller, no aircraft-identification officer—just a single Army lieutenant. McDonald passed on what Lockard had told him: "There are a large number of planes coming in from the north three points east."

Tyler pondered the information, then told McDonald not to worry about it. Tyler had heard a local station playing Hawaiian music that morning—always an indication that a flight of U.S. planes was due in from the West Coast. He was not wrong—a flight from the coast *was* on its way in. They would not be Pearl Harbor's only visitors that morning.

Up at Opana, Lockard and Elliott went on tracking all the blips for another 40 minutes, until they finally packed up their equipment. At 7:45, McDonald ended his shift and went back to his tent, where he told his tentmate, Private Richard Schimmel, "Shim, the Japs are coming." Minutes later, in they came, so close and low that Schimmel and McDonald were soon diving for cover on the mess-hall floor. They grabbed rifles and gas masks and rushed back to the Information Center to do their duty, but by then it was too late.

The Japanese attack on Pearl Harbor stunned the nation. The assault killed 2,345 American servicemen and 57 civilians, and wounded 1,282. Twenty-one major U.S. vessels were either sunk, capsized, run aground, or heavily damaged, including eight battleships. Of the 402 aircraft, 188 were destroyed and 159 damaged—155 of them on the ground. Japanese fighter planes had outmaneuvered and outfought American planes almost effortlessly.

The attack was also a failure. Admiral Yamamoto realized this the moment the results were transmitted to him, and he paused to write a short poem that reflected his penchant for one or both of those twin American passions of the time, bridge and baseball:

What I have achieved
Is less than a grand slam

Yamamoto understood where his attack had fallen short. By great good fortune, the Pacific Fleet's aircraft carriers—its most difficult-to-replace ships—were away from Pearl Harbor. And because they *were* still in the harbor, seven of the eight battleships at Pearl were salvaged. Save for the *Arizona*, whose hulk anchors the memorial at Pearl Harbor to this day, all were refitted and sent back out to see action before the war was over. The same went for 80 percent of the damaged airplanes. The Japanese missed the base's submarine yard entirely. A second attack might have forced the U.S. Navy and Army all the way back to the West Coast, had it hit the enormous aboveground oil tanks that constituted the only major fuel supply the military had in the Pacific. Now it was too late.

1941 TO 1945

THE ASSEMBLY LINE GOES TO WAR

AMERICA OUTPRODUCES THE WORLD

"No matter how long it may take us to overcome this premeditated invasion, the American people, in their righteous might, will win through to absolute victory," President Roosevelt declared through teeth gritted in anger, asking Congress for a declaration of war the following day in his Day of Infamy address.

The extended applause and atavistic cries that greeted those words spoke for the resolve of an entire people, now roused to wrath. What they would unleash would sweep all before it. Yamamoto had been right. Churchill comprehended this at once, writing after he heard the news of the attack on Pearl Harbor, "So we had won after all." Not so Hitler, who (displaying his usual juvenile mentality) rushed to tell his generals: "Now it is impossible for us to lose the war. We now have an ally who has never been vanquished in three thousand years."

Hitler was under no obligation to go to war with the U.S. under the Axis nations' Tripartite Pact, but he did so gleefully, certain that Japan would keep America tied down and out of the European war, and that the Japanese might even be obliging enough to attack the Soviet Union.

It was a vain hope—as Admiral Yamamoto already knew. Much as he had predicted, the Japanese "ran wild" in the Pacific for the next six months. They overran U.S. bases on Wake Island, Guam, and elsewhere, scored stunning victories over the Royal Navy and the British army in the Indian Ocean, at Singapore, and at Hong Kong. They also handed the U.S. the most humiliating defeat in its history when they somehow caught General Douglas MacArthur's planes on the ground the day *after* Pearl Harbor, and defeated and captured the rest of his command in the Philippines. Then, in June of 1942, a clever trap lured four critical Japanese carriers to their destruction at Midway Island and essentially broke the back of the empire's naval and air power. From that point on, Japan would be on the defensive—and Yamamoto would soon be a casualty, his plane ambushed and shot down over Bougainville Island, one of the Solomons, on April 18, 1943.

The main reasons for Japan's defeat were the ones Yamamoto had named: the automakers of Detroit, the oil fields of Texas, and the rest of the enormous industrial base of the United States, which had lain so underused for more than a decade. Now, it geared up at astonishing speed. By 1943 to 1944, the U.S. economy was producing one ship a day and one new aircraft every five minutes. Between 1940 and 1943, industrial output more than doubled in Germany and the Soviet Union, it more than tripled in the United Kingdom, and it more than quadrupled in Japan. In the United States, it increased 25 times over. By 1944, the United States was making 40 percent of all the world's armaments.

The heart of the Arsenal of Democracy that Roosevelt had insisted the U.S. make itself into was Detroit, along with nearby Michigan cities such as Flint and Dearborn, where the factories of the great auto plants were quickly converted to churning out weapons of war. Among many other things, they would produce 75 percent of all U.S. aircraft engines, 56 percent of all American tanks, 87 percent of aerial bombs. Chrysler reduced the time it took to

Back at El Segundo: Women and men work side by side at the Douglas aircraft plant in the little California town, turning out Dauntless dive-bombers.

BY THE END OF THE WAR, 427,000 OF THE 665,000 MOTOR VEHICLES THE RED ARMY POSSESSED WERE FROM THE WEST, MANY OF THEM SUPERB TWO-AND-A-HALF-TON DODGE TRUCKS.

manufacture a Swedish Bofors anti-aircraft gun from 450 hours to ten. Pontiac reduced the time it took to manufacture a Swiss Oerlikon anti-aircraft gun from 428 hours to 346, and cut the cost by 23 percent along the way. By March of 1942, General Motors' Saginaw plant had produced 28,728 Browning machine guns, and cut their cost from $667 apiece to $141.44.

The U.S. supplied the Soviet Union with 15,000 aircraft, 7,000 tanks, 350,000 tons of explosives, 2,000 locomotives, 11,000 railcars, three million tons of gasoline (including high-quality aviation fuel), 540,000 tons of rails, 51,000 jeeps, 375,000 trucks, 15 million pairs of boots, and three-quarters of its stocks of copper. By the end of the war, 427,000 of the 665,000 motor vehicles the Red Army possessed were from the West, many of them superb two-and-a-half-ton Dodge trucks. American farmers supplied Soviet troops with five million tons of food, or enough for a half-pound of concentrated rations for every Soviet soldier, every day of the war.

Workers at a Detroit Chrysler plant roll out the new model for 1942, a Sherman tank.

It was true that the Soviets did the great bulk of the fighting against Germany, pinning down and then thrashing some 262 Axis divisions, while the Western allies never had to face more than 88. But behind each Soviet soldier stood an American farmer and assembly line worker. "Wartime Russia survived and fought on American aid," John Keegan would write. "It was in American boots and trucks that the Red Army advanced to Berlin. Without them its campaign would have foundered to a halt in western Russia in 1944."

U.S. factories turned out quality as well as quantity. While German land weapons were usually better than those produced by the Americans (or anyone else), the difference was not great enough to compensate for the U.S. lead in production. By the end of the war, the Americans were producing the most impregnable battleships, the largest—and smallest—aircraft carriers, the farthest-ranging submarines, the fastest fighter planes, the most powerful heavy bombers. They came up with radar (based on a British design) and sonar. By 1943, the U.S. Navy's Grumman F6F Hellcat was outrunning and outmaneuvering the Zero, which it shot down at a kill-to-loss ratio of 19 to 1, all but eradicating the Japanese planes from the skies above the Pacific.

THE WHEEL DEAL: THE JEEP

Of all the United States' mass-produced instruments of war, probably the most durable and useful was a low, tough all-terrain vehicle that seemed virtually indestructible: the Model T of the Second World War.

The vehicle was probably named for its initials, G.P.—inevitably pronounced as "jeep." The G.P. stood for "general purpose," and no name was ever more appropriate. The jeep was designed to go anywhere and do anything, and so it did. Throughout the war, it would be driven everywhere around the world, not just by Americans but also by British, French, and Chinese. Before the war was over, there were three jeeps turned off the assembly line every four minutes, 634,569 in all.

Its advantages were legion and obvious. The jeep stood just 37 inches off the ground, with a removable canvas roof that presented a low profile to the enemy, and blackout headlights and taillights. It could carry up to seven men, if two were willing to ride sidesaddle on the front bumper. Its flat hood could serve as a dining table, a staff conference table, even an altar if need be. An M1 carbine could fit through an opening in the fixed cover just below the windshield—or the windshield could be folded down, in order to accommodate a wounded man on a stretcher. It had no doors, allowing for quick exits and entrances.

The jeep weighed just 2,554 pounds, making it light enough to fit into gliders and be dropped with commandos behind enemy lines, and to bounce over all but the worst roads. It had heavy wheels with split rims, allowing it to keep going for a long way even with a flat tire, and an electrical system that was waterproof and situated high in the vehicle.

THE ARSENAL OF DEMOCRACY: THE INDUSTRIES THAT WON THE WAR, 1940 TO 1945

With the coming of the war, the enormous U.S. industrial base switched to war production with almost frightening alacrity and efficiency. By V-J Day, American factories had produced 300,000 planes, 88,000 tanks, 6.5 million rifles, and 40 billion bullets. The average American soldier could draw on four tons of supplies; the average Japanese, just two pounds, and by the end of the war, the U.S. was supplying 28.7 percent of Britain's military equipment, and 29.1 percent of all its food. The Soviet Union's dependence was even greater, as Joseph Stalin acknowledged at the Tehran Conference in 1943, toasting, "To American production, without which this war would have been lost."

Airplanes

Iron ore

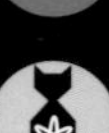
Nuclear

Ships

Submarines

Tanks

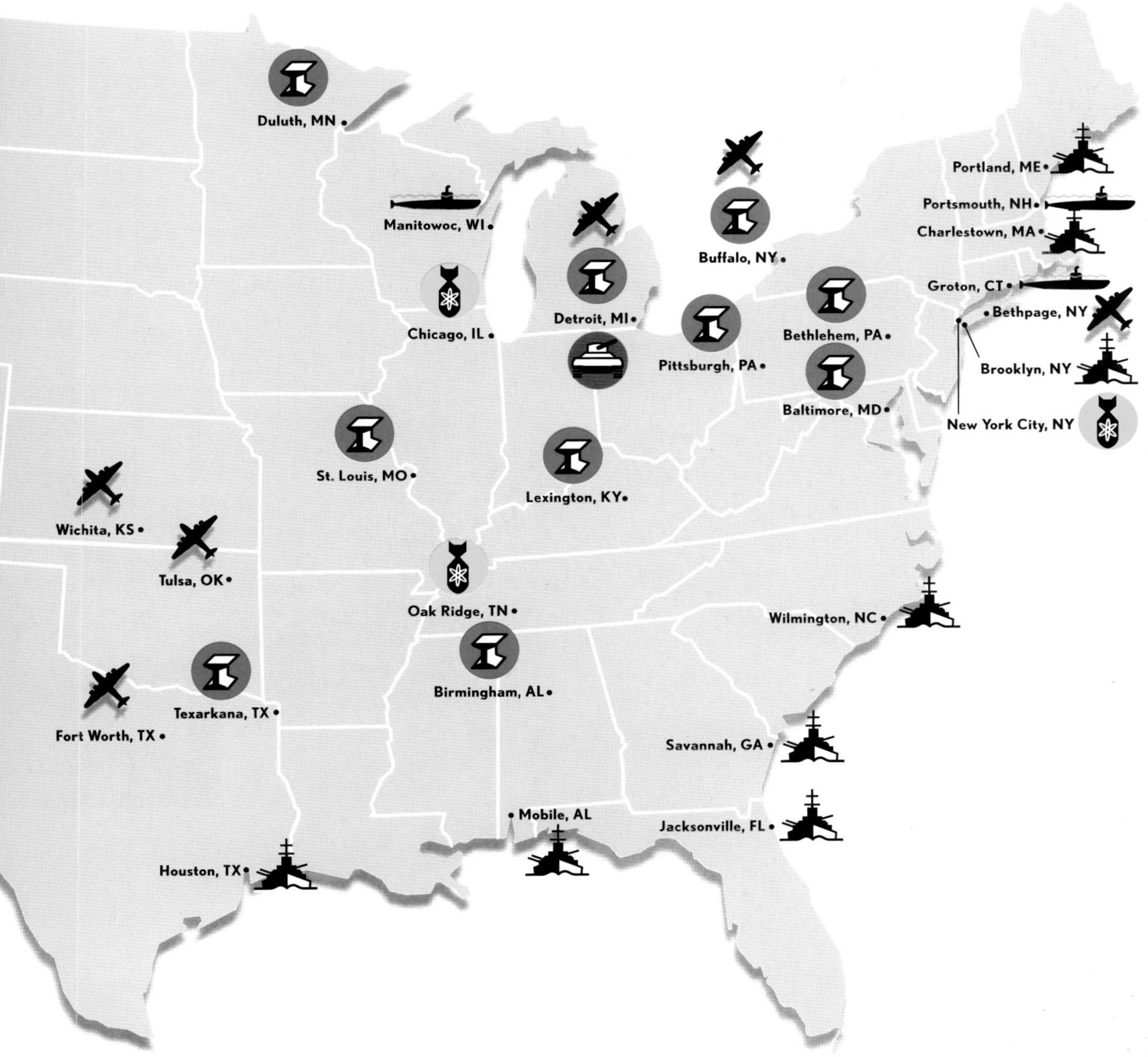

Duluth, MN
Manitowoc, WI
Chicago, IL
Detroit, MI
Buffalo, NY
Portland, ME
Portsmouth, NH
Charlestown, MA
Groton, CT
Bethpage, NY
Brooklyn, NY
New York City, NY
Bethlehem, PA
Pittsburgh, PA
Baltimore, MD
St. Louis, MO
Lexington, KY
Wichita, KS
Tulsa, OK
Oak Ridge, TN
Wilmington, NC
Birmingham, AL
Texarkana, TX
Fort Worth, TX
Savannah, GA
Mobile, AL
Jacksonville, FL
Houston, TX

It's Our Fight Too!

THE FIGHT FOR FREEDOM

WINNING THE HOME FRONT

With some 15 million men in uniform, the nation would have to look for new sources of labor. It would turn to two groups that had previously been excluded from most of the industrial workplace—women and people of color, especially African-Americans.

For the first time, American women were allowed into the armed forces (though not to participate in combat), and some 200,000 joined. Yet the greatest contribution women made to the war effort was in the defense plants. On America's entrance into the war, 12 million women were already employed. Seven million more women went to work for wages, some two million of them manufacturing the materials of war.

In the munitions plants, women assembled tanks and bombs; they also welded, riveted, and cut steel. Half of all workers in ordnance and electrical manufacturing plants, and one-third of all workers in aircraft factories, were women. They were thought to be better than men for welding in tight corners, and made most of the bomb fuses because of their smaller fingers.

The war spurred yet another exodus of blacks from the rural South, with more than 400,000 African-Americans leaving the cotton and tobacco fields for the steelworks, defense plants, and shipyards of cities in both the North and South. War work was a tremendous opportunity for many of them, doubling their average yearly income from $566 to nearly $1,200, but that betterment did not come without costs. White-owned companies—at first, anyway—assigned blacks to the very worst jobs and paid white workers twice as much. Even so, many whites in all parts of the country were openly hostile to the idea of working with blacks under any circumstances.

"Rosie the Riveter," as songs and posters named her. During the war, American women went to work in percentages matched by no other nation, and they never returned to the home in the same numbers that they had been before 1941.

The worst conflicts came in Detroit, where Ford, reversing its longtime policy, tried to refuse to hire blacks. At Packard, now building PT-boat engines and the famous P-51 Mustang fighter, 3,000 white workers—with the encouragement of management—walked off the job when three blacks were promoted. A long series of brawls and face-offs away from the workplace came to a head when the government attempted to open new public housing to all defense workers and their families, regardless of color. White mobs attacked blacks throughout Detroit for two days in the summer of 1943, often aided by the police. Before the fighting was over, nine whites and 25 blacks were dead (with 17 of the latter shot by the police), and 800 people were injured. Germany's foreign-distribution propaganda magazine, *Signal*, had pictures to run with a story ecstatically explaining why America's "mongrelized" society could not win the war.

That was only the worst of the race riots that occurred in 47 cities, nearly all of them white-on-black attacks that usually began in defense plants. In Mobile, Alabama, white shipyard workers rioted when black welders were hired to work—ironically enough—on the "Liberty ships" that kept a lifeline of supplies open to Europe. Similar attempts to integrate defense plants led to brutal, often deadly assaults by white workers in Chester, Pennsylvania; in East Chicago, Indiana; and in Beaumont, Texas. In Harlem, a highly popular destination for servicemen of all colors passing through New York, military authorities insisted

DAVID KENNEDY, historian, Stanford University: "The precedent of what women accomplished in World War II lingered in the memory of the society at large and it was one of the things that energized the feminist movement a decade or two later."

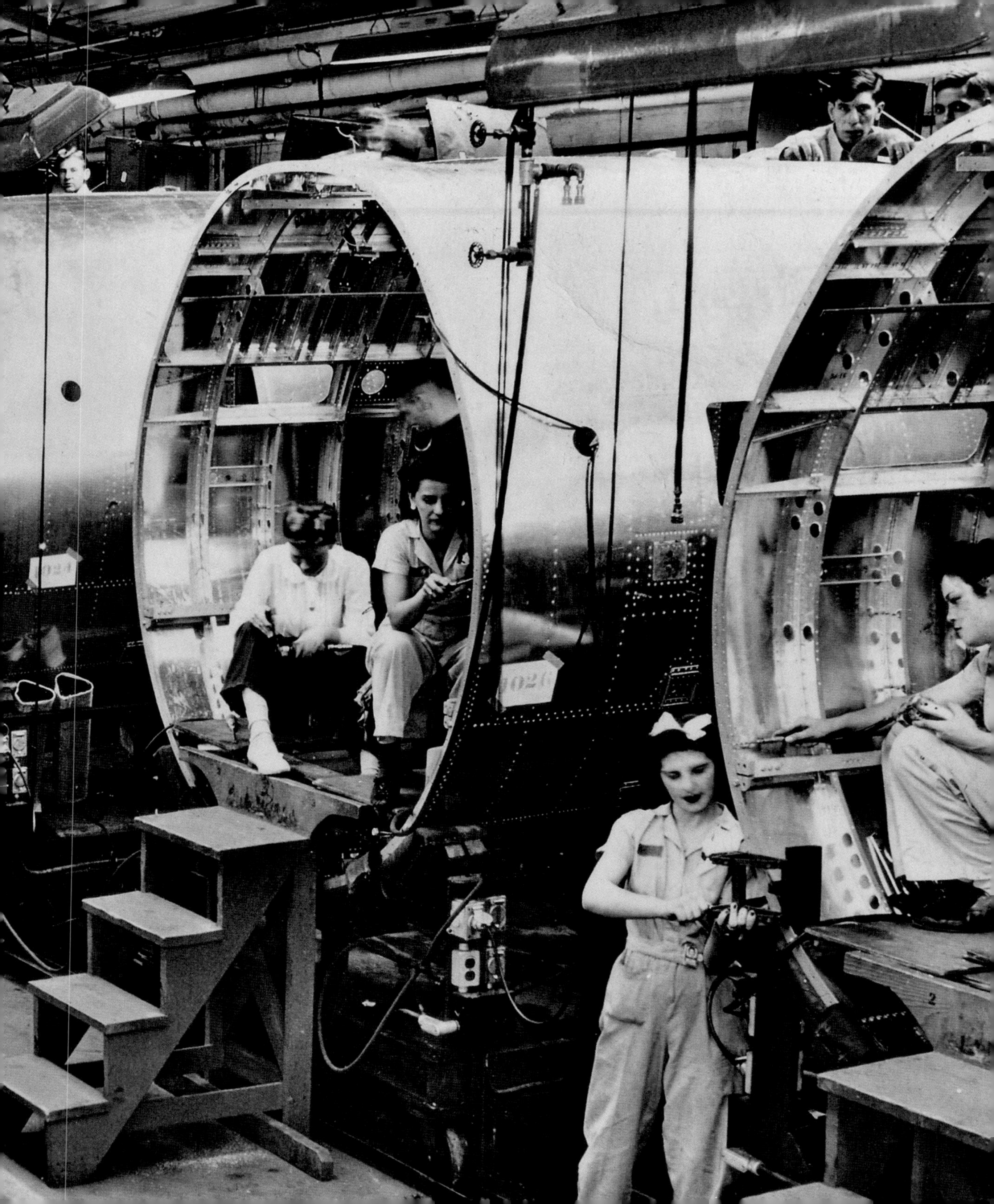
1026

on shuttering the fabled Savoy Ballroom to prevent "race mixing." In Los Angeles, running battles fueled by alcohol and the desire for women erupted between gangs of sailors and teenage pachucos from the Mexican-American barrios, who were known for affecting exaggerated zoot suits (thus, the fabled Zoot Suit Riots). The L.A. city council responded by making it a crime to wear a zoot suit.

Such scenes could be viewed as shocking. Yet they were, as well, the messy business of a democracy improving itself. "No country could have survived America's convulsive transformation of 1941–45 without altering its essence and its view of itself," William Manchester would write in *The Glory and the Dream*. "The home front was in reality a battleground of ideas, customs, economic theory, foreign policy, and relationships between the sexes and social classes."

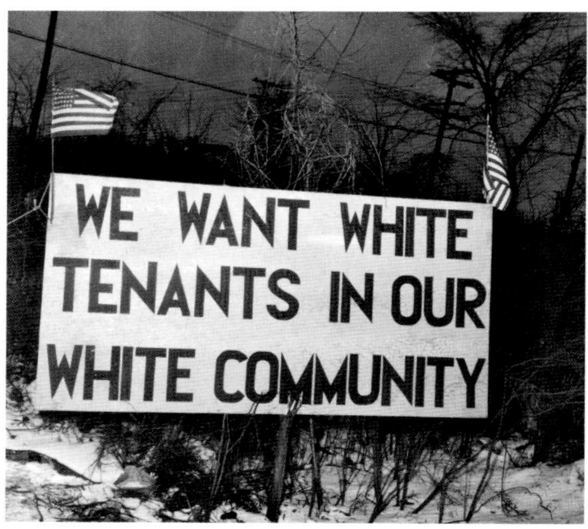

Above: A sign protests the integrated Sojourner Truth housing project in 1942 Detroit. White agitation against any and all black housing in the Motor City went back to the 1920s. Right: Lieutenant General Lucian K. Truscott Jr. talks to the black troops of the 92nd Infantry Division after they repelled a German attack near Viareggio, Italy, in 1944.

Here, in many different ways, the seeds of the civil rights movement were planted. James Farmer and the pacifist A. J. Muste led the first sit-ins in Chicago in 1943, desegregating restaurants and other businesses with a tactic that would be revived and become an integral part of the movement in 1960. A. Philip Randolph, the indefatigable activist who had struggled for 12 long years to organize the all-black Brotherhood of Sleeping Car Porters, secured a presidential commitment to equal pay for equal work, and to equal-opportunity hiring practices in defense plants, by visiting FDR in the White House in 1941 and threatening to lead a black "march on Washington." The president forestalled this in July with Executive Order 8802, creating a Fair Employment Practices Committee to hear complaints and pressing employers to banish discrimination from the workplace. It was the most important federal action on racial justice since the post–Civil War Reconstruction, and it would both spark the creation of similar state and local commissions and foreshadow the passage of the Civil Rights Act in 1964. (While Randolph got what he wanted from the White House, his march on Washington would not be abandoned, only delayed until 1963—when he would join Martin Luther King Jr. as one of the main speakers and organizers.)

If integrating American factories was difficult, integrating the armed forces was even harder. The Army had been rigorously segregated since black soldiers had had the gall to win far too many medals charging up San Juan Hill next to the Rough Riders

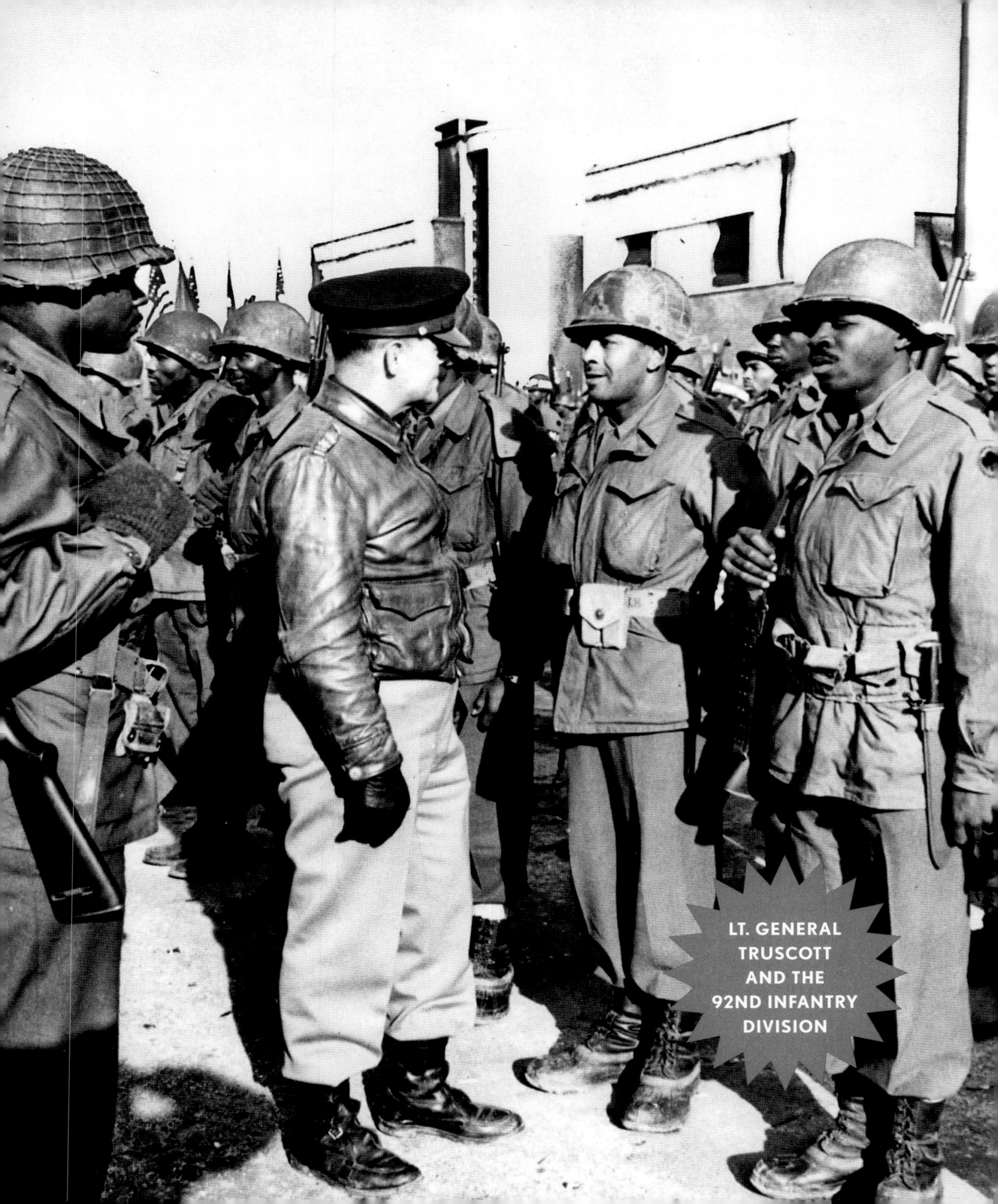
LT. GENERAL
TRUSCOTT
AND THE
92ND INFANTRY
DIVISION

"SOLDIERS WERE FIGHTING THE WORLD'S WORST RACIST, ADOLF HITLER, IN THE WORLD'S MOST SEGREGATED ARMY," NOTED HISTORIAN STEPHEN AMBROSE. "THE IRONY DID NOT GO UNNOTICED."

in the Spanish-American War of 1898. Despite an outstanding combat record in World War I (under the French flag), black troops were restricted almost exclusively to such duties as hauling equipment and digging ditches. More than a million African-Americans were inducted into the Army in World War II. They were sent to basic training camps that were usually in the Deep South, and often placed under white Southern officers, the premise being that the latter "knew how to handle them."

The result was misery. Black soldiers routinely received worse rations and billets than whites did. They were banned from many Southern towns, and often set upon by local white sheriffs and cops who greeted their very presence with expressions of vitriolic hatred. Black enlisted men and officers alike were repeatedly beaten, arrested, jailed, and even killed by white lawmen. Such incidents, along with the day-to-day indignities of existence in the Jim Crow South, proved to be a shock to young black men who had spent their whole lives in the North or the West. Their letters back home unified African-Americans in rage.

Resistance broke out everywhere, even in the training camps. A gifted young college athletic hero and black officer, soon to become a civil rights icon, Jackie Robinson was arrested and court-martialed for refusing to move to the back of a bus in Texas. He was acquitted, but discharged nonetheless. In Duck Hill, Mississippi—the site of two of the more brutal lynchings in American history just a few years before—black troops at nearby Camp McCain grew so outraged at their treatment that they marched into town on the night after the Fourth of July, 1943, and sprayed public buildings and homes with bullets for 12 minutes. "Soldiers were fighting the world's worst racist, Adolf Hitler, in the world's most segregated army," noted historian Stephen Ambrose. "The irony did not go unnoticed."

That irony began to slowly—finally—batter in some doors of prejudice. The Navy grudgingly worked blacks into combat postings, and eventually commissioned 58 black officers. The Marines also gave way and put blacks into combat, especially after they distinguished themselves as stretcher bearers in the bloodbath that was Peleliu, hauling their white comrades to safety on that Pacific island despite withering Japanese fire. The newly created Air Force proved especially resistant to integration, although the famed Tuskegee Airmen did serve with distinction in Italy.

The Army led all the services in integrating—black and white infantry platoons were even placed next to one another in Europe. African-Americans still were not supposed to do any real fighting, but again and again, under the exigencies of combat, they found themselves pulled into the fray. Not only did black drivers in the Red Ball Express (as the convoy system was known) keep supplies coming to the nearly encircled troops in the Battle of the Bulge, but other black supply soldiers also stepped up to hold the line at the worst moments of that conflict.

THE BLACK BIRDMEN: TUSKEGEE AIRMEN

The Tuskegee Airmen would become the Air Force's great integration success story, their fame following them down the decades. But things nearly didn't work out that way. The all-black unit trained largely under white and Puerto Rican officers at the Tuskegee airfield in Alabama. The men were then sent to Europe, where they won a unit Distinguished Service Citation for their work in providing air cover for the Allied invasion of Sicily.

Then, disgrace. Their white commanding officer, Colonel William Momyer, accused them of cowardice and incompetence, planting a negative story about them in *Time* magazine and recommending that they see little flight time. The accusations seemed to bear out everything that Senator James Eastland of Mississippi had said about blacks at the beginning of the war: "We are dealing with an inferior race.... They will not fight. They will not work."

When the House Armed Services Committee held a hearing to investigate Momyer's charges, one member even introduced into evidence a supposedly "scientific" report from someone at the University of Texas "proving" that blacks were of low intelligence and incapable of handling complex situations such as aerial combat. The committee duly voted to recommend that the squadron be broken up.

Sanity prevailed. The intervention of Colonel Emmett "Rosie" O'Donnell kept the airmen from being disbanded, and an evaluation ordered by air-combat pioneer General Henry "Hap" Arnold showed the Tuskegee fliers to be at least the equal to any others in the Mediterranean theater—whereas Colonel Momyer had been upbraided by his superiors for recklessly taking his men into Luftwaffe-dominated areas and losing much of his command. The colonel was sent home to conduct flight training. Along with other black airmen, the Tuskegee pilots were re-formed into the 332nd Fighter Group, commanded by Lieutenant Colonel Benjamin O. Davis Jr.—at the time only the fourth black man to have graduated from West Point.

Under Davis, the Tuskegee Airmen—known also as the Redtails or Redtail Angels, for the markings on their planes, and as the *Schwarze Vogelmenschen*, or Black Birdmen, by their German adversaries—fought the rest of the war in Italy and compiled a magnificent combat record, downing 111 Luftwaffe planes, sinking a destroyer, and wrecking numerous fuel dumps, trucks, and trains. They flew more than 15,000 sorties on 1,500 missions, received two more Distinguished Unit Citations (one for shooting down three of the new German jets while on a raid over Berlin) and were awarded several Silver Stars, and a total of 150 Distinguished Flying Crosses, eight Purple Hearts, 14 Bronze Stars, and 744 Air Medals.

Before the war was over, 150 of the Tuskegee Airmen would give their lives for their country.

FIGHTING ON TWO FRONTS

Every soldier would be needed. For all the advantages that American production provided to Admiral Chester W. Nimitz's hard slog across the Pacific, from Hawaii through Tarawa, the Marianas, and Peleliu to the Philippines—and for all the casualty-saving maneuvers of General Douglas MacArthur's adroit "island-hopping" campaign from Guadalcanal through Bougainville, Lae, and on to Bataan—the war against Japan was a mind-boggling enterprise, one paid for with more blood and treasure than the United States had ever expended before in all of its previous wars combined.

At the same time, the United States was launching a second front against what was, pound for pound, the greatest fighting machine ever assembled—joining with the British to drive the German Wehrmacht back through North Africa, then out of Sicily and up the Italian peninsula. In June of 1944, U.S. forces would face their ultimate test: a frontal assault on what the Nazis called Fortress Europe, in the greatest amphibious landing in history, directed against beaches on the northwest coast of France defended by Field Marshal Erwin Rommel, maybe the greatest of all the German commanders, commander of the famous "Ghost Division" during the 1940 invasion of France and the legendary "Desert Fox" of the North African campaign. Leading the Allied forces would be General Dwight D. Eisenhower, who had never seen action of any sort and was virtually unknown before he was 52. Ike would prove to be a capable tactician but above all an unsurpassed military politician, keeping the high-strung alliance command together. But everything depended on how the landing on the beaches of Normandy went.

Thirty minutes before midnight on June 5, 1944, some 1,100 planes and gliders landed 29,000 airborne troops throughout Normandy, with orders to seize key rail and road junctions and to ambush German units rushing to meet the invasion. A short time later, the greatest fleet ever assembled—6,939 ships from eight navies, in 59 convoys strung out along 100 miles of English coastline—set sail for five beaches along the northern coast of France. They carried 57,000 American troops; another 72,215 were British and Canadian; the rest were Poles who had escaped to Britain after their homeland was overrun almost five years earlier.

Above them was an aerial armada of 11,680 planes. Opposed by only a pathetic 300 Luftwaffe aircraft, their purpose was to blast the German defenses along the beaches out of existence, and then to protect the beachhead from any Wehrmacht reinforcements. To launch such an assault against a continent required a masterwork of logistical planning.

Of course, this being war, it all went wrong. Inexperienced pilots dropped many of the parachutists too high or too low, or scattered them all over the Normandy countryside. Some would drown in the sea or in the flooded hinterlands. Bad weather forced the B-24 bombers assigned to knock out the German defenses to drop their cargo blindly, relying on instruments. Out of fear of hitting the Allied fleet racing toward the beaches, most ended up dropping their loads into the countryside well beyond the German beach defenses.

And this being war, much of it worked out anyway. So many reports poured in of scattered airborne troops in so many different places that it froze many of the

"It's fatal to enter any war without the will to win it."

—General Douglas MacArthur

OMAHA
BEACH,
1944

German officers. The invasion caught Rommel on leave in Germany; soon after his return, he was badly strafed by a British plane and had to give up his command. Four of the five landing beaches offered little or no resistance and were quickly captured. Only on Omaha Beach, an American objective, did all the terrors of an amphibious landing manifest themselves. The landing craft were launched at a very distant 12 miles out to sea; they, in turn, let out their soldiers too soon, owing to nervousness or inexperience. Many died or floundered in the high surf.

There was no supporting fire from Allied ships afraid—once again—of hitting their own men. What's more, Omaha was the best fortified of all the German positions, with defensive obstacles narrowing the attackers into preplanned lanes of fire where they were mowed down helplessly, sometimes even before they could get out of the landing craft. Facing them was the crack German 352nd Division, well-trained veterans determined to hold their position.

Men had to advance through perfectly situated cross fires and minefields. The elite U.S. Army Rangers, who were supposed to lead the storming of the German pillboxes, lost 68 of their 130 men before they could reach the seawall. Only the desperate acts of courageous men kept the whole landing party from being wiped out. Staff Sergeant William Courtney and Private William Braher of the Rangers managed to scale the 100-foot Pointe du Hoc cliffs to the west of the beachhead, taking a key position. Sergeant Julius Belcher took a pillbox by himself. Soon they were followed by soldiers from the 1st Division—the Big Red One—whose Colonel George A. Taylor told them: "Two kinds of people are staying on this beach, the dead and those who are going to die. Now let's get the hell out of here."

With the help of fire from a destroyer, landed tanks, and other reinforcements, the troops at Omaha Beach were finally able to secure a shaky beachhead four miles wide and a mile deep. Behind them would come the deluge. By nightfall on June 6, the entire assault force was ashore. And five days later, 326,547 troops, 54,186 vehicles, and 104,428 tons of supplies had been landed on the beaches. By the end of June, there were 850,000 Allied soldiers in Normandy, and the breakout from the beaches was well underway. Soon after that, there were 1.5 million American troops in France—six times the number that would invade Iraq—and before the end of August they had both surrounded and annihilated the German armies there, in the battle of the Falaise Gap, and had liberated Paris.

FUSELAGE

1939
TO
1945

RAINING FIRE

THE WAR ON CIVILIANS

Coming when it did, World War II served as a showdown in the contest between democracies and dictatorships that had been escalating for more than a decade. The Great Depression had disheartened many in the West over the prospects of democracy. Individuals as diverse as Anne Morrow Lindbergh (author of a glum little prognostication, *The Wave of the Future*) and Joseph Kennedy (Roosevelt's ambassador to England before 1941) saw democracy as finished, soon to be supplanted everywhere by some derivation of fascism. In other fashionable circles, Communism was the coming thing.

The war settled these arguments decisively, in favor of liberal democracy. It also spurred major advances in both tolerance and the rights of minorities in America, and the national ideal retained an almost uncanny hold on even its most despised citizens. A Japanese military cult, for instance, had sent a number of agents to the United States before the war, trying to encourage people of color to rise up against whites in exchange for a promise of power after the empire's inevitable triumph. They found no takers. Even after 120,000 Japanese-Americans were forcibly removed from their West Coast homes to detention camps, 33,000 of their sons volunteered to join the U.S. armed services as soon as they were eligible, their infantry regiments becoming two of the most decorated units in the war.

The dream of a society of equals, drawn from all over the globe, may have been a partial explanation for the relatively humane war record of the United States. Despite the vastness and the desperation of the struggle it was involved in, the U.S. never resorted to the sorts of depredations against the helpless and the innocent that routinely characterized the behavior of its adversaries.

The one possible exception was the British and American effort to break the Axis from the air. The temptation was understandable, considering the awful casualties that the ground war was inflicting. Initially, all Allied bombing was intended solely to hit military targets; Roosevelt in 1939 had denounced the "inhuman barbarism" of German terror bombings of Poland. "Whatever be the lengths to which others may go," British Prime Minister Neville Chamberlain announced, "His Majesty's Government will never resort to the deliberate attack on women and children, and other civilians for the purpose of mere terrorism."

Above: Members of the Mochida family, photographed by Dorothea Lange, await an evacuation bus, 1942. Identification tags were used to aid in keeping a family unit intact during all phases of evacuation.

Opposite: An American fighter pilot in Tunisia, his plane "notched" with his kills against German and Italian planes and targets.

Yet attitudes began to change after the sustained bombing known as the Blitz burned down most of old London, and after it became increasingly clear just how hard it was to define or restrict bombing to "military objectives." One month after the stunning German raid on Coventry, England, in November 1940, the Royal Air Force lit up the center of Mannheim, Germany, with incendiaries. By the Casablanca Conference in January 1943, the Allied position had subtly shifted even further, to allow for the sort of bombing that would "undermine the morale of the German people." But a few American air commanders still thought they had a better alternative.

By 1942, hundreds of four-engine heavy bombers were pouring off the assembly line at the Boeing factory. The planes were immensely powerful and seemingly all but indestructible machines and could transport 6,000-pound bomb loads for 2,000 miles, at speeds of up to 250 miles per hour. Their ultimate incarnation had 14 machine guns, some mounted in Plexiglas turrets around the aircraft—and was so bristling with weaponry that its builders dubbed the B-17 the Flying Fortress. When they were flying in a "box formation," German pilots compared them to a *fliegendes Stachelschwein*, a "flying porcupine."

On August 17, 1942, a group of 12 B-17s from the Army Eighth Air Force, protected by RAF fighter planes, set off in the afternoon to attack the enemy's rail marshaling yards at Rouen, France. The lead plane, the *Butcher Shop*, was flown by a 27-year-old squadron commander named Paul Tibbets. Tibbets flew his mission without a hitch. Visibility was perfect, the Germans were caught by surprise, and the planes managed to drop half their bomb loads within the target area from a height of 23,000 feet. "[Y]ou couldn't describe it as pinpoint bombing," the squadron commander admitted. "We still had a lot to learn." But it was an encouraging improvement on night bombing raids.

"A feeling of elation took hold of us as we winged back across the Channel. All the tension was gone," Tibbets recalled. "We were no longer novices at this terrible game of war. We had braved the enemy in his own skies and were alive to tell about it."

Alas, it was not to be that easy. Visibility rarely turned out to be as good again in Europe as it was that sunny August day, and as the Germans adjusted to the B-17 and its tactics, American losses mounted sharply without inflicting any equivalent damage. Daylight bombing was temporarily suspended.

In lieu of it, the Allies listened to the advice of British Air Marshal Sir Arthur "Bomber" Harris and ordered what many considered to be terror bombing. An attack with high explosives and incendiary devices on Hamburg, Germany, by the RAF on July 24, 1943, created the war's first firestorm, with gale-force winds and fires that reached temperatures of up to 1,500 degrees Fahrenheit, incinerating people even in bomb shelters. Continued raids on the city over the next few days killed 50,000 people and destroyed 580 factories.

"Are we beasts? Are we taking this too far?" Churchill had asked two years before, in a rare moment of doubt, when RAF raids had first started inflicting significant civilian casualties. Now, Allied command fell almost easily in thrall to the idea of "area bombing," as it was euphemistically called. The rationale was that if targets could not be pinpointed then entire industrial neighborhoods would be razed, and if they were not destroyed, well, then at least the workers who manned the war plants would be annihilated.

Once the Luftwaffe was all but demolished, Allied planes could pound one German city after another into rubble, with the Americans now attacking by day and the British by night. The campaign reached an awful climax in a raid against the beautiful old city of Dresden. Dresden was a legitimate military target, a major military train depot and a leading manufacturer of munitions that was being fortified against the Soviet advance. But it was also stuffed with as many as 500,000 civilian refugees. In February of 1945, British incendiary bombs created a firestorm that burned down 15 square miles of the city center while the Americans hit the rail marshaling yards, killing 25,000 to 50,000 civilians—less than three months before Germany's final capitulation.

Prisoners in a concentration camp at Sachsenhausen, Germany, 1938. Terrible as the Dresden bombing was, it prevented the Nazis from transporting and murdering the last few Jews in the city, as Germany continued the Holocaust to the very end of the war.

B-29 BOMBER
ENGINE NO. 3
OSAKA, JAPAN

1939 TO 1945

"NOW I AM BECOME DEATH" THE ATOMIC BOMB

A young Eighth Air Force commander carried the lessons of Europe over to the Pacific theater. General Curtis LeMay soon found himself frustrated over how the high winds in the jet stream above Japan kept his bombers from achieving much accuracy. But with the Japanese air force all but annihilated by the last year of the war, he devised a novel and ruthless strategy. LeMay's new B-29 Superfortress aircraft swept in over the wood-and-paper cities of Japan's Home Islands at just 5,000 to 9,000 feet, loaded with as many incendiary clusters and magnesium bombs, and as much white phosphorus and napalm, as they could carry.

This campaign of systematic firebombing in 1945 destroyed 105 square miles at the heart of 64 Japanese cities between March and August. The raids killed at least 220,000 people and perhaps as many as 500,000. The worst hit was Tokyo, where just after midnight on March 10, 325 B-29s swooped down on the Japanese capital. Over the next three hours, 1,665 tons of incendiary bombs followed, killing more than 100,000 civilians, destroying 250,000 buildings, and torching 16 square miles of the city. The airmen at the end of the bomber stream were all but overwhelmed by the stench of burning human flesh.

Reduced nearly to starvation at home and sustaining staggering casualties at the front, Japan doggedly fought on. The terrifying kamikaze attacks by its planes on American ships, and the unbending defense of the islands of Iwo Jima and Okinawa almost to the last man, convinced some in Washington that American casualties for an invasion of the Home Islands could run as high as a million men. This was probably a greatly exaggerated estimate, but even a realistic one was likely to be higher than all American losses in the war to that date.

No one wanted to go on paying such a high price. The new president, Harry Truman, did not want to go on paying any price at all in American lives if there was any alternative. Just over three months after taking office, following FDR's cerebral hemorrhage, he learned of an option.

The theory that it was possible to create an explosion of almost unimaginable power by splitting the atom was confirmed back in 1939, in experiments conducted by a team of scientists led by Enrico Fermi, an Italian immigrant to the U.S. who had fled Mussolini's Italy. A trio of Hungarian refugee physicists teaching at Ivy League colleges—Leo Szilard and Edward Teller at Columbia and Eugene Wigner at Princeton—drove out to Peconic Bay, on Long Island, to impress this notion on the most famous scientific refugee of all, Albert Einstein. Alexander Sachs, a Russian émigré economist, prevailed on Einstein to write a letter to President Roosevelt about it because, well, Sachs knew the president.

By October 1941, Roosevelt had ordered up a huge, top-secret effort to develop an atomic bomb. Under the command of a blunt, no-nonsense Army engineer, General Leslie Groves, "the Manhattan Project" was originally headquartered in a single building in lower Manhattan, across Broadway from City Hall. Within the next four years, it would grow to become a $22 billion project (in today's dollars), employing 130,000 people at 14 sites across the

A U.S. Army Air Force B-29 Superfortress—the same type of plane that dropped the atomic bomb—flying from Tinian, from which the bomb flight was launched. It is continuing its bomb run over Osaka, Japan, June 1945, despite the loss of its No. 3 engine (second from right).

THE INNER WORKINGS OF THE A-BOMB

Little Boy, the first atomic bomb ever used, killed an estimated 140,000 people in Hiroshima, Japan, on August 6, 1945. Six feet long and weighing almost 9,000 pounds, it was triggered by a gun-type firing mechanism. When it reached the optimal altitude of 1,900 feet, a firing switch closed, activating the cordite powder charge.

The charge fired a tungsten-carbon and steel plug, which in turn propelled a "bullet" of hollow, uranium-235 rings down the "barrel" of the bomb at 1,000 feet per second, and into a uranium-235 target.
The collision set off a highly inefficient nuclear fission reaction that transformed only 0.6 grams of the 64 kilograms of uranium into energy. Those 0.6 grams unleashed a 15-kiloton, X-ray–heated fireball with a temperature of 7,200 degrees Fahrenheit, and created a firestorm two miles in diameter.
POWDER CHARGE
URANIUM-235 "BULLET"
URANIUM-235 TARGET

United States as well as in Canada and England.

The Hanford Site, where plutonium was produced, grew to encompass almost 1,000 square miles in the state of Washington. The facility in Oak Ridge, Tennessee, for both the enrichment of uranium and plutonium-production research, grew to 60,000 acres, becoming the fifth-largest city in the state, and consuming at its peak one-sixth of the nation's electrical power—or more than all of New York City. Meanwhile, at Los Alamos, New Mexico, some of the world's leading physicists worked under the direction of J. Robert Oppenheimer, a gaunt, intense, recovered tuberculosis patient who spoke Sanskrit, chain-smoked, and thoroughly despised himself: "I hardly took an action…that did not arouse in me a very great sense of revulsion and of wrong," he said 20 years later.

Oppenheimer had long-standing misgivings about the bomb, but he and Groves worked well together. On July 16, 1945, the physicist stood in a little hut in the New Mexico desert basin known as Jornada del Muerto ("Journey of Death"), listening to a solemn countdown, eyes trained on the Trinity test site before

him. As the countdown went on, the watchers put on their dark goggles, ready for something they could not imagine, for it had never been seen on this earth before. Then it happened—the mushroom cloud, the mind-bending radiance of the explosion. Oppenheimer thought of the *Bhagavad Gita*, the Hindu holy book: "Now I am become Death, the destroyer of worlds."

Having unleashed the building blocks of the universe, Oppenheimer rode in a simple jeep with General Thomas Farrell back to see Groves at base camp. Farrell told Groves, "The war is over." To which Groves replied, "Yes, after we drop two bombs on Japan." Oppenheimer was still hoping that he had at last attained Alfred Nobel's goal of discovering a weapon so powerful that no one would dare to use it.

He would be disappointed in this. When the bomb was dropped, on the Japanese cities of Hiroshima and Nagasaki, it caused death and destruction on a scale previously incomprehensible. It would not be used again, at least to this day, although men would continue to fight wars.

ON AUGUST 9, 1945, THE DROPPING OF THE SECOND ATOMIC BOMB, ON THE CITY OF NAGASAKI, KILLED 70,000 INDIVIDUALS AT ONCE. TENS OF THOUSANDS LATER DIED FROM THE EFFECTS OF RADIATION.

TOM BROKAW, journalist: “They’d been through it all and they wanted one thing: They wanted a better life for their families. And that’s what they dedicated themselves to.”

1941 TO 1945

THE WAGES OF WAR

HOW WORLD WAR II CHANGED AMERICA

It was, at least, the end of the Second World War, the most terrible war that ever was or ever will be fought by what would come to be known as "conventional methods." The conflict left every great nation on earth in ruins—save for America. The United States would emerge from the conflict exponentially stronger, with its cities and infrastructure intact, its economy fully recovered, its people's quality of life better than ever.

"The war gave a lot of people jobs," said Peggy Terry, who worked putting powder and detonators into anti-aircraft and incendiary shells and painting the red tips of tracer bullets. "It led them to expect more than they had before. People's expectations, financially, spiritually, were raised.... No bombs were ever dropped on us. Except for our boys that went out of the country and were killed, we came out of that war in good shape. People with more money than they'd had in years."

She remembered hearing a woman on a bus say that she hoped the war would not end until she could pay for her refrigerator: "An old man hit her over the head with an umbrella. He said, 'How dare you!'"

But it was a sentiment that many Americans shared. In six short years, America had moved from the Great Depression to being the wealthiest and most powerful country in the world. It would stay that way for a long time, with all sorts of benefits pledged to returning veterans under the GI Bill that Roosevelt had made sure to get passed, remembering the post–World War I slump.

Many women would leave the wartime factories where they had labored, to go home and start the baby boom. But many others were in the workplace to stay; the percentage of "working women" would never return to what it had been before December 7, 1941. African- and Hispanic-Americans were not going back to the cotton bolls, or the ghetto, or the barrio, either. Sons would not go back to their fathers' homes or jobs; farmers would not go back to their farms, although those who had never left found themselves richer than ever.

Paul Edwards, a New Deal agricultural worker before going to the war remembered: "[T]he war was a hell of a good time. Farmers in South Dakota that I administered relief to, and gave 'em bully beef and four dollars a week to feed their families, when I came home they were worth a quarter of a million dollars.... What was true there was true all over the United States.... And the rest of the world was bleeding and in pain. But it's forgotten now. World War Two? It's a war I would still go to."

Above: "The Big Three" make a cold peace at Yalta.

Opposite: American servicemen and women gather at a Red Cross club in Paris, exultant in victory and eager to go home.

SANDWICHES
Dolores
DINING ROOM ENTRANCE

CHAPTER ELEVEN BOOMERS

V-J DAY
TIMES SQUARE,
AUGUST 15, 1945

1945 TO 1980

AMERICA UNBOUND

THE CHALLENGES OF POWER

We are what we have been.

America in 1945 stood at a once unimaginable height, the most powerful nation the world had ever seen. The United States had already possessed the world's largest economy for some 60 years. Now, it was the only major power to have emerged from the worst war in human history relatively unscathed—its cities intact, its population larger than ever, its businesses thriving. It boasted far and away the world's greatest industrial base, its most productive farms, its biggest city, its busiest harbor, its tallest buildings, its leading aeronautics industry, its most prosperous citizenry, its strongest military, its only atomic weapons. With the installation of the United Nations headquarters in New York, it was also home of the world's titular capital. The U.S. was not only the colossus of its day but also the nation of the future, the envy of the world.

What would America do with this hegemony? Having just vanquished the corrupt philosophy—fascism—that claimed the ability to change the very nature of man, it would now take up an epic struggle against another philosophy—Communism—that made a claim just as false, and just as corrupting. The struggle would test the American character in ways that it had never been tested before.

Where once America's wars had been swift, periodic, and decisive, now they would be muddled, continual, and sometimes not even real wars at all. Where previously Americans had come from the crowded cities of the Old World to live on a desolate frontier (or, conversely, had come from isolated villages to live in New World cities more crowded than any that had ever existed), now they would try to live on a confusing new frontier that was neither city nor country, but an in-between place of almost unlimited abundance. Where they had tried to keep in silent subjugation all who did not fulfill their ideal of what an American should be, now they would have to embrace the ideals of inclusion they officially professed, or perish. As always, the United States would be all about the new—the "dawn land," as the peoples who greeted the Pilgrims called it, where the enduring human character wrestled with the ceaseless changes of modernity.

The first test the new American colossus faced, ironically enough, was the limits of its own power. Far and away the costliest war America had ever fought had been against itself, a conflict during which some 750,000 people perished. Now, many times that number faced annihilation within the first minutes of a nuclear war. The bomb appeared to give the U.S. an insuperable advantage, but perversely—in the hands of others, and when combined with air power and rocketry—it soon erased America's traditional defenses. Lincoln's boast about how a foreign army could not make a track on the Blue Ridge Mountains could be made irrelevant by a volley of missiles. New York had survived seven years of brutal British occupation during the Revolution. But as the writer E. B. White acknowledged in "Here Is New York," the famous essay he composed in 1949, the year that the Soviet Union developed an atomic bomb of its own: "The city, for the first time in its long history, is destructible. A single flight of planes no bigger than a wedge of geese can quickly end this island fantasy, burn the towers, crumble the bridges, turn the underground passages into lethal chambers, cremate the millions."

This was an existential shift, one that generated waves of paranoia and was quickly exploited by the demagogues. Joe McCarthy postured shamelessly in the House and the Senate, demanding to know—without a shred of irony—"Who lost China?" to Communism. Over the course of five years, FBI chief for life J. Edgar Hoover compiled some three million dossiers and launched 10,000 field investigations into the loyalty of American citizens, but failed to produce a single spy. The U.S. House of Representatives formed the House Committee on Un-American Activities to establish the idea that there could be an "American" way of acting and an "un-American" one. HUAC spent most of its time blacklisting everyone from screenwriters to schoolteachers (preventing their employment) and pressuring those they deemed politically suspect to testify about their politics and take loyalty oaths. Along with tainting many loyal Americans as subversives, such witch hunts also exposed and ruined the lives of numerous homosexuals, who were deemed to be "security risks."

There *were* subversives, though, as the American public began to discover. One was Alger Hiss, a State Department official who, despite having access to the highest levels of government, gleaned little of importance. Others made up the ring that included Ethel and Julius Rosenberg. They stole something very important indeed: atomic secrets that they passed along to Moscow.

The revelation of such activities was unsettling in the extreme. "[O]ne may imagine a large household whose children insist that they are pursued by a bogeyman," wrote the journalist and historian William Manchester. "Others in the family repeatedly assure them that there is no such thing as a bogeyman.... Then one evening when the family is gathered together one child notices that a closet door is ajar. He flings it open—and out steps a real bogeyman, ten feet tall and all teeth."

The bogeyman was real, if exaggerated. So were the expansionist ambitions of the Soviet Union, which was constantly puffing itself up in order to hide the fatal flaws of the Communist system. Confronted with what John F. Kennedy called "the burden of a long twilight struggle," Americans managed to construct a shaky consensus around George F. Kennan's idea of "containment"—the policy of containing the USSR and other Communist states more or less within the areas they already controlled, or which were at least not of vital interest to the West. It was a new interpretation of old, big-power politics, one that, it was believed, would obviate the need for a final, awful showdown.

Nevertheless, the world lurched terrifyingly close to war—one with the potential to be its last. In Berlin in 1961, lines of Soviet and American tanks confronted each another at Checkpoint Charlie in the divided city. The following autumn, the U.S. discovered that the Soviets had begun to spike Cuba (where American-backed expatriates had tried to snuff out Fidel Castro's revolutionary regime the year before) with intermediate-range nuclear missiles. The Cuban Missile Crisis was a reckless incursion on an American zone of influence, one that begged a response.

In their famous "Thirteen Days" of negotiation, President Kennedy and his advisers moved both sides back from the precipice, and the Cold War powers would never again come so close to mass destruction.

But their struggle continued to devolve into endless proxy wars throughout Asia, Africa, and Latin America. America's new Central Intelligence Agency fought these shadow wars with an untold number of assassinations and other "black ops," including the backing of military coups that overthrew democratically elected governments in Iran, Guatemala, Brazil, and Chile, and that brought shame, suspicion, and considerable "blowback" down on the United States.

Above: Children play beside the Berlin Wall, West Germany, 1962.

Opposite: Shoppers gather to watch John F. Kennedy calm the nation's fears during the Cuban Missile Crisis.

1945 TO 1955

A NEW MARSHALL IN TOWN

REBUILDING THE WORLD

Yet paradoxically, the strictures of the Cold War also forwarded the causes of tolerance and democracy, both in the United States and around the world. In the years immediately following World War II, the U.S. rebuilt and transformed the nations it had defeated, treating them more generously than any conqueror had ever dealt with a subject enemy. America's six-year occupation of Japan transformed that nation from a schizophrenic military dictatorship into a flourishing modern democracy. One of the first actions of the occupation's supreme commander, General Douglas MacArthur, was to outlaw the secret police; he also set up a $1 million-a-day food-supply network and freed communist and socialist dissidents from Japanese prisons. America introduced a new constitution for Japan that included a bill of rights, freedom of speech and of assembly, an independent judiciary, the right of unions to bargain collectively for wages, and equal rights for women (something still missing from the U.S. Constitution).

In Germany, society was rebuilt from the ground up, with three of the four zones controlled by the occupying Western Allies combined into a single democracy. The freedom of its citizens, and of the two million people in the free sector of Berlin, was defended with dogged determination. When the Soviets, who held on to East Germany, cut off the city in an attempt to force its capitulation in June of 1948, the U.S. Air Force, Britain's Royal Air Force, and the French responded by flying in up to 8,000 tons of food and vital supplies every month. Some 55 Allied pilots died in the massive operation known as the Berlin Airlift, but they kept coming. By May of 1949, the Russians had given up the siege.

Americans believed they had learned the lessons of why the peace after the First World War had gone so bad—the lack of forgiveness toward the defeated; the failure to establish global institutions that might check aggression, discourage isolationism, and prevent trade wars—and they were determined not to repeat their mistakes. Along with generosity toward the vanquished would come an attempt to forge a new, better system of collective security. The United Nations was a classic Roosevelt hybrid, designed by FDR to embody both the most pragmatic aspects of the former big-power balance-of-power arrangements and the idealism of the League of Nations. Every country would have a voice and a vote, but a Security Council made up of the leading nations would have veto power. The arrangement proved to be better in theory than in actual practice, but it was the first of a series of institutions—including the World Bank, the International Monetary Fund, and the World Trade Organization—designed to forge international cooperation and prosperity.

At the same time, the United States hastened to take up the "burden" of the old European empires, whose presumptions it had always hated and whose dismantling it had actively pursued even in the midst of World War II. If a single date could be assigned to the formal end of the British Empire, it might be February 21, 1947, when London informed the U.S. State Department that it was broke, unable to sustain its aid to shaky pro-Western governments in Greece and Turkey for more than another six weeks.

The Berlin Airlift: U.S. pilots regularly tossed candy out of their planes to children below.

FOOD AND
SUPPLIES, 1948

BY 1951, WESTERN EUROPE'S INDUSTRIAL PRODUCTION WAS 43 PERCENT ABOVE WHAT IT HAD BEEN BEFORE THE WAR, AND ITS FARM PRODUCTION WAS 10 PERCENT HIGHER.

The United States ran to the rescue, with President Harry S. Truman articulating the so-called Truman Doctrine in less than three weeks: "It must be the policy of the United States to support free peoples who are resisting attempted subjugation by armed minorities or by outside pressure."

This commitment would prove to be precariously ambitious and open-ended, but it yielded good results initially. U.S. aid kept both Greece and Turkey from falling to Soviet-backed insurgents. Four months later, Truman's secretary of state, the revered World War II military leader George Marshall, announced a more systematic approach. His Marshall Plan for massive assistance to Europe went against ingrained American beliefs in the virtues of isolationism. But a key Republican isolationist, Senator Arthur Vandenberg, had been in London during the assault of Germany's V-2 rockets and had seen the light, asking, "How can there be immunity or isolation when man can devise weapons like that?"

In April of 1948, the freighter *John H. Quick* set sail from Galveston, Texas, with 9,000 tons of wheat for the hungry citizens of Europe. Over the next four years, fleets of up to 150 ships followed with tons of

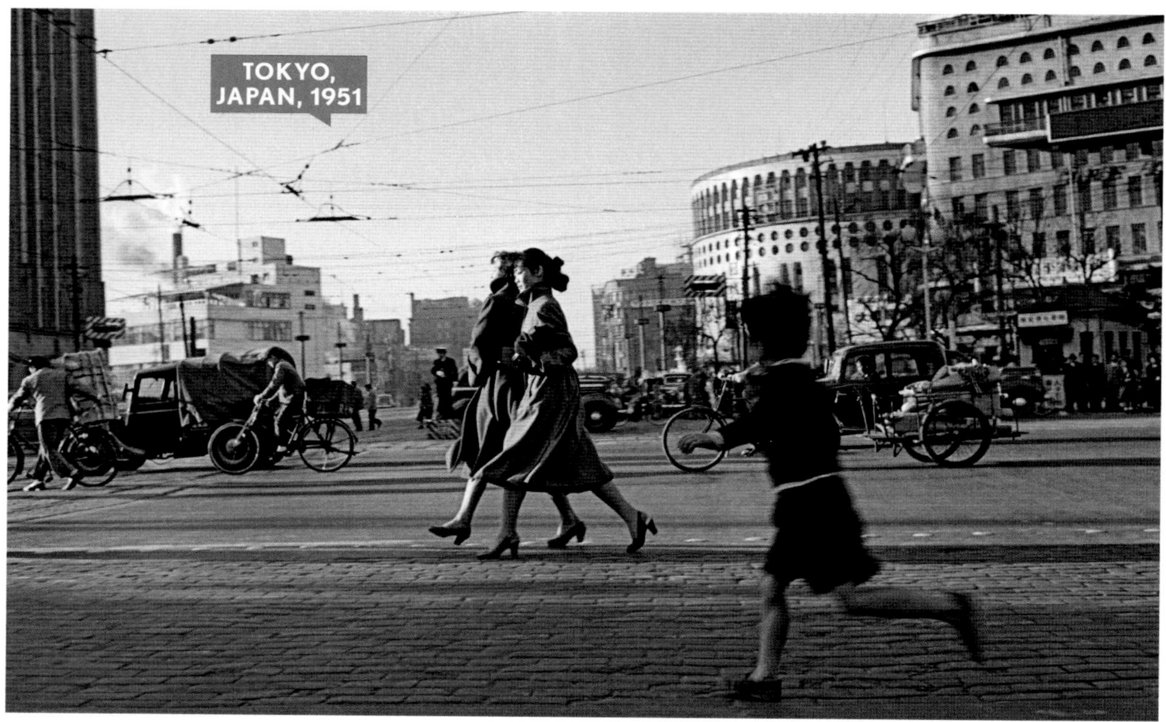
TOKYO, JAPAN, 1951

everything from tractors to fishing nets, from aircraft parts to flour, and with $20 million worth of horse meat. By the time the program ended in 1952, the U.S. had spent $13 billion on it; measured in terms of relative gross domestic product, it was the equivalent of nearly $517 billion in 2009 terms. It was the stimulus program to end all stimulus programs—and it worked. By 1951, Western Europe's industrial production was 43 percent above what it had been before the war, and its farm production was 10 percent higher.

In 1949, the Marshall Plan was joined by a further commitment to Europe: the first enduring military alliance in American history. NATO—the North Atlantic Treaty Organization—raised isolationist hackles, but it would secure for Europe a lasting peace such as it had not known since the days of the Roman Empire.

Opposite: Students stride through the rebuilt Ginza district of Tokyo, 1951.

Below: The U.S. ambassador to France, Jefferson Caffery, speaks at a ceremony in Bordeaux, France, 1948, welcoming the *John H. Quick* and its cargo of wheat on its arrival, the start of the Marshall Plan.

HEAR! HEAR!

HOW OUR BROTHERS

Died For Freedom

AND HOW WE ARE CARRYING ON THE FIGHT IN MISSISSIPPI

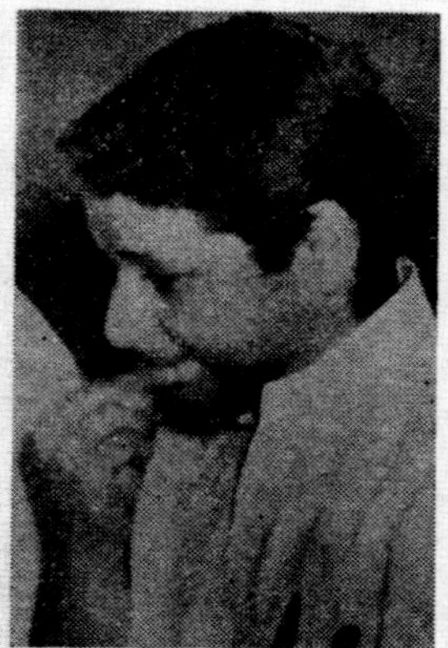

Mickey Schwerner

James Chaney

Andrew Goodman

HEAR

Mrs. Fanny Chaney

Courageous Mother of James Chaney

At New Zion Baptist Church

2319 THIRD STREET

THURS., AUG. 27, 1964

7:30 P. M.

1922
TO
1963

FREE AT LAST

THE CRUSADE FOR CIVIL RIGHTS

NATO and the Marshall Plan were so successful that American internationalists would come to propose similar arrangements everywhere. The reality was that both had been perfectly targeted to help what were already developed Western states get back on their feet. The hastily discarded possessions of the crumbling European empires would prove infinitely harder to make into viable states, and to win over to the U.S. side of the Cold War. And the effort would have to begin with finally confronting America's race problem.

The United States had no chance of gaining friends in the vast territories of the "Third World" if people of color were still accorded only second-class status at home. The State Department was mortified when delegates to the U.N. attempting to travel to Washington were repeatedly denied service at Jim Crow restaurants. As the situation in the Deep South was dramatically worse, Washington worried long and hard about a solution, while statesmen ventured the vague hope that America would evolve out of its racism in another generation, or two, or three.

They needn't have fretted. African-Americans began to break the fetters of their oppression, using every tool that both the Constitution and the nation's Christian heritage provided. One by one, then congregation by congregation and march by march, they stood up for their rights. In 1955, a middle-aged seamstress named Rosa Parks politely refused to move to the back of a public bus in Montgomery, Alabama. In 1960, four 18-year-old college freshmen named Ezell Blair Jr., Franklin McCain, Joseph McNeil, and David Richmond insisted on sitting at an "all-white" Woolworth's lunch counter in Greensboro, North Carolina, until they were served. In 1961, nine black and white Freedom Riders insisted on traveling together in a Greyhound bus from Washington, D.C., into the maelstrom of Anniston, Alabama, where they were attacked by a mob wielding knives, clubs, and iron pipes. In 1964, a serious young mathematics wiz from New York City named Robert Parris Moses led the intrepid men and women of his Student Nonviolent Coordinating Committee in registering the black people of McComb County, Mississippi, to vote—enduring beatings, jailings, and bombings.

And so it would go, through the long list of Americans—blacks and whites, women and men, Protestants and Catholics and Jews—who would stand up at last for civil rights, and in dozens of cases give their lives for that cause. The hundreds of thousands

Above: Separate drinking fountains for blacks and whites, 1950.

Opposite: Civil rights workers were registering black citizens to vote in Mississippi when they were murdered by local law officers in 1964.

of black men who had served their country in the global war for freedom were not about to submit again to the American version of apartheid upon their return home. They came up with a plan of action.

Rosa Parks and many others served willingly as the cutting edge of a campaign that had started back in 1922 when a 21-year-old white Harvard student named Charles Garland decided to give away most of his inherited $1.3 million fortune, declaring, "I am placing my life on a Christian basis." One of the recipients of Garland's philanthropy was the Legal Defense Fund of the NAACP—the National Association for the Advancement of Colored People—which was headed by an exacting black law professor named Charles Hamilton Houston.

Houston educated a generation of brilliant African-American lawyers, chief among them the son of a Pullman porter, named Thurgood Marshall. The professor set those young men and women to work tearing away at the state laws and disingenuous Supreme Court decisions that had effectively nullified the anti-discriminatory amendments to the Constitution. It was the work of decades. But by appealing to an increasingly liberal judiciary, Marshall—who would become the first African-American to serve on the high court—was able at last to remove a stain from the Constitution with the seminal 1954 decision of *Brown v. Board of Education*, which outlawed segregated schools.

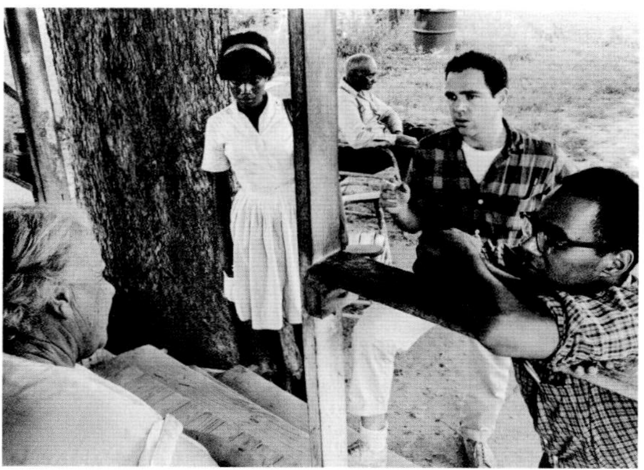

Above: Martha Prescod, Mark Miller, and Robert Parris Moses try to register black voters in the Mississippi Delta, 1964.

Opposite: City authorities turn fire hoses on peaceful black protestors during the Birmingham Movement in the spring of 1963.

Thousands of brave men and women like Parks would go on to make this ruling a reality, repeatedly putting their bodies on the line against dogs, fire hoses, clubs, and guns. Giving their protests a moral weight that turned the heart of the country was a 26-year-old Baptist minister who enlarged Parks's stand to a city-wide, yearlong bus boycott in Montgomery. Schooled in social protest by the writings of Gandhi and America's own Reinhold Niebuhr, the Reverend Martin Luther King Jr. and his fellow ministers found one method after another with which to press "the fierce urgency of now." In his quest, Dr. King, too, would endure beatings, jailings, blackmail attempts by the head of the FBI, a bomb that destroyed his family's home, and a stabbing that nearly pierced his heart.

Yet he would not desist, and with his eloquence, his ingenuity, and his gentleness, he kept his movement before the American people. On the night of June 11, 1963, John F. Kennedy finally submitted significant civil-rights legislation to the U.S. Congress, telling a national television audience: "We are confronted primarily with a moral issue. It is as old as the Scriptures and is as clear as the American Constitution."

"THE MORAL ARC OF THE UNIVERSE IS LONG, BUT IT BENDS TOWARD JUSTICE."
—MARTIN LUTHER KING JR.

THE ROUGH PLACES MADE PLAIN: THE CIVIL RIGHTS MOVEMENT, 1954–1968

Justice and equality before the law for all American citizens was made possible by the actions of millions of individuals, throughout not only the South but all of the nation. Whether they were putting their bodies on the line by riding on segregated buses, standing up to police dogs and fire hoses, or trying to register people to vote; or whether they fought in a courtroom, or took their seat in an integrated classroom, black and white Americans used every tool that democracy offered to win their mighty victory.

Desegregation

Legislation

Protest

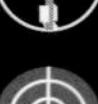
Assassination

Bombing

Riot

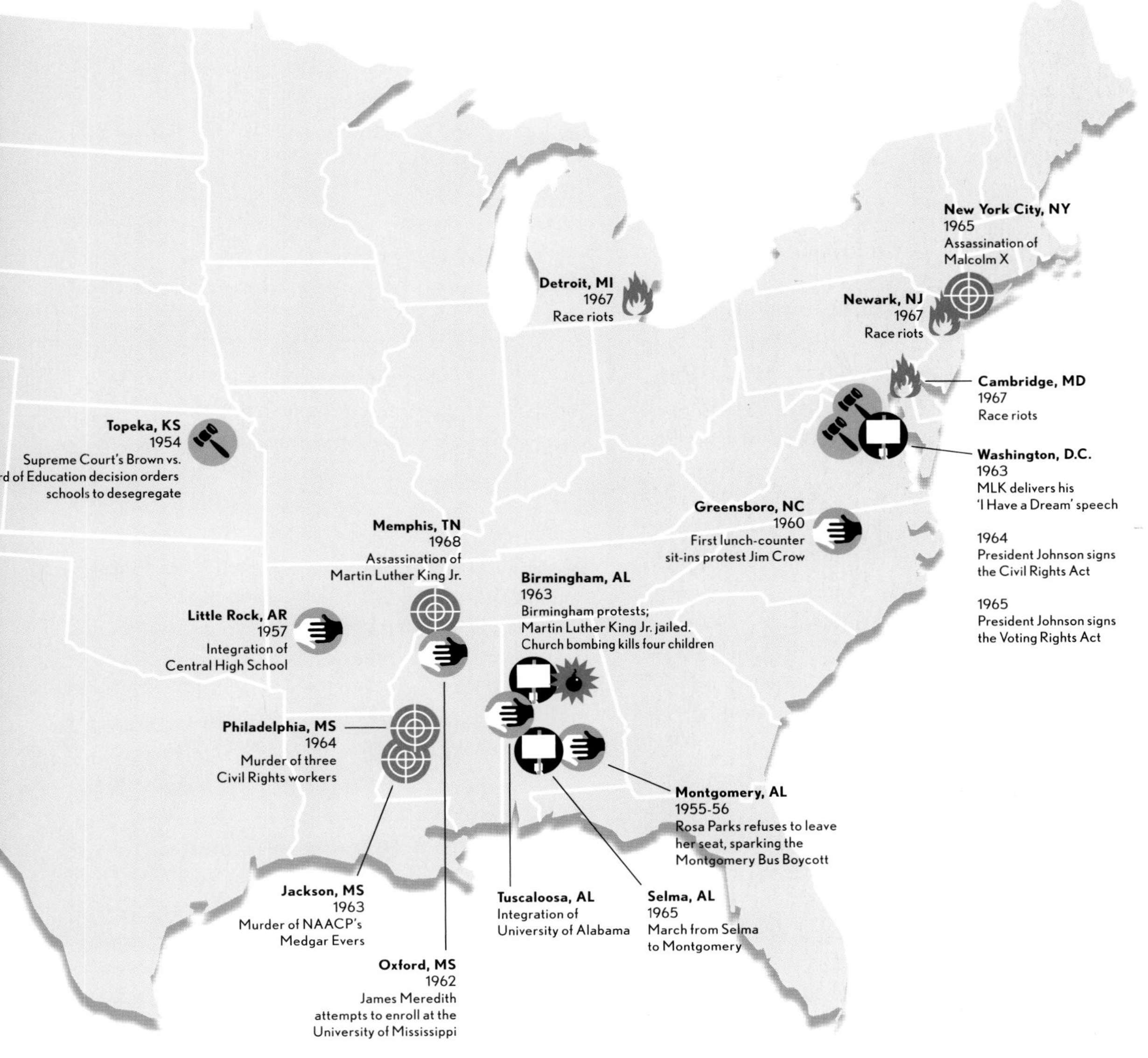
New York City, NY
1965
Assassination of
Malcolm X
Detroit, MI
1967
Race riots
Newark, NJ
1967
Race riots
Cambridge, MD
1967
Race riots
Topeka, KS
1954
Supreme Court's Brown vs.
-d of Education decision orders
schools to desegregate
Washington, D.C.
1963
MLK delivers his
'I Have a Dream' speech
1964
President Johnson signs
the Civil Rights Act
1965
President Johnson signs
the Voting Rights Act
Greensboro, NC
1960
First lunch-counter
sit-ins protest Jim Crow
Memphis, TN
1968
Assassination of
Martin Luther King Jr.
Birmingham, AL
1963
Birmingham protests;
Martin Luther King Jr. jailed.
Church bombing kills four children
Little Rock, AR
1957
Integration of
Central High School
Philadelphia, MS
1964
Murder of three
Civil Rights workers
Montgomery, AL
1955-56
Rosa Parks refuses to leave
her seat, sparking the
Montgomery Bus Boycott
Jackson, MS
1963
Murder of NAACP's
Medgar Evers
Tuscaloosa, AL
Integration of
University of Alabama
Selma, AL
1965
March from Selma
to Montgomery
Oxford, MS
1962
James Meredith
attempts to enroll at the
University of Mississippi

1954 TO 1980

THE ACTIVIST GENERATION

THE OPENING OF AMERICAN DEMOCRACY

The African-American civil rights movement would serve as a model and an inspiration for many other U.S. minorities and oppressed groups, including women. Liberation movements for Hispanics, for Native Americans, and for gays and lesbians followed closely, as for the first time millions of citizens were able to say without fear exactly what they were. César Chávez's overwhelmingly Hispanic United Farm Workers union battled both corrupt labor bosses and agribusiness to a draw in the picking fields of California. Native Americans battled FBI agents on the reservation around Wounded Knee, South Dakota. Gay pride parades became a staple of most major cities after homosexuals at a bar called the Stonewall Inn in New York's Greenwich Village refused to tolerate one more humiliating police raid.

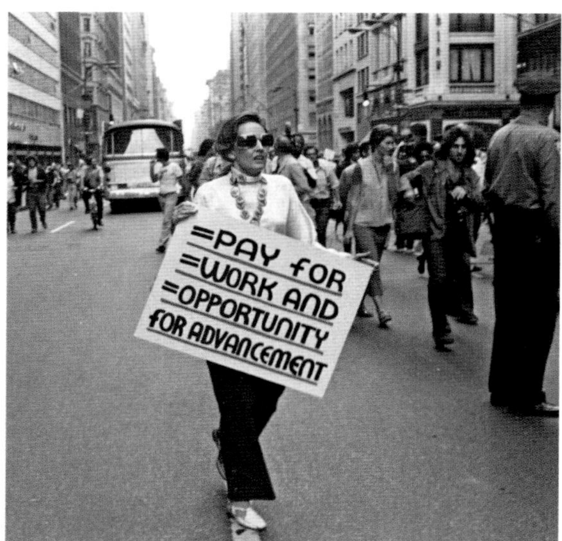

Over 40 years after the start of the "Third Wave" of feminism, American women had still not achieved equal pay with men, but they did constitute a majority of the workforce and the college population.

Barriers fell everywhere. Quotas limiting the number of Jews at many leading universities were abolished. Unspoken but rigid social strictures against Jews, Asians, Italians, Catholics, and most other non-WASP ethnicities at leading law firms, corporations, resorts, hotels, and country clubs were largely swept away in the years that followed.

Popular, crusading books of the 1960s were debated and translated into congressional hearings and then into effective government programs, whether they concerned poverty (as did Michael Harrington's *The Other America*), environmental degradation (Rachel Carson's *Silent Spring*), or consumer safety (Ralph Nader's *Unsafe at Any Speed*). Grassroots movements such as the campaign to end atmospheric nuclear testing received almost instant attention from the Kennedy administration, which signed a test-ban treaty with the Soviet Union. In the courts, justices now enforced the principle of "one person, one vote," guaranteed defendants a lawyer and the opportunity to hear their rights, and pulled down most censorship laws.

It was possible to believe that all the animal spirits, all the ambitions and desires and faiths that had driven American life, might at last be reconciled into something much greater than their parts. President Lyndon B. Johnson voiced just such a vision in a commencement address at Ann Arbor in 1964 when he first spoke of "the Great Society," one that "is not a safe harbor, a resting place, a final objective, a finished work. It is a challenge constantly renewed, beckoning us toward a destiny where the meaning of our lives matches the marvelous products of our labor."

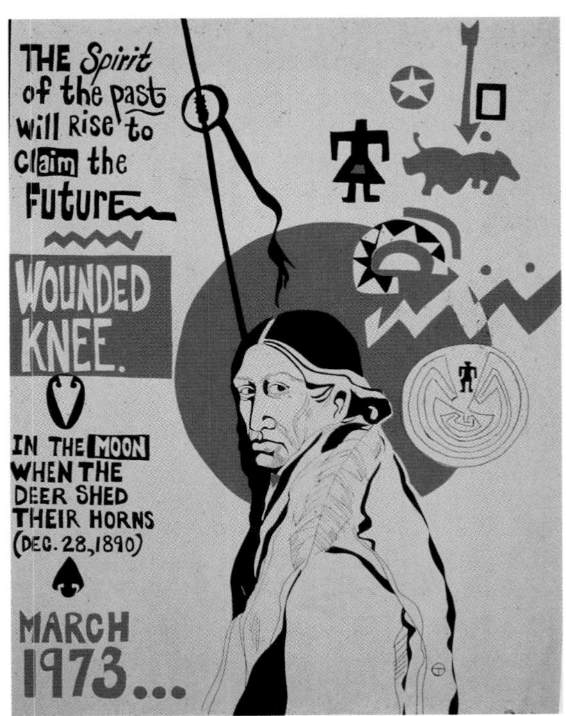

It was an ambition beyond that which had been ventured by almost any American since the arrival of the Pilgrims, with their dream of a shining "city upon a hill." Johnson's Great Society would go a long way toward making it reality, as his administration's civil-rights legislation encoded once and for all into law full rights for minorities and for women. Other laws, augmented by Richard Nixon's Environmental Protection Act would go on to preserve much of America's physical heritage, and improve the air Americans breathed and the water they drank. Medicare, Medicaid, and other social-welfare programs slashed poverty rates, and when combined with the seemingly invincible nostrums of Keynesian economics, they gave promise of at last actually banishing want—perhaps the oldest and most elusive of human dreams.

Above, left: A poster commemorating the Wounded Knee massacre of 1890. In 1973, Indian protests led to a violent clash at the village of Wounded Knee, leaving two Indians dead and a federal marshal paralyzed.

Above, right: Dick Ashworth, later one of the founding members of Parents, Families, and Friends of Lesbians and Gays, marches in the New York Gay Pride Parade, 1974.

1934 TO 1975

THUNDER FROM THE FIELDS

CÉSAR CHÁVEZ AND THE FIGHT FOR HISPANIC RIGHTS

Out of the hard fields of California's agricultural empire came a new voice in the 1960s. The big farmers—fast becoming known as agribusinesses—had long filled the nation's supermarkets with remarkably cheap fruits and vegetables by exploiting migrant workers.

These migrant workers—primarily Hispanic or Latino Americans—were paid a barely subsistence wage, and housed in filthy conditions in labor camps. There was little they could do about it. Under the *Bracero* program, agribusinesses would bring in as many temporary Mexican workers as they wanted to drive down wages and break strikes—then get the government to ship the laborers home again (sometimes before they had been paid at all) in actions such as the notorious 1954 "Operation Wetback" that deported 50,000 Mexicans.

Edward R. Murrow brought this state of affairs home to the American people with his groundbreaking 1960 television documentary, *Harvest of Shame*. Still, little was done. Much as with the African American civil-rights movement, justice for Latinos would have to come from the people themselves. And just as with the civil-rights movement, it did.

Enter a charismatic veteran of World War II and father of eight. César Chávez had spent most of his childhood in the fields of California and Arizona, after his parents lost their farm and store in the Depression. A second-generation Mexican-American, he left school when he was 14. Often, his whole family would earn only a dollar for an entire day's work.

In 1962, Chávez, along with Gilbert Padilla and Dolores Huerta, started the National Farm Workers' Association, later the United Farm Workers (UFW). Together, they fought big business in what would become known as *La Causa*. Learning from social activists ranging from Gandhi to Martin Luther King, Saul Alinsky to St. Francis of Assissi, Chávez brought the UFW's fight to national attention with a ten-year strike—*La Huelga*—that began in 1965. He won the support of Bobby Kennedy, convinced Congress to end the *Bracero* program, launched a nationwide grape boycott, and went on a 25-day hunger strike when violence threatened to overwhelm his movement. The UFW stuck to the picket lines under a slogan, "*Si, se puede*"—"Yes, it can be done"—that would echo down through the Obama campaign of 2008.

In 1975, Chávez and his union won the first collective bargaining rights ever achieved for American farm workers. It was a tremendous accomplishment. The UFW's ranks had swelled to 50,000 members, and wages in the fields had tripled.

Better conditions and a truly well-paid, national farm workers union would continue to elude Chávez, Huerta, and others in the years that followed. But for the first time, the nation had heard the voice of its growing Hispanic community, and it spoke for tolerance, for democracy, for a peaceful activism toward full human rights. Well into the twenty-first century, many would continue to reject that voice as illegitimate, foreign, illegal. They ignored the history of how many Hispanics had been disinherited in the first place, from a country that was originally theirs. But the Latino voice would not be stilled again.

Migrant workers during the California Grape Strike, 1968.

THE POWER
OF STEEL

1945 TO 1990

HEAVEN IS A BACKYARD

PROSPERITY AND SUBURBIA

The considerable advantages that America already enjoyed over the rest of the world in almost every economic sphere increased exponentially in the wake of World War II. The Marshall Plan restored Europe's physical plant and increased competition, but it also meant more customers in a time of unprecedented international trade.

By 1950, Detroit produced 80 percent of all the automobiles in the world. Even as so many of the beautiful old names and the beautiful old models were consolidated into the Big Three—Chrysler, General Motors, and Ford (now under the direction of Henry's grandsons)—American automakers were more dominant than ever. So were U.S. steelmakers and the producers in its other heavy industries. But Americans were moving ahead as well into newer realms: chemicals, pharmaceuticals, electronics, plastics, aeronautics, and something called information—as a company known as IBM, which specialized in business machines, began to build the first room-size vacuum-tubed computers, fulfilling the dreams of generations of science-fiction writers.

Americans had never had it so good. National output doubled between 1946 and 1956, and again by 1970. By 1960, the United States, with just 6 percent of the world's population, was accounting for two-thirds of its manufacturing output—and consuming one-third of all its goods and services. Personal incomes nearly tripled between 1940 and 1955. From 1950 to 1973, average per-capita income increased by 59 percent in America, while median per-capita income went up by 41 percent. By the 1960s, 83 percent of American households owned a television set, and the number of families owning two cars doubled between 1951 and 1958.

The new prosperity paid off in more than just owning things. A typical American family by 1951 enjoyed a diet of unmatched abundance, balance, and variety, and its effects were soon evident. Just as the first European children in the New World had been taller and healthier than their counterparts back home once they were exposed to fresh food and air, the average American child of 1950 was two to three inches taller than he or she had been in 1900. The average American woman in 1950 lived to be 71—20 years longer than she had back at the turn of the century. The average man's life expectancy, meanwhile, increased from 48 to 65. And with the advent of the postwar baby boom, some 40 percent of country's population was under 20 by 1964.

Above: The IBM 701 Data Processing System and its operator, 1951.

Opposite: Citizens of Pennsylvania parade to demonstrate all the products made possible by America's dominant steel industry, 1965.

THE FIRST OF THE DEVELOPMENTS THAT CAME TO BE KNOWN AS LEVITTOWNS, ON LONG ISLAND, HAD 17,447 HOUSES AND 82,000 RESIDENTS, AND SPRAWLED OVER 6,000 ACRES.

Unionized employees (a record 35 percent of the private-sector workforce was in a union by 1955) earned wages high enough for one parent to support a family, working in the most advanced industrial plants in the world. Not far from the factory stood the gleaming new glass-and-stone towers of the nation's burgeoning white-collar sectors, where record numbers of Americans sold one another insurance, real estate, stocks, and bonds, along with all the other financial instruments of the emerging post-industrial economy.

A blue-collar worker could count on his son (or even daughter!) making the leap to the white-collar world, thanks to a world-class public education system and greater access to universities than ever before. Or that worker might even make the leap himself, thanks to FDR's GI Bill of Rights, which guaranteed returning servicemen a chance for advancement, through unprecedented help in getting a college education—or a house, or a business loan. In the half-century after the war, the percentage of Americans graduating from college quintupled, from 5 to 25 percent.

Soviet premier Nikita Khrushchev was publicly dismissive of American life, after a helicopter tour of Washington, D.C., and its suburbs with President Eisenhower. Privately, he was stunned by American prosperity.

As for that house—in 1945, a 38-year-old contractor named William Levitt returned from his wartime service as a Seabee paving jungle airstrips on Pacific islands. He came home with a dream. Levitt, the son of Russian-Jewish immigrants, had an idea for building an entire instant community of identical houses. Each would be a two-story, 800-square-foot, two-bedroom Cape Codder, constructed atop a concrete slab on a 60-by-100-foot lot.

The GI Bill provided millions of potential customers, and the dream of home ownership—of *land* ownership—was still lodged deep in the hearts of most Americans. The first of the developments that came to be known as Levittowns, on Long Island, had 17,447 houses and 82,000 residents, and sprawled over 6,000 acres. Homes sold for $7,000. By 1990, they would be worth $135,000 to $150,000—and no two houses would look alike, after decades of ownership and improvement.

More Levittowns and their imitators followed, as Americans flocked to the suburbs. By the twenty-first century, a majority of the country lived in the 'burbs, and nearly 70 percent of American families owned their own homes. The suburbs were not quite a paradise, though. Often, Americans of color were not welcome, at least at first. The original Levittown forbade African-Americans from moving in until 1949—an exclusion that was legal in many states before passage of the federal Fair Housing Act of 1968.

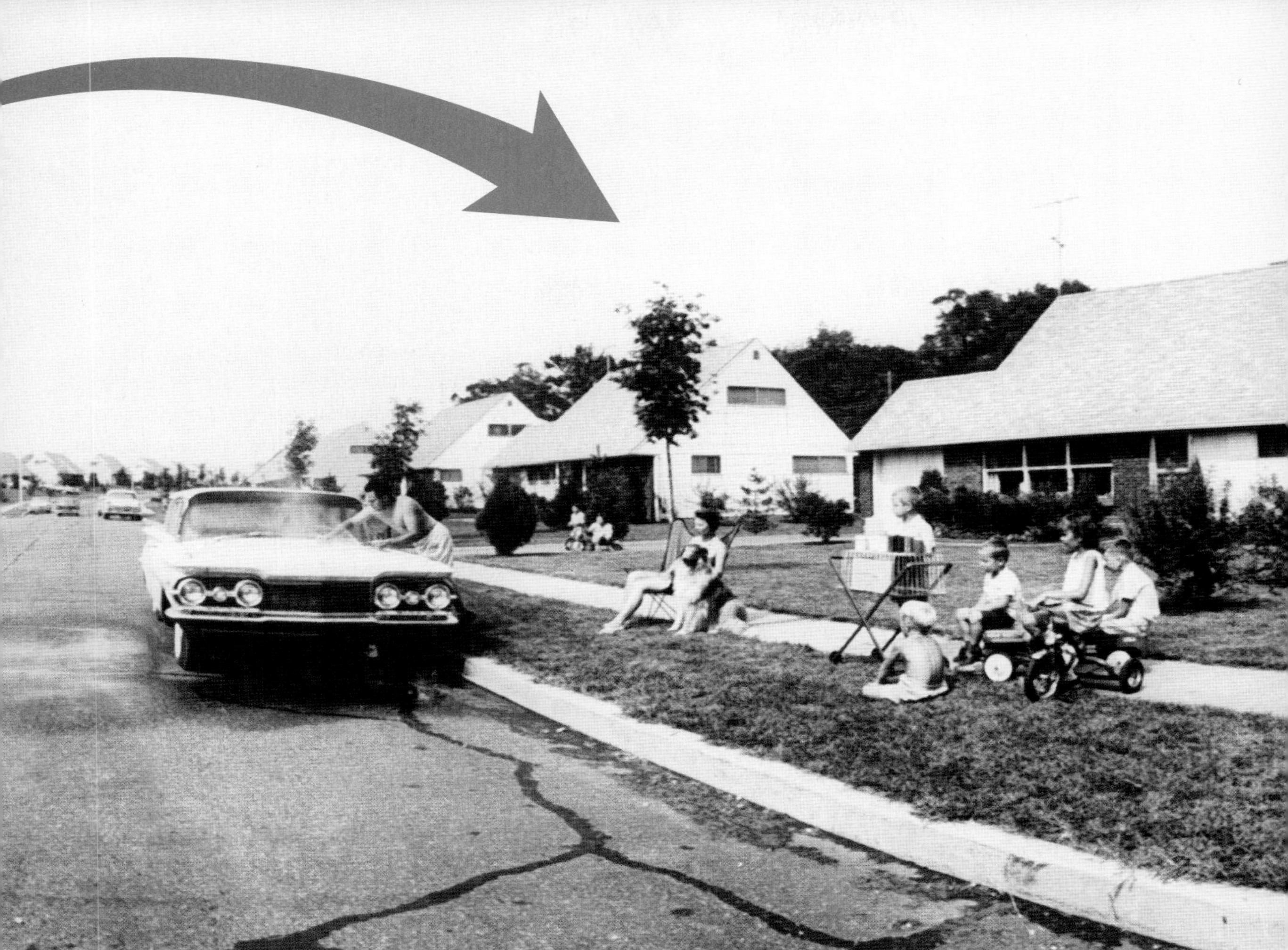

The suburban sprawl accelerated vast changes in how Americans would live and get about. By the end of the 1950s, there were 60 million cars on American roads—and more roads than ever. President Dwight D. Eisenhower's Interstate Highway System was sold to Congress as a Cold War defense measure, but it was in fact intended to accommodate suburbia. The largest public-works project in U.S. history, it was begun in 1956 and not officially completed until 1992. It would build the U.S. highway system out to nearly 47,000 miles of road, and cost over $450 billion in current, inflation-adjusted dollars.

The city that directly profited most from the new highway system was Detroit, but the way of life it enabled was that of Southern California. Millions flocked to its warm, sunny climate, making California the most populous state in the Union by 1960, and Los Angeles the country's second-biggest city by 1970. There, Americans drove their cars between the beaches and the huge new aerospace plants, the offices of the pop-culture industry, the subdivisions alighting on every hillside, and the gigantic, first-rate public universities that cost almost nothing to attend. Here was the good life at its zenith.

1957 TO 1969

TO INFINITY ...AND BEYOND

THE RACE TO THE MOON

Perhaps the most galling Cold War goad was the Soviet Union's success in launching Sputnik, the first man-made satellite, into orbit in 1957. Cultural panic ensued, followed by a raft of programs designed to improve American education in math and the sciences. In 1961, President Kennedy made the pledge that the U.S. would win the "space race" by landing a man on the moon before the end of the decade.

In order to do so, the U.S. turned whole cities—such as Houston, Texas, and Huntsville, Alabama—into hubs of cutting-edge technology and research. The drive to get to the moon made up for its $25 billion price tag many times over through advances in computer technology, electronics, and other fields.

And the race was won—eight years and 56 days after Kennedy's promise, when the *Apollo 11* moon lander, *Eagle*, touched down on the dusty bed of the Sea of Tranquility on July 20, 1969. The *Eagle*'s primitive computer system had failed and tried to abort the mission; mission commander Neil Armstrong had to override the computer and guide the craft in by hand, touching down with just 20 seconds' worth of fuel remaining. Armstrong then stepped out onto the surface of the moon, where he uttered the famous words, "That's one small step for man, one giant leap for mankind." Armstrong, together with fellow *Apollo 11* astronauts Buzz Aldren and Michael Collins, had changed the definition of what was possible forever.

It was, in many ways, the capstone to an era of unbounded American confidence and accomplishment. America—and Americans—led the world in almost every field of human endeavor. This cannot be considered too surprising since they were, after all, drawn from every part of the world, but the example of what free men and women under a free government could do was nonetheless exhilarating.

Above: The first astronauts, from the Mercury Project: (back row, from left) Alan B. Shepard Jr., Virgil I. "Gus" Grissom, L. Gordon Cooper; (front row, from left): Walter H. Schirra Jr., Donald K. Slayton, John H. Glenn Jr., Scott Carpenter.

Opposite: Shepard on his way to launch America's first manned flight, Cape Canaveral, Florida, May 1, 1961.

FIRST
U.S. TRIP TO
SPACE

1963

NICKELS AND NOVENAS

THE PROMISE OF AMERICAN LIFE

By the 1960s and '70s, American schoolchildren were thumbing through textbooks highlighting all the wellsprings of their country's prosperity: the Iron Belt and the Steel Belt, the Wheat Belt and the Corn Belt—monstrous glowing cauldrons of liquid metal and shimmering, endless fields of grain. Americans filed more patents than anyone else in the world, won more Nobel Prizes, even won the most Olympic medals. American cars filled the world's highways, American steel held up its buildings, American wheat filled its stomachs. American arts and culture—particularly its pop culture—dominated the world as never before, with entertainment emerging as a major industry.

Above: The Reverend Dr. Martin Luther King Jr., center, leads a triumphant march through Detroit after the victory of the Birmingham Movement, June 23, 1963. He was 34. Second from right is the insurgent mayor of Detroit, Jerome Cavanagh.

Opposite: Dr. King delivers an early version of his "I Have a Dream" speech at Detroit's Cobo Hall, later that day.

The moon landing was a crowning example of so much of what had always made America great: determination, courage, scientific knowledge, technical skill, and a rare genius for organization. Yet as great as that day was, there might have been a greater day. It might have been June 23, 1963, when the Reverend Martin Luther King Jr. traveled to Detroit. The trip came just weeks after the Birmingham Movement that Dr. King had led finally broke the official segregation in that ferociously resistant Alabama city.

The movement had won, and America had taken its own giant step forward. For the work he had just completed, Dr. King would win the Nobel Peace Prize the following year—the youngest man ever to do so. But many hard and wearying battles remained. He still had only the grudging support of the administration. President Kennedy, his reluctant ally, had just left on what was turning out to be a tumultuous state visit to West Germany.

Dr. King was on his own tour, a victory lap of sorts to raise badly needed money for the civil rights cause, and to promote awareness of the March on Washington—first dreamed up by A. Philip Randolph back in 1943—that was to take place later that summer. Traveling about the country with an entourage that included the great gospel singer Mahalia Jackson and a young Aretha Franklin, King touched down in Detroit and was greeted by a crowd as large and as ecstatic as the one Kennedy encountered in Berlin. A joyful, roaring mass of blacks and whites filled Woodward Avenue, breaking into spontaneous choruses of "We Shall Overcome" and "The Battle Hymn of the Republic."

At their front marched Dr. King, desperately trying to keep his arms linked with those of both Walter

WCHB

Reuther, the fiery head of the United Auto Workers, who had made his union a paragon of racial cooperation and social advancement, and Detroit's young reformist mayor, Jerome Cavanagh, who had come to power by beating the local political machine with a populist campaign that had started with just "nickels and novenas." The city he presided over seemed to exemplify everything that was best about the American experience. Detroit was booming, filled with magnificent buildings, and it boasted the highest percentage of minority home ownership in the country. Not only its cars but now also its music—including the exciting new Motown Sound of black musicians, promoted by a black entrepreneur—were exported all over the world.

Dr. King was all but carried along by the crowd to the city's Cobo Hall, where he gave one of his greatest speeches, working out some of the oratorical flourishes that he would make so famous in front of the Lincoln Memorial just two months later.

"I have a dream that one day, 'every valley shall be exalted, every hill and mountain shall be made low, the rough places will be made plain and the crooked places will be made straight, and the glory of the Lord shall be revealed and all flesh shall see it together,'" he told the crowd, quoting from Isaiah. "I have a dream this afternoon that the brotherhood of man will become a reality."

Historian Taylor Branch wrote that this was a seminal moment in American life: "In those few days, a president of Irish descent went abroad to Germany while a preacher of African descent went inland to Detroit, both to stir the divided core of American identity. The proconsul defended the empire of freedom while the prophet proclaimed its soul."

For all of the mighty strides it had taken, America still had a long way to go. Racism had not been banished, nor had any number of other prejudices, nor poverty, nor division. But then, American democracy had never claimed that man was perfectible. Instead, democracy as always remained a messy business, in dealing with man as he is, given to dissipation and corruption, hobbled by ignorance and self-interest. And yet if it had not delivered the millennium, it had produced, in America, what was probably the freest, most prosperous, most diverse society ever known to mankind.

All the crooked places might not ever be made straight, nor all the rough places be made plain. But the dream, it seemed, might now be a reality.

Above: President Kennedy visits the Berlin Wall, in 1963, a grim and vivid reminder of Soviet tyranny and the failure of the Communist dream.

Opposite: Absolution for Germany: Kennedy gives his famous *"Ich bin ein Berliner"* speech on January 26, 1963, declaring all free men citizens of Berlin.

CHAPTER TWELVE

MILLENNIUM

1963

IN SUNSHINE AND IN SHADOW

THE KENNEDY ASSASSINATION

On November 25, 1963, in a moment that marked just how far and how fast the United States had risen, the leaders of the world marched through the streets of Washington, D.C. Fifty-three years earlier, a similar collection of luminaries had gathered in London, then the de facto capital of the world, after the death of King Edward VII. The newsreel cameras there captured images of those powerful men, in their plumed hats and yards of gold braid, lumbering along on foot behind the riderless horse and the casket on the gun carriage—Kaiser Wilhelm of Germany and Austria's Archduke Franz Ferdinand, the sultan of Persia and princes from China, and other potentates from all the old empires that were about to vanish forever.

Now, the torch had been passed to England's former possession, not even two centuries old. Now, the leaders of the world walked behind another riderless horse and another casket on a gun carriage, this one carrying the mortal remains of President John Fitzgerald Kennedy. The mourners included, it seemed, everyone who had once mattered, everyone who still did matter, and many who were destined to play a part in the great trajectory of American history yet to come.

There was the towering, dignified figure of President Charles de Gaulle of France, in the uniform of the war the United States had helped him win; Prince Philip and Prime Minister Sir Alec Douglas-Home of the United Kingdom (the queen was pregnant and unable to travel); Emperor Haile Selassie of Ethiopia; Prince Norodom Sihanouk of Cambodia; and First Deputy Premier Anastas I. Mikoyan of the Soviet Union. There were Chancellor Ludwig Erhard of Germany and Mayor Willy Brandt of Berlin, where President Kennedy had spoken so memorably just a few months before, and President Eamon de Valera of Ireland, who had been born in New York City to an Irish mother and a Hispanic father. There were the presidents of Israel, Germany, Korea, and the Philippines; the premiers of Canada, Turkey, and Jamaica; the queen of Greece and the king of Belgium; the grand duke of Luxembourg; the crown princesses of the Netherlands, Norway, and Denmark. The delegations from 92 nations in all kept remarkably good time to the funeral dirge "Pray for the Dead" as it echoed through the stark streets.

It would not be accurate to say that this moment marked the pinnacle of American power, any more than it would be accurate to say that the funeral of Edward VII marked the pinnacle of the British Empire. America, in the years to come, would grow more powerful still—as well as richer, wiser, and more inclusive and democratic. In many ways, the assassination of President Kennedy would spur a new birth of freedom, particularly in the realm of civil rights.

Yet it was a turning point of sorts; President Kennedy's murder was a shock that continued to reverberate through the national psyche. America had seen presidents assassinated before. Always, it had succeeded in moving forward by exerting the great claim of a democratic society, which is that its well-being rests with no one man.

The Kennedy assassination was something else again. What made it so was partly the nature of the

The Mannlicher-Carcano 6.5 mm rifle that Lee Harvey Oswald used to assassinate President Kennedy on November 22, 1963. Kennedy was 46 at the time, his assassin, 24.

killing, conducted at long range, and by such a cretinous individual. But there were also the complications of a muddled investigation and the murder of the murderer himself—close-up and on national television, making it all horribly vivid but at the same time almost unbelievable.

The assassination would prove to be the first in a long string of events that diminished, as nothing had before, Americans' faith in their government. By the first decade of the twenty-first century, Kennedy's killing had come to support a flourishing industry, spawning untold numbers of books, movies, websites, and endless rumors. Recent polls reveal that 40 percent of the American people believe JFK was killed as the result of a conspiracy—a conspiracy hatched by the Mob, Castro, anti-Castro Cubans, the Soviets, the U.S. military, the CIA, the FBI, or all of the above. Nor did the credulity of the incredulous stop there. Similar polls show that more than one in three Americans believe that their government had somehow taken part in the terrorist attacks of September 11, 2001. There have come into existence conspiracy theorists around almost every major event in American history: the Japanese attack on Pearl Harbor, the assassination of Lincoln, the election of Kennedy, and on and on. One can even find books and websites outlining Custer conspiracy theories of one sort or another.

A stunned New Yorker learns the news. Later, the killing of Lee Harvey Oswald, by a small-time hoodlum and strip-club owner named Jack Ruby, would be viewed live, on national television.

New York
JFK
SHOT
TO
O DEATH

L.A.
ABLAZE,
1965

1963
TO
1968

MALCOLM, MARTIN, AND BOBBY

VIOLENCE SWEEPS AMERICA

Beyond this conspiratorial turn, the killing of President Kennedy seemed to trigger a violent turn in the nation, particularly in response to what were increasingly seen as intractable problems. During the next five years, bullets struck down one revered young leader after another. First, the radical black nationalist Malcolm X, in 1965; then, within the space of two sickening months in the spring of 1968, both Dr. Martin Luther King and Senator Robert F. Kennedy, the late president's brother, in the midst of his own run for the White House. Several years later, assassins would paralyze George Wallace, the demagogic governor of Alabama, and nearly succeed in killing President Ronald Reagan after he'd been in office for just two months. The term *lone gunman* became a household cliché.

By the mid-1960s, violence was on the rise everywhere—as "American as cherry pie," according to the black radical H. Rap Brown, who openly advocated riots as a form of racial "insurrection." He got his wish. The first "long hot summer," in 1964, saw urban disturbances break out in Rochester, New York, as well as in Philadelphia and in Jersey City, New Jersey. Six days of intermittent rioting that July in New York City—in Harlem and in Brooklyn's Bedford-Stuyvesant neighborhood—left one dead, 143 injured, and 461 arrested.

Much worse was to come. In August of 1965, 10,000 black rioters in the Watts district of Los Angeles chanted, "Burn, baby, burn!" as they put much of their neighborhood to the torch. Twelve thousand National Guardsmen, along with 2,500 city and county police, had to be called in to suppress the rioting, but not before 34 people were dead (28 of them African-Americans), more than 4,000 were arrested, 200 buildings were razed, and over $40 million worth of property was destroyed.

A riot in Cleveland in July of 1966 left four dead and 50 injured. In July of 1967, 26 died, 1,500 were injured, and $30 million worth of property was destroyed in Newark, New Jersey; that same year, riots in Detroit left 43 dead, 2,000 injured, 7,000 under arrest, 5,000 homeless, and 1,300 buildings destroyed; and the Motor City saw Sherman tanks rolling along its streets. In 1968 came the worst conflagration of all—rioting in cities across the country following the assassination of Dr. King. In the nation's capital, the violence left nine dead, 1,000 injured, and 6,000 arrested after four days of mayhem.

Above: Rioters mob an abandoned police car, 1965.

Opposite: The Watts riots started with the arrest of a black man for drunk driving.

These explosive riots were sparked at the complex intersection of race and economics. They reflected the subtler, more difficult challenge of the civil rights struggle. Eliminating official apartheid in the Jim Crow South required thousands of profiles in courage, but it was at least a tangible, obtainable goal. Eliminating the deeply entrenched social bigotry of whites in the South *and* North was something else again, as even Dr. King found out when his attempt to grapple with inadequate housing and employment for minorities in Chicago was met by stone-throwing white crowds and a stone-faced Mayor Richard Daley.

The economic aspect of the riots revolved around the beginnings of America's long process of deindustrialization. The decades after World War II had witnessed yet another vast exodus from the fields of the Deep South to the cities of the North. This time, it coincided with an influx of Hispanics coming up from Mexico, the Dominican Republic, Cuba, the American territory of Puerto Rico, and other parts of Central and South America and the Caribbean—millions of new migrants and immigrants seeking new opportunities.

Similar migrations had taken place after the Civil War and World War I. But now, new arrivals could not find jobs that might uplift them and their children. The old brick mills of New England sat dark and silent;

Top: The cofounders of the Black Panther Party, Chairman Bobby Seale (left) and Minister of Defense Huey Newton (right). Their movement for ghetto empowerment began with genuine idealism, but soon degenerated into general thuggery and even murder.

Bottom: Folk legend Joan Baez jokes with students occupying Berkeley's Sproul Hall as part of the 1964 Free Speech movement.

BY THE LATE SIXTIES, THE RADICAL STUDENTS FOR A DEMOCRATIC SOCIETY HAD OVER 100,000 MEMBERS IN MORE THAN 400 CHAPTERS.

the textile and shoe plants had fled to the South and then to the Third World, in search of ever-lower labor costs. New York Harbor, long the busiest port in the world, had all but emptied out, as container ships docked in New Jersey and the waterfront shed its jobs. The Big Three of Detroit had built 23 new automotive plants in Michigan in the years just after the war, all of them outside the city. Everywhere, urban manufacturers—long the first rung on the ladder to the unparalleled existence of the American middle class—were automating, shutting down, moving out.

So were many people. "White flight"—the escape of many white urban dwellers to their green patch of heaven in the Levittowns and elsewhere—was a well-documented phenomenon. Less noticed, but just as debilitating, was "black flight." Able for the first time to move into better city neighborhoods and even some suburbs, the black middle class pulled up stakes. Almost overnight, inner-city neighborhoods were transformed, their most prosperous, most well-educated, and most gainfully employed residents replaced by newcomers with little schooling and few marketable skills. These new arrivals found no jobs but instead—and also for the first time—a plethora of high-powered guns and addictive drugs. American crime rates spiked to record highs as the cycle of violence continued, and as more and more people and businesses moved out of the cities.

The wave of rebellion that swept American university campuses was, at first, directed against racism, a war in Vietnam that seemed to have less and less hope or reason, and the overbearing restrictions on college life. Students returning from the black-voter registration drives of the Mississippi Freedom Summer of 1964, where many had been beaten, were not about to tolerate university-imposed limits on the First Amendment.

Contrary to the stereotype, the student protestors were not usually flower children; they thought of themselves as political activists, and their courage and dedication were often impressive. By the late sixties, the radical Students for a Democratic Society had over 100,000 members in more than 400 chapters. The SDS took over the campuses of some of the leading universities, demanding that their administrations cease all support for the war effort, increase minority enrollment, make overtures to their surrounding communities, and give the students some say in their education.

When all of this failed to stop the war or to radically remake American society, the students began to search about in vain for new tactics. In 1968, incensed by the prevarications of the Johnson administration and its escalation of Vietnam into a senseless, bloody nightmare, many went to work for the insurgent Democratic presidential candidacies of Senator Eugene McCarthy and Robert Kennedy, and helped to bring a shocking and abrupt end to the Johnson administration. But when RFK was assassinated and McCarthy disengaged, they had nowhere to go. A merry band of anarchists calling themselves the Youth International Party, or Yippies, thought *they* knew where to go: the Democratic convention in Chicago, to protest the war and the party's nomination of Hubert Humphrey. Mayor Daley's police crushed the protest in brutal fashion before the TV cameras as the demonstrators chanted, "The whole world is watching!"

"There is a time when the operation of the machine becomes so odious, makes you so sick at heart, that you can't take part; you can't even passively take part and you've got to put your bodies upon the gears and upon the wheels, upon the levers, upon all the apparatus, and you've got to make it stop."
—Mario Savio
THE DRAFT
VETERANS
for
peace

1968 TO 1980

RADICAL TURNS

THE END OF NIXON—AND THE NEW LEFT

Yet the radical left's critiques of "Amerikkkan" society had no resonance among the members of the working class, who overall remained deeply patriotic and grateful for a prosperity well beyond anything their parents had known. Failing to rally the electorate and alienating most of their former student allies at the same time, the remnants of the sixties' "New Left" devolved into cells and revolutionary cults such as the Weather Underground and the Symbionese Liberation Army, specializing in pointless acts of violence that ranged from the pathetic to the appalling: the Days of Rage in the fall of 1969, the 1970 bombing of a University of Wisconsin–Madison science lab that killed a physics scholar, the 1973 assassination of a liberal black school superintendent in Oakland, California, the 1974 kidnapping of newspaper heiress Patty Hearst, and the gunning down of a couple of Brinks guards.

The Chicago police riot at the 1968 Democratic convention ended up helping to elect the Republican candidate Richard Nixon, who promised that he had "a secret plan" to end the war, but American troops remained in Vietnam for another four years. Before it was over, the U.S. had lost over 58,000 soldiers, and along with its allies had killed nearly 1.2 million enemy combatants; helped sink neighboring Cambodia into chaos and genocide; and dropped a greater tonnage of bombs than the U.S. had throughout all of World War II—without being able to hold up the South Vietnamese regime.

Nixon clung to power by tacking strategically from left to right and back again, easing Cold War tensions with historic overtures to China and the Soviet Union, and creating the Environmental Protection Agency—and also invoking the silent majority of Americans against what he called "campus bums," and egging on the efforts of the FBI and CIA to suppress protest movements.

Division and chaos seemed to multiply. Morale and command were slowly starting to unravel in Vietnam, where revelations about the My Lai Massacre of innocent civilians by U.S. troops came to light in 1969.

National Guard shootings at Kent State University left four students dead and shut down every college campus around the country in the spring of 1970. The leak of the Pentagon Papers the next year exposed the U.S. drift into war in Vietnam. It also had unintended consequences. In trying to seal the leak, and to ensure his re-election through illegal break-ins, wiretappings, and other political dirty tricks—and then by lying about all of it—Nixon undermined his own administration and became the first American president ever forced to resign.

Meanwhile, an Arab oil embargo, sparked by U.S. support for Israel in the 1973 Yom Kippur War, triggered America's first "oil shock." Skyrocketing fuel prices created both inflation and economic contraction—a condition dubbed *stagflation*. When combined with the enormous cost of the war in Vietnam, the oil shock made the U.S. financial system shudder, and pushed the country off the gold standard, thereby destabilizing its currency. Nixon was succeeded by his earnest vice-president, Gerald Ford. Though Ford managed to survive two assassination attempts and lead the nation beyond Watergate, he was criticized for his inability to tame inflation and

Demonstrators occupy the Civil War Sailors Monument—"renamed" the Peace Monument—in a 1971 demonstration in Washington, D.C., against the Vietnam War.

for granting Richard Nixon a presidential pardon. He was replaced by an equally earnest Washington outsider, the Democrat Jimmy Carter, who restored U.S. support for human rights abroad and made stalwart efforts to free the nation from dependence on foreign energy sources. But Carter proved ineffectual when the U.S. embassy staff in the Iranian capital of Tehran was held hostage by that country's radical new Islamic regime—a whiff of blowback for America's overthrow of the democratically elected Prime Minister Mohammad Mossadegh in 1953 and subjection of the country to 26 more years of kleptocracy under the Shah.

Richard Nixon (above) wins the Republican Party nomination in Miami in 1968, completing a stunning political comeback. Despite huge antiwar demonstrations, such as the one on the National Mall in 1971 (right), Nixon won election and re-election by invoking his "silent majority" against demonstrators.

MY SON WAS
KILLED!
IN VIETNAM
WHAT FOR?
America

1981
TO
2000

MORNING AGAIN IN AMERICA

THE REAGAN REVOLUTION

The country seemed to be coming apart—"a pitiful, helpless giant," in the phrase Nixon had used to justify what proved to be his pitiless, unhelpful invasion of Cambodia. The remedy was one that would have been considered fantastical just a few years before. Ronald Reagan was an amiable former actor, a lifelong admirer of Franklin Roosevelt, who was once considered too liberal to be nominated as a mayoral candidate in Los Angeles by a local Democratic committee. Within a few short years, Reagan had become a winning spokesman for the views of General Electric's conservative chairman, then a leader of the growing right-wing of the Republican party. As late as 1976, Reagan was considered too far right to win the GOP nomination even against the much-abused Gerald Ford.

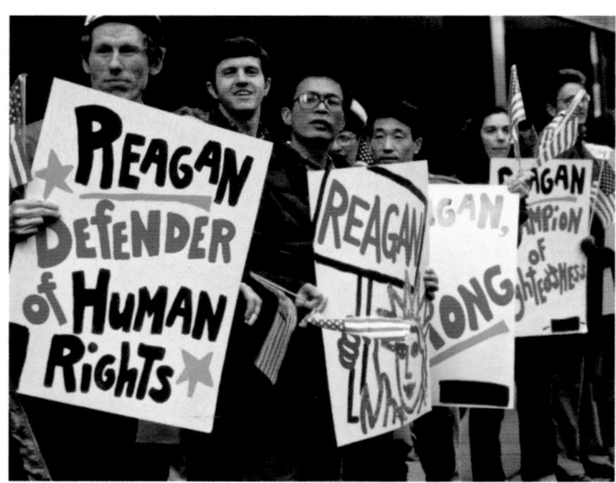

Above: Reagan supporters celebrate their candidate's commitment to human rights, 1984—always staunch when it came to Communist countries, but less so in the case of U.S.-supported regimes in Latin America.

Opposite: Ronald and Nancy Reagan on the stump, launching their 1980 general election campaign in Philadelphia, Mississippi.

Yet Reagan had taken the leadership of a grassroots conservative movement that had been quietly growing since the Scopes trial in the 1920s. The Cold War, the battles over civil rights, the vast cultural changes sweeping the U.S., and the crisis in political leadership had quickened its emergence, giving it cohesion and resonance.

Reagan was the candidate it had been lacking. Blessed with a genial disposition and a relish for the political arena, he banished from mind the "last angry man" persona of the right. Eight years as governor of California had both softened and honed his approach. He had largely acquiesced to the consensus for the social welfare state, while cheerfully pummeling the excesses—real and rhetorical—of the far left. His natural charm enabled him to shrug off serious criticism with an engaging grin.

The American people admired Reagan's optimism and faith, his sunny confidence in his nation's future and its abilities. It was all just a matter of will, whether it came to facing down the Soviet Union, or unleashing the power of the private sector, or finding the resolve to "just say no" to drugs, as First Lady Nancy Reagan urged the nation's youth.

A weary nation rallied to the message. Within two months of his inauguration, he psychically reversed the nation's recent twisted history of tragedy and failed presidencies when—despite being the oldest man ever elected as president—he survived an attempted assassination, a shooting at point-blank range.

Before his first term was out, the economy had started to turn around. It was soon spurred to a gallop by yet another great American grassroots boom. Out of a thousand garages and dorm rooms came the

CON VALLEY CEL
merica is Worki
LABOR DAY 19

electronic revolution, centered in the Silicon Valley of Reagan's beloved California. Contemporary versions of Samuel Morse and Andrew Carnegie stepped forward—people like Steve Jobs and Bill Gates, entrepreneurs who accumulated staggering fortunes while they transformed the world.

At the same time, Reagan stood in JFK's place before the Berlin Wall and demanded, in the name of freedom, "Mr. Gorbachev, tear down this wall!" And two years later, in 1989, the wall came down. The Soviet Union collapsed, gleeful Berliners ripped the wall down chunk by chunk, and Eastern Europe was freed. Ronald Reagan's adherents gave him the credit, pointing to the massive arms buildup he had instigated and the "Star Wars" nuclear-defense shield he had proposed. Credit should properly be shared with every other Cold War president, from Harry Truman, who set up the original framework to block Soviet expansionism with the Marshall Plan and NATO, right through to Carter, who had boycotted the 1980 Summer Olympics in Moscow, restored draft registration, and first armed and funded the Mujahideen resistance to the Soviets in Afghanistan. But it was undeniable that Ronald Reagan had conceived of victory as imminent—that he had believed in both containment and in "rolling back" the Soviet empire to help democracy flourish worldwide.

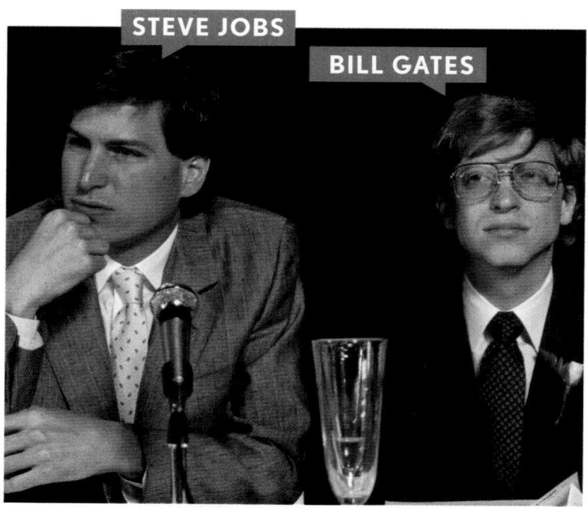

Above: Apple computer founder Steve Jobs and Microsoft's Bill Gates, the faces of the electronic revolution, during an interview in New York in 1984. Gates would become the richest man in America.

Opposite: Ecstatic Berliners pull each other over the Berlin Wall, as Communism collapses. Soon they would pull down that wall with their own hands.

His faith in the country was vindicated. America's triumph was not just over its Cold War enemy but also over its own friends and competitors. Many commentators had expected Japan to surpass the U.S. as the world's leading economy in the 1990s, citing its work ethic and its style of cooperative capitalism. Instead, Japan fell into a "lost decade" of economic stagnation, while the U.S. boomed on its enormous "peace dividend."

Once again, America's economy was the most dynamic in the world, as the country seemed to make the groundbreaking conversion from manufacturing to a postindustrial service economy as it grew ever richer. By the late 1990s, real wages in the U.S. crept upward for the first time in almost a quarter century. This was accomplished under the presidency of Democrat Bill Clinton, but the prevailing philosophy was still Reaganism—low taxes and limited government interference, leaving the creation of prosperity to the genius of the markets.

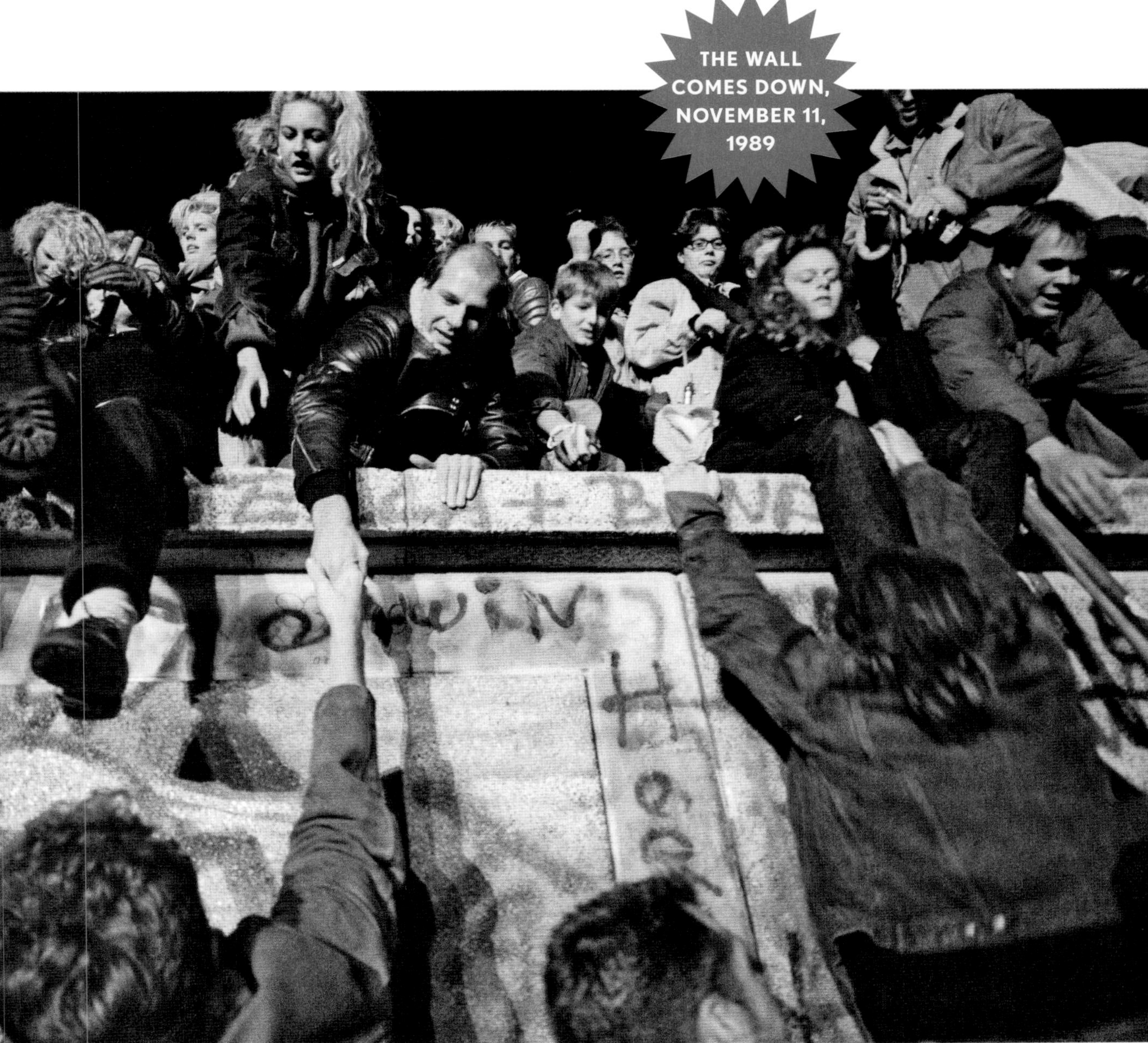

THE WALL COMES DOWN, NOVEMBER 11, 1989

1950 TO 2000

THE DREAM DERAILED

THE DOWNSIZING OF AMERICA

Even before Ronald Reagan gave a cheery last wave from the White House lawn and departed by helicopter, there were indications that the laws of physics and mathematics had not been suspended, and that serious problems remained. Reagan had managed to slow the rate of growth of the federal government, but budget deficits had ballooned, increasing by two-thirds as a percentage of GDP.

The tax cuts, a collapse in world oil prices, and Reagan's prodigious arms buildup did help to jump-start the economy, but they also created the largest peacetime deficit in U.S. history. Nor were the benefits of the boom well-distributed. The long-term trend toward more equitable distribution of America's wealth, begun with the New Deal, was now reversed. By 1998, according to some measures, income inequality in the United States was as bad as it had been since 1933; according to others, it was greater than it had *ever* been before. A small slice of the very rich got an enormous tax cut during the Reagan years. But thanks to payroll taxes needed to shore up the Social Security and Medicare systems, everybody else saw their personal income tax *increase*.

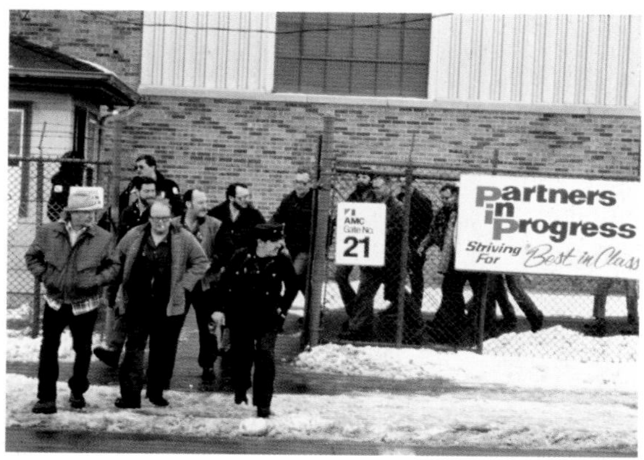

Above: Workers leave a Chrysler plant shortly before it closes down in 1988. "Foreman says these jobs are going, boys, and they ain't coming back/To your hometown," sang Bruce Springsteen.

Opposite: An unemployment office in Detroit, 1976.

There was also an accelerating flight of both American capital and manufacturers to foreign countries, primarily those in the Third World. Meanwhile, in those manufacturing sectors that remained, Americans were repeatedly beaten in quality and quantity even by foreigners competing on a level playing field. In the 1970s, the U.S. steel industry collapsed. American cars were now typically less fuel-efficient, less well-made, and more expensive than those built in Europe and Asia—especially in Japan.

The hometowns disappeared with the jobs. The one-time steel colossus of Pittsburgh lost over half its population between 1950 and 2000. Detroit, already devastated by the 1967 riot and by squabbles with predominantly white surrounding suburbs, now staggered along with its auto industry. Riots rocked Miami in 1989 and 1992, and Los Angeles in 1992. The L.A. conflagration killed 53 people and caused $1 billion worth of damage, exceeding the costs of the Watts Riot in 1965.

1981 TO 2010

THE BUBBLE MACHINE

THE RISE AND FALL OF THE CASINO ECONOMY

The accomplishments of the information revolution were real enough, but—much as occurred with blue-chip radio and utility stocks in the Great Crash of 1929—many of the first information companies were overvalued and poorly designed early on, leading to the collapse of the dot-com bubble by the end of the century. In the 1990s, books with titles such as *America: What Went Wrong?* and *The End of Work* began to appear. As the Nobel Prize–winning economist Joseph Stiglitz put it, Americans were asking, "Was the country creating hamburger flippers to replace its skilled manufacturing workers?"

The answer was no. Many of the jobs in the new, postindustrial economy were in fact high-paying jobs—in the burgeoning financial sector. By 2000, 40 percent of the nation's corporate profits were earned in finance.

Yet increasingly, America was morphing into a casino economy. This meant, among other things, literal casinos everywhere, along with new state lotteries and, later, myriad forms of Internet gambling. In the broader economic world, it meant that the Reaganist loosening of regulations everywhere, and virtual indifference to antitrust laws, created monopolies, cartels, and disaster. Sound companies of all sorts were repeatedly bought on debt, sliced, diced, reconfigured, and sold off again, often for no discernible purpose beyond the chance to rob them. The savings-and-loan scandals of the 1980s cost U.S. taxpayers an estimated $160 billion at the time, or $313 billion in today's dollars—an incomprehensible sum then, although it would be dwarfed by later bailouts.

Above: The New York Stock Exchange.

Opposite: Enron brokers field calls in 2000, not long before the company's crack up.

Bubbles—and scandals—quickly succeeded one another, with each more confusing to the American people than the last. The 2001 collapse of Enron, originally a natural-gas pipeline company turned bucket shop on a big-box-store scale, was at the time the largest corporate bankruptcy in American history. The company had been named America's most innovative large corporation six years in a row by *Fortune* magazine, but nobody—including Enron and its auditors—seemed to know exactly what it did, besides accepting bets on just about anything. Its failure sent a financial tsunami ripping through its hometown of Houston and through the financial world in general.

A hamburger, at least, was something that could be touched, smelled, tasted (and before that, of course, cut from a cow, shipped, and flipped). So much of the American economy now seemed to be based on financial instruments that could not be fully comprehended, even by those who had brought them into being—and then sent them tearing through the world financial system like so many minié balls, doing major

ENRON—
BEFORE THE
MELTDOWN

"The true measure of a career is to be able to be content, even proud, that you succeeded through your own endeavors without leaving a trail of casualties in your wake." —Alan Greenspan

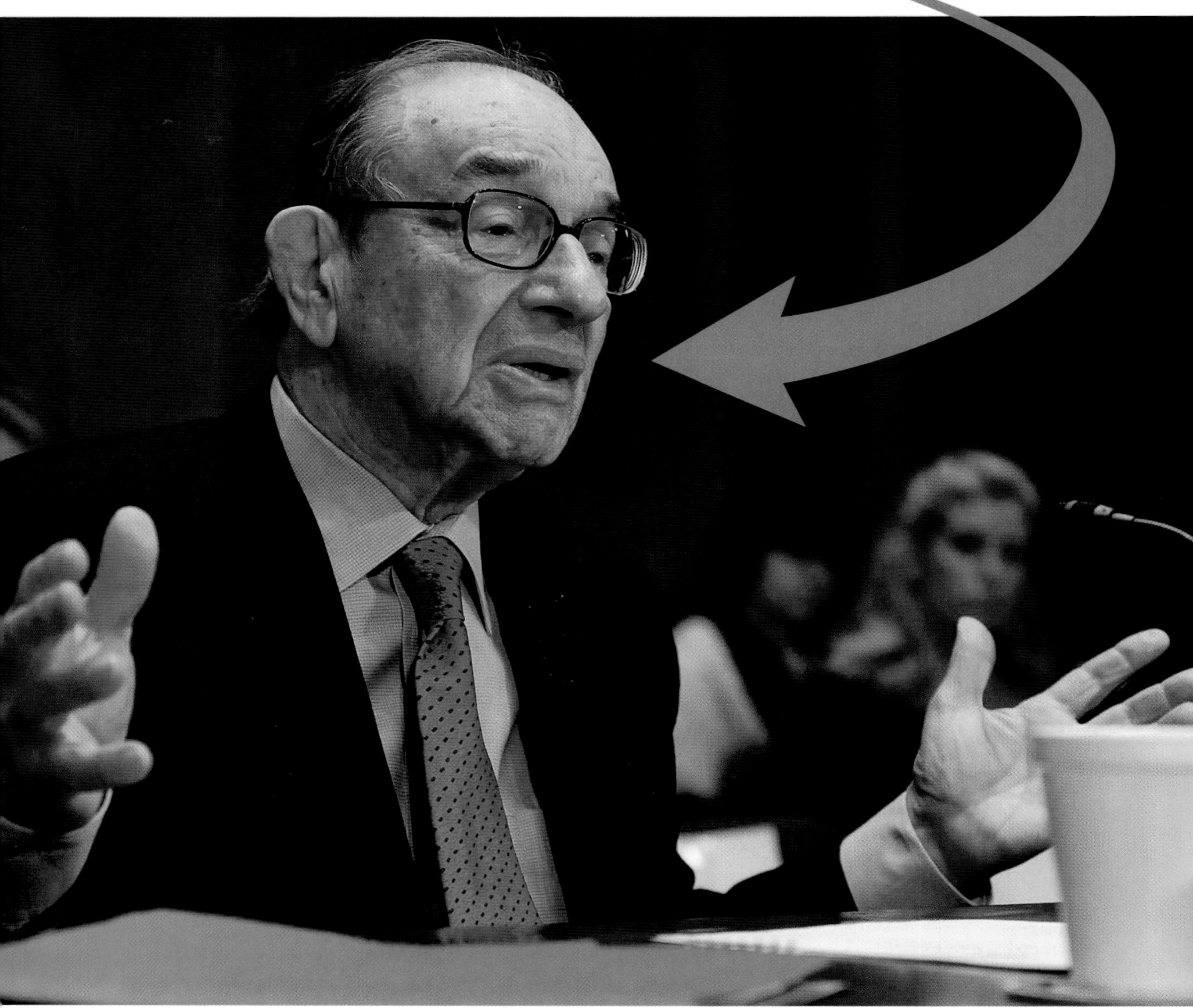

damage to vital organs. Even more disturbing, America seemed to have lost a democracy's most vital asset: its ability to learn and profit from its mistakes, even if they contradicted one's most cherished fantasies.

Far from learning from the savings-and-loan debacle, for instance, just over ten years later the Clinton administration, at the urging of a Republican Congress, agreed to undo the Glass-Steagall Act of 1933. That legislation had set up firewalls between commercial and investment banks, and ushered in almost 70 years of unprecedented prosperity and financial stability. In 1987, his next-to-last year in office, Ronald Reagan appointed the economist Alan Greenspan as chairman of the Federal Reserve. Greenspan was reappointed by Democratic and Republican presidents alike, and lionized by both parties, even though he had been a longtime member of Ayn Rand's bizarre cult of personality, with its unquestioning beliefs in the radical forms of laissez-faire economics and Social Darwinism that had been discredited almost a century before.

The results should have been perfectly predictable: a new bubble of incredible size. Or rather, a double bubble of real-estate speculation, inflated out of all proportion by all manner of hot air, and of so-called derivative financial instruments—hedges upon hedges, puts upon puts, bets upon bets of such complexity and such recklessness that no one could any longer calculate the full measure of risk involved. It all blew apart in a dizzying few days in the autumn of 2008, an explosion that threatened to take down the entire globalized financial system and that plunged America into its worst recession since the Great Depression.

A by-then-retired Greenspan found himself before a congressional committee that fall, admitting with chagrin and no little befuddlement that, contrary to his deepest beliefs, markets had *not* become perfectly self-regulating. It was a lesson one might have derived by perusing almost any chapter of American history, and the failure to do so would cost the country dearly. Congressional Budget Office estimates foresaw taxpayers losing, conservatively, $356 billion in bailing out all the Wall Street banks and other institutions that had become, as some argued, "too big to fail." The total of bailouts plus guarantees necessary to forestall financial collapse was $12 *trillion*—or almost *80 percent of the nation's gross domestic product*.

This level of indebtedness threatened to hinder America's ability to compete in the global economy it had done so much to create. No serious money was devoted to such looming problems as climate change. In an age when most industrialized (or postindustrial) countries spent an average of 3 percent of their GDP on infrastructure every year, U.S. spending dropped to 1.3 percent. China, Spain, and even Russia built high-speed, cutting-edge rail lines, while America did nothing. The Reagan administration had largely ended federal support for mass transit, housing, and development in the nation's cities.

A retired Alan Greenspan, testifying before Congress in 2009. The year before, he admitted that the financial meltdown left him in a "state of shocked disbelief" and that he had made a "mistake" in expecting deregulated banks to protect their shareholders— "a flaw in the model... that defines how the world works."

1950 TO 2010

THERE IS NO THERE THERE

THE URBAN CRISIS

Many American cities, from New York to Los Angeles, from Washington to Cleveland, had managed a resurgence of one sort or another after the riots and the meltdowns of the sixties and seventies thanks to their own resources and ingenuity—and to the renewed attractiveness of the urban experience after a generation spent marinating in the suburbs.

Detroit was not among the success stories. Its fortunes remained tied to the automakers, and by 2008 two of the Big Three were bankrupt, kept alive only through the intervention of the federal government. Ford, as resilient as ever, had managed to learn and retool, but Chrysler and General Motors were moribund. By then, the city had tried all the most discredited remedies for urban renewal, including casinos and a walled-off downtown complex called the Renaissance Center. Nonetheless, drugs and fires—many of them set deliberately on Halloween and during Devil's Night on October 30—savaged Detroit's handsome brick-and-wood neighborhoods. The beautiful old Hudson auto plant lay abandoned for over 50 years, its ruin used only as a backdrop for a television series about a male prostitute. The sumptuous Michigan Theater, erected on the site of the garage where Henry Ford built his very first car, was gutted, partly demolished, and converted into a parking facility.

Detroit lost more than half of its population between 1950 and 2010, going from over 1.8 million to 900,000, and from being the nation's fourth-largest city to its eleventh-largest. It was thought necessary by some city officials to abandon many of its sprawling, 143 square miles. With so many of its blocks reduced to just one or two occupied houses—or none at all—the city designed for cars could no longer afford to maintain itself over such a wide area. Charitable organizations launched plans to grow corn in its leafy, overgrown plots. Detroit—Motor City, Motown, FDR's "great arsenal of democracy," Joe Louis and Aretha Franklin's old town, heart of American soul—had become a desolate, eerie ruin.

Many of Detroit's neighborhoods and its factories (including Ford's once mighty River Rouge plant, above, and the Packard Motor Car Company, opposite) lay deserted and crumbling by 2010.

2001 TO 2010

A NEW CITY UPON A HILL

WAR AND REMEMBRANCE

In the new century, America was distracted from all domestic concerns—and its peace dividend swallowed up—by a new threat. E. B. White's "single flight of planes no bigger than a wedge of geese" finally did appear on September 11, 2001, in the skies over New York City and Washington, D.C. The destruction they caused was shocking and brutal. For the first time since the War of 1812, the American mainland was attacked by a foreign enemy. Once again, as they had during the Triangle Shirtwaist Factory Fire, New Yorkers witnessed the terrible spectacle of their fellow citizens forced by flames to jump from deadly heights. This time, they also saw firefighters and police hurrying stoically to their deaths as they tried to douse the blaze and rescue the survivors.

Americans rallied heroically after 9/11. They united behind swift military action to roust the perpetrators from their base in Afghanistan, and many also acceded to unprecedented restrictions on their civil liberties and to the invasion of Iraq, all in the name of rooting out Islamic terrorists and their backers, said to be preparing "weapons of mass destruction." But the weapons did not materialize, and America's wars in the Middle East soon bogged down into what seemed like a numbingly familiar and frustrating reprise of Vietnam. By early 2010, the wars had left 5,000 Americans and hundreds of thousands of Afghanis and Iraqis dead, emptied the U.S. Treasury, seriously diminished America's luster in the world, and opened deep partisan divides in a country already fissured by Republican attempts to remove President Bill Clinton from office for perjury in the 1990s, and by Democrats' anger over what they saw as George W. Bush's stolen election in 2000.

Above: The New York City Fire Department lost 343 firefighters attempting to rescue those trapped in the towers.

Opposite: The towers of the World Trade Center crumble to earth on September 11, 2001, taking some 2,600 lives with them, and covering lower Manhattan in a cloud of dust.

The partisan fury was only further inflamed by the election of President Barack Obama in 2008. American citizens concerned about the drift of the country took to the streets in conscious imitation of the nation's original activists, wearing tricornered hats and calling themselves "Tea Party Patriots." The Tea Partyers were inspired by a genuine exasperation with governement mismanagement and growing deficits. Critics charged that the movement lacked diversity and that its libertarian inclinations elided the fact that America had often operated by public-business partnerships.

While Americans were divided on his policies, the election of President Obama illustrated as nothing else what America still does best. Here was the son of a black Kenyan academic and a white college student from Kansas—a young man with an African (and Islamic) name, whose grandfather had ridden in

CHANGE WE NEED
Florida 4 Obama
Women 4 Obama
BUCS FOR
OBAMA BIDEN

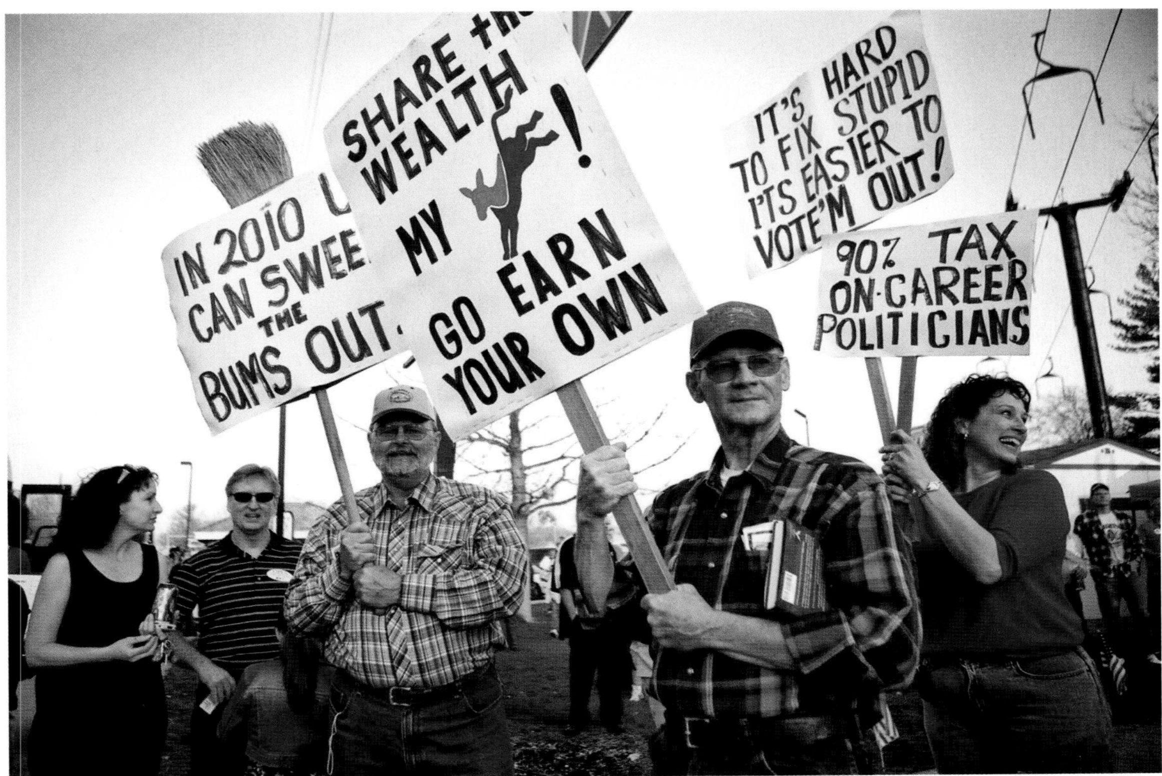

Patton's tanks against the German Reich. Here was a child born in Hawaii, the newest and most far-flung of the 50 states, who spent years in foreign lands, grew up without much money and often without one or both parents, worked his way through great universities, and dedicated his life to public service.

The election of such a man was vivid evidence of Americans' seemingly limitless belief in the possibility of change. Barack Obama's election was made possible by a new, grassroots media, an Internet campaign that went over, under, and right through the barriers raised by mainstream media and party potentates alike. But more than the latest technology, his election reflected the still young spirit of America, a nation constantly renewed and constantly animated by hope. Obama's ascension to the presidency reaffirmed for millions around the world that the United States is a true beacon of tolerance and democracy. The immigrants would continue to come, providing America with its lifeblood, as they always had.

"This work continues. This story goes on," George W. Bush proclaimed in his first inaugural address. Ten years into the twenty-first century, all that America has to offer is all that it has been. For all of its foibles, for all of the mistakes inherent in the rough, messy business of running a republic, the United States still offers the best hope of what our world can be.

Above: President Obama's first year in office was marked by vehement "Tea Party" protests.

Opposite: Supporters of Barack Obama, insisting "Yes, We Can," propelled America's first African-American president to a stunning win over Vietnam War hero John McCain.

EXTENDED READING LIST

CHAPTER 1: REBELS

General:

Alan Taylor, *American Colonies: The Settling of North America* (2002)

On the Plymouth:

Nathaniel Philbrick, *Mayflower: A Voyage to War* (2006)

On Jamestown:

Benjamin Woolley, *Savage Kingdom: The True Story of Jamestown, 1607, and the Settlement of America* (2007)

On Slavery:

Ira Berlin, *Many Thousands Gone: The First Two Centuries of Slavery in North America* (1998)

On the Boston Tea Party:

Benjamin Woods Labaree, *The Boston Tea Party* (1964)

Lexington and Concord:

John Ferling, *Almost a Miracle: The American Victory in the War of Independence* (2007)

CHAPTER 2: REVOLUTION

General:

Gary B. Nash, *The Unknown American Revolution: The Unruly Birth of Democracy and the Struggle to Create America* (2007)

On George Washington:

Rosemarie Zagarri, ed., *David Humphreys' "Life of General Washington": With George Washington's "Remarks"* (1991)

On the New York Campaign:

David McCullough, *1776: America and Britain at War* (2005)

On Valley Forge:

John Buchanan, *The Road to Valley Forge: How Washington Built the Army That Won the Revolution* (2004)

On Smallpox:

Elizabeth A. Fenn, *Pox Americana: The Great Smallpox Epidemic of 1775-82* (2001)

On Espionage:

Alexander Rose, *Washington's Spies: The Story of America's First Spy Ring* (2006)

On the Rifle:

Alexander Rose, *American Rifle: A Biography* (2008)

CHAPTER 3: WESTWARD

General:

Ray Allen Billington and Martin Ridge, *Westward Expansion: A History of the American Frontier* (2001)

On Daniel Boone:

John Mack Faragher, *Daniel Boone: The Life and Legend of an American Pioneer* (1993)

On the Trail of Tears:

Vicki Rozema, *Voices from The Trail of Tears* (2003)

On Lewis & Clark:

Paul Russell Cutright, *Lewis and Clark: Pioneering Naturalists* (1969)

On Jedediah Smith and the Mountain Men:

Robert M Utley, *A Life Wild and Perilous: Mountain Men and the Paths to the Pacific* (1997)

On Texas and the Alamo:

H. W. Brands, *Lone Star Nation: The Epic Story of the Battle for Texas Independence* (2004)

CHAPTER 4: DIVISION

General:

Daniel Walker Howe, *What Hath God Wrought: The Transformation of America: 1815-1848* (2007)

On Slavery in America:

Peter Kolchin, *American Slavery, 1619-1877* (1994)

Nell Irvin Painter, *Creating Black Americans: African American History and its Meanings, 1619 to the Present* (2006)

On Cotton and the Cotton Gin:

Angela Lakwete, *Inventing the Cotton Gin: Machine and Myth in Antebellum America* (2003)

On The Erie Canal:

Gerard Koeppel, *Bond of Union: Building the Erie Canal and the American Empire* (2009)

On Industrialisation:

John Steele Gordon, *An Empire of Wealth: The Epic History of American Economic Power* (2004)

On Whaling:

Eric Jay Dolin, *Leviathan: The History of Whaling in America* (2007)

CHAPTER 5: CIVIL WAR

General:

David S. Heidler and Jeanne T. Heidler ed., *Encyclopedia of the American Civil War: A Political, Social, and Military History* (2000)

On the Second Battle of Bull Run:

John J. Hennessy, *Return to Bull Run: The Campaign and Battle of Second Manassas* (1993)

On Civil War Medicine:

Frank R. Freemon, *Gangrene and Glory: Medical Care during the American Civil War* (2001)

On Robert E. Lee:

Emory M. Thomas, *Robert E. Lee: A Biography* (1997)

On Abraham Lincoln:

David Herbert Donald, *Lincoln* (1995)

On the Battle of Antietam:

John Michael Priest, *Antietam: The Soldiers' Battle* (1989))

On Newspapers in the Civil War:

Brayton Harris, *Blue & Gray in Black & White: Newspapers in the Civil War* (1999)

On the Emancipation Proclamation:

Ira Berlin et al., ed., *Free at Last: A Documentary History of Slavery, Freedom, and the Civil War* (1995)

CHAPTER 6: HEARTLAND

On Railroads:

Stephen E. Ambrose, *Nothing Like It In The World: The Men Who Built the Transcontinental Railroad, 1863-1869* (2000)

On the Lumber Industry:

Eileen M. McMahon and Theodore J. Karamanski, *Time and the River: A History of the Saint Croix* (2002)

On Cowboys:

Richard W. Slatta, *Comparing Cowboys and Frontiers: New Perspectives on the History of the Americas* (1997)

On Bison:

Andrew C. Isenberg, *The Destruction of the Bison: An Environmental History, 1750-1920* (2000)

On Chicago and the End of the Frontier:

William Cronon, *Nature's Metropolis: Chicago and the Great West* (1991)

CHAPTER 7: CITIES

General:

William E. Leuchtenburg, *The Perils of Prosperity: 1914-1932* (1958)

On Steel and Skyscrapers:

Thomas J. Misa, *A Nation of Steel: The Making of Modern America, 1865-1925* (1995)

On Andrew Carnegie:

Peter Krass, *Carnegie* (2002)

On Thomas Edison and Electricity:

Paul Israel, *Edison: A Life of Invention* (1998)

On Ellis Island and Immigration:

David M. Brownstone, Irene M. Franck and Douglass Brownstone, *Island of Hope, Island of Tears: The Story of Those Who Entered the New World through Ellis Island—In Their Own Words* (2003)

On Waste:

Martin V. Melosi, *Garbage In The Cities: Refuse Reform and the Environment* (2005)

On the Statue of Liberty:

Marvin Trachtenberg, *The Statue of Liberty* (1976)

On Hudson-Fulton Festival:

Kathleen Eagen Johnson, *The Hudson-Fulton Celebration: New York's River Festival of 1909 and the Making of a Metropolis* (2009)

CHAPTER 8: BOOM

General:

David M. Kennedy, *Over Here: The First World War and American Society* (1982)

On Oil:

Daniel Yergin, *The Prize: The Epic Quest for Oil, Money and Power* (2008)

On Spindletop:

Judith Walker Linsley, Ellen Walker Rienstra, and Jo Ann Stiles, *Giant Under the Hill: A History of the Spindletop Oil Discovery at Beaumont, Texas, in 1901* (2009)

On the Ford Company:

Douglas G. Brinkley, *Wheels on the World: Henry Ford, His Company, and a Century of Progress* (2003)

On L.A. Aqueduct and Mulholland:

Margaret Leslie Davis, *Rivers in the Desert: William Mulholland and the Inventing of Los Angeles* (1994)

On Suburbanisation:

Kenneth T. Jackson, *Crabgrass Frontier: The Suburbanization of the United States* (1987)

On Race Riots and Ghettos:

Janet L. Abu-Lughod, *Race Space, and Riots in Chicago, New York, and Los Angeles* (2007)

On Prohibition:

Edward Behr, *Prohibition: Thirteen Years that Changed America* (1997)

On the FBI:

Henry M. Holden, *FBI 100 Years: An Unofficial History* (2008)

CHAPTER 9: BUST

General:

David M. Kennedy, *Freedom From Fear: The American People in Depression and War, 1929-1945* (1999)

On Wall Street Crash:

Liaquat Ahamed, *Lords of Finance: The Bankers Who Broke The World* (2009)

On Hollywood:

David Wallace, *Hollywoodland: Rich and Lively History About Hollywood's Grandest Era* (2002)

On the Dust Bowl:

Timothy Egan, *The Worst Hard Time: The Untold Story of Those Who Survived the Great American Dust Bowl* (2006)

On the Hoover Dam:

Lesley A. Dutemple, *The Hoover Dam* (2003)

On Mount Rushmore:

Rex Allen Smith, *The Carving of Mount Rushmore* (1985)

On Louis v. Schmeling:

Lewis Erenberg, *The Greatest Fight of Our Generation: Louis vs. Schmeling* (2006)

CHAPTER 10: WORLD WAR II

General:

Studs Terkel, *'The Good War': An Oral History of World War II* (1984)

On Pearl Harbor:

Gordon W. Prange, *At Dawn We Slept: The Untold Story of Pearl Harbor* (1981)

On D-Day:

Harold Baumgarten, *D-Day Survivor: An Autobiography* (2006)

On Bombing Runs:

R. G. Grant, *Flight: The Complete History* (2007)

On the Atomic Bomb:

Richard Rhodes, *The Making of the Atomic Bomb* (1986)

CHAPTER 11: BOOMERS AND CHAPTER 12: MILLENNIUM

Terry H. Anderson, *The Movement and The Sixties: Protest in America from Greensboro to Wounded Knee* (1996)

George Brown Tindall and David Emory Shi, *America: A Narrative History* (2007)

Gary A. Donaldson, *The Making of Modern America: The Nation from 1945 to the Present* (2009)

Bernard Edelman ed., *Dear America: Letters Home from Vietnam* (2002)

Paul Levine and Harry Papasotiriou, *America Since 1945: The American Moment* (2005)

Sean Wilentz, *The Age of Reagan: A History, 1974-2008* (2009)

Howard Zinn, *A People's History of the United States: 1492 to Present* (Updated Edition, 2003

INDEX

Italic page numbers refer to illustrations.

PHOTO CREDITS AND ACKNOWLEDGMENTS

PHOTO CREDITS

Key: BAL: The Bridgeman Art Library, International; LOC: Library of Congress; NYPL: The New York Public Library

Still photography by Joe Alblas and Charlie Sperring

Pages 8-9: A&E Television Networks, LLC; 11: Erich Lessing/Art Resource, NY; 12: (top): The Trustees of The British Museum/Art Resource, NY; (middle left): John White/Private Collection/BAL; (middle right): John White/Private Collection/BAL; (bottom left): John White/Private Collection/BAL; (bottom right): John White/Private Collection/BAL; 14: William Hole/LOC Geography and Maps Division/LC-USZ62-73508; 16: Virginia Historical Society, Richmond, VA/BAL; 19: Private Collection/BAL; 20: Paul Revere/LOC/LC-USZ62-96234; 21: William Penn/LOC; 23: LOC Rare Books and Special Collections Division/LC-USZ62-44000; 25: NYPL/Art Resource, NY; 26-27: Paul Revere/Emmet Collection, Miriam and Ira D. Wallach Division of Art, Prints, and Photographs/NYPL; 29: Paul Revere/Worcester Art Museum, Worcehester, MA/BAL; 31: Emmet Collection, Miriam and Ira D. Wallach Division of Art, Prints, and Photograph/NYPL; 32: Art Resource, NY; 35: Benjamin Franklin/LOC Serials and Government Publications Division/LC-USZ62-9701; 36-37: A&E Television Networks, LLC; 38: Thomas Jefferson/LOC Manuscripts Division; 41: Doug Mindell/Lexington Historical Society; 42: Emmet Collection, Miriam and Ira D. Wallach Division of Art, Prints, and Photographs/NYPL; 45: LOC Prints and Photographs Division/LC-USZC4-1476; 46-47: Andre Basset/LOC/LC-USZ62-42; 51: LOC; 55: Private Collection/Peter Newark Military Pictures/BAL; 56: Collection of the New-York Historical Society/BAL; 62: Private Collection/Peter Newark American Pictures/BAL; 63 HIP/Art Resource, NY; 64-65: A&E Television Networks, LLC; 66: Samuel M. Lee/Smithsonian American Art Museum, Washington, D.C./Art Resource, NY; 69: LOC Prints and Photographs Division/LC-USZC4-509; 71: Georgetown University Library/Special Collections Research Center, Washington, D.C.; 72: Charles Balthazar Julien Févret de Saint-Mémin/Collection of The New-York Historical Society/1971.125; 73: William Clark/Yale Collection of Western Americana/Beinecke Rare Book & Manuscript Library; 76: Robert Fulton/Courtesy of ASME; 77: Robert Fulton Papers, Manuscripts, and Archives Division/NYPL; 78-79: The Metropolitan Museum of Art/Art Resource, NY; 80: Richard Canton Woodville/*War News from Mexico*, 1948, oil on canvas, 5 x 7 inches/Crystal Bridges Museum of American Art, Bentonville, AR; 82: Private Collection/Peter Newark American Pictures/BAL; 85: California Historical Society/FN-08767chs2010.207; 86: (left): *Untitled (Two Miners with Gold Nugget Stick Pins*/Collection of Oakland Museum of California, Prints and Photographs Fund; (right): Isaac W. Baker/*Untitled (Portrait of a Chinese Man)*/Collection of Oakland Museum of California, Gift of Anonymous Donor; 87: (left): Collection of Matthew R. Isenburg; (right): The Bancroft Library/1905.16242.25; 90-91: A&E Television Networks, LLC; 93: William Henry Brown/The Historic New Orleans Collection/Accession no. 1975.93.2; 94: The J. Paul Getty Museum, Los Angeles, CA/*Portrait of a Nurse and a Child*, 1850, Daguerreotype, 1/6 plate; 98-99: Frank E. Sadowski Jr./The Erie Canal website (http://www.eriecanal.org); 102: Lewis H. Hine/LOC/LC-USZ62-16435; 107: New Bedford Whaling Museum/1993.54.4; 110: Chester County Historical Society, West Chester, PA/103; 112: Schomburg Center/Art Resource, NY; 115: Kansas State Historical Society; 116-117: William Cheney/Photographs and Prints Division, Schomburg Center for Research in Black Culture/NYPL; 119: (top left): Augustus Washington/National Portrait Gallery, Smithsonian Institute/Art Resource, NY; (bottom left): The National Archives/111-B-4208-Taney; (middle): Missouri History Museum, St. Louis, MO; 120: H.C. Howard/LOC Prints and Photographs Division/LC-USZC4-4616; 122-123: A&E Television Networks, LLC; 124: Cook Collection/Valentine Richmond History Center; 126: J.B. Elliot/LOC Geography and Maps Division/g3701s cw0011000; 128: (top): LOC/LC-B8184-10037; (middle right): LOC/LC-USZ62-98334; (middle left): LOC/LC-B8184-10036; (bottom right): Verne Rhoades/LOC/LC-B8184-10582; 129: (full): LOC/LC-B813-3798; (top right): LOC/LC-BH82-1494; (bottom right): LOC/LC-BH82-1494; 130: Mathew Brady/Photography Collection, Miriam and Ira D. Wallach Division of Art, Prints, and Photographs/NYPL; 135: LOC/LC-B811-602; 136: Getty Images; 138: Mathew Brady/Private Collection/The Stapleton Collection/BAL; 139: (top): E. Howe Jr./U.S. Patent Office; (bottom): J.L. Plimpton/U.S. Patent Office; 141: Negative:T.H. O'Sullivan, Positive:Alexander Gardner/LOC/LC-B8184-7946; 142: Behring Center/Smithsonian Institution/Slide # 2004-40300; 144-145: William Morris Smith/LOC/LC-B8171-7890; 146: The National Archives/11-B-1769-Sherman; 147: George N. Bernard/LOC/LC-B811-3630; 148-149: George N. Bernard/BAL; 150: Collection of The New-York Historical Society/42793; 152: Collection of the New-York Historical Society/BAL; 153: Adoc-photos/Art Resource, NY; 155: LOC/LC-B817-7256; 156-157: A&E Television Networks, LLC; 158: John Hillers/National Anthropological Archives, Smithsonian Institution/Inv. 02695500; 160: The Huntington Library/photDAG59; 161: Andrew Joseph Russell/Private Collection/Peter Newark American Pictures/BAL; 163: Art Resource, NY; 166-167: Bibliotheque Nationale, Paris, France/Archives Charmet/BAL; 171: Solomon D. Butcher/Nebraska State Historical Society/RG2608.PH1053; 172: (top left): Solomon D. Butcher/Nebraska State Historical Society/RG2608.PH1274; (bottom left): Solomon D. Butcher Collection/Nebraska State Historical Society/RG2301.311; (middle right): The National Archives; 172-173: W.S. Prettyman/Oklahoma Historical Society/3948; 174: J.F. Gildden/U.S. Patent Office; 175: Solomon D. Butcher Collection/Nebraska State Historical Society/RG2608.PH758a; 177: LOC; 178: The National Archives/NWDNS-111-SC-93343; 180: Solomon D. Butcher Collection/Nebraska State Historical Society/RG2608.PH2430; 181: Private Collection/Peter Newark American Pictures/BAL; 182: Edward Curtis/LOC/USZ62-113085; 183: Edward Curtis/LOC/USZ62-40310; 184: John A. Anderson/Nebraska State Historical Society/RG2969.PH2222; 186: LOC/LC-BH831-365; 187: David Francis Barry/LOC/LC-USZ62-117640; 188: Yale Collection of Western Americana/Beinecke Rare Book & Manuscript Library; 190: Sumner Matteson/Milwaukee Public Museum; 191: Robert Benecke/Charles Swartz; 193: David Francis Barry/Adoc-photos/Art Resource, NY; 194: Getty Images; 196-197: A&E Television Networks, LLC; 198: Chicago Tribune, © Oct. 9, 1871/Chicago Tribune; 199: C.D. Arnold/Chicago Historical Society/ICHI-25216; 201: The Lionel Pincus and Princess Firyal Map Division/NYPL; 202: The New York Public Library Archive/NYPL; 203: Hagley Museum and Library; 207:LOC/LC-USZ62-101148; 208: Robert L. Bracklow/Collection of The New-York Historical Society/60609; 211: Lewis W. Hine/Photography Collection, Miriam and Ira D. Wallach Division of Art, Prints and Photographs/NYPL; 213: Schenectady Museum & Suits-Bueche Planetarium; 214: Schenectady Museum & Suits-Bueche Planetarium; 216: Schenectady Museum & Suits-Bueche Planetarium; 217: William J. Hammer Collection/Archives Center/National Museum of American History, Smithsonian Institution; 219: Time & Life Pictures/Getty Images; 220: (top left): Augustus F. Sherman/Statue of Statue of Liberty N. M. and Ellis Island; (top middle): Augustus F. Sherman/Statue of Liberty N. M. and Ellis Island; (top right): Augustus F. Sherman/Statue of Liberty N. M. and Ellis Island; (middle left): Augustus F. Sherman/Statue of Liberty N. M. and Ellis Island; (middle):

Liberty N. M. and Ellis Island; (bottom left): Augustus F. Sherman/Statue of Liberty N. M. and Ellis Island; (bottom middle): Augustus F. Sherman/Statue of Liberty N. M. and Ellis Island; (bottom right): Augustus F. Sherman/Statue of Liberty N. M. and Ellis Island; 221: Augustus F. Sherman/Statue of Liberty N. M. and Ellis Island; 223: Centennial Photographic Co./LOC/LC-USZ62-57385; 224: Jacob A. Riis/Getty Images; 227: Jacob A. Riis/Jacob A. Riis Collection/Museum of the City of New York; 228: LOC/LC-USZ62-55956; 228: LOC/LC-USZ62-55956; 229: Courtesy of Captain Larry Schneider/Fire Station 50, Los Angeles Fire Department; 231: LOC/LC-USZ62-22198; 234-235: A&E Television Networks, LLC; 236: Getty Images; 237: R.Y. Young/LOC/LC-USZ62-63542; 241: Collection of The Henry Ford/THF23828; 243: Collection of The Henry Ford/THF24982; 244: Rand McNally/Collection of the New-York Historical Society/BAL; 247: Los Angeles Department of Water and Power; 249: Los Angeles Department of Water and Power; 250: Carl Thoner/The National Archives/165-WW-492A-9; 251: The National Archives/165-WW-476-21; 253: Oberlin College Special Collections; 255: Jack Delano/LOC/LC-USF34-040841-D; 256-257: University of Tulsa Special Collections/Call No. 1989-004-5-7; 259: Time & Life Pictures/Getty Images; 262: American Antiquarian Society, Worcester, MA/BAL; 263: Collection of the New-York Historical Society/BAL; 265: Private Collection/Peter Newark American Pictures/BAL; 267: Getty Images; 268-269: A&E Television Networks, LLC; 270: Getty Images; 273: Charles Sheeler/Collection of The Henry Ford/THF22174; 274: Nebraska State Historical Society/RG3358.PH38; 275: Minnesota Historical Society/LOC# Ferrell III.275; 277: Security Pacific National Bank Collection/Los Angeles Public Library; 278: *New York Daily News* Archive/Getty Images; 281: *New York Daily News* Archive/Getty Images; 282: Arthur Rothstein/Getty Images; 284: Nebraska State Historical Society/RG3349.PH13; 286: Dorothea Lange/LOC/LC-USF34-018241-C; 287: Kansas State Historical Society/208994; 289: Dorothea Lange/LOC/LC-USZ62-118228; 290: Lewis H. Hine/*The New York Times* Picture Archives/Redux; 294: Ben Shahn/Art © Estate of Ben Shahn/VAGA, New York, NY; 295: State Archives of the South Dakota State Historical Society; 298: Vera Bock/LOC/LC-USZC2-837 DLC; 300: AP/Wide World Photos; 301: Private Collection/Peter Newark American Pictures/BAL; 302-303: A&E Television Networks, LLC; 304: William C. Shrout/Time & Life Pictures/Getty Images; 305: The National Archives/165-WW-566B; 307: Franklin D. Roosevelt Presidential Library and Museum, Hyde Park, NY; 308: TIME, December 22 © 1931 TIME, Inc.; 309: AP/Wide World Photos; 310: Franklin D. Roosevelt Presidential Library and Museum, Hyde Park, NY; 312: Fenno Jacobs/The National Archives/80-g-412712; 314: Gordon Coster/Time & Life Pictures/Getty Images; 315: Getty Images; 318: The National Archives; 320-321: Culver Pictures; 322: Arthur Siegel/Getty Images; 323: AP/Wide World Photos; 325: AP/Wide World Photos; 327: AP/Wide World Photos; 328: CphoM. Robert F. Sargent/The National Archives/26-G-2343; 329: Peter J. Carroll/AP/Wide World Photos; 330: Robert Capa by Cornell Capa/Magnum Photos; 331: Dorothea Lange/The National Archives/242-HLB-3609-25; 333: The National Archives; 334: AP/Wide World Photos; 337: AP/Wide World Photos; 338-339: AP/Wide World Photos; 340: The National Archives; 341: Getty Images; 342-343: Inge Morath © The Inge Morath Foundation/Magnum Photos; 344: Alfred Eisenstaedt/Time & Life Pictures/Getty Images; 346: Ralph Crane/Time & Life Pictures/Getty Images; 347: Henri Cartier-Bresson/Magnum Photos; 349: Walter Sanders/Time & Life Pictures/Getty Images; 350: Werner Bischof/Magnum Photos; 351: AP/Wide World Photos; 352: Danny Lyon/Magnum Photos; 353: Elliott Erwitt/Magnum Photos; 354: Danny Lyon/Magnum Photos; 355: Charles Moore/Black Star; 356-357: Bob Adelman/Magnum Photos; 360: Carmine Donofrio/*New York Daily News*/Getty Images; 361: (left): MPI/Getty Images; (right): Fred W. McDarrah/Getty Images; 363: Paul Fusco/Magnum Photos; 364: Arthur D'Arazien/Industrial Photographs, Archives Center/National Museum of American History, Smithsonian Institution; 365: Al Fenn/Time & Life Pictures/Getty Images; 366: Elliott Erwitt/Magnum Photos; 367: Robert W. Kelley/Time & Life Pictures/Getty Images; 368: Great Images in NASA; 369: Ralph Morse/Time & Life Pictures/Getty Images; 370: Francis Miller/Time & Life Pictures/Getty Images; 371: *The Detroit News* Archives; 372: AP/Wide World Image; 373: John Dominis/Time & Life Pictures/Getty Images; 374-375: Chris Niedenthal/Time & Life Pictures/Getty Images; 376: Central Press/Getty Images; 379: Wayne Miller/Magnum Photos; 380: AP/Wide World Photos; 381: AP/Wide World Photos; 382: (top) AP/Wide World Photos; (bottom): AP/Wide World Photos; 384: David Fenton/Getty Images; 386: Elliott Erwitt/Magnum Photos; 387: Leonard Freed/Magnum Photos; 388: Bernard Gotfryd/Getty Images; 389: Dirck Halstead/Time & Life Pictures/Getty Images; 390: Andy Freeberg/Getty Images; 391: Raymond Depardon/Magnum Photos; 392: Paul Williams/Time & Life Pictures/Getty Images; 393: Alex Webb/Magnum Photos; 394: Allan Baxter/Getty Images; 395: Paul S. Howell/Getty Images; 396: Mark Wilson/Getty Images; 398: Andrew Moore/Yancy Richardson Gallery, NY; 399: (top): Andrew Moore/Yancy Richardson Gallery, NY; (bottom): Andrew Moore/Yancy Richardson Gallery, NY; 400: Gilles Peress/Magnum Photos; 401: Steve McCurry/Magnum Photos; 402: Scout Tufankjian/Polaris; 403: Justin L. Fowler/AP/Wide World Photos.

ACKNOWLEDGMENTS

America: The Story of Us benefited from the tireless efforts of many who contributed to the documentary series that premièred on History. Historical consultants Professor Daniel Walker Howe and Professor David M. Kennedy were invaluable in bringing their knowledge and rigor to the project. The TV series was produced by Nutopia; Executive Producers Jane Root and Michael Jackson, with special thanks to the entire production team including Ben Goold, Kathryn Taylor, Ben Fox, and Alex Dwiar. Overseeing the project at History was Executive Producers Nancy Dubuc, Julian P. Hobbs, David McKillop with additional support from Libby O'Connell and Kristen Burns. Thanks to all.

Thanks also to Chris Beha, Sierra Fromberg, Marilyn Fu, Barabara Gogan, John House, Heather Hughes, Coco Joly, Parlan McGaw, Stephanie Myers, Lauren Nathan, Jamie Newman, Kenneth Partridge, Holly Rothman, Alex Tart, Kara Taylor, Shoshana Thaler, Anna Thorngate, Kate Winn, and Megan Worman.